Islamic FinTech

obstacles are black hat hackers, misuse and fraud cultures, natural system crash, rapid and repeated growth of devices, poor professionalism and skills, unskilled corporate governance, lack of confidence, non-etiquette and insufficient support and cooperation from decision makers and policy controllers. However, most of these challenges might be due to invention with new dimension, but with temporary effect, perhaps. Such challenges may not last long in the promising journey or the emerging era of the fintech with its skilled dynamism and friendly offerings. Shari'ah compliance eco-financial industries are not exception in coping up with the global emergence of fintech in their products and quality services, but within the rules of *Maqasid al-Shari'ah* (Divine objectives) in no parallel, but dichotomizing with the technological culture adapted in the conventional financial industries. The fintech with Islamic ethical compliance may be an added value to the existing solutions particularly in this socio-economic catastrophic era in the first quarter of the twenty-first century and the time ahead.

The world financial securities industries including capital market, stock market, money market, easy-pay, smart contract, social finance, digital currency, payment through apps, mobile banking, crowdfunding and global Waqf cooperation are among those facilities systemized by fintech with affordable technical solutions and less risk and minimum challenges. Economic and financial authorities, regulators, decision makers, operators and customers are moving with greater prospects towards transmitting the traditional financial system to fintech with promising benefits and better services with rational returns. Such achievement phenomena are realized not only among the socio-economically developing states but in a rising global dimension. The contemporary Islamic financial market is growing faster than conventional counterpart with an annual growth rate ranging from 13% to 23% with sustainability appreciated by all irrespective of religion, nationality, color, gender, status and/or age across today's world of economy. It is observed that Islamic financial industries capitalize on every digital opportunity in their technicalities, policies, system, products, services and marketing within the rules of *Maqasid al-Shari'ah* aiming at serving the customers with satisfaction and comfortness compatible with possible best offerings of the global practices of eco-culture. Hence, Islamic financial industries today foresee the emerging fintech is the pushing

Foreword

The world of today witnesses numerous catastrophes, namely the global attack by the novel coronavirus, negative hit on the global oil price, political turmoil in several parts of the world, and racial and ethnic war in many parts of the world, which destabilize in the world eco-peace and smooth forward of the socio-economic and financial movement. It has recently been predicted that the financial technology or fintech may play a significant role in rescuing the global economic future from the existing catastrophic status quo. In the contemporary century, the world has been enjoying with advancement of science and technology in the cyberspace in almost every sector of day-to-day life and culture, be one personal, private, domestic, social, political, economic, global or cyber. The economic, corporate, financial or trade sectors have still been dominated by traditional culture in coping up with gradual science and technological way uphill. It has been observed that, in the recent phenomena, the economic, financial and non-financial corporate sectors adapt borderless multiple smart mechanisms with sophisticated and complex technologies in facilitating the contemporary eco-financial movement in their technicalities, products, services and policies and promoting to maximize the friendly and easy-go with comfortness, rational cost-effectiveness and customer satisfaction with an ultimate goal in advancing the industry with dynamism and achievement, which is termed as financial technology or fintech. Despite such opportunities in the smart cyberspace (fintech) optimized by the financial industries, there are obstacles and challenges slowing the smooth way forward in true achievement. It may be recorded that among those

Mohd Ma'Sum Billah
Editor

Islamic FinTech

Insights and Solutions

palgrave
macmillan

Mohd Ma'Sum Billah
Editor

Islamic FinTech

Insights and Solutions

palgrave
macmillan

factor of the products and services with innovation to global platform with a furtherance legacy to position itself as an able alternative to the conventional counterpart with significant results and added benefits for all with universal value within the holistic spirit of *Maqasid al-Shari'ah*. To record that, among the Organization of Islamic Countries (OIC) and non-OIC other states leading the advancement of fintech for the Shari'ah-compliant eco-financial industries are the Kingdom of Saudi Arabia, Malaysia, the United Arab Emirates, Indonesia, Pakistan, Bahrain, Kuwait, Qatar, Turkey, Bangladesh, Oman, Brunei, Maldives, Sri Lanka, India, Iran, Sudan, Egypt, Gambia, Jordan, Uganda, Kenya, Afghanistan, Syria, Iraq, Hong Kong, Thailand, New Zealand, Ghana, Nigeria, South Africa, Bosnia, the United Kingdom, the Philippines, Singapore, the United States, Australia, Germany, Russia and Canada. The socio-political and financial authorities, corporate and professional entities, researchers and decision makers are among those who are earnestly pushing, supporting and innovating the legal framework, technical know-how, operational mechanisms of fintech in the Islamic financial industries in their innovative system, products, services and marketing. Digital currency, smart-contract, smart-payment, crowdfunding, capital market, Social Responsibility Investment (SRI) *sukuk*, Value based Intermediation (VBI), Impact investment, Waqf cooperation, Zakat management, online financial services, mobile banking and remittance are among those opportunities already in action through the fintech within the spirit of *Maqasid al-Shari'ah*.

Indeed, it is timely to have been initiated by a world-renowned Islamic finance authoritative scholar Mohd Ma'Sum Billah with this unique book (*Islamic FinTech: Insights and Industrial Solutions*) with numerous solutions to fintech within the rules of *Maqasid Shari'ah*, is the milestone of the contemporary fintech with the Islamic socio-economic and ethical value by contributing several notable chapters on specialized issues of fintech. It is thus, an honor for me to appreciate and acknowledge that, this unique book is a solution to core issues of *Shari'ah*-compliant fintech, which is rightfully produced by Mohd Ma'Sum Billah of Islamic Economics Institute, King Abdulaziz University, Saudi Arabia, along with the cooperation and intellectual contributions of reputable researchers from different parts of the world as contributors, which is timely to meet the global market demand of researchers, academia, professionals, industrialists, financial authorities, decision makers, technical experts, students and entrepreneurs. The book, therefore, may be a useful reference in understanding and technical know-how financial technology and mechanisms enshrined by the principles of *Maqasid al-Shari'ah* and may significantly contribute to industrial needs and applications of fintech in the contemporary Islamic eco-financial activities, *enSha Allah (swt)*.

National Commercial Bank (NCB) Sheikh Hamza Khalid Bawazir
Jeddah, Saudi Arabia
November 24, 2020

Preface

Fintech is an emerging chapter of the global economic and financial way forward, and the Islamic financial and Halal corporate industries are not an exception in moving towards transforming all mechanisms, products, activities and services smarter by financial technology (fintech) with promising outcome. Despite such a vibration in the global financial environment, it has been observed that, in the resource sector, there are numerous literatures on theoretical solutions of fintech available in the market and libraries besides online resources. But true enough to have been realized that there is no comprehensive literature addressing exclusively on the industrial solutions to fintech within the *Maqasid al-Shari'ah*. The impact of such a phenomenon is that professionals, industries, customers, promoters, researchers and even academia in the field of fintech are suffering having no specialized research work focusing on the practical know-how. This book is therefore timely to contribute with numerous applied solutions on fintech applicable in the contemporary Islamic financial and halal economic environments. The title "Islamic FinTech: Realization and Industrial Solutions" is by specialized treatment in focusing on *Shari'ah-compliant Fintech* solutions as ought to be practised and applicable in today's economy. The book however contributes with practical know-how concerning Fintech along with its corporate understanding, policies, structures, mechanisms, technical know-how and empirical analyses within the rules of *Maqasid al-Shari'ah*, which are divided into four parts with 24 chapters addressing specialized issues besides an introduction, a bibliography and an index.

Part I provides an overview of the emergence of Islamic fintech, which consists of four chapters addressing different core issues of fintech under the *Shari'ah*. *Chapter 1* contributes on "Emergence of i-Fintech in the Contemporary Socio-Economic Reality". *Chapter 2* focuses on "Fintech Versus i-Fintech: A Dichotomy", while *Chap. 3* contributes a scientific paradigm of "Fintech and *Maqāsid* Dichotomy Under the Prism of the Non-neutrality of Techniques".

Part II focuses on regulatory frameworks of Islamic fintech, which consists of six different classes of regulatory frameworks and experiences of fintech within *Maqasid al-Shari'ah* in six chapters. *Chapter 4* analyses on the "Central Banks and Financial Authorities: Towards the Advancement of I-Fintech". *Chapter 5* presents an "Analysis of *Fatwas* on Fintech". *Chapter 6* analyses on the "An Evaluation of Smart Contracts: Practices, Legality, and Shari'ah". *Chapter 7* provides "Digital Smart Contracts: Legal and *Shari'ah* Issues". *Chapter 8* discovers a model of "Judicial Procedures in i–FinTech: The Malaysian Experience".

Part III contributes on the Islamic fintech: its mechanisms and applications. The part analyses 13 different practical solutions and experiences besides technical know-how of Islamic fintech in 13 chapters. *Chapter 9* discusses on "The Forms and Effects of Cryptocurrencies in a Dual Banking System". *Chapter 10* analyses on "Islamic Fintech and Financial Inclusion". *Chapter 11* contributes "Enhancing Financial Inclusion Using FinTech-Based Payment System". *Chapter 12* analyses on "Islamic FinTech and Financial Inclusion" with a different approach. *Chapter 13* discusses on "Utilization of Digital Technology for Zakat Development". *Chapter 14* discovers the model of "i-FinTech and Its Value Proposition for Islamic Asset and Wealth Management". *Chapter 15* analyses on "The Opportunities of Digital Wallets from an Islamic Perspective" and scope of further research. *Chapter 16* analyses on "The Optimization of Blockchain for Greater Transparency in *Zakat* Management". *Chapter 17* contributes with "*Zakat* Digital Management Techniques". *Chapter 18* analyses on the "*Zakat* Calculation Software for Corporate Entities". *Chapter 19* provides a "FinTech in the MENA Region: Current State and Prospects". *Chapter 20* discovers on "The Risks of Islamic Fintech". *Chapter 21* discusses on the "TakafulTech for Business Excellence and Customer Satisfaction".

Part IV focuses on Islamic FinTech: its challenges and the professional way forward. The part contributes four different components of Islamic fintech, namely, SWOT, cryptocurrency challenges, digital currency literacy and professional development through research plan. *Chapter 22* contributes on "The Challenges of Cryptocurrencies and the Shari'ah Paradigm". *Chapter 23* analyses on the "Digital Technology and Its Impact on Islamic Social Finance Literacy". *Chapter 24* provides "The Direction of Future Research on i-FinTech".

Jeddah, Saudi Arabia — Mohd Ma'Sum Billah

Acknowledgements

There is no strength and power except in Allah (swt). To Him comes the praise, the Savant, the Wise, the Omniscient, the most beautiful names belong to Him. May the blessing of Allah (swt) and peace be upon Muhammad (saw) and all the Prophets (aws) from the first to the last.

First of all, I would humbly like to acknowledge King Abdulaziz University, Kingdom of Saudi Arabia, and its prestigious wing Islamic Economics Institute for supporting us with every facility in research, academic, human capital and professional development activities outreaching the global *Ummah*. It is also a great honor for me to humbly acknowledge His Excellency Professor Dr Abdulrahman Obaid Al-Youbi, *President of King Abdulaziz University*; Professor Dr Yousef Abdul Aziz Al Turki, *Vice President of King Abdulaziz University*; Dr Abdullah Qurban Turkistani, *Dean of the Islamic Economics Institute (IEI), King Abdulaziz University* (KAU); Dr Mohammad A. Naseef (*Vice Dean, IEI-KAU*); Dr Marwan G. A. Andejani (*Vice Dean, IEI-KAU*); Dr Hasan Mohammad Makhethi (*Vice Dean, IEI-KAU*); Dr Maha Alandejani (*Vice Dean, IEI, KAU*);

Dr Faisal Mahmoud Atbani (*Head, Department of Insurance, IEI-KAU*); Dr Adnan M. A. Al-Khiary *(Head, Department of Finance, IEI-KAU*); and Dr Albara Abdullah Abulaban (*Head Department of Economics*) for their continuous supports and encouragements towards dynamic professional development, excellent academic contributions and specialized scientific research activities. Heartiest appreciation is extended to my respected fellow-colleagues from the Islamic Economics Institute, King Abdulaziz University, Saudi Arabia, including my outstanding talented colleague Mr Mohammed Alabdulraheem (*Lecturer in FinTech and Islamic finance, IEI-KAU*). Further acknowledgement is also extended to individuals; experts; industrialists; academia; researchers including Ibtesam Azad (*an outstanding PhD candidate at both KSU (Riyadh) and MEDIU-Kuala Lumpur, carrying out her research on 'Digital Currency' in five different perspectives by treating with the Islamic ruling*), Mr Jahanzeb Khan (*Lecturer, ECE Dept, Faculty of Engineering, KAU*) and Mrs Rabia Khatoon (*Language Instructor, ELI, KAU*); and also public-private sectors including financial and fintech authorities, promoters, operators, universities, industries and professional firms whose direct and indirect supports with knowledge, experiences and resources are full-heartedly recorded.

Islamic Economics Institute
King Abdulaziz University
Saudi Arabia

Mohd Ma'Sum Billah, PhD

Contents

Notes on Contributors

Faraz Adam, MA is a Shari'ah scholar and director of Amanah Finance Consultancy from where he actively advises several global organizations in Islamic finance, banking, Zakat management and other sectors. He has studied Shari'ah with scholars for almost a decade and completed a Master's degree in Islamic finance and banking in the UK. He has further attained a number of industry qualifications. Adam has authored many research papers on cryptocurrencies and blockchain from a Shari'ah compliance perspective and advises a number of crypto-asset management and crypto-exchange platforms. Adam is passionate about establishing an economy which upholds justice, equity and growth for all members of society.

Suhail Ahmad, MBA is a PhD research scholar in the Department of Business Administration in the Sarhad University of Science & Information Technology Peshawar, Pakistan. After getting his graduation (i.e. BBA HONS) in Finance with *Distinction* and awarded (*Certificate of Merit*) from Govt. Post Graduate College of Management Sciences Thana Malakand, University of Malakand, Chakdara, Pakistan, he moved to his MBA/MS in Finance with research thesis (*Issues & Problems of Islamic Banking in Pakistan with Special Reference to Poverty Alleviation*) from the University of Malakand, Chakdara, Pakistan. His area of interest is Islamic finance, poverty alleviation through Islamic finance and microfinance. He has the will to alleviate poverty in the economy, not only in Pakistan but also in the globe. He published research papers in the field of finance, Islamic finance, microfinance, poverty alleviation and so on. His paper title "Developing and proposing a Model for Zakat Management System: A Case of the Malakand District of KP, Pakistan with Special Reference to Poverty Alleviation in the District" was published in *International Journal of Zakat* (Volume 04 No. 01, 2019), an Indonesia-based journal, and won the *Best Paper Award* of a cash prize.

Mezbah Uddin Ahmed, MSc is a Researcher at the International Shari'ah Research Academy for Islamic Finance (ISRA), Malaysia. He is also part of the Shariah audit team and one of the consultants of ISRA Consultancy Sdn. Bhd. (ICSB) for the development of the Islamic finance sector in the Republic of Tajikistan under the Islamic Development Bank (IDB) technical assistance project. His notable academic contributions include as an editor and writer of *Islamic Financial System: Principles & Operations (2nd edition)*—a globally reputed textbook published by ISRA. He also has several publications in reputed journals and on contemporary issues. Ahmed is Fellow of the Association of Chartered Certified Accountants (ACCA) and an AAOIFI Certified Islamic Professional Accountant (CIPA). He obtained a BSc in Applied Accounting from Oxford Brookes University, UK, and MSc in Islamic Banking and Finance (MIBF) from IIUM Institute of Islamic Banking and Finance (IIiBF), Malaysia. Before joining ISRA, he worked in audit and assurance with a Big-4 affiliate accountancy services firm in Bangladesh. He also has several years of experience providing lectures of ACCA and ICAEW courses. He has provided trainings on financial reporting (AAOIFI and IFRS standards) and auditing of Islamic financial institutions.

Nafis Alam is a professor and head, School of Accounting and Finance, Asia Pacific University of Technology and Innovation, Malaysia. Alam's expertise is centred on banking regulation, financial stability and corporate finance. His scholarly articles have been published in leading journals including *The World Economy*, *Emerging Markets Review*, *Pacific Basin Finance Journal*, *Journal of Asset Management*, *Journal of Banking Regulation*, *Review of Islamic Economics and Journal of Financial Services Marketing*, among others. He has co-authored five books in Islamic Finance—among them is *Encyclopaedia of Islamic Finance*, which is the first of its kind and has sold over 1000 copies worldwide. As a frequent traveller, he has given lectures on finance and Islamic finance across the world, including Harvard Islamic Finance forum at

Harvard Law School; a Gulf Research Meeting at Cambridge University, UK; Durham University Summer School; Seoul International Finance Conference (SIFIC); World Islamic Economic Forum (WIEF); and OIC Asia Trade and Economic Forum. Alam has served as a visiting associate professor at various universities in the UK and Indonesia. He was featured as a Professor of the Month by *Financial Times* (FT) in 2014 and received an award for Upcoming Personality in Islamic Finance in 2016 presented by GIFA and hosted by the Indonesian government.

Laily Dwi Arsyianti, PhD is an assistant professor at IPB University. She holds an *amanah* as Deputy Head of Department of Islamic Economics, Faculty of Economics and Management. She graduated the Bachelor in Economics (Hons) from the same university, and did her Master of Science in Finance and PhD in Islamic Banking and Finance from the International Islamic University of Malaysia. Her area of interest includes Islamic wealth management, Islamic social finance, and behavioral finance. She has written 32 papers in SCOPUS indexed journals and national accredited journals. She also has presented selected papers in various reputable conferences, especially those that are organized by IRTI-IDB and Bank Indonesia.

Ayman Mohamad Bakr, MBA is a PhD student at the Department of Islamic Economics and Finance at Istanbul Sabahattin Zaim University. He holds two Bachelor's degrees, one in electrical electronics engineering from Bilkent University and the other in mathematics from Southern New Hampshire University from which he earned two outstanding academic achievements rewards. Bakr received his master's degree in business administration with distinction from Strathclyde University. He has lots of industrial experience, more than ten years of which are in an international financial institution. He has written several research papers and his interests are e-waste, circular economy, econometrics of FX rates and trade, waqf, and waqf worldview.

Houssemeddine Bedoui is a global lead Islamic finance expert at the Islamic Development Bank (IDB). As part of his work at the Islamic Development Bank, he actively contributes to the structuring, launch and implementation of innovative products and processes for the market. Besides, Bedoui is ATD certified trainer (MTP: Master Trainer Program). He has several entrepreneurial experiences putting Islamic finance principles and products into practice. Prior to his job at the IDB, he was a consultant in Europe in management advisory and ethical/sustainable finance and worked with many think-tanks to develop Islamic finance in France. He has a Master's from Telecom SudParis Engineering School (INT), France; an MBA from IE Business School (Spain); a PhD from ENS (École Normale Supérieure, France); and he is also an alumnus from Harvard Kennedy School (CID, Center for International Development). Bedoui is the co-editor of IRTI's French journal. His research interests comprise Islamic capital markets, fintech, social entrepreneurship and finance, competitiveness and Islamic banking; his articles have appeared in several academic journals and presented his research works at various international conferences.

Irfan Syauqi Beik is an associate professor at the Department of Islamic Economics, Bogor Agricultural University (IPB), Indonesia, and holds the position of the Director of the Centre of Islamic Business and Economic Studies (CIBEST) at IPB. Besides being an academician, Beik has been appointed as the Director of the Centre of Strategic Studies at the National *Zakat* Board of the Republic of Indonesia (BAZNAS) since August 2016. He is also a member of the National Shari'ah Board of the Indonesian Council of Ulama (DSN-MUI) and the Deputy Chairman of the Indonesian Association of Islamic Economist (IAEI). Beik is a member of Shari'ah supervisory council in several Islamic financial institutions. In addition, Beik has published books and scientific articles at both national and international journals and has contributed regularly in various national newspapers in Indonesia.

Abderrazak Belabes serves as an associate professor of economics, Islamic Economics Institute, King Abdulaziz University, Saudi Arabia. He holds an engineering degree in electronics, a Master's in Science in econometrics and a PhD in economic analysis and policy from the School of High Studies in Social Sciences (EHESS, Paris). His main research interests—beyond the subject matter—focus on the economic methodology, in the broadest sense of the term, which includes the distinction between the existence of the object (ontology), its representation (imago) and the way to know it (epistemology). This led him gradually to the deconstruction of the discourse on Islamic economics, finance and banking to better understand the complex interactions between religion and economics, and the inconsistencies between intention and action, theory and facts, beyond the conceptual smokescreen. This approach is a continuation of his PhD thesis which investigated the complex interaction between ideology and economics beyond the Schumpeterian dichotomy "science/ideology". It aims to identify the conditions for the emergence of a discourse, its limitations and inconsistencies in the light of research works on comparative literature, archaeology of knowledge, history and philosophy of science, sociology of knowledge, history of economic life and institutions and ethics of science and technology.

Ahmed Belouafi is Professor of Islamic Economics and Finance at the Islamic Economics Institute (IEI), King Abdulaziz University (KAU). He holds a Master's in Money Banking and Finance and a PhD in Economics from Sheffield University (UK). Belouafi taught several Islamic Economics and finance courses at the University of Birmingham (UK), London Open College (UK), and at Economics Department and IEI at KAU in Saudi Arabia. In the academic year 2013–2014, he was awarded a teaching excellence certificate of the executive education of IE Business School (Madrid, Spain). Belouafi is a member of the editorial board of King Abdulaziz University Journal: *Islamic Economics* and other international journals. He authored/edited more than 40 papers and publications in the form of articles in international refereed journals, books, chapters in books, academic reviews and monographs. He has participated in many national and international symposiums in the IEs and IF domain. Among his research interests are financial and monetary reform, sovereign money, complementary currencies, Islamic finance education and curricula, financial crises and financial stability and fintech in the MENA region.

Mohamed Cherif El Amri is working as an assistant professor at the Faculty of Business and Management Sciences Specialized Islamic Economics and Finance, at Sabahattin Zaim University. He completed his Bachelor's degree in Islamic Studies from Ibn Tofail University in Morocco. He had his Master's in Islamic jurisprudence and its principles, while his PhD in Islamic banking and finance from International Islamic University Malaysia. He worked as an intern at several Islamic financial institutions, such as the Islamic Capital Market Business Group, Securities Commission, Kuala Lumpur Malaysia and Maybank Islamic. He worked as a researcher at the Institute of Islamic Banking and Finance, Malaysia. He was an Associated Consultant at Amanie Advisors, Kuala Lumpur,

Malaysia. He is a member of the Scientific Committee of the *International Review of Entrepreneurial Finance Journal* and *Journal of Islamic Economics and Finance*. He has multiple research publications and presentations in the field of Islamic Finance and Economics.

Hurriyah El Islamy, PhD is the Best National and Global Islamic Finance Activist/Proponent Award Winner (Bank Indonesia 2018) who serves the executive board of Badan Pengelola Keuangan Haji Indonesia (Presidential Decree 74/2017) and the IsDB's APIF Supervisory Committee. Recently awarded "Anugerah Tokoh Alumni" (Best Alumni) by International Islamic University Malaysia, she is also FAA certified Assessor, IFN Advisory Board member, Shariah Board Member and Strategic Advisor of Islamic Fintech Alliance and was the head of Professional Development in AAOIFI prior to which she served as AAOIFI Shariah Central Board Working Group member. Until recently, she was IMF expert in Islamic Finance and a member of the Islamic Finance Advisory Council of the AIFC. With over two decades of experience globally, she served, among other things, as director, Group Head Shariah and Governance and Group Legal—Islamic Banking and Capital Markets of CIMB Group; director, Head of Legal Capinnova Investment Bank; head of AML and Compliance and Legal Counsel Kuwait Finance House Bahrain; and chairperson, Audit and Legal Committee of Bahrain Associations of Banks. She was trained in Leadership in General Counsel (2019) and Negotiation and Leadership (2012) by Harvard Law School, received multiple academic awards including from the University of Strathclyde in Glasgow, graduated as the Best Overall LLB student from International Islamic University Malaysia, wrote multiple articles in several disciplines including Islamic finance and was IFN Correspondence on Legal Frameworks. She has been providing advice and consultancy to regulators and/or entities in several jurisdictions on Islamic finance related matters.

Sahibzada Ghisaul Haq is a professor and the Dean of Faculty of Management Sciences, Sarhad University of Science & Information Technology, Peshawar, Khyber Pakhtunkhwa, Pakistan. He holds PhD in economics from Glasgow University, UK. He is one of the top supervisors and supervised many doctorate scholars in the university in the field of economics and management sciences. He has a vast experience in the field of economics and management sciences. He published different research papers in the field of economics, and Islamic economy and Islamic finance. He also worked on SMEs' financing in Khyber Pakhtunkhwa, Pakistan.

Hichem Hamza holds PhD in Economics from the University of Economics and Management in Clermont-Ferrand, France. He started his career at Tunis Higher School of Business in 2003. Since 2016, he is an associate professor and researcher at the Islamic Economics Institute—King Abdulaziz University. His research interests include Islamic finance and banking, monetary and financial economics, Awqaf (Endowments) and non-profit organization. His articles have appeared, among others, in *Research in International Business and Finance*, *Studies in Economics and Finance*, *International Journal of Islamic and Middle Eastern Finance and Management*, *Journal of Islamic Accounting and Business Research*, and *Borsa Istanbul Review*.

S. M. Rashed Jahangir, MSc is a PhD student at the Department of Islamic Economics and Finance at Istanbul Sabahattin Zaim University. He graduated from Northern University Bangladesh with BBA major in Finance. Later, he completed his master's degree at Anadolu University in Turkey. He is one of the authors of a book, titled *Microfinance Improved Knowledge-Skills Empowered Organization in Difficult Terrains of Bangladesh*. Jahangir is also an author of the two recently published reports: "Improving the Takaful sector in Islamic countries" (funded by the Standing Committee for Economic and Commercial Cooperation of the Organization of the Islamic Cooperation (COMCEC), one of the four Standing Committees of the OIC), and "Islamic finance report: focus on Turkey". Besides, he has written several articles on general finance, the stock market, and the energy market. Furthermore, he has presented many papers at various international conferences. His areas of research interests include Islamic finance, capital markets, financial technology (FinTech), and savings-based finance (SBF) or rotating savings and credit association (ROSCA).

Khoutem Ben Jedidia is Associate Professor of Economics at the High Institute of Accounting (ISCAE), Tunisia. She completed her undergraduate studies at the Faculty of Economics and Management of Sfax in 1993 and subsequently taught there. She has received an honorary Presidential Prize in Economics. Then, she received a Master's degree of Advanced Studies in Money, Finance and Banks from University Lumière Lyon II, France, in 1994, and completed her PhD in

Economics at University Lumière Lyon II in 1998. Her first academic job was as an assistant professor on the Faculty of Economics and Management of Sfax, 1999–2004. She is a member of Research Unit in Islamic Economics and Finance, University of Zitouna, Tunisia. Jedidia's publications and research areas pertain to Islamic banking, financial intermediation and financial development. Her articles have appeared in *Journal of Policy Modeling*, *Economics Bulletin*, *International Economic Journal*, *Journal of Religious Ethics*, *Etudes en Economie Islamique*, *International Journal of Islamic and Middle Eastern Finance and Management*, *Journal of Islamic Accounting and Business Research*, among others.

Noor Suhaida binti Kasri is a senior researcher at International Shari'ah Research Academy for Islamic Finance (ISRA). She is also the Head of ISRA's Islamic Capital Market Unit. Prior to joining ISRA, she had almost 12 years of experience as a Malaysian advocate and solicitors as well as a Syarie lawyer. During her legal practice, she was appointed as one of the members of the Malaysia's Investigating Tribunal Panel, Advocates and Solicitors Disciplinary Board and headed the Shariah Legal Clinic of Kuala Lumpur Bar Legal Aid Centre. Kasri received her Doctor of Philosophy in Islamic Banking Finance and Management from the University of Gloucestershire (in collaboration with Markfield Institute of Higher Education), UK, under the sponsorship of ISRA. Her Master's in Laws was from King's College of London under the funding of the British Chevening Scholarship Award. Her Bachelor of Laws and Diploma in Shariah Legal Practice were from the International Islamic University of Malaysia. She has written a number of research papers, textbook chapter and articles and presented in conferences locally and globally.

Ainul Azam bin Ahmad Khamal, LLM graduated with an LLM (Hons) from the University Malaya in 2000 having earlier read laws at the International Islamic University, Malaysia, and graduated with an LLB (Hons). He is an alumnus of Asian Institute of Management, Manila, which he attended in 2007. Founded Messrs. Ainul Azam & Co. in 2003, a boutique legal firm specializing in Mergers & Acquisitions ("M & A"), scheme of arrangements and restructuring, corporate finance, corporate and commercial transactions, information and communication technology and intellectual property as well as corporate and dispute resolution. He is also a Registered Trademark Agent and a member of the Malaysian

Intellectual Property Association (MIPA) since 2005. He is a passionate observer on company and corporate law issues, namely, shareholders' rights, "derivative action", "minority oppression" and directors' duties. He has appeared as counsel in courts. His published legal article "There and Back Again—Recent Perspectives on the Law of Derivative Action in Malaysia" [2017] 5 MLJ cxxiv is available online at lexisnexis.com, an article which discusses the impact of sections 347–350 of the Companies Act 2016 to the law on statutory derivative action. His latest legal article, "There and Back Again: The Journey Continues—Recent Perspectives on the Law of Derivative Actions in Malaysia" [2019] 6 MLJ cxxii.

Khairul Azmi Mohamad was academically trained in the field of common law and Islamic law. After graduation, he served as a lecturer at the Law Faculty of the International Islamic University, Malaysia. He was later appointed as the Information and Research Chief of the State Government of Johor under the office of the Chief Minister of Johor. He was entrusted to lead Ilmuwan Foundation as its executive chairman. It was a foundation that involved in research and development as well as consultancy activities in the fields of education and human capital development. Here he was entrusted to lead a strong team of academics and professionals, a five-year government project on Japanese Technical Education Technology Transfer. He worked with various Japanese top universities representing numerous unique expertise. His research is mainly focused in the field of politics especially on the Malaysian politics as well as the Islamic politics. He has published seven books and wrote more than 70 academic papers. He has deep interest in *Siyasah Syar'iyyah* and *Maqasid Syariah*. Professionally, he is an Advocate and Solicitor of the High Court of Malaya.

Mustafa Omar Mohammed is presently the Head and an associate professor at the Department of Economics, International Islamic University Malaysia (IIUM), where he has been teaching for more than 15 years now. He has published more than 50 referred journal articles and presented more than 70 papers, mostly at international conferences. He is actively involved in funded and commissioned research projects. His present research areas of interest are in *Waqf*, *Zakat*, Islamic Microfinance and *Maqasid al-Shari'ah*. He has supervised more than 45 dissertations at PhD and master levels. He is also a journal editorial member and reviewer panel to 11 academic entities. He has received several quality awards for teaching and research. He was part of a committee responsible for setting up the Institute of Islamic Banking and Finance and, recently, the Department of Islamic Finance at IIUM. He also has long experience in translations, Arabic and English. He undertook projects for several organizations, including MIFC, IBFIM, AIBIM, IFSB—affiliates of the Central Bank of Malaysia. He offers consultancy and has conducted several training on Islamic economics, banking and finance in several countries including Kazakhstan, Singapore, Sri Lanka, Bangladesh, Philippines, Indonesia, South Africa and Uganda. Mohammed holds a Bachelor's and a Master's degree in Economics from IIUM and PhD in Finance from Universiti Sains Malaysia.

Hazik Mohamed is a business strategist with substantial market research, operational management and start-up experience. He consults for MSMEs and MNCs on various business-related issues including operational process optimization, investment management and strategic market penetration. Specialized in PhD research in behavioural research and decision-making analysis, applicable in many industry applications including marketing and understanding consumer (or user) behaviour as well as policy formulation and regulatory implementation. He has spoken extensively on blockchain-based applications in Kuala Lumpur (Malaysia), Lahore (Pakistan), Lyon (France), Turin (Italy) and Singapore, proposed a multi-dimensional approach to poverty alleviation in Jakarta (Indonesia), developed a socio-development and financial inclusion index in Islamabad (Pakistan) as well as discussed early warning indicators in macro-prudential policy in Manama (Bahrain). His past corporate clients include the UNCDF on a variety of consulting work, the ASEAN Secretariat, Oman Tourism (Sultanate of Oman) as their market-based representative, SME Bank (Malaysia) for specific strategic advisory, EDC@SMCCI (Enterprise Development Centre of Singapore Malay Chamber of Commerce for MSMEs), where he served as an independent consultant. Mohamed is the published author of *Belief and Rule Compliance* on behavioural economics and *Blockchain, Fintech and Islamic Finance*. He regularly contributes thought leadership articles to industry-specific magazines and reputable academic journals to bridge the gap between academia and industry. Professionally, he is working on AI-driven and blockchain-based innovations, business growth strategies for start-ups and the digital transformation of the economy. Despite his hectic schedule, he also teaches Business Economics and Corporate Finance at Putra Business School.

Kazi Mohammad Mortuza Ali, MCom holds BCom (Hons), MCom, LLB., and is a qualified professional of Chartered Insurance Institute (ACII) London. He is also a graduate from Norwegian Shipping Academy, Oslo. He is presently serving as Director General (DG) of Bangladesh Institute for Professional Development (BIPD). He served as CEO and Chief Consultant of Prime Islami Life Insurance Limited (PILIL) during October 2002–April 2019. He was the Director (CEO) of Bangladesh Insurance Academy during 1995–2002. Before joining the Insurance Academy, he served Bangladesh Shipping Corporation during 1974–1995 in different positions, including GM (Operation), DGM (Marketing & Research) and AGM (Insurance & Claims). He served as specialist member of the "Committee" formed by the Government of the People's Republic of Bangladesh for reforming Insurance law and enacting new laws. He served also as a Member of the "Committee" formed by the Honorable President's Secretariat of the Government of the People's Republic of Bangladesh to investigate into alleged "Insurance Claim & Maritime Fraud". Mortuza Ali has provided Consultancy Service under ADB project as "Insurance Regulatory Specialist" for the Enhancement of Governance and Capacity of Insurance Sector of Bangladesh and Third Capital Market Development Program: Capacity Building of Insurance Development and Regulatory Authority as Insurance Regulatory Expert. Ali presented several papers on health insurance, micro-insurance and risk management in international seminars in Egypt, Malaysia, Singapore, Hong Kong, Vietnam, India, Australia, the Netherlands, Japan, Indonesia, China, Thailand and Bangladesh. He received several awards including S.K. Desai Award from Insurance Institute of India, Mumbai. He received World Leader Business Person Bizz Award 2013, 2014 and 2015 from WORLDCOB, Texas, USA, and Best Manager Award from Europe Business Assembly (EBA), UK, 2013. He secured prizes of FAIR essay competition in 2010–2011. More than 70 articles and 11 books/booklets of Mortuza Ali have been published so far.

Aishath Muneeza is an associate professor at INCEIF. She is the first female Deputy Minister of Ministry of Islamic Affairs and is the Deputy Minister of Ministry of Finance & Treasury of the Republic of Maldives. She is also the chairwoman of Maldives Center for Islamic Finance. She is considered as the founder of Islamic finance in Maldives. Her contribution to Islamic finance includes structuring of the corporate sukuks and sovereign private sukuks of the country including the Islamic treasury instruments. She also drafted the Islamic Capital Market framework of the country and is the only registered Shari'ah adviser for Islamic capital market in the country since 2013. She played a key role in the setting up of the Tabung Haji of Maldives, Maldives Hajj Corporation, and was the first chairperson of it. She sits in various *Shari'ah* advisory bodies nationally and internationally and is the chairman for many of these *Shari'ah* advisory bodies including the apex Shari'ah Advisory Council for capital market in Maldives. She has assisted more than 11 institutions to offer Islamic financial products/services. She won various national and international awards for her contribution made towards the development of Islamic finance industry. She is also a role model and a mentor for females who aspire to build their careers in Islamic finance industry and is the Vice President of Women on Boards, an NGO advocating women representation on boards of companies. She is an invited speaker in Islamic finance conferences and events held in different parts of the world. She was listed in 2017 as number seven among the 50 Influential Women in Business and Finance by ISFIRE, which is an official publication of Islamic Bankers Association based in London, and she is among the most influential 500 in Islamic Economy. She is a member of the Association of Shari'ah Advisors in Islamic Finance Malaysia (ASAS), Malaysia. She holds a doctorate in law from the International Islamic University of Malaysia.

Zakariya Mustapha, LLM practises law in Nigeria, where he is an advocate and solicitor of Nigeria's Supreme Court since 2008. In 2010, he joined Faculty of Law Bayero University Kano, Nigeria, as a lecturer where he taught conventional and Islamic banking and finance law, alongside other Islamic law courses until 2017. He specializes on legal and *Shari'ah* issues in Islamic banking and finance and offers legal and Islamic financial advisory services about legal framework, dispute resolution and Shari'ah-compliant product development in Islamic banking and finance. He has published numerous articles, and he has presented research papers in national and international conferences. He holds an LLB, LLM, BL with membership of Nigerian Bar Association and Nigerian Institute of Management (Chartered). He is pursuing his PhD in Islamic finance law at faculty of law University of Malaya, Kuala Lumpur.

Priyesta Rizkiningsih, MSc is a senior researcher in the Center of Strategic Studies, the National Board of *Zakat*, the Republic of Indonesia

(Puskas BAZNAS). Previously she worked as a research assistant at the Central Bank of Indonesia. She holds a master's degree in Islamic Finance and Management from Durham University, UK, with a full scholarship from Indonesia Endowment Fund for Education. Her research interests are Islamic social finance as well as governance and social reporting.

Aroua Robbana, MSc is a holder of Msc in Islamic finance from the International Centre for Education in Islamic Finance (INCEIF). She is pursuing her PhD at the International Islamic University Malaysia (IIUM). Her research interests comprise Islamic finance, Islamic economics, *Zakat* and fintech.

Abdul Aziz Yahya Saoqi, MSc received a bachelor's degree in Islamic economics from Tazkia University in Indonesia with cum laude predicate. Moreover, in 2015 he received a scholarship from Maybank Islamic Berhad to continue a master's degree in Islamic finance at International Islamic University Malaysia and completed the same in 2017. In the years 2018–2019, he served as a research fellow at Central Bank of Indonesia in Islamic Economics and Finance Department. From 2019, he has been with BAZNAS Center of Strategic Studies (Puskas BAZNAS) of the Republic of Indonesia holding the position of senior researcher in the organization. Amid his career, he has been involved in several national strategic projects in the Islamic social finance area. In Central Bank, he was involved in designing Shariah and Internal Audit Standards for Zakat Institution and other projects related to Islamic social finance issues. In BAZNAS Center of Strategic Studies, he leads significant and impactful projects and surveys such us National Zakat Literacy Index and Shariah-Compliance Index for Zakat Institutions across the nation and other related projects. Besides, he is also an active speaker in webinars that discuss the issue of Islamic social finance.

Randi Swandaru, MSc is head of the Division of Zakat Utilization at the National Board of Zakat, the Republic of Indonesia (BAZNAS). He is responsible for managing the zakat fund for economic empowerment programs with the aims of alleviating poverty. He leads four economic empowerment programs, namely BAZNAS Zakat Community Development, BAZNAS Microfinance, BAZNAS Institute of Mustahik Breeder Empowerment, and BAZNAS Institute of Mustahik Economic

Empowerment. He graduated the master's program of Islamic Finance and Management at Durham University in 2017 as the best academic performance student. He also received several awards such as Young Southeast Asian Leaders Initiative (2020), Obama Foundation Leaders Asia Pacific (2019), Future Leaders Connect British Council (2018) and third place in Indonesia Financial Authority Financial Inclusion Competition.

Ahmed Tahiri Jouti holds a PhD in Islamic Finance and Economics and serves management board at Al Maali Group (Dubai—Casablanca) in charge of Al Maali Auditing & Al Maali Dubai. He led many consulting assignments related to Islamic Banks, Takaful, IT providers and government agencies in Morocco, Algeria, Spain, France, Ethiopia, Somalia and KSA in terms of strategic plans and visions, corporate and Shari'ah governance systems, product development and market surveys, policies in terms of risk management, accounting, internal control and marketing, implementation of IT systems; associate editor at *ISRA International Journal of Islamic Finance*—Kuala Lumpur, Islamic finance news correspondent—Morocco and Algeria; international trainer in Islamic Banking, Takaful and Shari'ah Auditing. He has given many training sessions in Morocco, Algeria, Tunisia, Ethiopia and France. Worked as an auditor—Head of Mission in Societe Generale.

Kazi Mohammad Tarique is an assistant professor, School of Business Studies, University of Liberal Arts, Bangladesh. He has completed his undergraduate degree in Business Administration from North South University, Dhaka, Bangladesh, in 2001. After that in 2005 he completed his Master's in International Finance from London Metropolitan University (UK). In 2017, he completed his PhD in Business Administration from International Islamic University Malaysia. His PhD work titled "A Maqasid (Objective) Based Performance Evaluation Index for Islamic Banks" received RM 63,000 grant from the Malaysian government. He has been teaching in different areas of finance, banking and Islamic banking and finance in both graduate and undergraduate levels for last 14 years. He also delivers lecture at the Bangladesh Bank Training Institute as a guest lecturer on Islamic banking. His research interests include Islamic banking and finance, service quality and multi-criteria decision-making. His 14 journal articles have appeared in peer-reviewed journals including 5 in *Scopus*. He also presented papers in different international conferences in Malaysia and Indonesia.

Tajudeen Olalekan Yusuf bagged his Bachelor's and Master's degrees in Insurance and Management from the University of Lagos. As a lecturer in the department of Actuarial Science and Insurance, University of Lagos, he travelled to England in 2004 to obtain his second Master's degree in Islamic Management, Banking and Finance (with Distinction) from the Loughborough University and a PhD in Insurance in Nottingham University Business School in 2009. He is an associate professor in the Faculty of Management Sciences, University of Lagos. As an academic, Yusuf has travelled to several countries, including the USA, the UK, Malaysia, Japan and Kenya to deliver lectures and participate in learned conferences, seminars and workshops. His 50 articles have been published in referred and peer-reviewed journals both locally and internationally in Islamic finance and risk management. He is an Associate Member and Chartered Insurer of Chartered Insurance Institute of London. He is the Chairman of the Lagos State Muslim Pilgrims' Welfare Board and the founder and Fellow of the Institute of Islamic Finance Professionals (IIFP) in Nigeria. As an Islamic scholar, Yusuf is one of the Imams of the University of Lagos Muslim Community and former staff adviser for the Muslim Students' Society of Nigeria, University of Lagos Branch. Yusuf is an oratory speaker who regularly gives lectures on varied Islamic subjects in public, radio and television. His hobbies are travelling and keeping tab on current affairs. He has also authored Islamic books such as *Winning Souls for Allah*, *Conquering Shaytan*, *Mosque: Basics and Management*.

Muhammad Hasbi Zaenal is a deputy director in the Center of Strategic Studies, the National Board of Zakat, Republic of Indonesia (Puskas BAZNAS), and research fellow in Islamic Economic Studies and Thoughts Centre (IESTC). He graduated from Al-Azhar University (Bachelor's degree) and Universiti Kebangsaan Malaysia (Master's and PhD). His previous experiences include as researcher at the Research Center for Islamic Economics and Finance, School of Economics, Universiti Kebangsaan Malaysia from 2011 to 2014 and research assistant at Islamic Research and Training Institute, Islamic Development Bank from 2013 to 2017.

Nor Razinah Mohd. Zain is an assistant professor at the IIUM Institute of Islamic Banking and Finance (IIiBF). She actively participated and published on Dispute Resolution, Islamic Banking, Islamic Social Finance and Islamization of Knowledge since 2013. She was trained in mediation for conflict solution and trauma conciliation by Prof Johan Galtung, the Founder of Peace Research Institute Oslo, Norway, in 2014. Prior to joining IIiBF, she was an Advocate and Solicitor of the High Court of Malaya (non-practising). She is the acting Editor for *Journal of Islamic Finance* and Islamization Coordinator for IIiBF. She is also an active member of the International Council of Islamic Finance Educators (ICIFE) and Association of Sharīʿah Advisors in Islamic Finance (ASAS). Recently, she and her team successfully proposed the use of dispute resolution to the Malaysian government, which leads to the establishment of the National Unity and Reconciliation Council in overcoming interfaith and interracial disputes. She also has researches relating to FinTech, smart contracts and their impacts on regulations and Sharīʿah principles. She contributed a chapter of a book titled "Settlement of Islamic Finance Disputes in the United Arab Emirates", in an edited book titled *Dispute Resolution in Islamic Finance*, 2019. Her latest research on Islamic Social Finance can be found in the Global Islamic Finance Report 2019, organized by the Cambridge Institute of Islamic Finance.

Abdolhossein (Pejman) Zameni is Senior Lecturer in Finance, Segi University, Malaysia. Zameni obtained a BSc in Industrial Engineering at the Mazandaran University of Science and Technology in Iran. In 2006, in order to pursue his education in an international environment, he moved to Malaysia and obtained his MBA in Finance at Multimedia University. In 2014, he was awarded a PhD in Finance by the National University of Malaysia (UKM). Zameni has experience in the delivery of educational programmes at undergraduate levels, as well as business experience within the fields of finance, accounting and industry.

About the Author/Editor

Mohd Ma'Sum Billah, DBA, PhD, MBA, MCL, MMB, LLB (hons), is Professor of Finance, Insurance, Fintech and Investment, Islamic Economics Institute, King Abdulaziz University, Kingdom of Saudi Arabia. Billah had been serving and contributing both academic and corporate industries for more than 25 years with management, teaching, research, solution proving and sharing of strategic and technical know-how towards the advancement of Islamic finance, fintech, business and insurance (*Takaful*) besides *Halal* standard. Billah has published 36 books and chapters in books besides more than 200 articles in journals and social media. He had been presenting in more than 300 conferences, seminars, executive workshops and industrial trainings in different parts of the world. In addition, he had also been affiliated with corporate, academic and financial industries including central banks, international corporate organizations, governments and NGOs in his capacity as a member in boards, director, advisor, strategic decision maker, transformer and reformer with strategic solutions and technical know-how. Among the areas of his interest and contributions are Islamic finance, insurance (*takaful*), crowd-funding, investment, *Zakat*, *Waqf*, capital market (*Sukuk*), social finance, SDGs, petroleum finance, trade, fin-tech, Crypto-asset and cryptocurrency models, standards, strategies and technical know-how.

List of Figures

List of Tables

Introduction

If we can recall back to 11 years when financial giant Lehman Brothers filed for bankruptcy on September 15, 2008, the financial world was shaken by a discovered paradigm. The conceptual origin of FinTech was discovered in 2008, but the central idea with reality began years after only in the recent years (2013 might be recorded) mainly through some applications like crowdfunding, smart payment and cryptocurrency. This anticipated that the next wave of economy would completely change the face of the financial industry, eventually leading to the invention of a new breed of financial innovation—financial technology (fin-tech). Fin-tech is the recently discovered smart financial solution and innovation that aims to dominate the traditional financial platforms to offer smart financial products and services. It is an emerging industry that uses smart technology to advancing financial activities and due performance. The use of smartphones for the mobile banking, investing services and digital currencies is one of the experiences of fin-tech aiming to make financial services more efficient, friendly, productive, less cost in high return and accessible to all levels of mankind. Numerous existing financial institutions design and adapt fin-tech solutions aiming at improving and developing their services smartly, to maximize the opportunities for the providers, consumers and the decision-makers as well.

In the smart economic chapter of the contemporary reality, the emergence of fin-tech is significantly realized with utmost appreciation. The Shari'ah alternative of fin-tech is no exception, which ought to have been appreciated in the core components of economics and finance within the rules of *Maqasid al-Shari'ah*. The mindset of fin-tech under the Shari'ah is however a smart digital financial solution with virtual action with a borderless liberty to maximize the legitimate (Halal) opportunity for all with less effort, within an affordable cost and by economic time. The growth of the fin-tech under the Shari'ah discipline is among the fastest of the financial components of the contemporary world economy. Despite its successful journey, it is not free from any undesirable catastrophe; one may be due to regulatory weakness, poor securities, uncertainties, inadequate operational mechanisms, lack of professionals, malpractices, manipulative attacks and lack of market confidence. It is thus undeniably admitted that there are huge demands in fin-tech in the economic culture, but not sufficient solutions of it under the *Shari'ah* principles, yet despite the global market desires one to move on in parallel with the conventional counterpart.

No doubt that the growth of Islamic finance today is significantly realized, and its fin-tech is no exception. It is thus timely to meet the market demand across the world by producing an efficient fin-tech platform under the *Shari'ah* ethical principles. Despite all the advancement scenarios along with minor shortcomings of fin-tech, it is further hypothetical queried; what is the limitation of the fin-tech under the *Shari'ah* principles? What are the strength, weaknesses, opportunities and threat in the fin-tech? What shall be the true model of a *Halal* fin-tech? How may the operational mechanism of a *Halal* fin-tech be? What are the added significant results anticipated in the fin-tech particularly for the socio-economic environment? This book however aims at addressing core components of fin-tech with possible industrial solutions within the *Maqasid al-Shari'ah* in enabling operators, consumers, traders, issuers, promoters, facilitators, managers, decision-makers, academia, researchers, students and other relevant professionals to understand the *Shari'ah* fin-tech and its practical mechanisms. Among the issues to be covered by the project are an understanding of fin-tech from *Shari'ah* and corporate perspectives, its global phenomena and the worldview, the *Shari'ah* model of fin-tech, its SWOT analysis, conventional practices and the *Shari'ah* dichotomy, regulatory standard, technology, system, mechanisms, strategies, products and services, business plan, innovation, opportunities, risk factors and *takaful* solution. An attempt will however be made in this research to establish an Islamic fin-tech model touching on core issues along with possible industrial solutions, aiming at meeting the contemporary global market demand.

PART I

Emergence of Islamic FinTech

CHAPTER 1

Emergence of i-FinTech in the Contemporary Socio-Economic Reality

Mohd Ma'Sum Billah, Suhail Ahmad, and Sahibzada Ghisaul Haq

Abstract The objectives of the study are to describe the emergence of FinTech and its implications for Islamic finance industries both in Pakistan and also on the global scenario. It includes FinTech's emergence and adaptation by different countries around the globe. It refers to the useof modern and advanced technological applications in financial services and activities. FinTech is a newly emerging innovative tool of operations and financial activities for organizations, firms, and companies. The Islamic financial services industry adopts FinTech in their business operations and activities to gain easy access to their different products, services, and other contracts and activities for customers and stakeholders. FinTech in the Islamic financial service industry is practiced by different countries around

The authors acknowledge that this article is a revised version of their original research, intended for publication for the benefit of academia, researchers, industrialists, and students.

M. M. Billah (✉)
Islamic Economics Institute, King Abdulaziz University, Jeddah, Saudi Arabia

S. Ahmad • S. G. Haq
Sarhad University of Science & Information Technology, Peshawar, Pakistan

M. M. Billah (ed.), *Islamic FinTech*,
https://doi.org/10.1007/978-3-030-45827-0_1

the globe. Prominent countries like, Malaysia, UAE, the UK, Indonesia, and the USA have adopted Islamic FinTech in their regions and use it to promote Islamic financial services to stakeholders in their regions. The study is qualitative in nature and uses conducted interviews from financial experts in the Islamic financial industry, bankers, and also with scholars of Shari'ah and jurisprudence. In Pakistan, the concept is new and still in its infancy. There is a lack of the necessary awareness about Islamic FinTech. Awareness campaigns such as seminars, conferences, workshops, road shows, and other types of activity are required for introducing an awareness of Islamic FinTech into countries. The Islamic financial industry needs to adopt joint ventures and alliances with highly technological companies around the globe, such as Samsung, Apple, and other dominant companies, for making and developing new Shari'ah-compliant products and services for customers. For the target segments of Islamic FinTech, Pakistan firms, companies, and organizations are focused on the young generation as their population is increasing along with their use of technology like mobile or smart phones, the Internet, and other advanced technologies. Similarly, FinTech also targets the female population and provides different financial services, products, and other related activities to them. Islamic FinTech has a great future in Pakistan, once the proper marketing and awareness campaign is launched and circulated throughout the country. The role of the State Bank of Pakistan cannot be ignored in introducing and boosting FinTech to different Islamic financial services organizations and institutions in the country. The study is original in nature and has not previously been published.

Keywords FinTech • Islamic FinTech • Islamic finance • Digitization

An Overview

FinTech is the combination of two words: "Fin" and "Tech." "Fin" is abbreviated from "Finance" and "Tech" from "Technology" (Aslam, 2017). Meaning "Finance Technology" it has been shortened to "FinTech" (Kanwal, 2017). FinTech refers to the use and application of technology in the finance industry, providing financial services in a new and modern mode of technological innovation to the customer (Rahim, 2016). It covers a wide range of activities, such as payments, financing, security, and the safety of customers' funds and information. It also covers operations and risk management (Abdullah, 2016).

Thus, FinTech is the combination of finance and technology, using technological innovation in financial transactions and different services and products. Within the Islamic financial sector, FinTech ensures Shari'ah compliance of products and services practices with social and ethnicity practices. It began with the aim of accelerating financial services to customers so they can conveniently reach services offered by the financial industry. The FinTech industry is growing rapidly all over the globe. It invested up to US$ 12 billion in 2014 compared to US$ 4 billion in 2013 (Abdullah, 2016).

The use of mobile devices like smart phones, tablets, and iPhones has had a global impact on FinTech, because customers around the world increasingly use these devices to access financial transactions and services. The percentage of customers using such devices to gain easy access to financial transactions, products, and services is for the UK 26 percent, Canada 28 percent, Hong Kong 36 percent, China 50 percent and India 58 percent (Aslam, 2017). Digital financial inclusion is a means to provide people with digital financial services (Manyika, Lund, Singer, White, & Berry, 2016). The Indian economy is considered a digital economy around the globe. It has one billion cellphones; 330 million people use the Internet, and smart phone users are up to 240 million.

According to the vice-president of the Asian Development Bank, the bank is trying its best for its member countries to develop and implement a digital financial economy in the development of small and medium enterprises, which will work for the welfare of the individuals.

Objectives of the Study

The objectives of this study are to present FinTech and its entry onto the financial scene and the implications of FinTech for Islamic finance industries in Pakistan, including its emergence and adaptation by different countries around the globe. This study also has a positive step in making an addition to the literature in the field of FinTech and its adaptation by Islamic financial service industries around the world for further studies and research purposes.

Commonly Used Concepts of FinTech

There are some concepts of FinTech which are normally used around the globe in order to practice technological innovation within financial transactions and other financial activities.

Digital Coin or Crypto Currency

FinTech is a digital asset constructed through technological applications (cryptography), forming a secure medium of exchange, and controlling for additional currency units known as crypto currencies. Crypto currencies have different forms around the globe, such as bitcoin, ripple, and prime coin (Augur, 2016; Park, Pietrzak, Alwen, Fuchsbauer, & Gazi, 2015).

Crowdfunding

Crowdfunding is a technological method by which a large pool of individuals combine and invest their funds for certain projects or an activity (Suleiman, 2016). It is a method of using the Internet and other technological instruments to collect money from individuals to enable small-scale entrepreneurs to boost their businesses (Bradford, 2012). It connects individuals through a network, and collects some portion of their funds for a collective business course of action such as financing, the operation of activities, and learning (Botsman, 2015). Crowdfunding is a digital economy formed by individuals through a distributed network to jointly form a fund for a specific course of actions, e.g. projects, venture, alliances, and other related means of financial activities.

P2P Lending

P2P lending means peer-to-peer lending, also called social lending, in which lenders and borrowers manage their transactions through an online platform. It is a social lending in which lenders agree to loan money to borrowers through an online platform. This lowers the cost of traditional lending and minimizes the time framework (Augur, 2016).

ROBO Advisory Firms

The ROBO advisory firm is a class of financial advisor that provides financial advice in portfolio management in digitized form, with minimal human intervention. It provides financial services according to mathematical or algorithmic rules (Summerfield, 2017). The author further argues that the FinTech concepts and activities are not only limited to the above, but that there are FinTech lists available, like block chain, electronic commerce (E-Commerce), B2B (Business to Business), B2C (Business to Consumer), G2P and other concepts and platforms under the umbrella of FinTech.

Literature Review

This study summarizes and presents the relevant literature and researches undertaken by scholars, academics, and researchers in the field of Islamic FinTech and Islamic financial service industries around the globe. Digital technology in Islamic finance plays a remarkable role in providing services to customers in a more convenient way. It can provide the fastest form, and the customer can easily access the services and products of the Islamic finance industries in their home, workplace, and other public places. There is no need for time consumed for wondering about the branch network of Islamic financial institutions, because due to FinTech all such types of activities are changed through a digitized form of services by the Islamic financial institutions. FinTech in Islamic finance should strictly follow and implement the basic rules of Shari'ah principles and jurisprudence, and strongly discourage activities like paying interest, bribery, gambling, cheating, and unethical financing activities (Abdullah, 2017).

FinTech in the Islamic finance industry plays an important role in supporting and encouraging its services and products to customers in a faster and modern way, via the use of technology. It is an innovative opportunity in the financial sector and cannot be ignored by the Islamic financial industry around the globe because digital customers and mobile banking customers are on the rise, particularly in Malaysia, concludes Omar, M., assistant-governor of the Central Bank of Malaysia. He further argued that the Islamic finance industry is boosting up with more investment in FinTech and their new and emerging players in this field. Moreover, he concluded that they are trying to redesign and revise their existing model of the Islamic finance industry in a new and more digitized form, as is now emerging via FinTech. According to Nazrin Shah (financial ambassador in the Malaysian International Islamic Finance Center) "in the world of FinTech the Islamic finance industry plays its role in changing the financial world of digitized form by adopting the new phenomena of FinTech but keeping and ensuring Shari'ah teachings and ethical norms and values." The ROBO advisory firm is established in New York and named as Wahed Invest Corporation, which works in various portfolio managements in the light of Shari'ah and ethical Islamic finance all over the world (Summerfield, 2017).

Nilish Chadha (co-founder of Wahed Inc.) argued that, "it is the future of wealth management and ethical business. They developed their technology to combine portfolio management and investments in a socially responsible manner" (Summerfield, 2017). As Malaysia is a hub for the Islamic financial industry, it also focuses on FinTech to Islamic financial institutions not only in their region but also globally so that other economies of the world can benefit from the newly emerging innovations in the sector. They have established cross-border currency channels called Investment Account Platforms. These are Shari'ah-based investment platforms for Islamic banks to reposition themselves to play the role of an investor and not just as credit providers' institutions in the marketplace. Similar to the FinTech trend around the globe, Canada has also contributed to the Islamic financial industry the applications and strong support of FinTech. Gold money is recognized as gold-based financial products according to the teaching of Shari'ah (Summerfield, 2017).

"Ethics Venture" established a charitable crowdfunding platform in Malaysia called "Global Sadqah." It is working for social finance and its objectives are to enhance and benefit the poor community (IFN, 2017). "Hello Gold" is a Malaysian company working as an online Shari'ah-compliant platform which uses a block chain. It operates within the country and planned to do business in Indonesia, Philippines, and Thailand and to enter into China by 2019 (Vizcaino, 2017). In the United Arab Emirates a crowdfunding firm named "Beehive" operates to enhance Islamic banking in the country for development of SMEs (Small & Medium Enterprises) and similarly in Indonesia, "Blossom Finance" operates for encouraging SMEs to provide Shari'ah-based financial services.

Islamic crowdfunding is practiced in the UK by Javed Khan, the owner of PropTech, a real estate firm. It works in real estate and initially focused on the residential sector, but now has a plan to enter the commercial sector. It serves as Islamic crowdfunding in real estate and its services are Shari'ah-compliant. It has planned to target Pakistan as well as Saudi

Arabia (KSA) in the future. Similarly in the US, the firm "Life beyond Boarders Studio" has set up a FinTech firm known as "Hajj builder" for the Muslim community to perform Hajj and Umraah by different programs of savings, investments, and travel (IFN, 2017).

FinTech is a newly emerging trend around the globe. The world is a global village and any innovations and new ideas that appear in one region can impact another region of the globe. Financial technology is being used in the Pakistani financial industry, because the large young generation makes frequent use of the Internet and mobile devices (Kanwal, 2017).

According to the State Bank of Pakistan newsletter in 2015, various banks have developed branchless banking for their customers. These include United Bank Limited (UBL), Muslim Commercial Bank (MCB), Habib Bank Limited (HBL), Meezan Bank, Bank of Punjab, Bank Alfalah, and many others working with mobile companies to facilitate and work as FinTech to provide products and services to customers. These banks provide conventional financing as well as Islamic financial services to customers. Among them, some banks are Islamic banks and some of them are conventional banks, and have separate branches, which provide and ensure Islamic financial products and services.

In January 2016 the State Bank of Pakistan framed a committee called the Digital Financial Services and Payments System (DFSP) for digital financial inclusions in the country, which aimed to formulate, plan, and implement financial inclusion strategies in the country. Islamic banking and financial institutions launched branchless baking and customers can access services through mobiles, smart phones, the Internet, and other modern technologies. Similarly, debit card, credit card, online payments, and other activities are in operation by different banks and Islamic financial service institutions in the country (SBP, 2018).

Limitations of the Study

The study is limited to the financial sector of Pakistan. In the financial sector, this study focuses only on Islamic banking and other Islamic financial institutions and will exclude other financial sector of the country. The study adopts the interview methods of survey and data collection, in which detailed responses are gathered in formal sessions of interviews with the respondents. Only professional bankers and Shari'ah experts and scholars are the target populations for the study, and particularly professional bankers of the rank of branch managers and above are considered for interview sessions. In addition, Shari'ah experts and scholars are considered for responses, since they have the knowledge of Shari'ah, technology, and the banking and financial sectors.

Methodology

The study is qualitative in nature and conducts interviews with financial experts from the Islamic financial industry, bankers, and with scholars of Shari'ah and jurisprudence. In addition, previous studies from different scholars, researchers, and some discussions, formal and informal sessions, are also included in the study. For the survey, a total of ten respondents participated in the survey, in which five are experts in banking professional and five are experts in Shari'ah, these scholars having knowledge of information and communication technologies.

The following questions were asked of the experts in the subject domain (Table 1.1).

In the interview session, the professional bankers' responses are recorded in the following words:

Table 1.1 List of questions answered by the subject experts

S. No.	*Statement*	*Bankers and Shari'ah experts*	*Total*
Q1.	What do you know about FinTech?	Professional bankers = 6 + Shari'ah experts = 4	10
Q2.	Do you think FinTech adaptation in the banking and financial industry is fruitful in today's business environment?	Professional bankers = 8 + Shari'ah experts = 2	10
Q3.	How you experience the FinTech in your bank & financial industry in providing products and services to the customers?	Professional bankers = 7 + Shari'ah experts = 3	10
Q4.	How you will strengthen the Islamic finance in the adoption of FinTech in your Bank/ Organization?	Professional bankers = 4 + Shari'ah experts = 6	10
Q5.	Is FinTech in the Islamic finance industry in Pakistan playing their role in uplifting the Islamic financial industry in the country?	Professional bankers = 5 + Shari'ah experts = 5	10

Q1:

- *"FinTech is the emerging financial service and technology for the sake of business development, especially in the financial sector in the twenty-first century." (n = 6).*

Q2:

- *"Yes of course; today the World is a global village and all the countries across the globe are not far away from a click of the mouse. All the sectors are using the technology and no one can deny the importance of technology in this revolutionary phase towards information and communication technologies. As I am a professional banker, so I am concerned with the financial sector, so the financial and banking sectors even cannot operate without the technology in today's business environment, in which everywhere is the slogan and adoption of technology and moving at fast speed from conventional ways of business to modern adoption of information and communication technologies. And last but not least, I think that FinTech is of the utmost necessity in the banking and financial industry in providing their products and services to their customers in a very fast way." (n = 8).*

Q3:

- *"Well, I have experience of about 30 years in the banking profession, since the early 90s in Pakistan; we have a totally manual form of documentation, account opening, customer's facilitation, deposits, drawings, and all the other operations. These manual forms of operation were time consuming and also required more personnel to facilitate and provide services to the customers. But as the technology emerges in the banking and financial sectors, so the way of business and operations is totally changed and has expedited the whole system of operations. For example; when without FinTech, if we served twenty customers in a day, so with the adaptation of the newly emerging technology of FinTech, now we serve twenty customers in an hour. Let us see the difference of operations in a fast way. So, FinTech enhances the banking and financial services industry in a revolutionary way of business." (n = 7).*

Q4:

- *"The Islamic finance industry is growing around the globe. In Pakistan the growth rate is not different from the rest of the countries across the globe. As the financial industry adopt FinTech, so the Islamic banks and other financial institutions providing Islamic financial services can also adopt this new way technology, in which they can facilitate their customers and provides services to their customers within the shortest possible time. FinTech has strengthened the business services of the Islamic finance industry by providing them the services, products, and transactions which are fully Shari'ah based, which will definitely achieve their targets and promotethe Shari'ah form of business." (n = 4, 6).*

Q5:

- *"Why not: in Pakistan, the population of the young generation is increasing and information & communication technologies are much used by the young as compared to the other people in the country. Islamic finance targets this population of the country and provides services to them by adopting the new way of business, i.e. (FinTech). By the use of FinTech in the Islamic finance industry in Pakistan, the young generation is aware and can be motivated towards Islamic finance in the country. So by the use of FinTech, the Islamic financial sector can enlarge their customer profile up to these young populations in Pakistan, which results in the promoting and enhancement of the current Islamic finance sector to a maximum level of operations, customer volume, assets, and many more in Pakistan." (n = 5).*

In the interview session, the responses of Shari'ah experts are recorded in the following words:

Q1:

- *"FinTech is the combination of finance and technology. It means the uses of modern technology in the financial sector." (n = 4).*

Q2:

- *"Yes, the financial sector cannot ignore the role of modern technology in their services and operations like the online banking system in which customers can know about their account details, can do deposit, drawings, and transfers through ATMs, and many more." (n = 2).*

Q3:

- *"It is very good to practice the technology in the financial sectors by the banks and other institutions such as, Takaful, Ijarah, and Mudarabah companies, etc. Through the usage of technology in Islamic banking and financial instructions, customers can benefit up to the maximum level as compared to the age of the manual form of documentation."* (*n* = 3).

Q4:

- *"It is the Shari'ah and teaching of Islam, which provides a detailed and comprehensive set for every aspect of life. It is not only limited to the financial aspect of life. Due to FinTech in Islamic financial sectors, it has enhanced and captured the customers towards the Shari'ah-based services, transactions, and other products offered by them in the market to their customers."* (*n* = 6).

Q5:

- *"Yes, FinTech's role cannot be negated in the promotion of Islamic finance in Pakistan. Due to FinTech usage, Islamic banking and other financial institutions offering Islamic financial products and services to their customers is a remarkable change in their operations and facilitations to the customers. Due to which the Islamic finance industry promotes and attains the economic development of Pakistan."* (*n* = 5).

Countries Adopt FinTech with Maqasid al-Shari'ah

Table 1.2 shows information on FinTech and its growth in the Islamic financial industry in countries around the world. It indicates that Malaysia, the UK, Indonesia, UAE, and the US followed by other countries are incorporating Islamic FinTech, which plays a vital role in promoting FinTech in Islamic finance.

Figure 1.1 shows that Islamic FinTech firms are managing different types of operation and forms of their business activities around the world. It shows that 35 percent of Islamic FinTech firms operate in crowdfunding, 17 percent operate their business activities in bank software, 13 percent of firms are practicing in payments and remittances, and 12 percent in P2P business activities. Figure 1.1 also shows that 11 percent of Islamic FinTech companies are carrying out activities in personal finance and management, such as investment, financing, and trading activities of individuals and institutions. While the shares of block chain and crypto currency and digital banking are 5 percent and 4 percent respectively, InsurTech and data and analytics have a share of only 2 percent and 1 percent respectively. It seems that the Islamic financial service industry around the globe

Table 1.2 Top Islamic FinTech countries across the globe

S. No.	*Country name*	*No. of Islamic FinTech companies working*
1.	Malaysia	18
2.	UK	16
3.	Indonesia	15
4.	UAE	12
5.	US	11
6.	Egypt	4
7.	India	4
8.	Pakistan	3
9.	Singapore	3
10.	Jordan	2
11.	Switzerland	2

Source: IFN (2017)

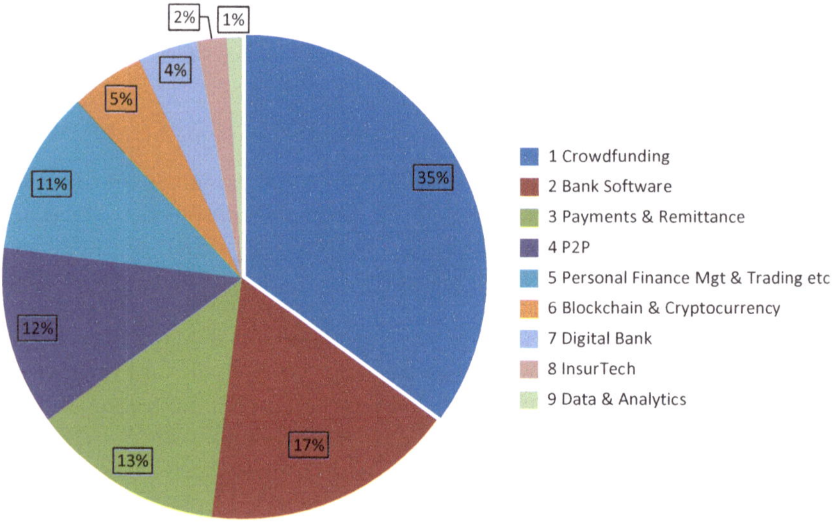

Fig. 1.1 Different types of business around the globe by Islamic FinTech organization. (*Source:* IFN, 2017)

is playing an important role in introducing and promoting Islamic FinTech to different regions in the world.

Final Remarks

To conclude: FinTech is a new concept for developing countries, but developed countries around the world are now familiar with FinTech. And different businesses are adopting this new technology within their various types of business. Alongside existing financial services and product developers, other financial fields such as insurance, property business, Hajj, and similarly for the Sadaqah and Zakat collection and distribution, are all also adopting this new trend in technology across the world.

Pakistan, for example, is a developing country, and is not isolated from the rest of the world. When there is a new technological evolution in the world, Pakistan also adopts the innovation. The FinTech concept is new and still in its infancy in Pakistan, but most of the organizations in the country are adopting this innovation, especially for financial products and services in the banking and financial services industry. Similarly, when the FinTech concept was introduced into the country, the conventional banking and financial industries quickly adopted it. Islamic banks, financial institutions, Takaful, and other products and service providers have also adopted this innovation in their respective fields and organizations for an easy and fast access to their products and services to their customers in the country. Bankers and Shari'ah experts are trying to see the Shari'ah-compliance aspects of the products and services provided through these innovations and technology.

FinTech is a new emerging trend and innovation in the twenty-first century. It is practiced in most of the country. Malaysia as the hub of the Islamic financial service industry in the world is practicing Islamic FinTech and has had fruitful results with it. Customers are facilitated and benefited through Islamic FinTech in Malaysia. Similarly, countries such as the United Kingdom, Indonesia, United Arab Emirates, the United States of America, Egypt, India, Singapore, and Jordan are launching FinTech into their Islamic financial service industries.

Pakistan is also playing its role in introducing FinTech into the Islamic financial service industries in the country, and provides services through new emerging trends and ideas in financial transactions and services to the customers of the region. But as it is still in its infancy stage there is therefore a lack of awareness about FinTech in Pakistan; 72 percent of firms, companies, and institutions do not even know about it. FinTech in the Islamic financial industry targets the youth of the country, because there is a large population of the young generation in Pakistan.

Due to targeting the young population, FinTech can develop and grow according to expectations, but could also expand beyond expectations if fully concentrated and focused on this segment of the population. Financial institutions around the world are practicing different types of Islamic FinTech in their regions. Most of the organization, firms, and companies in the world are carrying out Islamic FinTech activities such as crowdfunding, bank software and networking, payments and remittances, P2P, and personal finance such as financial management, saving investment, and trading activities. Similarly, some of the companies operate Islamic FinTech such as block chain and crypto currencies, digital banking and financial institutions, InsurTech, PropTech, and data security and analysis.

Recommendations

Whenever a new trend or innovation emerges it faces various challenges and hurdles in the development phase, and thus needs effort to promote it. FinTech is also a new emerging field in the Islamic financial industry in the global economies. It also faces challenges in order to raise it to the desired level of its emergence. As it is in its infancy stage, many individuals are not aware of it, and do not even know the word FinTech. So it is necessary to arrange awareness seminars, workshops, symposia, road shows, and campaign for the introduction and awareness of Islamic FinTech to Pakistan.

Marketing is also needed, as due to marketing the public can be made aware of, and fully introduced, to the concept and practices of FinTech for companies. Another major challenge is if FinTech companies are complying with Shari'ah law and Islamic ethical values and norms. Because whenever a service is not certified by Shari'ah laws and concepts, so the customers' (Islamic financial services customers) attention cannot be focused and cannot be motivated by such financial services through FinTech.

Smart phone usage is expected to increase from 16 percent in 2016 to 51 percent in 2020. Similarly, urban areas in Pakistan need to focus and coordinate these areas through FinTech applications. Islamic financial institutions are required to make use of and to adopt the services of advanced technology companies like Samsung, Apple, and Dell, etc., in order to adopt FinTech and introduce a new mechanism of products and services to customers. FinTech is ensuring Shari'ah-compliant and ethical businesses and services.

Islamic financial institutions are required to make an investment in digital banking and financial services and then plan and provide different types of partnership, alliances, and other related ventures to launch FinTech into different segments of the market, especially as the numbers of mobile, smart phones, and Internet users in the country are increasing. The Islamic financial service industry can target these segments and introduce new products, services, and other financial transactions which are compliant with Shari'ah law and ethical norms and values, to the target populations of the country.

Likewise, there is a great opportunity for Islamic financial services industries in Pakistan and around the globe for FinTech to target the female segment. The financial services using mobile users in Pakistan is about 15 percent, but consisting of only 2.9 percent of women. FinTech can also benefit the poor in the country because it provides services and products at lower cost and at a minimum time frame, compared to the involvement of conventional methods of intermediaries in financial transactions and services. By introducing and practicing Islamic FinTech Islamic financial service industries can completely achieve their target of Shari'ah-compliant products, services, and other transactions in the country, and can achieve their target goals.

References

Abdullah, O. (2016). Impact of Fintech to Islamic Finance. Retrieved May 20, 2018, from www.islamicfinance.com/2016/04/impact-fintech-islamic-finance/

Abdullah, O. (2017). Fintech and Shari'ah Governance. Retrieved from www.islamicfinance.com

Aslam, H. (2017). FinTech and the Future. *Pakistan Today*. Retrieved May 15, 2018, from www.pakistantoday.com.pk/2017/03/20/fintech-the-future/

Augur, H. (2016). A Beginner's Guide to Fintech Terminology. Retrieved from https://dataconomy.com/2016/07/a-beginners-guide-to-fintech-terminology/

Botsman, R. (2015). The Sharing Economy Lacks a Shared Definition. *Portuguese Competition Authority, 21*, 1–11.

Bradford, C. S. (2012). Crowdfunding and the Federal Securities Laws. *Columbia Business Law Review*, 1–150.

IFN. (2017). Unlocking the Potential of Islamic Finance. *IFN Fintech Newsletter. Kuala Lumpur Malaysia*, 1–13.
Kanwal, M. (2017). FinTech in Pakistan: Challenges, Opportunities and Recommendations. Retrieved May 17, 2018, from www.techjuice.pk/fintech-in-pakistan-challenges-opportunities-and-recommendations/
Manyika, J., Lund, S., Singer, M., White, O., & Berry, C. (2016). *Digital Finance for All: Powering Inclusive Growth in Emerging Economies.* New York: McKinsey Global Institute. Retrieved from https://www.mckinsey.com/~/media/mckinsey/featured%20insights/Employment%20and%20Growth/How%20digital%20finance%20could%20boost%20growth%20in%20emerging%20economies/MGI-Digital-Finance-For-All-Executive-summary-September-2016.ashx
Park, S., Pietrzak, K., Alwen, J., Fuchsbauer, G., & Gazi, P. (2015). Spacecoin: A Cryptocurrency Based on Proofs of Space. *2015: 528, Tech. Rep.*
Rahim, F. A. (2016). *Fintech Pitch for Islamic Bank: Three New Areas of Services.* Master Thesis, INCEIF Malaysia, 1–7.
SBP. (2018). *General Guidelines Digital Financial Services (DFS) – Innovation Challenge Facility* (pp. 1–10). Agricultural Credit & Microfinance Department, State Bank of Pakistan.
Suleiman, H. (2016). Crowdfunding and the Opportunity Presented in the American Islamic Financial Sphere. *Journal of Islamic Banking and Finance, 33*(4), 61–71.
Summerfield, R. (2017). Innovation in Islamic Finance. *Financier Worldwide Magazine.* Retrieved from www.financierworldwide.com/innovation-in-islamic-finance#.XJNbhskza1s
Vizcaino, B. (2017). FinTech Platforms Add Islamic Finance Capabilities. Retrieved January 10, 2019, from www.reuters.com/article/us-islamic-finance-fintech/fintech-platforms-add-islamic-finance-capabilities

CHAPTER 2

Fintech Versus I-Fintech: A Dichotomy

Faraz Adam

Abstract As conventional financial institutions and conventional start-ups are capitalising on innovative technologies, Islamic financial institutions are yet to take advantage of such technologies. Data shows that more than $50 billion has been invested in Fintech globally since 2010; just 1% of this was channelled to the MENA region, which has a quarter of the global Muslim population (Smith, M. (2017). A Tale of Two Cities, Global Investor, viewed 13 July 2019. [online] Available at. https://fowgilive-blobstorage.blob.core.windows.net/files/GISep2017binder%20(2).pdf). The top ten global Fintech deals in 2018 were all in the US, Europe and China (Fintech Global. (2018). 2018 Is Already a Record Year for Global FinTech Investment—FinTech Global. [online] Available at: https://fintech.global/2018-is-already-a-record-year-for-global-fintech-investment/). Interest in Fintech from the Middle East has grown exponentially in the past couple of years. Fintech sandboxes and government-driven initiatives have been accelerating demand for Fintech. With the MENA region being a major Islamic finance hub, it is of no surprise that Islamic financial institutions are looking to benefit from Fintech. Practitioners believe that Fintech will offer Islamic financial institutions opportunities to thrive and develop further services to a broader market to

F. Adam (✉)
Amanah Advisors, Leicester, UK
e-mail: mfa@amanahadvisors.com

M. M. Billah (ed.), *Islamic FinTech*,
https://doi.org/10.1007/978-3-030-45827-0_2

help the industry grow further. This has given rise to a sector called 'Islamic Fintech'. Does such a term have any substance to it? and what does it mean? How is it different from Fintech? These questions need deliberation and answers. This chapter begins with a brief introduction to Fintech and after that addresses the notion of 'Islamic Fintech'. Thereafter, the landscape of the Islamic Fintech sector is viewed, citing some real use cases of the disruptive technology. Consequently, to demonstrate the dichotomy between Fintech in the conventional finance sector and the Islamic finance sector, six case studies are presented. Three cases are of conventional platforms, while the other three are of Shariah-compliant platforms. Subsequently, the question of dichotomy is answered. The chapter ends with some of the challenges Islamic Fintech is facing and will need to address to excel.

Keywords Fintech • Shariah • Conventional • Innovative Technology

Introduction to Fintech

Fintech is derived from the contraction of finance and technology and stands for financial technologies (Investopedia, 2019). Fintech is empowering and reshaping the service provision of financial institutions. Fintech refers to the technology-driven innovation happening within the financial services industry. This term has become a buzzword to describe the smart design and delivery of financial services and products using technology. That being said, Fintech is also being used to refer to start-up companies which have harnessed new technologies challenging traditional business models, in addition to the sector which comprises of all such companies. Companies in the Fintech industry are usually involved in offering products and services typically offered by financial institutions. However, these Fintech firms are delivering these products and services by leveraging innovative technology and thereby making the entire service affordable, user-friendly and accessible. The number of Fintech firms is predicted to increase, given that Fintech firms are small and agile but possessing enough strength to disrupt well-established business protocols. We learn that Fintech is an umbrella term referring to an array of things, including technologies, innovative methods, companies and new services reshaping the financial services landscape. However, at its core, the thrust behind Fintech is to provide financial services by leveraging the latest software and technology.

The impact of Fintech has been felt in many sectors such as banking, remittance services, lending, deposits, insurance, crowdfunding, wealth management, data management and customer services. According to research conducted by PwC, 73% of the financial sector executives are of the view that banking is the most likely sector to be disrupted and impacted by Fintech (PwC, 2017).

Islamic Fintech

Before considering Islamic Fintech, what is the Shariah position on Fintech? Technology is neutral from a Shariah perspective as it is only an enabler. However, like every financial product or service, Fintech innovations for Islamic financial services are required to adhere to Shariah guidelines. Fintech dealing with financing, investments and investment advisory services must be developed and structured to meet Shariah requirements. Services-based Fintech solutions such as mobile payments, money transfer and trading platforms are universally applicable for both conventional and Islamic finance, and require very little modification for Shariah compliance. Crowdfunding and peer-to-peer (P2P) financing platforms need to have clear Shariah protocols in place to ensure Shariah compliance. The firms operating such platforms should have a Shariah board to oversee the financing and investment processes and to ensure that they comply with the prevailing Shariah standards and acceptable practices. Islamic Fintech firms dealing in investment advisory services need to ensure that their advice is tailored around Shariah-compliant ventures only; the recommendations must not lead customers to be involved in financial instruments which are not Shariah-compliant (GIFR, 2017).

Fintech can be likened to a knife; it can be used in permissible and impermissible ways. A knife can be used for a virtuous action such as cutting fruits to serve one's guests, or it can be used for heinous crimes like murder. The knife is, of course, not to blame, but the user and the way they used this tool. Similarly, Fintech is technology. It can be deployed in rewarding and permissible avenues, or it can be used to execute unlawful transactions. As a tool, Fintech is lawful. It is the usage which is of crucial concern. This is supported by the juristic maxim that states:

> *The fundamental principle is that things are permissible for use until proof of prohibition becomes evident.* (Zakariyah, 2015)

In and of itself, it is *Mubah* (lawful). It is the use of this tool and technology which needs to be considered for Shariah compliance.

Some may argue that the term 'Islamic Fintech' is a misnomer; however, when it is used, the term is being used in the industry to refer to Shariah-compliant Fintech use. Fintech can be applied to conventional financial services or Shariah-compliant financial services. Thus, Islamic Fintech refers to the use of financial technologies in a Shariah-compliant manner. The working definitions of Islamic Fintech include:

1. A digital delivery of Islamic finance.
2. The usage of Fintech utilities: KYC / AML, Blockchain and DLT, Cyber, Payments, Big Data & Machine Learning in Islamic Finance
3. Any Fintech in Muslim market demography that delivers an unmet financial need and or financial inclusion objective
4. Any Shariah-compliant Fintech fund investing in digital infrastructure or economic development anywhere in the world. (Hasan 2018)

Islamic Fintech has enormous potential to boost the Islamic finance industry. Despite being disruptive, Islamic Fintech will accelerate much-needed innovation in the Islamic finance industry. Several countries are seeking to spearhead growth in the Islamic Fintech landscape. The Dubai International Financial Centre (DIFC) has planned to invest $100 million in Fintech start-ups. 'Regulatory sandboxes' have been established in Bahrain and Malaysia to drive Fintech growth (Islamic Fintech Report, 2018).

Islamic banks are already embracing Fintech to increase financial inclusion and offer more products and services to enhance the customer experience. An obvious benefit of embracing Fintech is the potential savings in cost. Fintech allows digital banks to have leaner virtual operations cutting traditional fixed costs.

The investment management industry has also incorporated Fintech. Fintech has led to the development of Shariah-compliant Robo-adviser platforms such as Wahed Invest. These Robo-advisers are digital platforms that offer automated, algorithm-driven financial planning services with minimal human supervision. Such a service typically collects data from the clients through surveys to understand the investment objectives, risk tolerance and return expectations. This data allows the platform to offer advice and automatically invest client wealth and build a diversified portfolio. Robo-advisory services have many benefits. The first benefit of such services is the relatively lower fees as opposed to human financial advisers. Another powerful feature of such Fintech is the automated rebalancing of the client's investment portfolio. Research suggests that recalibrating and rebalancing the client's investment portfolio back to the preferred asset allocation periodically improves return and reduces volatility (Todorof, 2018).

Another novel outcome of Fintech is Smart Sukuk™, where blockchain and smart contracts are used to develop Sukuk. Blockchain is a shared, immutable ledger that facilitates the recording of transactions and tracking assets. One of the outstanding features of blockchain technology is the ability to code smart contracts. Smart contracts execute transactions automatically and register the transactional information onto the blockchain without any human intermediary or involvement. The conditions within such a contract are agreed mutually among the transacting parties. Smart contracts play a considerable role in developing trust in blockchain technology. These innovative tech-based contracts effectively eliminate all the paperwork, thereby smoothening and streamlining the entire process. It can prove to be cost-effective and time efficient. For example, Blossom Finance has developed the idea of Smart Sukuk™ which uses an Ethereum smart contract to collect funds, issue ownership certificates using the ERC20 token standard, remit money across borders, disburse payments proportionately to ownership interests in the underlying assets. All these processes occur automatically using the blockchain and smart contract. Smart Sukuks standardise and automate much of the legal, accounting and payment features of Sukuk offerings. All the necessary information is visible and updated in real time on a single blockchain (Khatri, 2018).

Another Islamic Fintech manifestation is peer-to-peer (P2P) financing. P2P financing is a form of crowdfunding and involves investors financing borrowers without a conventional intermediary like banks. P2P financing uses the internet to connect cash surplus and deficits smartly and smoothly. One such example is the Beehive platform which directly connects creditworthy businesses looking for funding with investors looking to support their growth. The process simply involves a business to apply for finance on the Beehive platform. If an application is approved, the business is listed on the Beehive marketplace. Thereafter, investors provide the finance and receive monthly repayments and profits (Beehive, 2019).

Fintech in the Islamic social finance sector is also gaining momentum. It is argued that traditional Zakat management structures have limited transparency and traceability. The collection and distribution of Zakat are not as efficient as they could be. Blockchain enthusiasts have proposed blockchain-based Zakat system integrated with mobile, web interfaces and analytics can play a significant role in driving transparency and efficiency in the sector. The transparency will be a result of the blockchain, which brings all stakeholders to a common platform. The efficiency will be in integrating different interfaces with the blockchain. Furthermore, the digital technology increases awareness and accessibility. Analytics can assist in identifying need and highlight where resources are needed (Hussain, 2019).

Case Studies: Fintech Versus I-Fintech

To understand the dichotomy between Fintech and Islamic Fintech, six case studies in total are being presented. There are two case studies each for the following three categories: banking, crowdfunding and crypto-exchanges. In each category, there is one case study for conventional finance and one case study for Islamic finance.

Banking

The European Central Bank (ECB) considers a Fintech bank to be one which has "a business model in which the production and delivery of banking products and services are based on technology-enabled innovation" (European Central Bank, 2018)

Fintech revolutionises traditional-banking business models. Fintech offers speed and convenience such that products are delivered and accessed online, increasing the customer convenience. Fintech brings more products to the customers. Fintech allows for remote access to a range of products. Digital-only banks in the form of mobile banking apps are not burdened with overheads for brick-and-mortar branches. The savings in the delivery of products and services allow for better rates and cheaper deals than their traditional counterparts. Fintech banking allows for greater personalisation of products. The technology gathers more data on customers, which then can be used to personalise products and services for its customers (Central Bank of Ireland, 2014).

Case Study 1: Monzo

Digital banks such as Monzo, Starling, Atom, Digibank (India), Finn by Chase, Citi's new digital-only app are intrinsically more adaptable, agile to customer demand, more user-friendly and more customised than traditional banks. Digital banks have a head start than their traditional counterparts by launching as digital platforms using the latest technology from the outset.

Monzo started with one product, a prepaid debit card account named Mondo. It was in April 2017 that it received its banking licence. Monzo transformed into a smart bank for the smartphone generation which does away with things like bricks and mortar branches, cheque books and the like; instead, it hinges around an app. In its own words, Monzo says it is "Focused on building the best current account in the world and ultimately working with a range of other providers so that Mondo can be an intelligent hub for your entire financial life".

Monzo Plus allows customers to add extra features to their accounts with payments starting from £3 a month. Customers can benefit from features like travel insurance or rewards. Monzo Pots are means to set money aside with one's main Monzo account. Multiple pots can be set up for different purposes. Monzo offers 'Savings Pots' which earn interest. Monzo offers overdraft facilities with a daily charge for every day the account is overdrawn by more than a specific amount. The benefit of being a digital platform reduces many traditional overheads. This allows Fintech start-ups to invest the extra funds into providing user-friendly facilities and innovative services. One of the features offered on the Monzo app is budgets. Monzo helps its customers budget by keeping track of their spending. Spend is automatically categorised into a befitting category (Monzo, 2019).

Monzo offers a number of non-Shariah-compliant facilities such as interest-bearing saving pots and overdraft facilities. The saving accounts and overdraft facilities are technically in the ruling of *Qard* (loan) from a Shariah perspective. In Islam, a *Qard* is a gratuitous contract, and it is commendable for a lender to provide a loan to a borrower who needs money. Both the Qur'an and Sunnah promise reward to a lender who provides a loan to a person in need. The Shariah prohibits the lender from deriving any conditional benefit from the borrower. Thus, any profit or additional return in lieu of the loan is impermissible and non-Shariah compliant. Both the Qur'a and the Sunnah have prohibited the lender from charging the borrower any additional amount. The Qur'an emphasises that the lender is entitled to receive the principal amount only. It states:

> *O you who believe! Fear Allah and give up what remains of your demand for usury, if you are indeed believers. If you do it not, take notice of war from Allah and His Messenger. However, if you turn back, you shall have your capital sums: Deal not unjustly, and you shall not be dealt with unjustly.* (al-Qur'an, 2:278-279)

A famous juristic maxim states: "Any loan which draws an increment is Riba" (Ibn Abi Shaybah).

Case Study 2: Insha

The year 2018 saw Albaraka Turk, part of the Al Baraka Banking Group, launching its Insha app in Germany for a branchless and digital banking facility. Insha's website states that an account can be opened in eight minutes via the mobile app. The app provides detailed expense reports, allowing customers to see which month they spend the most, where and how many times they shopped. Customers can transfer funds from their apps to all SEPA countries and to Turkey at any time. Other features include an ATM map, a 'nearest mosque' locator and a Zakat calculator. Insha has a Shariah compliance certificate from the Shariah board where it states that the accounts work on a Mudaraba basis and interest-free finance principles (Getinsha.com, 2019).

Crowdfunding

Traditionally, businesses have had to approach banks for business loans or private investors for investment. However, with the rise of the internet and financial technologies, the past decade has witnessed a boom in an alternative source of funding called crowdfunding. Crowdfunding involves businesses and entrepreneurs pitching their business ideas to potential investors purely through online platforms. Anyone can invest as there are no prior stipulations for those wanting to be part of the crowdfunding. The person seeking finance will present their business model digitally and will earmark a funding target. After that, investors who like the idea of the business are at liberty to invest.

There are six common crowdfunding models: reward-based, donation-based, micro-lending, peer-to-peer, peer-to-business (P2B) and equity. Reward-based platforms showcase products, services and projects which are incentivised with a reward in lieu of the donation. Such platforms commonly offer tiered structures to reward the largest pledgers with the highest value or most unique reward. Donation-based platforms are very similar in structure to rewards-based platforms; however, there is no promise of any reward. The donations are philanthropic and altruistic. Another type of crowdfunding platform is micro-lending. This allows funds to be channelled to those struggling in poverty. The funding empowers them to start a business, acquire skills or study. Debt-based crowdfunding platforms have also gained popularity. Debt-based platforms can be split into two core categories; peer-to-peer (P2P) and peer-to-business (P2B). P2P platforms enable financiers to lend to individuals with annualised interest rates. On the other hand, P2B platforms enable everyday financiers, the government and institutions to finance a range of businesses. As with P2P lending, interest rates are based on a myriad of factors including the risk band and term of the loan. The sixth common type of crowdfunding platform is equity-based platforms. Several crowdfunding platforms offer an equity stake. They facilitate investments into a start-up, early stage and growth companies for a pro-rata equity stake in the company (Hu, et al., 2016).

Case Study 3: Crowdcube

Crowdcube takes advantage of technological developments to enable small businesses to attract investments from professionals, venture capital firms and any interested investor on a digital platform. Launched in February 2011, Crowdcube has since facilitated £689 million in pitches, has 755,590 registered members and 883 successful raises (Crowdcube, 2018)

Crowdcube provides three options for investing: equity, venture funds and minibonds. Equity grants investors share in the start-up and a potential to earn high returns for high-risk investments. A return is gained in the event the company makes an 'exit' in the future. Different types of exits include a trade sale, IPO or share buyback. The primary way investors profit from these equity investments is by selling their share for more than the initial purchase price. There is no active secondary market on Crowdcube. Some companies may pay dividends. The second option of venture funds facilitates a professional fund manager to build and manage the portfolio. The third option is minibonds. This allows the lender to receive a steady fixed-rate return.

Crowdcube is another example of a Fintech crowdfunding platform. The crowdfunding platform showcases a number of non-Shariah-compliant businesses as well as using non-Shariah-compliant methods for fundraising such as bonds.

Case Study 4: EthisCrowd

EthisCrowd is arguably one of the world's first real estate Islamic-crowdfunding platform. This platform facilitates investment in entrepreneurial, business, trade and real estate activities in 'Emerging Asia'. Ethis has a network across Singapore, Indonesia, Malaysia and Australia. The expertise of EthisCrowd is manifest in how it crowdfunds the construction of affordable and commercial housing, mostly in Indonesia, through private and institutional investors, as well as Islamic banks (Islamic Fintech Report, 2018).

According to the Islamic Fintech Report 2018, the company boasts 24,373 community members with $5.59 million in crowd-investments made and $1.64 million of pay-outs to crowd-investors. As per the date of the report, the total value of projects by EthisCrowd in 2018 was $52.8 million. The process of Ethis is straightforward. Investors sign up, browse and select the campaigns they want to invest in. They can then invest directly into the bank accounts of the project. Thereafter, investors will receive monthly project updates by email and on their dashboards on Ethis.

Ethis uses two different Islamic contracts and structures for its investments. The first is an Istisna' (manufacturing) contract. The Istisna' contract is structured in the following way:

1. The project developer appoints Ethis Pte Ltd. (Singapore) as the crowdfunding agent.
2. The investors appoint Ethis as the agent (wakeel) through a Wakalah agreement to execute an Istisna' agreement with the developer for a quantified amount of housing units.
3. The investors sign an Istisna' facility letter and appoint PT Ethis as the agent to act on behalf of the investors.

4. PT Ethis enters into an Istisna' contract with the project developer to fund the construction of the specified number of housing units. The agreement is governed by Indonesian law allowing PT Ethis to take legal action in cases of any misconduct by the project developer.
5. The investments are transferred into PT Ethis's Singapore-dollar-denominated bank account in Indonesia.
6. Payments are made to the project developer based on the milestones of the construction.
7. The project developer develops the agreed housing units.
8. Upon the initiation of the construction, the project developer transfers the conditional ownership of the housing units to PT Ethis through sale certificates (PPJB). Upon the completion of construction, PT Ethis disburses the remaining sale price to the developer, and the Istisna' contract is concluded.

Upon the completion of the Istisna' agreement, the next contract is a Murabahah contract which facilitates the sale of the housing unit to the end-user. The Murabahah is structured in the following manner:

1. PT Ethis selects the project developer as an agent. The project developer's role is to find potential buyers of the units.
2. The project developer sells the units to end buyers approved by Bank Indonesia and the financing bank, commonly Bank BTN Syariah.
3. PT Ethis transfers the sale certificate (PPJB) of the units to the end house buyers.
4. Through a standing instruction on the bank account of the project developer, the proceeds from the sale of the housing units are shared between PT Ethis and the project developer.
5. The financing bank makes both transfers, for example, 70% to PT Ethis and 30% to the Project Developer (as the Wakalah fee from PT Ethis).
6. PT Ethis transfers the investment amounts and the profits to the investors (EthisCrowd, 2017).

Ethiscrowd is an exceptional display of Islamic Fintech. The power of innovative technology is harnessed to connect global investors to invest in the growth of the real economy and provide real estate to those in need.

Crypto Exchanges

Another area of exponential growth in the Fintech industry is crypto-assets. There have been extensive debates on the nature of crypto-assets. Crypto-assets are digital assets which are based on cryptography, peer-to-peer networking, and blockchain (Drescher, 2017). These technologies allow the regulation of the creation of new units, verification of transactions, and the securing of transactions without the intervention of any middleman. The removal of middlemen is argued to be a manifestation of decentralisation and greater transparency. There are various classifications of crypto-assets. One such classification is as follows (Tatar, 2017):

1. Cryptocurrencies

Cryptocurrencies are the most common type of crypto-asset. Examples include Bitcoin, Litecoin and Dash. These seek to serve as decentralised alternatives to fiat currency by facilitating the transfer of value as a medium of payment.

2. Platform tokens

Platform tokens facilitate the development of decentralised projects. The most common platform token is Ethereum. Ethereum's decentralised platform gives a hardware and software base for the development of decentralised applications (dApps). The introduction of smart contracts allows new projects to be built upon the Ethereum platform. New projects can use Ethereum's platform to issue their ERC20 token.

3. Utility tokens

Utility tokens are usually ERC20 tokens built on the Ethereum platform. These tokens serve a specific purpose in mind, customised for the project that issues them. They are used and spent on specific services such as distributed storage, in-app currency or for more operational purposes. The value is derived from the expected use and need of such tokens.

4. Transactional tokens

These crypto-assets serve as a remittance. Ripple is a well-known transactional token used for remittance. These tokens allow fast cross-border payments while providing transparency during the process (Haeems, 2018).

5. Equity Tokens

These tokens are said to represent equity in the issuing company, giving token holders votes as shareholders, participation in future dividends reflecting some form of ownership in the project as well (Karpan, 2019).

Case Study 5: Binance

Binance—derived from the words binary and finance—released their whitepaper in mid-2017 outlining their goal to build a digital asset exchange. The token launched during the Initial Coin Offering (ICO) was the BNB. Binance set their initial conversion rate at $0.10 per BNB. After two weeks of the ICO coming to an end, the Binance exchange went live. The BNB was functional from the very beginning; users could immediately receive discounts on trading, withdrawals and listing fees when they used BNB. The Binance platform was capable of processing 1.4 million orders per second. This resulted in Binance being well ahead of other ICOs at the time. The BNB coin was valued at $0.10 in June 2017 (Grabowski, 2019). Two years later, in June 2019, it was valued at $30. This was due to many features:

1. Quarterly burns

Binance has a strategy of quarterly burns. Every three months, Binance burns BNB from its reserves relative to the amount of trading volume on their exchange. This strategy will continue until only 100 million BNB (50% of the initial supply) remains (Fitzner Blockchain Consulting, 2019).

2. Launchpad sales

Binance was one of the first exchanges offering the ability to purchase tokens directly from their platform. Customers could participate directly in vetted ICOs. Binance facilitated near instant liquidity as trading pairs became available almost immediately after the close of the ICO (Fitzner Blockchain Consulting, 2019).

3. Lottery system

Initially, Binance employed a first-come-first-serve system for those wishing to take part in Launch pads. However, this was causing issues among customers and did not seem to be the most efficient way to serve everyone. Therefore, Binance switched over to a lottery system where BNB ownership would dictate the ability to participate in Launchpad sales. Only those who win the lottery are eligible to participate in the Launchpad sale (Fitzner Blockchain Consulting, 2019).

4. Binance chain and the BEP2 standard

Binance recently launched their native blockchain in which BNB will be the native token and will be used for all transactions that occur on the network. Furthermore, Binance launched Binance DEX, a decentralised exchange on top of this native blockchain. The Binance DEX allows traders to issue and exchange Binance-based digital assets without having to deposit onto a centralised exchange. With the introduction of Binance chain, customers can create a new token standard BEP2, which is a competitor to Ethereum's ERC20 standard (Fitzner Blockchain Consulting, 2019).

Binance is an example of a conventional Fintech product. The cryptocurrencies listed on Binance are not screened according to Shariah screening norms. Likewise, the exchange is not structured to ensure all facilities are Shariah compliant.

Case Study 6: Rain

Rain is a cryptocurrency trading platform in the Middle East, headquartered in Manama, Kingdom of Bahrain. It is licensed and regulated by the Central Bank of Bahrain (CBB). Rain enables traders to buy, sell, and store bitcoin and other cryptocurrencies, in a regulated, secure, and compliant way. Shariyah Review Bureau has reviewed Rain's brokerage service and has determined that the sale, purchase and custodian activities of Rain are in compliance with Shariah principles. The Shariah certification covers a suite of four cryptocurrencies (bitcoin, ethereum, litecoin and XRP).

Conclusion

The case studies highlight the distinct dichotomy between Fintech use in the conventional markets and Fintech use in the Islamic markets. It is this type of usage of Fintech in Shariah-compliant services which has given birth to the term 'Islamic Fintech'. Islamic Fintech has now become a sector in and of itself within the broader framework of Islamic finance and economics. The sector is still in its infancy. There are many Shariah and regulatory questions that need to be answered for the development of this sector. Human capital in this sector is also a scarce resource. However, global forums and summits being staged in the Islamic world give hope for a new breed of Shariah scholars and practitioners who will take the Islamic finance industry further by harnessing the power that lies in Fintech. Further, the user experience and interface design for Islamic Fintech applications need to improve. In the immediate term, accessibility, transparency and efficiency need to be considered in all Islamic Fintech initiatives.

This chapter has analysed the dichotomy between Fintech and Islamic Fintech. It has been argued that Fintech in and of itself is just a tool and that the Shariah compliance of any Fintech product or service will be determined on the way it is delivered. Fintech can be used to deliver conventional finance or Shariah-compliant finance. Thus, in and of itself, Fintech has been deemed lawful from a Shariah compliance perspective. Fintech has impacted banking, remittance services, lending, deposits, insurance, crowdfunding, wealth management, data management and customer services. The gradual use of Fintech in delivering Shariah-compliant facilities has given birth to a new sector called Islamic Fintech. Islamic Fintech refers to the use of financial technologies in a Shariah-compliant manner. A number of countries have come forward to spearhead growth in the Islamic Fintech landscape. The DIFC (Dubai International Financial Center) has planned to invest $100 million in Fintech start-ups. Bahrain and Malaysia are among the leading countries which are involved in Islamic finance to have set up a 'regulatory sandbox' for Fintech growth. The chapter further features a number of Islamic financial institutions which have deployed Fintech in various services such as banking, wealth management, advisory, Sukuk issuance, Zakat management and P2P financing. Six case studies are presented to show the dichotomy between the use of Fintech in conventional finance and Islamic finance. Islamic Fintech is still in its early phase and faces a number of challenges until the full power of Fintech is leveraged. The need for more experts in Shariah, finance and technology to come together and deliver cannot be greater.

References

Beehive. (2019). *How It Works | Peer to Peer Lending | Investment in UAE | Beehive.* [online] Available at: https://www.beehive.ae/how-it-works/

Callahan, T. (2018). *ADAB Solutions to Launch First Islamic Crypto Exchange (FICE) in 2019 in Compliance with Shariah Law—Ibinex News.* [online] Ibinex News. Retrieved July 2, 2019, from https://news.ibinex.com/2018/11/03/adab-solutions-to-launch-first-islamic-crypto-exchange-fice-in-2019-in-compliance-with-shariah-law/

Central Bank of Ireland. (2014). *What Is "Fintech" and How Is It Changing Financial Products?* [online] Available at: https://centralbank.ie/consumer-hub/explainers/what-is-fintech-and-how-is-it-changing-financial-products

Crowdcube.com. (2018). *Online Investing, Equity Crowdfunding, Business Finance: Crowdcube.* Retrieved May 25, 2019, from https://www.crowdcube.com

Drescher, D. (2017). *Blockchain Basics: A Non-Technical Introduction in 25 Steps.* Berkeley, California; New York, NY: A press.

EthisCrowd. (2017). *EthisCrowd—Islamic Crowdfunding.* Retrieved June 14, 2019, from https://www.ethiscrowd.com/how-it-works/

European Central Bank. (2018). *Fine-tuning licensing for fintech banks.* [online] European Central Bank—Banking Supervision. Retrieved June 20, 2019, from https://www.bankingsupervision.europa.eu/press/publications/newsletter/2017/html/ssm.nl171115_1.en.html

Fintech Global. (2018). *2018 Is Already a Record Year for Global FinTech Investment*—FinTech Global. [online] Available at: https://fintech.global/2018-is-already-a-record-year-for-global-fintech-investment/

Fitzner Blockchain Consulting. (2019). *Binance: A Case Study of BNB's Success.* [online] Medium. Retrieved June 24, 2019, from https://medium.com/future-vision/binance-a-case-study-of-bnbs-success-5820cb86edc3

Getinsha.com. (2019). *Insha—The New Face of Interest-free Digital Banking.* Retrieved July 2, 2019, from https://www.getinsha.com/en

GIFR. (2017). Islamic Finance in the Digital Age: Fintech Revolution. Global Islamic Finance Report. [online], Available at: http://www.gifr.net/gifr2017/ch_17.pdf

Grabowski, M. (2019). *Cryptocurrencies: A Primer on Digital Money.* Abingdon, Oxon; New York, NY: Routledge.

Haeems, A. (2018). *What Is a Crypto-asset?* [online] Medium. Retrieved June 1, 2019, from https://medium.com/babb/what-is-a-crypto-asset-1f0fcc517887

Hasan, M. (2018). *Islamic Fintech in Simple Terms | Ethis Crowd Blog*. [online] Ethis Crowd Blog. Retrieved July 10, 2019, from https://www.ethiscrowd.com/blog/understand-islamic-fintech-simple-terms/

Hu, J., Vanhullebusch, M., Harding, A., & Jiao, S. (2016). *Finance, Rule of Law and Development in Asia: Perspectives from Singapore, Hong Kong and Mainland China*. Leiden; Boston: Brill Nijhoff.

Hussain, S. (2019). *Blockchain and Fintech for Islamic Social Finance*. Retrieved June 6, 2019, from https://www.linkedin.com/pulse/blockchain-fintech-islamic-social-finance-syed-shahid-hussain

Investopedia. (2019). *Financial Technology—FintechDefinition*. [online] Available at: https://www.investopedia.com/terms/f/fintech.asp

Islamic Fintech Report 2018 Current Landscape & Path Forward. (2018). Retrieved June 6, 2019, from https://www.dinarstandard.com/wp-content/uploads/2018/12/Islamic-Fintech-Report-2018.pdf

Karpan, A. (2019). *Cryptocurrencies and Blockchain Technology*. New York: Greenhaven Publishing.

Khatri, Y. (2018). *Microfinance Firm Plans Issuance of Shariah-Compliant Blockchain Bonds*. [online] CoinDesk. Retrieved June 29, 2019, from https://www.coindesk.com/microfinance-firm-plans-issuance-of-shariah-compliant-blockchain-bonds

Monzo. (2019). *Your 31 Most-asked Questions About Monzo, Answered*. Retrieved June 29, 2019, from https://monzo.com/blog/2019/06/14/monzo-most-asked-questions/

PwC. (2017). *Customers in the Spotlight: How FinTech Is Reshaping Banking*. [online] PwC. Retrieved June 29, 2019, from https://www.pwc.com/gx/en/industries/financial-services/publications/fintech-is-reshaping-banking.html

Smith, M. (2017). *A Tale of Two Cities*, Global Investor, viewed 13 July 2019. [online] Available at. https://fowgiliveblobstorage.blob.core.windows.net/files/GISep2017binder%20(2).pdf

Tatar, J. (2017). *Cryptoassets: The Innovative Investor's Guide to Bitcoin and Beyond*. New York: Mcgraw-Hill Education.

Todorof, M. (2018). Robo Advice in Islamic Finance. SSRN Electronic Journal. Retrieved July 1, 2019, from https://papers.ssrn.com/sol3/papers.cfm?abstract_id=3337712

Zakariyah. (2015). *Legal Maxims in Islamic Criminal Law: Theory and Applications*. Leiden; Boston: Brill Nijhoff.

CHAPTER 3

Fintech and Maqāsid Dichotomy under the Prism of the Non-Neutrality of Techniques

Abderrazak Belabes

Abstract 'Fintech' and *'Maqāṣid al-Sharī'ah'* remain rare apart from some vague expressions conveyed, for instance, in the HBKU Workshop *Fintech and Islamic Finance* held at the London School of Economics in London, on 23 February (Djafri, Fares. (2017). Summary Report of the 'LSE—HBKU Workshop on Fintech and Islamic Finance', hosted by the Center for Islamic Economics and Finance (CIEF), College of Islamic Studies, Hamad Bin Khalifa University at the London School of Economics on February 23, 2017: 4-5; 7) and a chapter 'Fintech and Shariah Principles in Smart Contracts' (Rahim, N. F., Bakri, M. H., & Yahaya, S. N. (2019). Fintech and Shariah Principles in Smart Contractsm. In A. Rafay (Ed.), *FinTech as a Disruptive Technology for Financial Institutions* (pp. 207–220). Hershey P.A.: IGI Global: 210; 214) published in a recent book *FinTech as a Disruptive Technology for Financial Institutions.* The only writing devoted entirely to the subject *Fintech in the light of Maqāṣid al-Sharī'ah* (Mohammed,

A. Belabes (✉)
Islamic Economics Institute, King Abdulaziz University, Jeddah, Saudi Arabia
e-mail: mfa@afinance.org

M. M. Billah (ed.), *Islamic FinTech*,
https://doi.org/10.1007/978-3-030-45827-0_3

M. O., & El Amri, M. C. (2019). Fintech in the Light of Maqāsid al-Sharī'ah. In U. A. Oseni & S. N. Ali (Eds.), *Fintech in Islamic Finance: Theory and Practice* (pp. 93–112). London: Routledge) was recently published in a collective book on 'Fintech in Islamic Finance'. In spite of its interest, this writing remains very brief and has difficulties overcoming the dominant discourse on the *maqāṣid* in Islamic finance often associated with the five imperative necessities (*al-dharūriyāt al-khams*), in this case: the preservation of religion (*dīn*), being (*nafs*), understanding (*'aql*), offspring (*nasl*), and what is beneficial to human beings (*māl*). The word '*māl*', generally translated as 'wealth' or 'property', corresponds in its broadest sense to the idea of what is beneficial to human beings, as demonstrated by a recent critical study (Belabes, A. (2019). Book Review of 'Islamic social finance' edited by Valentino Cattelan. *Journal of King Abdulaziz University: Islamic Economics, 33*(2), 98–106; 184).

This discourse does not distinguish between the general purposes (*al-Maqāṣid al-'āmah*), the specific purposes (*al-Maqāṣid al-khāṣah*) and the auxiliary purposes (*al-Maqāṣid al-juziyah*), knowing that this field of knowledge requires a finesse of mind and a rigor of understanding (Al-Dihlawī, S. W.-A. (1992). *ḤujjatAllāh al-Bālighah [The Conclusive Argument from God]*. Beirut, Lebanon: Dar Ihya al-Ulum, 1; 21) in the field of jurisprudence methodology (*uṣūl al-fiqh*). To refer to classical authors in the domain, such as al-Juwaynī, his best student al-Ghazālī, or al-Shātibī, is a necessary but not sufficient exercise. Yet one must read their respective writings carefully with the language of Sībawayh, rather than that of Shakespeare or Molière, and seize the real epistemological spans far from any essentialism under the effect of a constant desire for generalization, as some linguists rightly point out (Wittgenstein, [1933-1934]1965: 68).

Keywords Fintech • Maqāsid • Prism • Non-Neutrality • Mechanisms

Introduction

The sketch of applied sciences shows that the reflection on the purposes deals in a general way with the fact, be it a being or a thing, of having a goal assigned either by a superior will, or by a natural end in reference to the function to fulfill (Belabes, 2014: 51-55). Thinking about purposes in the field of FinTech cannot ignore the progress of research on the non-neutrality of technics, stemming from philosophy, history and ethics, in that some technics end up invading the horizon of ends by intrinsically giving themselves their own laws. This shows the usefulness of the chapter which explores the interactions between *Maqāsid* and FinTech under the prism of the non-neutrality of the technics in order to identify some unavoidable questions.

After drawing attention to the need to use moderately the adjective 'Islamic' and the word *maqasid al-Shari'ah*, the chapter evokes the illusion of neutrality and pure instrumentality of technics, before illustrating the ethics of the digital through the case of exponential technologies. The notion of FinTech associated with those of exponential technology and singularity must be approached as a complex system, based on a particular belief of 'transhumanism', and not as a simple means. The conclusions recall the main findings and make some recommendations.

The Need to Use Moderately the Adjective 'Islamic'

Among the most controversial subjects in specialized scientific circles during the last decade appears what is commonly called 'Islamic finance', with a questioning on the nature of its products and its role in the city with regard to the initial intentions. Is it a separate form of finance, fundamentally different from the practices that exist in the world apart from speculative finance, in particular ethical and solidarity finance? Do the principles of Islamic finance really reflect what is happening in the world of finance described as Islamic? Is there a coherent entity that could be described as 'Islamic finance' with regard to what is generally referred to as 'conventional finance' in the same way as polarizations like 'East/West' (Said, 1978), 'Us/the others' (Todorov, 1989) based on representations closed in on themselves and detached from reality? What has given that sense of common belonging on which the myth of a common identity has been built (Corm, 2009)?

This vision, which emphasizes the predominant role of religion in guiding behaviors and decisions, prevents us from treating the real with discernment by observing the facts as 'they are' and not by referring only to our feelings with regard to what we would like 'to be' or 'not to be'. As said by Myson, one of the most illustrious sages of ancient Greece, 'we must not scrutinize the facts based on the words, but scrutinize the words based on the facts' (Laërce, 1999: 145). This vision tends to lock the reflection into a vague thought that puts the critical spirit almost in suspense. This leads to an almost systematic exclusion of what is not called 'Islamic', to make it insignificant, devoid of value, or almost so.

If the facts are approached in such a simple way, why are we giving so much trouble? Is not the certainty of social science a hindrance to a reflection worthy of the name? Does it not lead to dogmatism, the tendency to assert without debate, or proof, what we advance with its corollary autism, which is a form of withdrawal, refusing reality and hearing others? In the world of certainty, there is no room for questioning or for substantive debate. There are only answers, solutions ready, denying time, space, cultural diversity, which is common to all humanity.

The Muslim countries have undergone since the end of the eighteenth century, with the campaign of Egypt undertaken by Napoleon Bonaparte in 1798, a process of colonization that destroyed some internal social structures and emptied others of their real substance. This dual effect demonstrates the limits of the approach based on the intensity of religious beliefs and practices, the approach that emphasizes the structural and institutional separation of the social spheres of religion and religious leadership, and the approach that considers that Islam played an important role in the ideologies of resistance to European colonial rule.

The central question is more about how to read the sacred texts, under whatever pretext, than to claim it, purely and simply, under the effect of emotion, reaction or ideological positioning. However, the critique of any ideology is itself a prisoner of another ideological referent (Mannheim, 1956), which refers to all the symbolic mechanisms by which Man understands himself in a given culture (Ricœur, 1997), and interprets sacred texts for personal, partisan or institutional purposes, whether banks, investment funds or insurance companies.

In this context, can one speak on the real practice of finance that stands out from the usurious and speculative financial system? Or talk about finance that refers to Islam? Is there really an agreement on the content of the adjective 'Islamic' in light of the various interpretations of the Islamic bank that have emerged in the Muslim world since the beginning of the twentieth century, starting with that of Saint Petersburg in 1908 (Belabes, 2016) and Cairo on the same date (Belabes, 2018), without any interference in view of the historical sources consulted so far?

The appeal of the discourse stems more from the endogenous nature of the language that refers to the centrality of the Islamic heritage—or rather its interpretation by the elite of the business world—than its religious dimension to comply scrupulously with the injunctions of the sacred texts without recourse to the stratagems or artificial means (*ḥiyal*), of any nature whatsoever, to circumvent the prohibition.

The tangible answer to the question, 'Is Islam compatible with banking practice?' is in fact 'How do the concerned people justify it according to the understanding of each, most often conducted in the name of an aggiornamento, or a renewed reading of the sacred texts, given the constraints and priorities of the moment?' The discourse that tends to associate everything with Islam—and therefore its opposite created by a whole kaleidoscope of distorting mirrors, reflections and boomerang-type occurrences—proves not only reductive, but dangerous because it underlies the idea that Islam would be the solution to the crises that the Muslim countries are living under the slogan 'Islam is the solution' (*al-Islāmhuwa al-ḥal*), just as it would be the explanatory factor; an idea supported by those who claim that the backwardness of Muslim countries has its origins in religion.

The word 'bank attributed to Islam or claiming to act in its name' is more reflective of the historical reality over a long period than that of 'Islamic bank', no matter what the marketing managers may think who make it an advertising slogan playing on feelings and concerns for the respect of the divine commands.

The rhetoric of 'Us' (Muslims) and 'the others' (the rest of the world, which is reduced most often to the West) constituted a serious obstacle to tackle in a serious and thorough manner substantive issues that do not directly concern others (Westerners in the first place), starting with the production of concepts that reflect the reality of each human group (*'umrānbasharī* or city) in the sense of Ibn Khaldūn (2001: 46), beyond any globalizing position that leads to the intermingling of the senses. However, any city that does not bother to produce concepts that reflect its existence, with the problems, risks and challenges that flow from it, is condemned to consume those of others, because nature hates emptiness.

Maqāṣid al-Shari'ah: A Formula to Use with Caution

In the literature on Islamic finance, the notion of *maqāṣid al-Sharī'ah* is generally used with reference to the classical legal literature, a tool of preeminence or superiority of consideration (*tarjīḥ*) to give more weight to an opinion after careful consideration of the evidence of each other in the absence of formal proof of the *Qurān* and *Sunnah* in a determined, clear, unequivocal way. *Maqāṣid* therefore constitutes a legal tool at the disposal of prominent jurisconsults (*mujtahidūn*) who pronounce judgments (*fatwa*) based on the *Qurān*, *Sunnah*, consensus (*ijmā'*) and reasoning by analogy (*qiyās*).

The first maxim of the science of legal rules (*al-qawā'id al-fiqhiyah*) states that 'things are evaluated according to their purpose' (*al-umūr bi-maqāṣidihā*) (Zarqa, 1993: 47-53). It is one of the five major maxims in the field of financial transactions (Nadvi, 2015: 53-61). The second maxim that follows states that 'contracts are determined according to their purposes and meaning, not their terms and forms' (*al-'ibrahfī al-'uqūd li-al-maqāṣidwa-al-ma'ānī la-li-alfādhwa-al-mabānī*) (Zarqa, 1993: 54-78). In other words, in terms of contract, what is considered, in the first place, is intention and semantics, not terms and syntax.

This illustrates the close connection between the injunctions (*ḥukm*: *Ḥ*), the rule of jurisprudence (*qā'idah*: *Q*), and the finality (*maqṣad*: *M*), which can be summed up through the formula 'triptych ḤQM' as illustrated in the Fig. 3.1.

The paradox is that most of those who engage a discourse on *maqāṣid al-Sharī'ah do* not even master the meaning of the basic notions of the foundations of jurisprudence, in the first place the notion '*maṣlaḥah*', generally translated in a simplistic way as *'public interest'*. Rather, the specialized scientific literature uses the notion of *'maṣlaḥahmursalah'* which refers to a utility (*manfa'ah*) which is neither recognized (*mu'tabarah*)

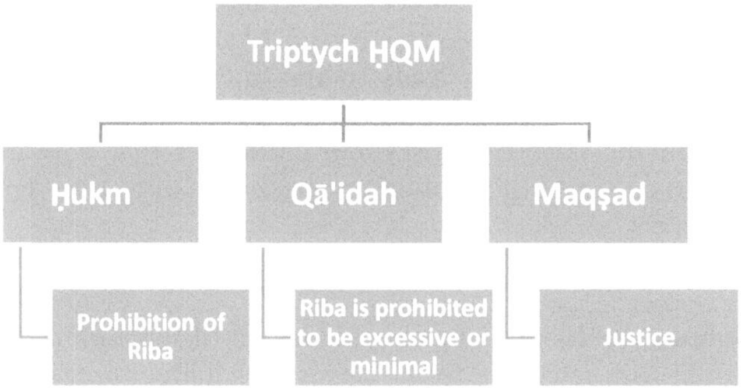

Fig. 3.1 Illustration of the triptych ḤQM

nor canceled (*mulghāt*) by a text of the *Qurān* or the *Sunnah*. However, the jurisconsults have stipulated rules (*dhawābit*) so that the *maṣlaḥah* is not fictitious (*mawhūmah*) in the sense that its disadvantages outweigh its benefits. The use of *maqāṣid* does not amount to follow passions (al-Masri, 2005: 11). The consideration of purposes must be taken into account with caution and wisely: it is not a question of using them to the detriment of the explicit texts of *Qurān* or *Sunnah*, nor to justify infrequent situations or allegations that are not based on solid evidence.

Moreover, the discourse on *maqāṣid al-Sharī'ah* of Islamic finance does not distinguish between general purposes (*al-maqāṣid al-'āmah*), specific purposes (*al-maqāṣid al-khāssah*) and partial purposes (*al-maqāṣid al-juziyah*). The general purposes of *Sharī'ah* with reference to Bin Bayyah (2010: 69-71), as illustrated in Fig. 3.2, cover all areas of life. But on closer inspection, it appears that the principle of worship (*'ibādah*) derives from that of justice, which consists in recognizing the merits, rights and value of God through the Uniqueness of the Lordship (*Tawḥīd al-Rubūbiyah*), the Uniqueness of Worship (*Tawḥīd al-Ulūhiyah*) and the Uniqueness of Names and Attributes (*Tawḥīd al-Asmā' wa al-Ṣifāt*).

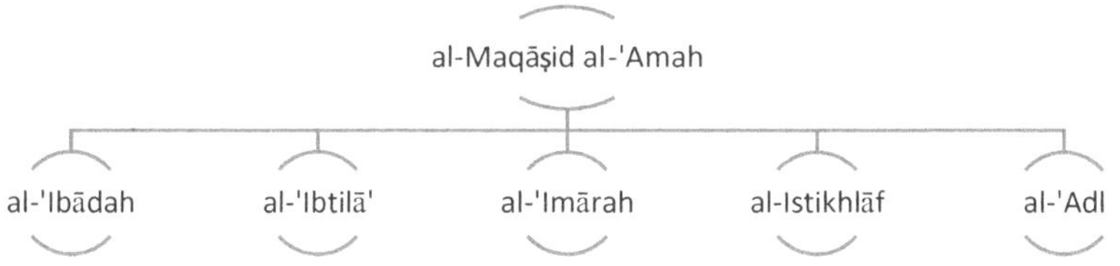

Fig. 3.2 Illustration of the general purposes of *Sharī'ah*

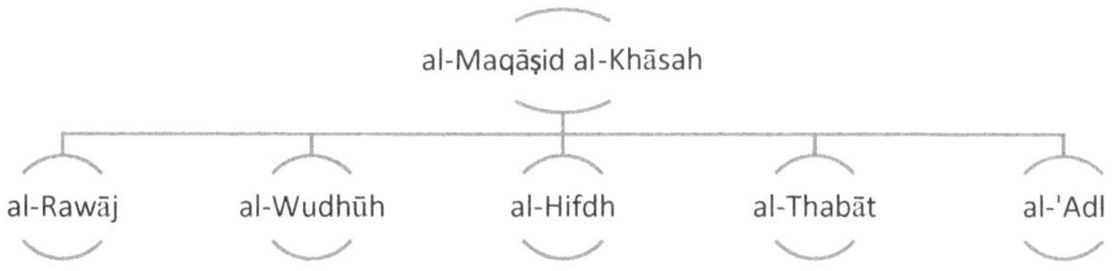

Fig. 3.3 The specific purposes of *Sharī'ah* in terms of financial transactions

The specific purposes (*al-maqāṣid al-khāssah*) in reference to Ibn Ashur (2001: 106-109), as illustrated in Fig. 3.3, relate to a particular area such as financial transactions (*al-mu'āmalāt al-māliyah*).

The partial purposes concern the reasons (*'ilah*) that led to the initial injunctions (*aḥkām*). For example, the loan with interest (*ribā*) has been prohibited by all religions because of the exploitation of the weakness of others in need. This is an act contrary to justice (Nadvi, 2015: 109) (Fig. 3.4).

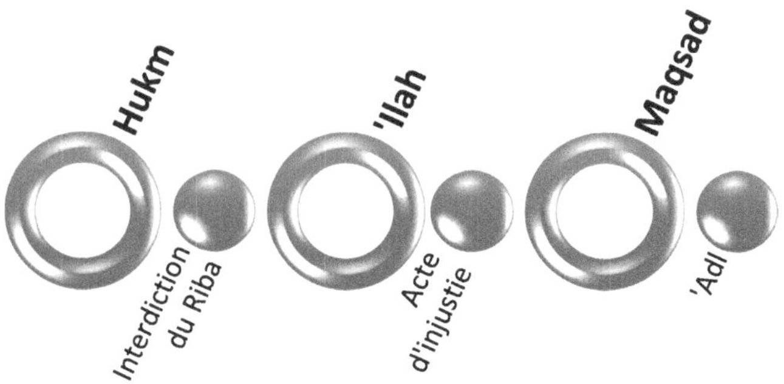

Fig. 3.4 Illustration of the partial purposes of *Sharī'ah* concerning the prohibition of *ribā*

Fig. 3.5 Justice as a fundamental value common to the three forms of purpose

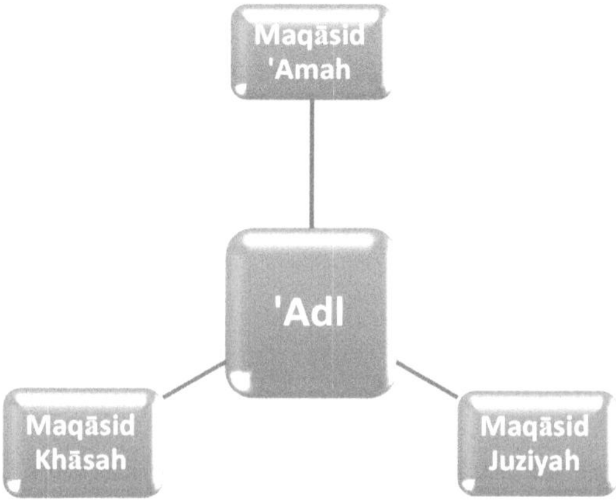

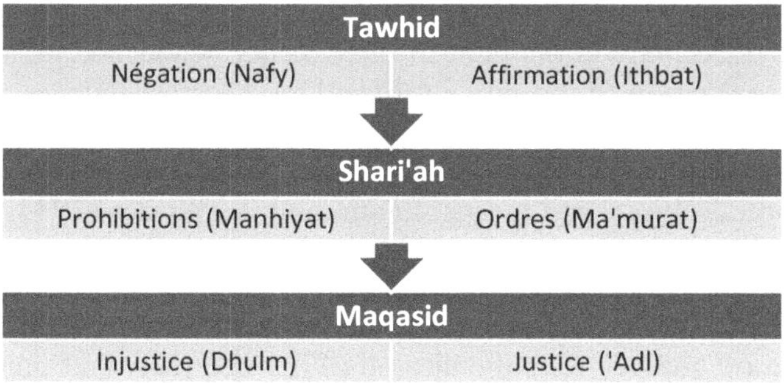

Fig. 3.6 Coherence of the concepts of the main Islamic sciences

It should be noted that the justice is a fundamental value common to the three forms of purpose set out above, as illustrated in Fig. 3.5.

This indicates the coherence of the concepts derived from the science of monotheism (*tawḥīd*), that of *Sharī'ah* and that of the purposes, as illustrated in Fig. 3.6, from which a close link appears between the concepts of 'negation' (*nafy*), 'prohibition' (*manhiyāt*) and 'justice' (*'adl*), on the one hand, and between the concepts of 'affirmation' (*ithbāt*), 'orders' (*ma'mūrāt*) and 'injustice' (*dhulm*), on the other hand. These sciences draw from a single source: revelation (*waḥy*), which includes *Qur'ān* and *Sunnah*.

Some authors believe that interest is contrary to the nature of things because money cannot generate money. This argument stated by Aristotle is taken up by Thomas Aquinas and gradually moves to the moral tradition of Western Christianity (Francotte, 1988: 295-296). In this reading, the reason for condemning the loan based on interest is that money cannot generate money. For the same injunction, in this case the condemnation of the loan based on interest, there may be several reasons arising from the analysis of the sacred texts or from the observation of economic life in the cities. This cause can be associated with a partial purpose (money cannot generate money) or a general purpose (condemnation of injustice). In other words, if the questioning of the purposes of beings and things is not limited to the religious field, it cannot ignore the observation of facts in order to better refine the tools of analysis. For example, the notions of 'clarity' (*wudhūḥ*) of Ibn Ashur (2001: 473) and 'transparency' (*shafāfiyah*) of Bin Bayyah (2010: 28) cannot be sufficient today in the face of the increasingly complex production systems resulting from an unrestrained race for competitiveness. Hence the need to refine them through the notion of traceability in the light of the repeated scandals experienced by the industrialization of the agriculture and food sector (Belabes, 2018).

Aristotle's analysis of money, as a technical intermediary of exchange, raises the question of the ethical relationship that humans should have with technical objects and means. Before him, Sophocles (1941: 26) had the choir of one of his most famous tragedies, Antigone, say: 'Ingenious in his industry beyond what one can imagine, he sometimes goes towards evil, sometimes towards good'. This premonition that technology can lead to both good and evil tests the illusion of the neutrality and pure instrumentality of technology, a subject that is not addressed in the literature on the ***maqāṣid*** of Islamic finance, which functions, under the influence of mimetic desire, as a distorting mirror of the globalization on world economy dominated by financialism, that is, a system in which the real economy plays a secondary role to the financial economy. The backing of tangible assets in transactions seems superficial; it focuses more on form than spirit of contracts.

The Illusion of Neutrality and Pure Instrumentality of Technics

After defining the technics in the following way: 'Wherever there is research and application of new means according to the criterion of efficiency, it can be said that there is technics' (Ellul, 1977[2004]: 38), Jacques Ellul (1954: 91) adds: 'In fact, there is strictly no difference between the technique and its use. We will therefore formulate the following principle: man is faced with an exclusive choice, to use the technics as it should be according to the technical rules, or not to use it at all; but impossible to use other than according to the technical rules'. Considered in itself and for itself, Cornelius Costariadis (1978: 241-248) also notes that technical activity does not take into account the value of the purposes proposed to it, efficiency appears as the only value. In this way, as Bruno Latour (2000: 39) points out, 'certain technics end up invading the entire horizon of ends by giving themselves their own laws'. Thus, although it is often believed that a technic is never good or bad in itself, but that its quality depends on the use made of it: beneficial if its use is measured and reflected, evil if not. Historians also show that a technic is never neutral because it always redefines social relationships (Jarrige, 2016). In fact, some technics are powerful forces that reshape human activity and its meaning. With the development of modern technology, it is nothing less than individual habits, perceptions, self-conceptions, ideas about space and time, social relationships, moral and political boundaries, which have been strongly restructured (Winner, 1986).

If the technical system has no purpose, it means that technical progress is not toward something but is from itself. At least that is what Ellul (1977[2004]: 279) argues: 'It can be said that the technique never goes forward for something but because it is pushed from behind'. At first sight, there is no possible purpose for the technics (Ellul, 1977[2004]: 274). But the author goes further by showing that the technical system is autonomous, that it grows without voluntary human intervention and even that technical progress is accelerating. His conclusion is that there is no point in proposing purposes for technical progress or discussing its purposes. We can always talk indefinitely, this is pointless. This may satisfy those who undertake such an exercise for one reason or another, but it has no scientifically rigorous value (Ellul 1977 [2004]: 288).

When Man is forced to achieve results, he ultimately has no choice but to take the most effective means, the one that will guarantee his survival under the effect of competitive rivalry. However, the most effective means corresponds, as we have seen, precisely to the technics in its general sense. Once the constraint of result brings a constraint of means, by using the technics, Man gives birth to the technician environment. This environment in turn conditions the individuals living there and when the organization is sufficiently widespread, we see the implementation of the technician system. Therefore, Man is condemned to enter into technological progress and to submit to it.

Technics has become an autonomous phenomenon: autonomy in relation to economics, politics, culture, morality and, ultimately, autonomy in relation to Man himself. There is an automaticity of technical progress: an advance in one field inevitably leads to another in a neighboring or more distant field. There is dissolution of the ends (assignable by a human community) in the means of technics. From this point of view, the discourse on the *maqāṣid al-Sharī'ah* of FinTech seems disconnected not only from reality, but also from the progress of research on the non-neutrality of the technics in reference to philosophical, historical and ethical literature. It is simply an oxymoron: if the ends dissolve in the means of technics, the word *maqāṣid* of technics becomes meaningless.

The Ethics of the Digital: The Case of Exponential Technologies

The progress of scientific research on the non-neutrality of technics calls for the development of a research program on the ethics of means, commonly referred to in Arab literature as the 'jurisprudence of means' (*fiqh al-wasāïl*), which is just as important as the study of purposes (*fiqh al-maqāṣid*), since means are the instruments and tools necessary to achieve the targets stated (Bourkani, 1987). However, such an ambitious program, to say the least, cannot be limited to a purely legal approach (*fiqhiyah*), commonly understood in a narrow sense, namely, the study of legal injunctions (*al-aḥkām al-shar'īyah*) resulting from their detailed evidence, whereas the original meaning of the term in Arab culture refers to a thorough understanding of things. In view of these considerations, that has been cruelly lacking for the dominant discourse on *maqāṣidal-shar'īyah* of Islamic finance, a question arises: Is technics a simple means or is it to be regarded as a complex medium that calls to a systemic thinking worthy of the name?

If we refer to the history of societies, technics appears to be a set of skills that can improve the living conditions of human beings. In our contemporary societies, the question of technics is often characterized by the desire to produce more and more to encourage consumption. However, Man must not devote his existence solely to a technics mastery aimed at ever-increasing productivity, but must devote time to activities that are not subject to productivism. If he considers technics as his sole purpose, he risks reducing his existence to a technical mastery of reality (Heidegger, 1980: 9-48). In this sense, technics must be applied responsibly: Man must be attentive to consequences of technics, because it can challenge certain natural balances and threaten the environment, but also threaten all aspects of human life, including the most intimate. Hence the importance of a reflection on modern technics and its effects. It is therefore a question of reflecting on which technics we are prepared to renounce in order to preserve a world fit for future generations; it is not a question of renouncing all technics but those that threaten the dignity of present and future human beings (Jonas, 2013).

As soon as certain means, more precisely the most sophisticated ones, are not neutral, they bring a new normativity into the life of human societies that tend to impose a 'good use' in the face of forms considered outdated. Is not he who does not have a smartphone perceived by some

Islamic economic researchers as backward, stingy or technophobic? This representation raises the question of alienation, which tends to deprive humans of what constitutes their essential being, their 'raison d'être' (Bontems, 2018). Sophisticated means, led by the Internet, which have become in a few decades the driving force behind profound transformations in the lives of individuals, companies and institutions (Benghozi *et al.*, 2014: 11), serve as much to create problems, in their ability to release new parameters to vary, as to solve (Bonoist, 2015).

One of the limits of the writings on *maqāsid* of technology (Mohammed, 2017: 137), beyond the question of non-neutrality developed by philosophers, ethicists and historians, is the lack of approach to technics as a system consisting not only of interacting entities (Bertalanffy, 1952: 148), but which refers to a belief, that is, an opinion that has the character of an intimate conviction and that excludes doubt. If some applications of technology are based on a belief that is opposed to monotheism, the word '*maqāsid* of technology' is an oxymoron that combines two contradictory terms. If we take as an example exponential finance which constitutes a new field of research aimed at the effect of exponential technologies, that is, those whose price/performance ratio doubles every eighteen to twenty-four months, on the world of finance, we must not limit our analysis to the ambient discourse according to which these technologies will massively increase the intelligence at humanity's disposal and solve its major problems.

A concept in vogue for two decades in Silicon Valley is beginning to make its way into the workshops dedicated to Islamic FinTech, that of singularity, that is, the point in time when all the advances in technology, particularly in artificial intelligence, will lead to machines that are smarter than human beings (as shown in Fig. 3.7). This inflection point will take place in 2045 according to Ray Kurzweil's predictions (Reedy, 2017) and in 2047 according to Masayoshi Son's predictions (Galeon, 2017). The association between exponential technologies and Islamic finance is all the easier as Islamic finance seems to have grown exponentially in recent years. The adoption of exponential technologies will somehow accelerate the trend.

Through this approach, where the discourse on FinTech is treated in a systemic way, as shown in Fig. 3.8, behind the notion of singularity is hidden transhumanism, that is, the search for an unlimited improvement of the physical and mental faculties of the human being by all possible means: chemical, genetic, mechanical or numerical, in particular through artificial

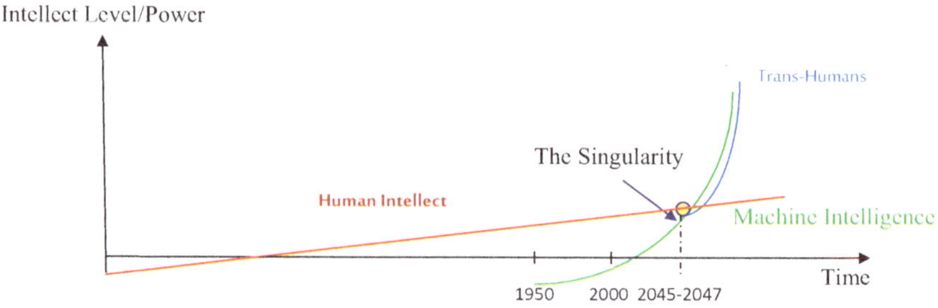

Fig. 3.7 The Singularity Timeline

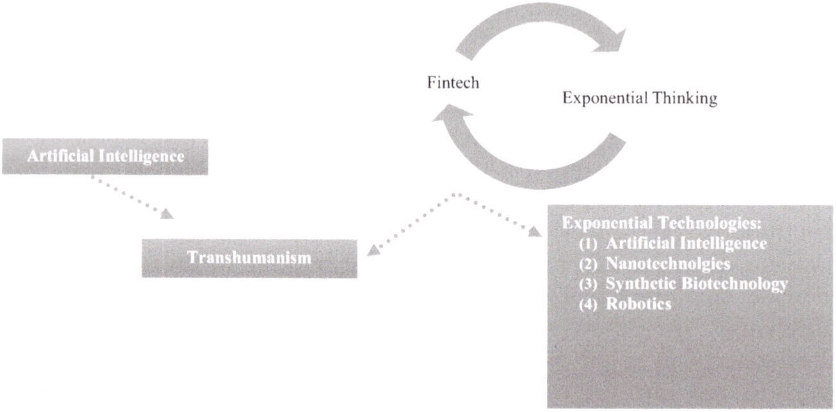

Fig. 3.8 Line between Fintech, Exponential Thinking and Transhumanism

intelligence. The significant development of NBIC technologies (Nanotechnologies, Biotechnologies, Information Sciences and Cognitive Sciences) has appeared to transhumanists as a historically unique opportunity to implement their ideas. They were encouraged to move forward in this direction by the famous principle of the physician Dennis Gabor, which indicates that everything that can be done, sooner or later science realizes it. Transhumanism defends the idea of transforming/overcoming Man to create a posthuman, or transhuman, with capacities superior to those of current human beings. This transformation can be envisaged at the individual level, but also at the collective level, leading to a new humanity. Different faculties of the human being would be concerned: physical, mental, cognitive.

If transhumanists assimilate life to an information system, humans and their major constituents—reason (*'aql*), soul (*rūh*), psyche (*nafs*)—are in their eyes only a database that can be collected and transferred in an electronic chip. However, the reason, which has an extraordinarily complicated structure and highly dynamic functions, is not limited to the brain. It is important to distinguish between the reason that controls behavior and orientation (*al-'aql al-tasarufī al-irshādī*) that is in the heart and the reason that perceives and imagines (*al-'aql al-idrākī al-tasawurī*) that is in the brain (Ibn Al-'Uthaymin, 2006: 51). Moreover, the soul, qualified as 'consciousness' because of the narrow-mindedness, is not acquired through artificial intelligence, but through revelation (Ibn Kathīr, 2002: 1422, 5: 116). God said: '*And they ask you*, [O Muhammad], *about the soul. Say, «The soul is of the affair of my Lord». And mankind have not been given of knowledge except a little*' (Qur'ān, 17: 85).

Although the predictions announced by transhumanists would only be illusory and fanciful, ethics must be renewed so that fundamental decisions are not delegated to a technology or superintelligence. A fundamental debate will have to begin to sort out the effects of announcements, demiurgic promises and the reality of scientific progress. It is not a question of rejecting out of hand all innovations like gene therapy, bionic prostheses and intracerebral neural implants, but to remain vigilant about the systemic role of the uses that will be made.

Conclusion

The exploration of the interactions between *maqāṣid* and FinTech under the prism of the non-neutrality of technics invites more rigors in the use of the notion of *maqāṣid al-Shar'iah*. The latter has been used so much wrongly that it becomes imperative to reason the use so that it is used in moderation and does not become counterproductive.

In the introduction to his book '*al-Muwāfaqāt fī Usūl al-Sharī'ah*' (The Reconciliation of the Foundations of Sharī'ah), which is a major reference for the research in the field of *maqāṣid al-Shar'iah*, imam al-Shātibī wrote:

> It is not permitted for the reader of this book to consult it in a useful or profitable manner without a thorough mastery of the sciences of Shari'ah, whether it is its foundations or its branches, the revealed texts or the writings

of eminent scholars in this field; avoiding imitation and passionate attachment to the legal doctrines in force.

Does this mean that most of those who quote this book inaccurately have not read it, simply browsed it, only consulted a tiny part, or have not properly understood what they have read altogether?

Moreover, reflection on the aims and purposes of technics cannot be successfully completed without a mastery of the relevant literature, particularly in the field of philosophy, history and ethics. In reality, these three fields of knowledge are intimately linked and essential to the development of complex thinking to link the themes of compartmentalized specialties to the major issues of our time. Thus, after having stressed that the moral development of Man is conditioned by the technics by which he will be able to provide for his needs and free time to develop spiritually, Henri Bergson ([1932]1984: 329-331) considers that done to spiritualize matter, the technics has finally materialized the spirit. Hence the need to understand that more technical power requires more wisdom so that the force that can be an instrument of liberation does not become an instrument of alienation.

In this context, the discourse on the *maqāṣid* of FinTech seems meaningless. To hold it in these terms shows a lack of mastery of the writings on the purposes, the technics, or even both at the same time. This is true both for the jurist, legal scholar (*fuqahā'*), financiers and computer scientists who have ventured into discursive speculation on this theme to give the impression of being up-to-date without remembering the word of God valid at any time, in any place, for any subject: 'And do not pursue that of which you have no knowledge' (Qurān, 17: 36). Talking for nothing has become a common practice in Islamic financial circles.

This lack is the result of a deficiency in educational programs that neglect philosophy, history and ethics. It hinders the development of a critical mind among students beyond purely technical considerations. This is valid both for the financial and engineering sciences including contemporary Islamic science programs that focus more on imitation, parsimony and rhetoric than on critical reflection, careful observation and in-depth analysis of facts. Most students graduate with the certainty that they hold the absolute truth. In the world of certainty, there is no room for questioning or fundamental debate. There are only answers, ready-made solutions. Slogans such as 'Islamic finance as a solution to the global economic crisis' or 'Islamic microfinance: Solution to poverty alleviation' reveal this way of thinking that perpetuates the culture of sufficiency driven by a centric view of the world.

But in Islamic financial circles, what is more important is not so much the scientific content as the membership of business networks whose religious sensitivity is revealed, against all expectations, as the factor with the least importance (Belabes, 2013; Luxembourg, 2016). This confirms the result from the observation of the halal market that it does not consist in promoting Islam through consumption, but relies on the moral values associated with a religion to sell products (Bergeaud-Blackler, Bernard, 2010: 83). The adjective 'Islamic' refers to what is 'home-made', that is, made by Muslims. This is part of the world of sacred signs that reminds us of *'Ilnomedellarosa'*, Umberto Eco's famous novel that has become a worldwide bestseller. The semiology would be of great use to deepen the understanding of this captivating spectacle.

References

Al-Dihlawī, S. W.-A. (1992). *ḤujjatAllāh al-Bālighah [The Conclusive Argument from God]*. Beirut, Lebanon: Dar Ihya al-Ulum.

Al-Masri, R. Y. (2005). *Fiqh al-Mu'āmalāt al-Mālīyah*. Damascus: Dar al-Qalam.

Belabes, Abderrazak. (2013). Les réseaux de la finance islamique à la Place de Paris [The networks of Islamic finance at the Paris financial centre], paperpresented to the workshop 'Les figures de l'entrepreneuriat religieux' [The figures of the religiousentrepreneurship], organized by École des Hautes Études en Sciences Sociales, Institut d'études de l'Islam et des sociétés du monde musulman, Centre d'études interdisciplinaires des faits religieux, Chaire éthique et normes de la finance de l'Université Paris 1 Panthéon-Sorbonne, Paris, EHESS, June 14.

Belabes, A. (2014). Al-ab'ād al-maqāṣidiyah li-al-tamwīlfī 'ālammurakab [Maqāṣid Dimensions of Finance in a Complex World]. *Journal of King Abdulaziz University: Islamic Economics, 27*(3), 45–93.

Belabes, Abderrazak. (2016). Enquête sur une initiative de créationd'unebanque par des entrepreneurs musulmans de Saint-Pétersbourg au début du XXe siècle [An Inquiry of an initiative to establish a bank by Muslim entrepreneurs in St. Petersburg in the early 20th century]. Paper presented to the Chair 'Ethics and Financial Norms' of the University of Paris 1 Panthéon-Sorbonne, 20 January.

Belabes, Abderrazak. (2018). Istiqṣā' fikratinshā' bank Islāmī bi-miṣrfī 'ām 1908 [An Inquiry of the idea to establish an Islamic bank in 1908]. Paper presented to the Wednesday Seminar, Islamic Economics Institute, King Abdulaziz University, Jeddah, November 7.

Belabes, A. (2019). Book Review of 'Islamic social finance' edited by Valentino Cattelan. *Journal of King Abdulaziz University: Islamic Economics, 33*(2), 98–106.

Benghozi, Pierre-Jean, Bureau, Sylvain, & Massit-Folléa, Françoise. (2014). *L'Internet des objets: Quels enjeux pour l'Europe ?*, Les Editions de la MSH.

Benoist, J. (2015). Le sujet de la technique : maîtrise, aliénation, expérimentation. *Sociétés, 2015/3*(129), 17–27.

Bergeaud-Blackler, F., & Bernard, B. (2010). *Comprendre le halal.* Liège: Edipro.

Bergson, Henri. (1932 [1984]). *Les deux sources de la morale et de la religion*, Paris: Presses Universitaires de France.

von Bertalanffy, L. (1952). *Problems of Life: An Evaluation of Modern Biological Thought.* New York: J. Wiley & Sons.

Bin Bayyah, A. (2010). *Maqāṣid al-Mu'āmalātwaMarāṣid al-Wāqi'āt.* London: Al-Furqan Islamic Heritage Foundation.

Bontems, V. (2018). La machine respectueuse. L'éthique des techniques de Simondon à l'ère des robots. *Revue française d'éthique appliquée, 2018/1*(5), 22–33.

Bourkani, O. W. (1987). *Fiqh al-wasāïl fi al-Sharī'ah al-islāmīyah.* Doha: Kitab al-Ummah.

Corm, G. (2009). *L'Europe et le mythe de l'Occident, la construction d'une histoire.* Paris: La Découverte.

Costariadis, C. (1978). *Les carrefours du Labyrinthe I.* Paris: Seuil. Dihlawi.

Djafri, Fares. (2017). Summary Report of the 'LSE—HBKU Workshop on Fintech and Islamic Finance', hosted by the Center for Islamic Economics and Finance (CIEF), College of Islamic Studies, Hamad Bin Khalifa University at the London School of Economics on February 23, 2017.

Ellul, J. (1954). *La technique ou l'enjeu du siècle.* Paris: Economica.

Ellul, Jaques. (1977 [2004]). *Le système technicien*, Paris: Le Cherche Midi.

Francotte, A. (1988). Aristote et le prêt à intérêt. *Les cahiers de l'analyse des données, 13*(3), 295–318.

Galeon, Dom. (2017). Softbank CEO: The Singularity Will Happen by 2047 So, what do we do then? *Futurism.com*, March 1st.

Heidegger, M. (1980). *Essais et conférences.* Paris: Gallimard.

Ibn Al-'Uthaymin, M. i. S. (2006). *Tafsīr Sūrat al-'Imrān [An Exegesis of Sūrat al-'Imrān].* Riyadh: Dar Ibn al-Jawzi.

Ibn Ashur, M. a.-T. (2001). *Maqaṣid al-Shariah al-Islamiyah [The Purposes of Shari'ah].* Amman: Dar al-Nafais.

Ibn Kathir, I. (2002). *Tafsīr al-Qur'ān al-'Adhīm (An Exegesis of the Noble Qur'ān).* Riyadh: Dar Taybah.

Ibn Khaldūn, A. a.-R. (2001). *Al-Muqadimmah [An Introduction to History].* Beirut: al-Maktaba al-Asriya.

Jarrige, F. (2016). *Technocritiques.* Paris: La Découverte, collection Essai.

Jonas, H. (2013). *Le principe de responsabilité: Une éthique pour la civilisation technologique*. Paris: Flammarion.

Laërce, D. (1999). *Vies et doctrines des philosophes illustres*. Paris: Librairie Générale Française.

Latour, B. (2000). La fin des moyens. *Réseaux. Communication—Technologie—Société, 18*(100), 39–58.

Luxembourg, M.-L. d. (2016). La finance islamique en France: que valent ces paroles ? *Archives de sciences sociales des religions, 175*, 159–180.

Mannheim, K. (1956). *Idéologie et utopie*. Paris: Marcel Rivière.

Mohammed, H. F. (2017). Al-maqāsid al-shar'īyahwa al-tatbīqāt al-fiqhiyah li-al-tiknūlūjiyahwa al-ikhtira'āt al-hadīthah (dirāssahfiqhiyah fi al-ru'yah al-maqāsidiyah li-al-thawrah al-tiknūlūjiyah) [Legitimate purposes and applications jurisprudence of technology and modern inventions (Doctrinal study at Makassed vision of the technological revolution)]. *Journal of the Iraqi University, 36*(2), 137–160.

Mohammed, M. O., & El Amri, M. C. (2019). Fintech in the Light of Maqāsid al-Sharī'ah. In U. A. Oseni & S. N. Ali (Eds.), *Fintech in Islamic Finance: Theory and Practice* (pp. 93–112). London: Routledge.

Nadvi, A. A. (2015). *Al-MadkhalilaQawā'īd al-Fiqh al-Mālī (Introduction to Financial Legal Maxims)*. Jeddah: Scientific Publishing Center, King Abdulaziz University.

Rahim, N. F., Bakri, M. H., & Yahaya, S. N. (2019). Fintech and Shariah Principles in Smart Contractsm. In A. Rafay (Ed.), *FinTech as a Disruptive Technology for Financial Institutions* (pp. 207–220). Hershey P.A.: IGI Global.

Reedy, Christianna. (2017). Kurzweil Claims That the Singularity Will Happen by 2045, Get ready for humanity 2.0., *Futurism.com*, October 5th.

Ricœur, P. (1997). *L'idéologie et l'utopie*. Paris: Le Seuil.

Said, E. (1978). *Orientalism*. New York: Pantheon.

Sophocle. (1941). *Antigone*. Clermont-Ferrand: Sorlot.

Todorov, T. (1989). *Nous et les Autres. La réflexion française sur la diversité humaine*. Paris: Seuil.

Winner, L. (1986). *The Whale and the Reactor: A Search for Limits in an Age of High Technology*. Chicago: Chicago University Press.

Zarqa, M. (1993). *Sharh al-qawā'id al-fiqhiyah li-Ahmad Zarqa*. Damascus: Dar al-Qalam.

PART II

Regulatory Frameworks of Islamic FinTech

CHAPTER 4

Central Banks and Financial Authorities: Towards the Advancement of I-Fintech

Nafis Alam and Abdolhossein (Pejman) Zameni

Abstract In the year 2007 British banks witnessed the first run on to their very own banks due to various scandals that tarnished the trust and reputations of the banks and the banking industry. Simultaneously, the sub-prime crisis was happening to major banks in the US, France and some other countries that were sharing a high systemic risk. When a systemic risk is high and at the same time if banks don't keep enough reserved capital to compensate their clients during a crisis period, this situation could lead to a recession, high unemployment, and eventually economic collapse. Since then, stakeholders lost their trust in the banking system globally and were demanding for a more socially responsible, ethical, and systemic stable form of banking. True enough, in the wake of the 2008 global financial crisis (GFC), Islamic finance banking and the Fintech industry were proliferating to fill the existing void in the finance industry by their innovation and a different approach to business transactions. At that time, the faith inspired in the form of ethical banking was enjoying

N. Alam (✉) • Abdolhossein (Pejman) Zameni
Asia Pacific University of Technology and Innovation, Kuala Lumpur, Malaysia
e-mail: Nafis.alam@apu.edu.my

M. M. Billah (ed.), *Islamic FinTech*,
https://doi.org/10.1007/978-3-030-45827-0_4

steady growth. Advancement in technology was also facilitating the rapid growth of revolution in Islamic-Fintech (i-Fintech) industry.

Keywords Fintech • Central Bank • Authorities • Regulation • Shariah

Introduction

Needless to mention that, Islamic finance and i-Fintech are blooming and evolving rapidly. The reality is that the combination of Islamic finance and i-Fintech which is based on trust and moral creates efficient and satisfactory financial services for the customers. The main reason behind the evolution of Islamic finance and i-Fintech is its business model that proved its worth and value by avoiding situations like a sub-prime crisis. Losing trust on the conventional banking industry, penetration of internet and technology globally, lack of accessibility of funds to everyone no matter with or without track record with banks, speed of transactions, and transaction cost along with clients' craving for a trustworthy financial system among other reasons are key enticements behind the growth and expansion of the i-Fintech. The system that has an ethical principal embedded in it. The system that looks after the benefits of both sides, borrowers and lenders, equally and fairly.

A system-wide crisis is able to destroy and tarnish public confidence. For instance, financial crises also raise borrowing costs, leading to a credit crunch and recession. The spread and advancement of Fintech can bring more depositors and borrowers across the nation together, which consequently financial institutions can better diversify their sources of funding and lending opportunities and this makes them safer. For example, M-Pesa in Kenya, Alipay in China and Paytm in India have brought financial services literally to our fingertips.

On the other hand, any innovation in technology is accepted in Islam as long as it complies with the Shariah rules. But what is i-Fintech? Wintermeyer and Basit (2017) define i-Fintech as follows:

1. The DIGITAL delivery of i-Finance
2. The use of Fintech utilities: KYC[1] / AML, Blockchain, and DLT, Cyber, Payments, Big Data & Machine Learning in i-Finance

[1] KYC: Know Your Customer, AML: Anti Money Laundry, DLT: Distributed Ledger Technology.

3. Any Fintech in Muslim market demography that delivers an unmet financial need and or financial inclusion objective
4. Any Shariah-compliant Fintech fund investing in digital infrastructure or economic development anywhere in the world.

Indonesia, followed by the US, the UAE, and the UK, holds the most significant number of i-Fintech startups. Indonesia, by having the world's largest Muslim population, has the highest number of startups, which is more than 30, with a readily increasing number of i-Fintech establishments registering with the country's i-Fintech Association. The United Arab Emirates (UAE) and Malaysia follow as the next two largest Muslim-majority countries by some startups, reflecting the broad Islamic economy strategies that both countries have put in place (DinarStandard, 2018). All these progress in i-Fintech would be impossible without the support of the Central Bank and financial authorities of the respective countries.

Worth mentioning that Islamic finance and i-Fintech not necessarily go hand in hand. Digitisation and disruption are an undeniable fact for existing business and finance environment. Given this, i-Fintech can be considered a rival to the Islamic finance market which potentially is able to cannibalise its market.

Central banks and financial authorities by supporting the i-Fintech due to its benefits towards society are able to smoothen the development, expansion, and penetration of it. Drawing upon this argument, some of the success factors for i-Fintech that could be considered and practised by central banks and financial authorities are highlighted. Islamic-Fintech's role is to expand technology innovation into the Islamic banking product and services. If i-Fintech is positioned appropriately among its stakeholders due to its inherent ethical values, it is able to outperform its rivals and gain significant sustainable competitive advantages. The advancement and accessibility of technologies are one of the determining factors in this rivalry. High and fast-growing Muslim population that needs financial products and services is another advantage and opportunity for promotion, expansion, and penetration of i-Fintech into the Muslim society (Bakar & Rosbi, 2018). The median age of Muslims worldwide is 24 years as opposed to 32 globally, 15 of the top 50 countries with smartphone penetration are Islamic economics and 72% of the unbanked population lives in the Organisation of Islamic Cooperation (OIC) member countries (main Islamic finance markets) compared to 49% worldwide (DinarStandard, 2018). Relying on these factors, i-Fintech should be able to accelerate and take off more rapidly than its rival, conventional Fintech, but of course, it needs the continuous supports of central banks and financial authorities.

Additionally, central banks and financial authorities can initiate collaboration with other central banks in order to promote those Islamic banks that are advanced in i-Fintech and are capable of quickly and efficiently advertising their new products and services globally. Hence, this can entice clients to engage with Islamic banking and i-Fintech products and services. Study of Alaabed and Mirakhor (2017) on the role of Fintech in accelerating the implementation of risk-sharing Islamic finance shows that i-Fintech is closer to the spirit of Shariah as it eradicates two main risks in the banking industry, explicitly uneven maturity and leverage. Another example of i-Fintech that could be backed by central banks and financial authorities is the Shariah-compliant P2P lending. The Shariah-compliant P2P lending such as crowdfunding, remittance, and mobile wallet are predominantly suitable for the needs of a considerable portion of the population in Islamic countries and also is able to accommodate part of the population that is left out of the possibility to transact with a conventional banking and financial institution. Shariah-compliant P2P lending provides the facility to engage in financial transactions, for example, pay their bills or send money abroad.

On the other hand, the biggest and main problem of i-Fintech stakeholders is how to come up with innovative Islamic products rather than imitating the existing products that are aligned with the utmost ethical values that are shared by so many. Currently, the Islamic finance market is too far behind in a total number of clients and the level of sophistication of the products and services accessible in its portfolio (Todorof, 2018). This is where central banks and financial authorities need to intervene and assist and support local banks to encourage them to come up with innovative Islamic products consistent with i-Fintech.

Study of Firmansyah and Anwar (2019) related to Indonesian and Singaporean i-Fintech companies show that most of the i-Fintech firms are able to raise fund and finding sufficient skilful human resources for their operations. Besides, they mention that most of the participating firms agreed that they have enough support from the government. In general, the lack of regulations is one of the challenges faced by i-Fintech firms (Firmansyah and Anwar, 2019). In a nutshell, the governments, central banks, and financial authorities of mostly different Islamic countries or the International i-Fintech organisations need to provide supportive regulations for the i-Fintech sector, not too loose or too strict. The too lax i-Fintech regulations will not protect the customers and investors right and will deprive them of investing in or using the i-Fintech products and services. On the other hand, the too rigid regulation in a country may hamper the development of i-Fintech. Consequently, the i-Fintech regulations should protect all parties involved in the i-Fintech practice, the firms, customers, and investors.

The i-Fintech landscape maps over the wide range of products and services globally from Islamic Exchange-Traded Fund (ETFs) to cryptocurrencies, to name but a few: Islamic RoboAdvice with access to Shariah-compliant ETFs, Islamic alternative asset market place such as property, Islamic trade finance play; Shariah-compliant initial coin offering (ICO) that allows for fees and risk sharing backed by halal instruments using a token, Shariah-compliant universal payment system backed by grains, and EthisCrowd Fintech company that is using e-Wakalah (agency contract) and Istisna (contract to construct an asset) contracts that allow for crowdfunding of new real estate developments in Indonesia (Wintermeyer, 2017).

In addition to this, other key emerging trends in i-Fintech that are worth mentioning are such as Islamic Digital Challenger banks and Sukuk (bond) ETFs, Murabaha (asset-backed interest free loan) instruments around buying and selling goods in addition to Takaful (insurance), Blockchain; these are revolutionising Islamic banking by incorporating standard Islamic finance contracts to smart contracts and reducing the service cost up to 95% with an unchangeable record of ownership and assets.

The i-Fintech industry will be able to see steady and robust growth soon if it is ensured that the provided services and products have at least a few important attributes. Hence, the offered services and products of the i-Fintech in order to provide high customer experience need to be accessible, more automated, user-friendly, packaged decently, and transparent. The accessibility of the i-Fintech can be fulfilled by smartphones, internet, and developed applications. At the same time, the new offered package to clients should be able to add value by mitigating frictions, convenient to use and most importantly serve the purpose. For i-Fintech products and services to be transparent, it needs to be certified by authorities that are recognised and respected by both consumers and institutions. Generally, i-Fintech services are able to benefit the unbanked to create a new form of credit history, and moving from there, at the next phase, they can be enjoying the benefits of borrowing and lending and some other services via i-Fintech.

Study of Saksonova and Merlino (2017) highlighted if i-Fintech industry intends to advance rapidly, the main strategies and foundations that are required in the framework of i-Fintech development are, "ability to manage and analyse big data, technological infrastructure improvements, creating a reliable transaction system, human resources in digital marketing, establishing cooperation, collaboration and investment with relevant stakeholders and Fintech product innovation." Furthermore, governments and regulators, educational institutions such as universities, and also existing banks and financial institutions play an important role in the i-Fintech ecosystem. The lesson needs to be learned is that the rapid advancement in i-Fintech should be considered and supported seriously by central banks and financial authorities.

Report of DinarStandard (2018) specifies that i-Fintech has an ample room for growth, but beforehand it needs to address its unaddressed opportunities in various areas rapidly. According to the report of DinarStandard (2018), the three most major unaddressed areas of which are: "1) the leveraging of big data and AI in providing Islamic banking services, 2) the use of Blockchain in facilitating the growth of Islamic trade finance, which at the US$186 billion is a fraction of the global US $12 trillion trade finance industry, and 3) the use of AI in facilitating investments, in particular addressing institutional investor needs." Practically speaking, if the i-Fintech industry expects to grow and develop quickly and have a higher market share in the worldwide finance industry, a rigorous strategic effort is needed across government entities, financial investors, and financial institutions, to fill the numerous gaps in the i-Fintech ecosystem.

Fintech technologies are aggressively enhancing and disrupting twentieth-century i-Fintech services, operations, business models, and customer engagement. DinarStandard (2018) report outlines the Islamic finance services segment into 12 categories (Shariah deposit and investment account, sukuk, ijarah financing, Islamic private equity, musharaka and mudaraba, muharaba working capital/supply chain, wakalah LOC, bank treasury, Islamic retail private wealth, Islamic institutional fund, and takaful and re-takaful), correlates to the six broad service areas (deposits, business and consumer financing, treasury, trade financing, wealth management, and insurance) identified globally, serving the same underlying needs of retail consumers and businesses, as well as the institutional needs of financial service providers, adjusted of course for the Islamic faith-based requirements of customers.

In order for the i-Fintech industry to proceed more rapidly on those aforementioned service areas, it needs to manage its operations, including back, middle, and front office by utilising and incorporating the big data, artificial intelligence (AI), quantum computing, P2P finance, open banking, mobility, blockchain, cloud adoption, and cybersecurity in its daily operation activities (DinarStandard, 2018).

Most notably, to support i-Fintech firms, additional dedicated accelerators and incubators are needed globally. Currently, there are a few in Singapore, Turkey, and the UAE to facilitate the adoption of financial technology among Muslims. And the more, the merrier. Promoting and establishing additional incubators is the role of central banks and financial authorities. If Islamic banking institutions (IBIs) intend to stay competitive, the rational response to the existing and evolving revamp in banking and financial services industry would be to find ways to collaborate with i-Fintech rather than acknowledging them as a threat.

As one of the application of the i-Fintech, Shariah-compliant P2P lending is helping to close or narrow the massive credit gap existing in Muslim countries, by preserving more of the local money within the local financial market and allow local banks to generate more profit at a price, which will be lower for all stakeholders (Todorof, 2018).

Moreover, technology is able to offer readily available standardised contracts to mitigate the risks of some financial products. The neutrality of Fintech can contribute to the success of i-Fintech segment too. The neutrality component of Fintech is one of its attractive aspects as the making of the Islamic finance framework more up-to-date for its clients and also it can prevent the accusations of blindly copying the Western system.

Interestingly, Fintechs can be applied and utilised with the same success rate in conventional and Shariah-compliant settings by allowing i-Finance practitioners to pick which Fintech components to include or develop in their practice in order to upsurge their efficiency and inclusion while still are sticking to Shariah and Islamic values.

But on the other hand, technology and innovation in the financial market should be able to bridge the gap between i-Fintech and conventional financial market instruments and products. Furthermore, technology advancement can provide greater transparency to bankers, Islamic courts, and clients, which would ultimately enable all stakeholders to scrutinise the transactions that take place in a Shariah finance/banking environment.

One of the main critiques against i-Finance is that whether Islamic finance is ethical by reference to the *Maqasid* due to the design of synthetic products using a form over substance method to imitate the economics and risk profile of conventional products. It is expected from Shariah Supervisory Boards to ensure Islamic finance products meet both the spirit and the letter of the law to attract more investors and clients for Islamic finance and Fintech products and services. Meanwhile, central banks and financial authorities can facilitate the process by supporting the i-Fintech.

The underlying ethical and Islamic values under the Islamic finance and i-Fintech are identical, but on the flip side, growth and flourishing of i-Fintech will cannibalise the Islamic banking institutions (IBIs) existing and potential future market share. Even though i-Fintech is able to serve the unbanked segment of the society, the growth of i-Fintech is considered a threat to IBIs. For instance, with the formation of i-Fintech firms, it can potentially serve the less creditworthy companies, individuals and small and medium Enterprises (SMEs) by proposing simple, low-cost alternative financing instead of tedious and lengthy procedures offered by IBIs. Due to several disadvantages of conventional and Islamic banking institutions, such as lengthy procedures and processes, high finance cost and a limited amount of available cash and credits, in which this can cause a credit crunch for clients, bank clients are reducing their dependence to the banks as the primary sources of financial service providers. Bank clients are increasingly relying on Fintech providers instead. In a nutshell, Fintech and i-Fintech are both a threat and an opportunity to both conventional and IBIs.

Islamic finance and i-Fintech may be a nascent sector, but its fast growth has led to skills shortages. In this regard, Samina Akram, managing director of London-based Islamic and ethical finance consultancy Samak Consultants, explains, “One of the major challenges the industry faces is a shortage of adequately trained talent. So because it’s such a young sector, the right talent can flourish, no matter what their gender” (Everett, 2018). This point should be taken care by central banks and financial authorities in conjunction with the education industry.

The road ahead presents a balance of opportunities and challenges to i-Fintech. By the year 2100, 50% of the world’s population will be living in MENA and Sub-Saharan Africa (SSA). Not to mention that the potential existing customers of the i-Fintech are about 1.8 billion, globally (Wintermeyer & Basit, 2017). These markets consist of a large portion of the unbanked populations, people without having access to the bank accounts. On the other hand, smartphones penetration's rate is high in these societies. Needless to highlight that, these societies are profoundly underserviced and diverse while both the needs and the rewards for servicing these markets are pronounced. This serves as an impetus for i-Fintech in addressing financial inclusion. With the availability of Shariah-compliant crowdfunding and P2P financing tools, this creates opportunities for individuals and SMEs that require financing but thus far do not qualify for the funding from traditional IBIs.

In view of this, among others, one of the supreme and profound future developments, to expand the access of the i-Fintech mostly to Islamic regions and also to other non-Islamic regions, is to introduce i-Fintech passport scheme. For instance, the Gulf Cooperation Council (GCC) could introduce regional Fintech passporting to drive certification schemes to offer more considerable client access to i-Fintech. Furthermore, the i-Fintech passporting scheme could be extended to MENA and Sub Saharan Africa as well as the rest of the world to provide access to certified Shariah-compliant products. This service could be initiated and collaborated among the MENA, Sub-Sahara, and GCC countries by their central banks and financial authorities.

The i-Fintech sector cannot just isolate itself from non-Islamic Fintech institutional and capital markets. While there are developments in the institutional and capital markets, i-Fintech also needs to catch up simultaneously and speed up its innovations and developments; otherwise, it will lose its market share to conventional Fintech firms and easily would be substituted with non-Islamic Fintech services and products.

Drawing upon our earlier argument, i-Fintech has an ability to transform the lives of millions of people around the globe and to help turn the i-Fintech hubs into Fourth Industrial[2] Revolution digital leaders (Klaus, 2016). Thus, there is a substantial need and there is a gap for digital infrastructure investment, especially in countries with emerging economies. Therefore, the global requirement for digital infrastructure investment is

[2] The term 'Fourth Industrial Revolution' was coined by Klaus Schwab, the founder and executive chairman of the World Economic Forum. It is characterised by a fusion of technologies that is blurring the lines between the physical, digital, and biological spheres collectively referred to as cyber-physical systems. It is marked by emerging technology breakthroughs in a number of fields, including robotics, artificial intelligence, nanotechnology, quantum computing, biotechnology, and the internet of things (IoT).

an opportunity for Islamic banks, asset managers, and investors to harness through i-Fintech both in Islamic and non-Islamic economies.

Dubai, Malaysia, and Iran as a number of key Islamic Finance hub together account for more than 80% of the industry's total assets, followed by the UK (Everett, 2018). Drawing on that, the i-Fintech industry is young and has been predicted to continue growing, the Muslim world population is young too, and they fit in the middle- to low-income (countries) bracket. Further to this, the 2008 Global Financial Crisis (GFC) created interest in non-Muslims population to search for more ethical and transparent means of investment. This has created an expectation that the i-Fintech industry to become the go-to option for different classes of investors due to religious and non-religious reasons. Generally, as awareness of these sector's ethical approach continues to grow, most probably its acceptance also will rise among millennials and women. Subsequently, if countries that intend to grow and penetrate faster to dominate the i-Fintech market need to work on an adequate and practical regulatory framework for the i-Fintech sector. Islamic Fintech is the future of the Islamic finance industry.

If i-Fintech wishes to offer its ethical values to more non-Muslim population and protect more clients against financial crisis such as 2008, it requires to quicken its digital infrastructure's development by collaborating more with Fintech companies or establish its own i-Fintech department. No matter whether it is a digital solution or Blockchain technology, i-Fintech must ensure their back office is rightly real-time and adaptable.

The current disruption in the banking and finance industry could be perceived as a win-win situation for both IBIs and i-Fintech firms. Through suitable and planned collaborations, the i-Fintech industry will be able to acquire the innovative practices of the newly emerged i-Fintech start-ups and also are able to learn the pros and cons of doing business with established and reputable IBIs. Therefore, with proper and effective collaborations, and after considering all of the aspects of the business such as threats and opportunities that must be in accordance to Shariah, collectively they will be able to benefit from the growth multiplier that Fintech can bring to the table. The future of i-Fintech is bright.

With around 1.8 billion existing Muslim population globally, Islam is the fastest-growing religion in the world, and the population of Muslim is expected to surpass Christians in not far future (Lipka & Hackett, 2017). Thus, i-Fintech could position itself as a solution providing financial inclusiveness to as many people as possible, including non-Muslim who are looking for a more efficient and ethical financial system. The main advantages of i-Fintech over its conventional counterpart are its transparency, being beneficial to the two parties, and Shariah-compliant component (Kelana, 2018).

Moving forward, in order for i-Fintech to flourish, authorities such as central banks and financial authorities need to set the policy instruments guarding the Fintech work process from upstream to downstream (Pollari, 2016), proactively train specialist and qualified human resources for i-Fintech, secure the system from malware attacks (Saksonova & Merlino, 2017), clarify the legal certainty of online-based clients (Rusydiana, 2018), reaching to low-income clients, educate people about Shariah and last but not the least providing comprehensive framework in governance, accounting, and Shariah auditing.

Unlike the i-Fintech, since a few decades ago, the Islamic Finance industry has begun experiencing extraordinary innovation and expansion. True enough, according to Thomson Reuters, assets under the Islamic finance are expected to rise to $3.9 trillion by 2023 (DinarStandard, 2018). To the contrary, i-Fintech has started its baby steps, and it is at the very beginning of an exciting, transformative journey for the industry. On the positive side, the primary driver and backbone for the growth of the i-Fintech are young, digitally native Muslim demographic that is on average younger than the worlds non-Muslim population.

For instance, Rusydiana (2018) points out that only 36% of Indonesia's population as the world's largest population Muslim country having a bank account. On the other hand, the smartphone's penetration rate in Indonesia is about 70% which provides fertile terrain for i-Fintech's rapid boost. Given the importance of such a vast opportunity in Indonesia, the prospects for i-Fintech in Indonesia seem very bright. Hence, the i-Fintech industry by the support of central bank and financial authorities should be able to grab the current opening and provide accessible financial services to the unbankable population in Indonesia which traditional financial institutions are not able to provide.

The number of countries that are joining the i-Fintech/Fintech league is increasing everyday—along with several other newcomers such as the Maldives and Sri Lanka—which intend to issue a sovereign Islamic paper. The Asian continent is anticipated to be the leader of the international Shariah-compliant debt and equity markets by leveraging on progressive, practical, and sophisticated regulations, and attracting potential global investors into the region.

Furthermore, moving forward digitisation could bring savings for banks and their clients in terms of time, effort, and money. In addition, technology enables the i-Fintech industry both to lower its overheads and to reduce transactional risks, for instance, by using blockchain. Islamic-Fintech is capable of driving the Islamic Finance industry to its next phase of evolution and opportunity. The followings are a few suggestions to i-Fintech developments for different stakeholders, namely *Government agencies, Financial institutions & startups, and Investments*, by DinarStandard (2018).

Government agencies need to increase the number of 'regulatory sandboxes' to facilitate the test and evaluation of the i-Fintech products and services before authorising it to be populated. Increase in the number of regulatory sandboxes allows the i-Fintech segment to be able to compete with the conventional Fintech markets. Central banks and government agencies by developing 'Fintech innovation hubs & knowledge sharing' platform can encourage i-Fintech firms to share their best practices that can promote to develop consistency and generate best-in-class operating models. Government agencies need to recognise and assess cybersecurity, money laundering (ML) and know-your-customer (KYC) risks associated with Fintech firms and technology providers. Government agencies in order to pave the way for i-Fintech firms are urged to promote the General Data Protection Regulation (GDPR) compliance and other trust factors to support consumers right and simultaneously promote for consumer awareness of i-Fintech's practicality and credibility.

'Incumbent financial institutions' need to engage more with i-Fintech startups and 'innovation hubs' for the future of their organisation and growth. They need new approaches to drive change and deliver innovation to their existing clients. On the other hand, i-Fintech 'startups' in order to have access to capital and clients need to effectively engage with incumbent financial institutions too. If i-Fintech startups intend to gain more market share they need to enhance their customer experience, engagement, and Islamic finance's social impact potential through Fintech adoption.

Going forward, the i-Fintech segment for its development and opportunity creation relative to conventional Fintech industry needs more attention and 'investments' from venture capitalist and private equity entities. While the positive news is that corporate investors such as established Islamic banks are now investing in i-Fintech projects, the scale and scope of the investment need to be scaled-up intensely.

To sum up, moving forward, new disruptive technologies are able to play a vital part in removing obstacles for both inhabitants and financial institutions. Given this, central banks and financial authorities have a key role in providing the right infrastructure; physical infrastructures such as payment and settlement systems and soft infrastructures like rules and guidelines. In line with this, in order to move towards financial inclusion, it is necessary that central banks fulfil their main mandate. Central banks and innovators relationship is reciprocal; one is unable to achieve financial inclusion without the other's help. Policymakers, central banks, and financial authorities can help address the market-failures and risks posed by innovation.

References

Alaabed, A., & Mirakhor, A. (2017). Accelerating Risk Sharing Finance via FinTech : NextGen Islamic Finance. In The 1st International Colloquium on Islamic Banking and Islamic Finance, 1–10. Tehran.

Bakar, N. A., & Rosbi, S. (2018). Robust Framework Diagnostics of Blockchain for Bitcoin Transaction System: A Technical Analysis from Islamic Financial Technology (i-FinTech) Perspective. *International Journal of Business and Management, 2*(3), 22–29. https://doi.org/10.26666/rmp.ijbm.2018.3.4

DinarStandard. (2018). *Islamic Fintech Report 2018: Current Landscape & Path Forward.* Retrieved from https://www.dinarstandard.com/wp-content/uploads/2018/12/Islamic-Fintech-Report-2018.pdf

Everett, C. (2018). Islamic Finance Growth Means New Opportunities for Women – Raconteur. Retrieved March 28, 2019, from https://www.raconteur.net/finance/islamic-finance-growth-means-new-opportunities-women

Firmansyah, E. A., & Anwar, M. (2019). Islamic Financial Technology (FINTECH): Its Challenges and Prospect. *Advances in Social Science, Education and Humanities Research (ASSEHR), 216*(Assdg 2018), 52–58.

Kelana, I. (2018). Here Are Some Advantages of Using Fintech Syariah. Retrieved May 14, 2019, from https://republika.co.id/berita/ekonomi/syariah-ekonomi/18/08/28/pe58om374-ini-beberapa-keuntungan-gunakan-fintech-syariah

Klaus, S. (2016). The Fourth Industrial Revolution: What It Means and How to Respond | World Economic Forum. Retrieved April 3, 2019, from https://www.weforum.org/agenda/2016/01/the-fourth-industrial-revolution-what-it-means-and-how-to-respond/

Lipka, M., & Conrad Hackett, C. (2017). Why Muslims Are the World's Fastest-Growing Religious Group. *Pew Research Center*. http://www.pewresearch.org/fact-tank/2017/04/06/why-muslims-are-the-worlds-fastest-growing-religious-group/.

Pollari, I. (2016). The Rise of FINTECH Opportunities and Challenges. *The Finsia Journal of Applied Finance*. Retrieved from https://search.informit.com.au/documentSummary;dn=419743387759068;res=IELAPA

Rusydiana, A. S. (2018). Developing Islamic Financial Technology in Indonesia. *Hasanuddin Economics and Business Review, 2*(2), 143–152. https://doi.org/10.26487/HEBR.V2I2.1550

Saksonova, S., & Merlino, I. (2017). Fintech as Financial Innovation – The Possibilities and Problems of Implementation. *European Research Studies Journal, XX*(3), 1. https://doi.org/10.1021/ja00368a049

Todorof, M. (2018). Shariah-Compliant FinTech in the Banking Industry. *ERA Forum, 19*(1), 1–17. https://doi.org/10.1007/s12027-018-0505-8

Wintermeyer, L., & Basit, A. B. (2017). The Future of Islamic FinTech Is Bright. *Forbes*. https://www.forbes.com/sites/lawrencewintermeyer/2017/12/08/the-future-of-islamic-fintech-is-bright/#15165ed65faf

CHAPTER 5

Analysis of Fatwas on FinTech

Mohamed Cherif El Amri and Mustafa Omar Mohammed

Abstract By the end of the twentieth century, the global financial system began experiencing a rapid financial technological development, which culminated in the first decade of the twenty-first century, with extraordinary increase in innovations of financial instruments (mostly technological). Today, a new wave of technological innovations often called "Fintech" is gradually dominating the financial sector. According to KPMG (2017), "the total global investment in Fintech companies increased from US$9 billion in 2010 to over US$25 billion in 2016. Venture capital investment has also risen steadily, from US$0.8 billion in 2010 to US$ 13.6 billion in 2016". According to consultancy Accenture, more than US$50 billion has been invested in Fintech globally since 2010.

Keywords Fatwa • FinTech • Shari'ah • Principles • Application

M. C. El Amri (✉)
Istanbul Sabahattin Zaim University, Istanbul, Turkey
e-mail: Mohamed.amri@izu.edu.tr

M. O. Mohammed
International Islamic University Malaysia, Kuala Lumpur, Malaysia

M. M. Billah (ed.), *Islamic FinTech*,
https://doi.org/10.1007/978-3-030-45827-0_5

Introduction

By the end of the twentieth century, the global financial system began experiencing a rapid financial technological development, which culminated in the first decade of the twenty-first century, with an extraordinary increase in innovations of financial instruments (mostly technological). Today, a new wave of technological innovations, often called "FinTech" is gradually dominating the financial sector. According to KPMG (2019), the total global investment in FinTech companies grew from US$9 billion in 2010 to over US$135.7 billion (with 2693 deals) in 2019. Out of this, investment in fintech companies in the Americas reached US$64.2 billion (almost 1337 deals). Likewise, the USA fintech companies alone received the highest investment of US$59.8 billion (almost 1144 deals), the second-highest investment was received by Europe to a tune of US$58.1 billion (with 753 deals), and Asia Pacific fintech companies received the investment of US$12.9 billion (across 547 deals).

Meanwhile, in the Muslim world, particularly the Middle East and North Africa (MENA) region, MAGNiTT & ABU DHABI Global Market, (2019) stated that there are 310 FinTech start-up companies in October 2019 in MENA. According to MAGNiTT & ABU DHABI Global Market, (2019), "A total of $237M has been invested in 181 deals since 2015 in MENA-based FinTech startups. 2017 was the breakout year for FinTech venture investment across MENA, with large investments including Network International ($30M), PayTabs ($20M) and Souqalmal ($10M)". The report added that "In 2018, FinTech overtook more traditionally invested industries, such as e-commerce and transport, and became the most popular by number of deals across MENA. Despite this, funding amounts are still low, given that investment has predominantly been at the early stage of investment". As of July 2020, there are at least 142 fintech companies that offer Shari'ah-compliant products and services (IFNFINTECH, 2020). Noticeably, the prospect of FinTech for Islamic finance is very high, mainly because Islamic finance is an infant industry with a growth rate of 11.4% year-on-year and total worth estimated at USD 2.44 trillion (2Q19 (Islamic Financial Services Board, 2020). Despite the established views on the merits of FinTech, the extent of its compliance with the Shari'ah still occupies a large space of intellectual discourse in the Islamic finance industry, particularly among Shari'ah scholars. The permissibility and non-permissibility of FinTech are mainly expressed through Shari'ah *Fatwas* (decrees) from various individual scholars or prominent Shari'ah institutions, such as OIC Fiqh Academy, Accounting and Auditing Organization for Islamic Financial Institutions (AAOIFI), IFRS, and Shari'ah Advisory Council of central banks. The extant literature has mostly been silent on the analysis of these Fatwas, in any case. The present chapter critically analyses Fatwas issued concerning FinTech.

The chapter is structured into six sections, including the introduction. Section "Literature Review" that follows reviews the extant related works to identify the research gap. Sections "Overview of FinTech" and "Overview of Fatwas" provide the overviews of FinTech and Fatwas, respectively. Section "Analysis of Fatwas in FinTech" analyses Fatwas in FinTech. The final section "Conclusion" concludes the chapter and provides some suggestions for future research.

Literature Review

Most of the discussions in the literature on the Shari'ah compliance of FinTech represent individual scholar's view rather than fatwa in the real sense of the word. The discussion is skewed towards individual applications of FinTech such as bitcoin and its technology platforms such as blockchain rather than FinTech in general and its various ecosystems. Furthermore, discussion of the so-called FinTech Shari'ah compliance has mostly been general and disjointed. There are few studies on institutional fatwas. The FinTech Shari'ah compliance literature based on individual and institutional fatwas can be largely classified into three: (1) cryptocurrency, (2) bitcoin, and (3) blockchain. The literature on bitcoin is dominant. There is hardly any extensive and intensive study of Fatwas on FinTech, and hence this chapter is very significant in analyzing these literatures on various fatwas related to the subject to identify the gaps and provide suggestions for future research.

There are few studies that discussed FinTech Shari'ah compliance in relation to cryptocurrency. The themes of these studies focus on analyzing the permissibility and merits of cryptocurrency relative to the various aspects of Islamic economics and finance. For example, in terms of permissibility Oziev and Yandiev (2017) applied analytical, descriptive and theoretical methods to investigate the effect of cryptocurrency on the financial system, analyze the extent to which cryptocurrency fulfills the Shari'ah requirements for money and its circulation, and evaluating how the features of cryptocurrencies (e.g., bitcoin) compare to fiat currency.

Regarding the merits of cryptocurrency, Muedini (2018) examined the usability of cryptocurrencies (including bitcoin) in the context of Islamic law. The author argued for the significance of cryptocurrencies to Islamic finance. He said cryptocurrency is a better solution for government-controlled currency problem, and that cryptocurrencies, especially bitcoin, provide many solutions that were troubling the early Muslim scholars. He cited some of the merits of cryptocurrencies as follows. The supply of bitcoin and other cryptocurrencies is fixed, which is different from the conventional fiat currencies. This feature eliminates potential gharar (uncertainty) and inflation as well. Furthermore, unlike fiat and precious metal coins, cryptocurrencies such as bitcoin may not be modified, manipulated, or forged. Moreover, the peer-to-peer transactions of cryptocurrencies eliminate the need for any banking entity, removing third party risk of controlling an individual's money.

Meanwhile Bakar, Rosbi, and Uzaki (2017) evaluated the operation of cryptocurrency from the perspective of Islamic finance. The study also examined the structure of cryptocurrency based on Shari'ah standards. The study is informative and is aimed at providing the Islamic-minded investors with the right perspective and details about bitcoin investments. The study also cautioned that the manager of the bitcoin account is anonymous, and thus in case of any unexpected incident, it is hard to trace the real account holder.

Studies on the Shari'ah compliance of bitcoin are equally few. This literature discussed various views of Muslim scholars on the Shari'ah permissibility of bitcoin. Abubakar, Ogunbado, and Saidi (2018) classified this group of literature into two. Their findings show that some Muslim scholars entirely oppose bitcoin and find it to be contradictory to the principles of Shari'ah. On the other hand, there are Muslim scholars who opine that bitcoin does not violate Shari'ah principles and can therefore be adopted but with some conditions. For example, Charles W. Evans (2015) compared fiat money and bitcoins and drew a conclusion that bitcoins are free from Riba and incorporated the principles of *maslahah* and risk-sharing.

Bergstra (2015) described bitcoins as a currency-like informational commodity and conclude that there is higher than 99% probability that bitcoins will disappear, and the investors will get disappointed. Nevertheless, he is of the view that bitcoin or other similar cryptocurrencies could be introduced as an effective instrument for the development of Islamic finance. The author recommended the following for effective implementation of bitcoin in Islamic finance: (1) applying circulation theory of bitcoin that uses payment system free from interest, (2) treating bitcoin-like system as a money-like exclusively informational commodity with the implication that such a system need not support debt, (3) the idea that Islamic Finance imposes different requirements compared to conventional finance on the use of money to achieve social and economic objectives, and (4) recognizing that the aspects of mining, gambling and lack of trust are problematic from the perspective of Islamic Finance and hence the need to modify order to ensure compliance with the Shari'ah.

Adam (2017) considers bitcoin as *Māl* (wealth) and *MuTaqawwim* (lawful). However, from the *Maqāṣid al-Shari'ah* perspective, bitcoin fails to fulfill the role of money prescribed by the Shari'ah and thus cannot be considered to possess *Thamaniyyah* (intrinsic value). The author also opined that bitcoin has failed to meet the conditions of circulation, marketability, equity (*'adl*), transparency, and *hifẓ al-Māl* (wealth preservation). Regarding circulation and marketability, the author explains that bitcoin's volatility raises uncertainty resulting in investors hoarding and storing it instead of investing, making bitcoin illiquid and inflating the bubble even more. He further explained that the mysterious network makes the clarity in bitcoin the problematic as each trader and merchant remain anonymous. More disputes can be triggered by the lack of a regulatory system. Adam (2017) argued that due to its cryptic essence, bitcoin has failed to meet the objective of *hifz al-Māl* [preservation of wealth]. Therefore, he added, bitcoin has become an enticing opportunity for hackers and fraudsters in the absence of regulatory controls and sophisticated technologies, as there is an additional layer of anonymity shielding for their privacy within the industry. He said investments in bitcoins and cryptocurrencies do not represent the real economy and do not encourage an economy's real development. Besides, he added, bitcoin investments do not benefit society or the real economy, as investments in bitcoin do not increase utilities, labor, or the manufacturing of goods. Nevertheless, the author concludes that notwithstanding his arguments, any return on bitcoin investments will be Shari'ah-compliant and lawful.

Contrary to the view of Adam (2017), other scholars have taken a strong position in relation to Bitcoin. For example, Alshaikh (2019) opined that Bitcoin is prohibited in its current application and status. He emphasized that there is a need for creating a cryptocurrency which meets Shari'ah requirements and the needs of the people in the advanced digital world. In another study, Alshammari (2019) and Jumaili (2019) concurred with Alshaikh that cryptocurrencies do not meet the Shari'ah definition of currencies since the issuer of those currencies remain anonymous, which is a form of gharar or uncertainty.

On the other hand, Abu Hussain (2019) undertook a critical review of the reasons provided by scholars who consider cryptocurrencies non-Shari'ah compliant. Specifically, he rebutted the following four reasons provided by those scholars: ambiguous nature of cryptocurrencies, anonymity of the issuer, anonymity of the contracting parties, and instability of their values. Regarding the first reason, Abu Hussain (2019) argues that the nature of the cryptocurrencies is not ambiguous because the nature of the currencies can be known from the programmers who mine them. With regards to the anonymity of the issuer of those currencies, the author argues that this reason is not valid because the issuers of most of those currencies are announced to the public. For example, he said, the government of Venezuela is known by the public to have issued a cryptocurrency backed by oil, in addition to Goldman Sachs, and OneGram who also issued cryptocurrencies. Similarly, he argues that the reason cited for the anonymity of the contracting parties does not hold water in cup. This is because the information of those institutions involved in cryptocurrencies in various countries is readily available within the public domain. Finally, the reason that the values of these currencies fluctuate and hence are unstable is unfounded. These currencies are normally backed by assets and commodities, thus maintaining a relatively stable value due to such indexation. The author has therefore, proposed that scholars should be selective in identifying the non-Shari'ah elements in those cryptocurrencies rather than issuing blanket fatwas for their total prohibition.

Unlike the literature on cryptocurrencies and bitcoin, studies on blockchain from Islamic perspective see blockchain as a tool or instrument that can technically be used to enhance the efficiency of Islamic finance. These works have not largely emphasized the Shari'ah compliant or fatwa aspects of blockchain except in the area smart contract. Major studies on FinTech Shari'ah compliance related to blockchain include Abojeib and Habib (2019) who discussed how the technology of blockchain and smart contract could help Islamic social finance institutions to enhance governance, reduce transaction costs, increase transparency, and increase confidence, which in turn increases market accessibility and business flexibility. Alzubaidi and Abdullah (2017) explored the ability of a digital currency to provide a safer alternative to the existing fiat money system for blockchain applications in the Islamic financial system. The paper explored the potential and ability to implement a digital currency that fulfills the features of money under Shari'ah principles and offers a currency that is more robust than fiat currency.

Elasrag (2019) focused on examining the disruptive technology "Blockchain" and its potential applications in Islamic finance. The author explained how blockchain could turn around the Islamic finance industry. The paper discussed the various blockchain technologies that Islamic finance offers, and the challenges Islamic finance face in its blockchain application. In the same vein, Evans (2015) examined autonomous blockchain management systems (BMS) like bitcoin and the distributive compliance with the requirements of Islamic banking and finance. He demonstrated that the concepts of *Maslahah* (public interest) and reciprocal risk-sharing (as opposed to risk-shifting) could be integrated into a BMS.

Although the literature of fatwas on Islamic FinTech focusing in three areas: cryptocurrencies, bitcoin, and blockchain are largely from individual perspective, there are few with detailed fatwas issued by institutions. For example, the National Shari'ah Board—Indonesia Council of Muslim Scholars published fatwas on the application of FinTech, in two areas: information technology payment and electronic money. The references to the fatwas in these two areas are: 117/DSN-MUI/II/2018 for fatwas on information technology payment and, 116/DSN-MUI/IX/2017 for fatwas on electronic money [Dewan Syariah Nasional—Majelis Ulama Indonesia website]. The South African Islamic Seminary Fatwa Center declared that bitcoin is acceptable for trade, but should be licensed by government authorities for it to be considered a currency (Oziev & Yandiev, 2018).

Oziev and Yandiev (2017) cited other cases of institutional fatwas as follows. The Turkish government's religious authority declared bitcoin and other cryptocurrencies as unlawful. A similar view is shared by the Fatwa Center of Palestine. Meanwhile Oziev and Yandiev (2017) also cited views by prominent personalities in Fatwa institutions. For example, the Grand Mufti of Egypt Shaykh Shawki Allam forbids bitcoin and cryptocurrency, which he claims facilitate illegal and hidden transactions or activities, with untraceable feature. In contrast, Mufti Muhammad Abu Bakar, a Shari'ah expert and compliance official at Blossom Finance in Jakarta, see bitcoin as non-Shari'ah compliant although he approved the application of blockchain. Mufti Abdul QadirBarakatullah, a member of the Shari'ah Committee in Al-Ryan Bank, formerly the Islamic Bank of Great Britain is convinced that that cryptocurrencies are effective tool for enhancing development of Islamic finance. Sheikh Dr. Adnan Al-Zahrani,

Ex-chairman of the Shari'ah Supervisory Board of Al-Jazeera Bank, sees cryptocurrency as one type of currencies/money that evolved with time.

AlQaradaghi (2018) examined bitcoin based on four assumptions to derive Shari'ah rulings related to the currency. He discussed in the first assumption three major issues namely, public acceptability of bitcoin, the issuing authority and the stability of the currency. Firstly, he queried whether bitcoin has the features of the currency accepted by the public, issued by the government and is stable. He concluded that such crypto-currencies as bitcoin do not meet the specification of currencies that are accepted widely by the public. Secondly, since there is no government backing for bitcoin, it does not fulfill an important Islamic principle related to the issuance of currency which should be by the sovereign authority, that is the government. Finally, the value of bitcoin is relatively unstable as it experiences constant fluctuation.

The second question is whether bitcoin can be treated as credit card: He concluded that the parties involved in the credit card (Owner of the credit card like Visa Company, bank, customer, and the shops where the card is used) remain anonymous in the case of bitcoin. The third question relates to whether bitcoin can be treated as an asset or commodity. He explained that bitcoin is neither an asset nor a commodity because it does not have the features of wealth as defined by the jurists. In the final assumption, AlQaradaghi questioned whether bitcoin is a financial right. He argues that bitcoin is devoid of financial right as it does not represent a financial asset that can be easily sold and bought.

Overview of FinTech

FinTech is a compound word (financial technology) that is derived from "Fin" for finance and "Tech" for technology. It is defined as companies or representatives of companies that incorporate financial services with modern and innovative technologies (Dorfleitner, Hornuf, Schmitt, & Weber, 2017). Conceptually, it is a new kind of financial service focusing on the broad types of users of IT businesses, combined with IT technology and other financial services such as payment, remittance, and wealth management. All technical processes, from updating financial software to programming a new form of financial software, are included in FinTech. The entire financial service process is influenced by these technical procedures (Park, 2015).

Financial technology is broadly applied to any kind of new transaction in the areas of business, ranging from the invention of digital money to double-entry bookkeeping. The essential features of FinTech related products and services that attract customers are convenience, transparency, efficiency, and automation where traditional banks are yet to enhance their services in these areas (EBF, 2015; Mackenzie, 2015).

Based on the unique models of business, FinTech industry can be divided into four major segments: financing, asset management, payments, and other FinTech (Dorfleitner et al., 2017). Figure 5.1 summarizes the segments of FinTech as follows:

Dorfleitner (2017), as shown in Fig. 5.1 above, classified the conventional FinTech into four main segments. The four main segments are: financing, asset management, payments and other. Dorfleitner (2017) further categorized, in the original figure, the four FinTech segments into 17 sub-segments shown in Table 5.1 below.

According to the author, the financing segment of FinTech ensures the availability of financing for both private individual and businesses. Dorfleitner (2017) further divided the financing segment into two sub-segments: (1) crowdfunding (based on the participation of a large number of contributors) and (2) credit and factoring (no involvement of crowd participation). The author included in the asset management segment FinTechs that provide guidance, disposal and asset management, and aggregated personal wealth metrics. He subdivided the asset management

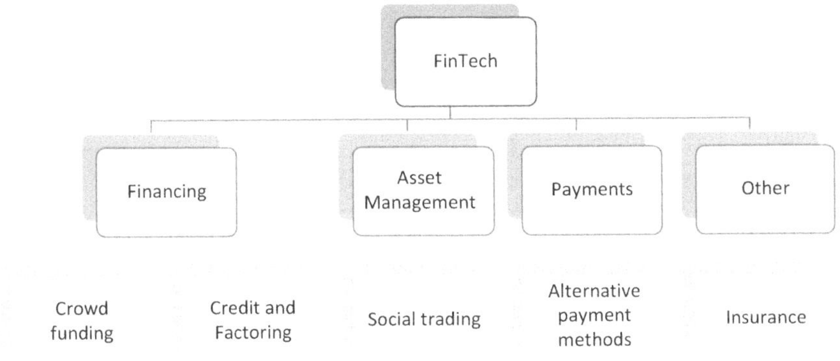

Fig. 5.1 Segments and Sub-segments of FinTech. (Source: Adapted from Dorfleitner (2017). The original figure comprises 17 sub-segments)

Table 5.1 Sub-segments of the four FinTech segments

Categories	*Segments*			
	[a]*Financing*	*Asset Management*	*Payments*	*Other*
Sub-segments	Crowdfunding	Social funding	Alternative payment methods	Insurance
	Donation-based crowdfunding	Robo-advice	Blockchain and cryptocurrencies	Search engine and comparison sites
	Reward-based crowdfunding	Personal Financial Management	Other FinTechs	Technology, IT and infrastructure
	crowdinvesting crowdlending	Investment and Banking		Other FinTechs

[a]As shown in Fig. 5.1 above, Financing segment also includes credit and factoring sub-segment, which does not appear in this table because it does not have other sub-categories

segment into four sub-segments: Robo-advice, social trading, investment and banking, and personal financial management. Another main segment is the payments; which includes the blockchain and cryptocurrency sub-segments. Both sub-segments offer virtual currencies (cryptocurrency) as an alternative to typical fiat money. FinTech companies that cannot be categorized based on these three functions of a conventional bank, that is, asset management, financing, and payment transfers, are defined by another payment sub-segment called 'other FinTechs'. This segment includes a sub-segment called insurance or InsurTechs, which facilitates the acquisition of insurance. The insurance sub-segment provides peer-to-peer insurance, where, in the event of loss, a group of policyholders come together and assume mutual responsibility. Another sub-segment related to 'other FinTechs' is called the "search engines and comparison sites" which enables the Internet-based search and comparison of financial products or financial services. Meanwhile, the sub-segment referred to as "Technology, IT and Infrastructure" provides technical solutions for financial service providers.

Islamic FinTech has largely tried to adopt some of these segments and subsegments. In financing segment, Islamic FinTech has made headways in crowdfunding (Abdullah, 2016; Achsien & Purnamasari, 2016), while in the asset management segment, evident progress can be seen in investment and banking, robo-advice and personal financing management. With regards to payments, Islamic FinTech is progressing in terms of alternative payment system, but slow in the application of cryptocurrencies and blockchain (Elipses, 2019). Another area where progress is slow is insurance (COMCEC, 2019). The slow adoption of Islamic FinTech is attributed to, among others, Shari'ah compliance, financial inclusion, digital awareness, trust deficit, security, infrastructure, regulations, and impact investment conservative culture, human resource quality, digital transformation, data quality and digital literacy (Aziz & Anim, 2020; Mohamed & Ali, 2019).

Overview of Fatwas

Fatwa or Futya is the singular form of the word Fatawi, or Fatawa. Literally, it means to clarify something for someone, interpretation of dreams, and to answer a question (Ibn Mandhur, 2003). Scholars have provided the technical meaning of fatwa more or less similar to its literal definition. Technically, therefore Fatwa refers to a ruling or a response by a Muslim jurist (Mufti) to a question or issue raised by an individual or group (Mustafti) on Shari'ah matters that are either dubious or obscure in nature, or have newly arisen without known precedent (Ministry of Awqaf & Islamic Affairs, 1983).

The qualification of a Mufti, as explained by Al-Mawsu'ah al-Fiqhiyyah of the Ministry of Awqaf & Islamic Affairs (1983), includes the following conditions, among others. The Mufti must be a Muslim who has reached the age of puberty and has complete legal capacity. The Mufti must be known for his moral standing, good personality trait, and as a just person. Intellectually, he must have a mastery of the Arabic language, be conversant in the sciences of Quran and Sunnah, Ijma' (consensus) of the scholars, and also be knowledgeable in Islamic Jurisprudence. Moreover, he should be well-versed on the subject of the objectives of Shari'ah, and is well-acquainted with the custom of the people, their culture, and their situations on the ground (Ministry of Awqaf & Islamic Affairs, 1983).

Kamali (2016) explained that traditionally fatwa began as a private practice, and was not bounded by any influences or control from the state. He further explained that the muftis would often respond to issues on problems of the people or those that are related to the community. Hence, Fatwa was seen as a community service. He said it was the people who established the standard for fatwas although the muftis would often advice government on religious matters by issuing fatwas.

Based on Al-Mawsu'ah al-Fiqhiyyah (1983), a fatwa is only permissible when it complies with the Quran and the consensus of qualified scholars (ijma'). It further stated that fatwa should not be based on someone's speculation and assumption. Moreover, it explained that the mufti should not just choose a random position if there are any contradictory opinions and explanations in the source. Rather, he should verify and consider his preference (*al-tarjih*) for developing a favored stance.

A Muslim scholar or institution is expected to thoroughly study and research, and carefully review, evaluate and verify the issues presented before issuing a fatwa. Such investigations include knowing the nature of the incident or issue, the context and reasons why the issue happened, the precedence of similar cases, the appropriate Shari'ah tools and principles to apply and the relevant rules. The fatwa must be relevant to the time and place bearing in mind the maxim that real life events are not linear as they change relative to places and time. For example, if an individual asks the mufti the extent to which alcoholic perfume is permissible. Based on Shari'ah ruling, any form of alcohol that intoxicates is unlawful. In other words, the reason why alcohol was prohibited is intoxication. In one of the hadith narrated by Ibn Umar, the Prophet, May Peace Be Upon Him, cursed ten types of persons related to alcohol, which include the manufacturer, the seller, the buyer, the consumer, and the one who carries and distributes it [Abu Dawood, Hadith no. 4899]. Then the Mufti has to research about the process of producing modern alcohol, which has several purposes including as an antiseptic agent. He or she should understand at what stage in the production process does alcohol become intoxicant. When people use alcoholic perfume, do they become drunk? Is wearing alcoholic perfume similar to one who transports or distributes alcohol as mentioned in the hadith? Hence, a fatwa can only be issued when all these situations are taken under due considerations.

Today, only authorized Shari'ah and fiqh councils and academics can issue a fatwa. Nevertheless, within a limited scope, a scholar can issue a fatwa on issues that are adirectly raised by people to him or her. Therefore, it can be concluded that currently, we have platforms for both individual and collective fatwas (official and non-official) based on the nature of the issues and the corresponding knowledge and wisdom of the Mufti as an individual or collectively as an institution.

Analysis of Fatwas in FinTech

As discussed in section "Literature Review" of this chapter, fatwas on Islamic FinTech have largely focused in three areas: cryptocurrencies, bitcoin and blockchain from individual and institutional perspectives. These groups of literatures are not catching up with the development in the applications of Fintech in the Islamic finance industry, which continue to grow extending to several ecosystems. The present discussion in the literature has largely been on the Shari'ah permissibility and non-permissibility. There is a huge research gap in terms of fatwas on the processes, on product development, on Shari'ah review and audit of Islamic Fintech practices, among others.

Mohammed and Siti Norbaya (2019) argued that although Islamic law is vital for the validity of Islamic FinTech, such discussion among scholars remain insufficient. This view is supported by Mustafa, Shahnawaz, and Eleftherios (2020) who stated that the Shari'ah compliance related to cryptocurrency and block-chain remain the biggest challenge that Islamic finance is facing. In the same vein, Hasan, Hassan, and Aliyu (2020) emphasized that Shari'ah compliance was one of the major challenges for the growth of Islamic FinTech.

As stated in section "Overview of FinTech" above, Islamic finance has made headways in the Fintech ecosystem and business models in terms of payment, crowdfunding, wealth management, cryptocurrencies, bitcoin, blockchain, insurance, and robo-advisory. In relation to the payment system, there are several institutional fatwas. For example, the fatwa discussed in section "Literature Review" above by the National Shari'ah Board—Indonesia Council of Muslim Scholars on information technology payment and electronic money. The fatwas are very detailed. They first spelt out the models for information technology payment and electronic money systems, which include purchase and sale orders, online factoring and sale. The fatwas included the online Shari'ah offer and acceptance, the electronic procedures to execute the various contracts involved such as Qard (loan), Ijarah (leasing), Wakalah (agency), Musharakah (partnership), and Murabahah (sale). The fatwas also detailed out the electronic procedures, electronic documents with the necessary coding, signature, symbols, and access; electronic certificates, and Shari'ah ways of verifying the transactions. The fatwas stated that the negative elements such ar riba, gharar and tadlis or deceptions that must be avoided. The institution showed how these fatwas were harmonized with the common law in Indonesia.

In the area of crowdfunding, Islamic finance has adapted the mainstream donation based crowdfunding, crowdlending and crowdinvesting to conform to Shari'ah principles. In applying donation-based crowdfunding and crowdfunding lending, Islamic finance institutions ensure that the activities are free from interest, gharar, and deception. Several Islamic organizations widely adapt these two modes of crowdfunding, and there are several fatwas on them. Meanwhile, crowdinvesting is less popular. Those who use it, adapt it as an equity or partnership mode of investing such as Mudarabah and Musharakah.

As stated earlier, much of the fatwas are on cryptocurrencies, bitcoin, and blockchain. This is because the first two areas have become popular for individual or retail investment. Besides, many people find it convenient to make purchases with these electronic monies. In terms of Islamic insurance, the Islamic Fintech penetration is very slow (COMCEC, 2019). There is a general consensus in most of the jurisdictions that efforts need to be doubled in this regard. The growth of fatwas would be proportionate to the FinTech application in Islamic insurance or Takaful.

Another area that is witnessing the increasing application of Islamic FinTech is the Islamic social finance especially Zakat and Waqf. For example, Zakat institutions continue to take advantage of the rapid growth in Islamic financial technologies and digital services to enhance the collection of Zakat and its distribution (Al Azizah & Choirin, 2018). Through FinTech, Zakat institutions are largely able to lower their operational costs, enhance governance structures, recognize faster payments, and provide more developed products and solutions (Banna & Alam, 2020).

Conclusion

Islamic financial institutions continue to increasingly adopt FinTech applications and solutions to enhance their financial and operational performances. FinTech is able to improve financial efficiency, reduce operational costs, promote transparency, enhance governance, and facilitate payments and flow of funds between these institutions and their various stakeholders, especially the customers. Fatwas on the application of Islamic Fintech have largely remained general and focus on only three aspects: cryptocurrencies, bitcoins, and blockchain. Meanwhile fatwas on detailed application of other FinTech ecosystem remain to a great extent unfulfilled. Most of the Shari'ah views on FinTech are issued by individual scholars through the media and other public forum or platforms rather than through in-depth constructive studies. Such drawbacks could potentially slowdown the pace of adopting Shari'ah compliant FinTech. This implies that major challenges of digital transformation still prevail in the Islamic finance landscape. These challenges include lack of appropriate technical knowledge and capabilities, traditional and conservative cultures, lack of awareness and, lack of talent and expertise who are versed with both the technical and Shari'ah knowledge.

Therefore, to move forward, Islamic finance institutions would be required to promote awareness campaigns on FinTech, build capacities in talents and expertise, and encourage institutional fatwa bodies to issue regular Shari'ah standards on FinTech. This would necessitate Shari'ah scholars to be well informed, resourceful, and innovative in issuing Fatwas on the subject. They need to understand FinTech and the various issues, and to consult all the relevant parties related to Fintech especially individuals with good technological literacy and basic Shari'ah understanding. Secondly, governments or central authorities in Muslim nations should support efforts through the relevant institutions to produce Shari'ah standards to guide the Fatwas of Shari'ah scholars in relation to FinTech. Thirdly, promoting public awareness would involve public and private institutions offering short-term (training and courses) and long-run (diploma and bachelor) programs that integrate Shari'ah and FinTech. Finally, interested Shari'ah scholars in the area need to undertake serious scientific research and publish them. The findings from the present study provide a fertile ground for future research to leverage on. They could conduct extensive and intensive research on fatwas related to detailed application on the various Islamic FinTech ecosystems.

References

Abdullah, A. (2016). Crowdfunding As An Emerging Fundraising Tool: With Special Reference to The Malaysian Regulatory Framework. *Islam and Civilisational Renewal, 7*(1), 98–119.

Abojeib, M., & Habib, F. (2019). Blockchain for Islamic Social Responsibility Institutions. In *FinTech as a Disruptive Technology for Financial Institutions* (pp. 221–240). IGI Global.

Abu Hussain, O. (2019). Alhukm Al-shar'i Litta'amul Bil'umulat Al-iftiradiya. In *Virtual Currencies Under Evaluation* (pp. 107–134). Sharjah: University of Sharjah.

Abu-Bakar, M. M. (2018). Shariah Analysis of Bitcoin, Cryptocurrency, and Blockchain. (Shariah Analysis in Light of Fatwas and Scholars' Opinions).
Abubakar, Y. S., Ogunbado, A. F., & Saidi, M. A. (2018). Bitcoin and Its Legality from Shariah Point of View. *SEISENSE Journal of Management, 1*(4), 13–21. (Muslim scholars' opinion on bitcoin).
Achsien, I. H., & Purnamasari, D. L. (2016). Islamic Crowd-funding as The Next Financial Innovation in Islamic Finance: Potential and Anticipated Regulation in Indonesia. *European Journal of Islamic Finance, 5*(June), 1–11.
Adam, M. F. (2017). Bitcoin: Shariah Compliant. *Amanah Finance Consultancy*, 1–54. (Islamic Fiqh Analysis of Bitcoin).
Al Azizah, U. S., & Choirin, M. (2018). Financial Innovation on Zakat Distribution and Economic Growth. In International Conference of Zakat.
AlQaradaghi, A. (2018, March 15). Al'umulat Al-raqamiya Al-'iliktruniya bayna Al-hil Wa-ttahrim, bayna Alwaqi' Walmashhud: Dirasa Fiqhiya Iqtisadiya ma'a bayan Albada'il Almaqbula Shar'an. *I-FIKR*. Retrieved from https://ifikr.isra.my/library/pub/10167
Alshaikh, G. (2019). Al-ta'sil Alfiqhi Lil'umlat Alraqmiya-Bitcoin Namudhajan. In *Virtual Currencies Under Evaluation* (pp. 15–50). Sharjah: University of Sharjah.
Alshammari, A. R. (2019). Al-ta'sil Alfiqhi Lil'umlat Al'iftiradiya. In *Virtual Currencies Under Evaluation* (pp. 51–84). Sharjah: University of Sharjah.
Alzubaidi, I. B., & Abdullah, A. (2017). Developing a Digital Currency from an Islamic Perspective: Case of Blockchain Technology. *International Business Research, 10*(11), 79–87.
Aziz, M. R. A., & Anim, N. A. H. M. (2020). Trust Towards Zakat Institutions Among Muslims Business Owners. *Jurnal Ekonomi & Keuangan Islam, 6*(1), 1–9.
Bakar, N. A., Rosbi, S., & Uzaki, K. (2017). Cryptocurrency Framework Diagnostics from Islamic Finance Perspective: A New Insight of Bitcoin System Transaction. *International Journal of Management Science and Business Administration, 4*(1), 19–28.
Banna, H., & Alam, M. R. (2020). Islamic Banking Efficiency and Inclusive Sustainable Growth: The Role of Financial Inclusion. *Journal of Islamic Monetary Economics and Finance, 6*(1), 213–242.
Bergstra, J. A. (2015, January 1). Bitcoin and Islamic Finance. Semantics Scholar. SemanticsScholar.org, pp. 1–19.
COMCEC. (2019). Improving the Takaful Sector in Islamic Countries. Ankara, Turkey. Available at: www.comcec.org *E-book: http://ebook.comcec.org. ISBN: 978-605-7751-05-8.
Dewan Syariah Nasional – Majelis Ulama Indonesia. Retrieved September 22, 2020., from https://dsnmui.or.id/kategori/fatwa/page/2/

Dorfleitner, G., Hornuf, L., Schmitt, M., & Weber, M. (2017). *FinTech in Germany*. Cham: Springer International Publishing.

EBF. (2015). *The Digital Transformation of Banks and the Digital Single Market*. EBF Discussion Paper Nr. 015782. Brüssel: European Banking Federation.

Elasrag, H. (2019). *Blockchains for Islamic Finance: Obstacles & Challenges*. University Library of Munich.

Elipses. (2019). *The Global Islamic Fintech Report*.

Evans, C. (2015). Bitcoin in Islamic Banking and Finance. *Journal of Islamic Banking and Finance, 3*(1), 1–11.

Hasan, R., Hassan, M. K., & Aliyu, S. (2020). Fintech and Islamic Finance: Literature Review and Research Agenda. *International Journal of Islamic Economics and Finance (IJIEF), 3*(1), 75–94.

Ibn Mandhur, M. i. M. (2003). *Lisān al-ʿArab* (1st ed.). Beirut: Dar Sadir. Retrieved from https://waqfeya.com/book.php?bid=4077

IFNFINTECH. (2020). IFN Islamic Fintech Landscape. Retrieved January 25, 2020, from https://ifnfintech.com/wp-content/uploads/2020/01/Landscape-21-01-2020.jpg

Islamic Financial Services Board. (2020). *Islamic Financial Services Industry Stability Report 2020*. Kuala Lumpur.

Jumaili, I. A. A. (2019). "Isdar Al'umulat Al'iftiradiya bayna Dhawabit Al-shar" Wamutatallabat Al'asr. In *Virtual Currencies Under Evaluation* (pp. 85–106). Sharjah: University of Sharjah.

Kamali, M. H. (2016). Moderation in Fatwa and Ijtihad: Juristic and Historical Perspectives. *Islam and Civilisational Renewal, 7*(3), 303–324. https://doi.org/10.12816/0035262

KPMG. (2019). *The Pulse of Fintech*. Amstelveen, Netherlands: KPMG.

Mackenzie, A. (2015). The FinTech Revolution. *London Business School Review, 26*(3), 50–53.

MAGNiTT, & ABU DHABI Global Market. (2019). *MENA FinTech Venture Report*. Retrieved from https://magnitt.com/research/50675/2019-mena-fintech-venture-report

Maloney, C. (2018). Islamic Scholar Says Bitcoin Is Compliant with Sharia Law as Price Surges. Retrieved from https://www.ccn.com/bitcoin-declared-compliant-with-sharia-law-price-surges/

Ministry of Awqaf & Islamic Affairs. (1983). *Al-Mausu'ah Al-Fiqhiyah Al-Kuwaitiyah* (1st ed.). Kuwait: Ministry of Awqaf & Islamic Affairs. Retrieved from https://waqfeya.com/book.php?bid=878

Mohamed, H., & Ali, H. (2019). *Blockchain, Fintech, and Islamic Finance: Building the Future in the New Islamic Digital Economy*. Berlin: De|G PRESS.

Muedini, F. (2018). The Compatibility of Cryptocurrencies and Islamic Finance. *European Journal of Islamic Finance, 10*, 12–19.

Mustafa, R. R., Khan, S., & Thalassinos, E. I. (2020). FinTech, Blockchain and Islamic Finance: An Extensive Literature Review. *International Journal of Economics & Business Administration (IJEBA)*, *8*(2), 65–86.

Rahim, N. F., Bakri, M. H., & Yahaya, S. N. (2019). Fintech and Shariah Principles in Smart Contracts. In *FinTech as a Disruptive Technology for Financial Institutions* (pp. 207–220). IGI Global.

Oziev, G., & Yandiev, M. (2018). Cryptocurrency from Shariah Perspective. Retrieved July 20, 2018, from https://papers.ssrn.com/sol3/papers.cfm?abstract_id=3101981

Park, J.-G. (2015). Fintech and Information Security. *Communications of the Korean Institute of Information Scientists and Engineers*, *20*(4), 23–32.

CHAPTER 6

An Evaluation of Smart Contracts: Practices, Legality, and *Sharī'ah*

Nor Razinah Mohd. Zain and Khairul Azmi Mohamad

Abstract The increasing usage of blockchain technology in digital investment, cryptocurrency, and financial technology (FinTech) has led the global financial market to a new innovation of concluded contract. Instead of depending on legally drafted documents, smart contract is concluded through the computerized algorithm. Based on the smart contract, the legal relationship between the involved parties is completed online without being limited to time and space. Thus, the application of smart contract needs to be explored from both Common Law and *Sharī'ah* perspectives. By adopting qualitative research design and doctrinal legal analysis, this research evaluates the best practices of the selected Commonwealth countries in accepting the application of smart contract. While evaluating the practices on smart contracts from the majority of

N. R. Mohd. Zain (✉)
IIUM Institute of Islamic Banking and Finance, International Islamic University Malaysia, Kuala Lumpur, Malaysia
e-mail: mumtaz_razi@iium.edu.my

K. A. Mohamad
Harun M. Hashim Law Centre, International Islamic University Malaysia, Kuala Lumpur, Malaysia

M. M. Billah (ed.), *Islamic FinTech*,
https://doi.org/10.1007/978-3-030-45827-0_6

Commonwealth countries, Malaysia is selected to represent the Commonwealth country with a majority Muslim. Additionally, the practices on smart contracts as applied in Australia and United Kingdom are also appreciated. The evaluation of smart contract from *Sharīʿah* perspective is done by investigating the views of the four main Islamic schools of legal thought, which are, *Mālikī's*, *Ḥanafī's*, *Shāfiʿī's*, and *Ḥanbalī's*. A comparative legal approach is considered in analysing similarities and differences between the perspectives of Common Law and *Sharīʿah* relating to the smart contract. These approaches are necessary to be carried out in ensuring the workability of smart contracts in blockchain for *Sharīʿah*-compliant start-ups. This is essential especially to those Muslim countries that stand with Common Law background. As a part of the findings, the researchers found that as long as the smart contract fulfils the required legal elements as required under Common Law and the principles of *Sharīʿah*, it can be used and referred to by the concluding parties.

Keywords Smart Contract • Blockchain • FinTech • Common Law • *Sharīʿah*

Introduction

Starting from the unleashed of cryptocurrency-based technology in 2008, the world is introduced for the first time on the potentials of technology in advancing the global financial market. The potentials of this financial technology or FinTech are considered disruptive and may change the traditional financial services system as available currently. From the famous first cryptocurrency Bitcoin, new cryptocurrencies emerge rapidly and have been applied in the global financial market. Among others are Ethereum, XRP, Bitcoin Cash, Tether, Litecoin, EOS, and Binance Coin. Cryptocurrencies can be understood as digital or electronic currencies that can be created online, stand without any central issuing or bound to any regulating authority. It heavily depends on the blockchain technology that has computerized ability to track and record any existing transactions that completed within its digital platform. Even though cryptocurrencies are considered disruptive in nature due to their lack of regulations and monitoring, the blockchain technology that exists behind it is treated like the eighth wonder of the world.

The innovative technology of blockchain captures the attention from either governments, or public, or private sectors. Reaching towards 2020, the increase of dependency on blockchain grows consistently without any sign of dropping. The technological magic of the blockchain to make records without fail has become the influential factor for its adoption. According to *Statista Report 2017*, the size of blockchain market is estimated to reach 339.5 million US dollars (Statista, 2018). This trend indicates the popularity of blockchain technology in all sectors. Furthermore, it is estimated to grow up to 2.3 million US dollars by 2021 (Statista, 2018). Such forecast estimates the increasing demands towards blockchain and its adoption. From those numbers, a shift in the global financial market can be predicted where FinTech based transactions will be more likely to be used and depended on. The records made by the blockchain technology are closely related to the usage of smart contracts in the adopted digital platform. With the frequent use of blockchain technology, it is foreseeable that the usage of smart contracts will be increased, and it gains more importance in FinTech-based transactions. This can be done through a simple click either through smartphones or through other electronic devices such as laptops.

The global financial market has seen the raise of alternative financial services system that derived from the divinely revealed laws of *Sharīʿah*. After almost 40 years of its re-emergence in the modern economic system, this alternative financial services system has successfully stood as a counterpart of the conventional financial services system. It is well-known as Islamic financial services system (IFSS). Instead of depending on interests-making system, the IFSS depends on unique principles such as profit and loss sharing between Islamic financial institutions and their customers; prohibitions of interests (*riba*), speculative or uncertainty (*gharar*), and gambling (*maysir*); and *Sharīʿah*-compliance transactions. In describing the compliance nature of *Sharīʿah* in IFSS, International Shariah Research Academy for Islamic Finance or ISRA (2018) explains that:

> *Sharīʿah* compliance is the raison d'etre for the existence of the Islamic banking and finance industry. Shariah compliance is achieved by meeting not only the prerequisites of the pillars and conditions of the Shariah contract used, but ensuring that the underlying asset as well as the underlying purpose of entering into such a contract is in compliance with the Shariah.

> Compliance with Shariah ensures that the rights of the contractual parties are protected and contractual obligations are met out in a responsible and lawful manner. ISRA (2018)

Thus, it is essential to look closely on the Common Law and *Sharīʿah* perspectives relating to the application of smart contract in the blockchain technology. This research is carried out to: (1) explore the Common Law and *Sharīʿah* perspectives regarding the application of smart contract; (2) to investigate the views of Muslim scholars from *Maliki's*, Ḥanafī's, *Shāfiʿī's*, and Ḥanbalī*'s Islamic schools of legal thought; and (3) to discover the* best practices of the selected Commonwealth countries (with majority are from Muslim countries) in accepting the application of smart contract.

This chapter is organized into several sections. After this introductory section, it follows with a section that explains the smart contract and its application. The third section provides the analysis of traditional elements of contracts under Common Law. Subsequently, it follows with the section that details out the traditional elements of contracts under the principles of *Sharīʿah*. The fifth section elaborates similarities and differences of traditional elements of contracts both under Common Law and *Sharīʿah*. Here, the available modern Islamic legal rulings (if any) are provided relating to smart contract's application. The sixth section elaborates the latest best practices of the selected Commonwealth countries, especially among Muslim countries, in applying smart contracts. Before the conclusion, the seventh section discusses the findings and recommendations (if any).

The Application of Smart Contract

Blockchain and smart contract—When Satoshi Nakamoto introduced Bitcoin, he/she or they also introduced blockchain technology in 2008. This was significantly done through an online white paper famously known as *Bitcoin: A Peer-to-Peer Electronic Cash System*. Instead of discussing about the blockchain technology, he/she or they described that Bitcoin depends on "a system for electronic transactions without relying on trust … with the usual framework of coins made from digital signatures, which provides strong control of ownership" (Nakamoto, 2018).

According to Mohd. Zain, Engku Ali, Adewale, and Abdul Rahman (2019), the blockchain technology normally used as a technology that operated behind the digital currency. Later on, it receives acceptance from private and public sector, and continues to provide digital ledger or recording system. It grows more significantly with the usage of smart contracts that enable parties to conclude agreement relating to crypto-assets regardless of their time and places. While the parties conclude their agreement online, the blockchain technology records it. This gives to the birth of basic form of smart contract. Nowadays, in a ready FinTech start-up, the parties may agree or disagree to certain computerized terms as available online. With a simple click in the online platform, they may transfer their crypto-assets or properties' certificates. The blockchain technology simultaneously records any exchange made by the parties.

Williams (2017) emphasizes on the advantages of having smart contract through the blockchain technology where it is more transparent, less cost in term of documentation and representation, fast-track agreement, controlled-based networks by users, and decentralization. In describing the function of blockchain towards smart contracts, Hsiao (2017: 688) stipulates that:

> By combining peer-to-peer networks, cryptographic algorithms, distributed data storage, and a decentralized consensus mechanism, it provides a way for people to agree on a particular state of affairs and record that agreement in a secure and verifiable manner … encrypted … into smaller database referred to as "blocks". Every block contains information …. Since, blockchain is always kept in synchronization, there is only ever one true record of ownership-essential to prevent anyone trying to double spend their assets by sending it multiple parties at the same time … it is impossible to edit … once it has been properly updated, parties have mathematically-enforced confidence that the record of their ownership will persist into the future.

Nevertheless, with the increasing usage of blockchain, this technology is not free from security risks such as online hacking, encroachment of private data, and attacks from online viruses. Thus, it opens a new discussion on cyber security systems and regulations.

Understanding smart contract—In understanding on what exactly meant by smart contracts, it is important to evaluate the available definitions. According to Agnikhotram and Kouroutakis (2019), there is no consensus among modern scholars in the definite definition of smart contracts. Majority of modern scholars are heavily depending on the definition of smart contract as provided by Nick Szabo who is among the first theorists on the smart contract's application. His research can be traced back to 1994 with the dependency on the usage of vending machines. Due to such absence of definite definition, there is a wide gap in understanding smart contract from a legal sense. Moreover, majority of regulators tend to leave it out or draft smart contract's definitions in various manners. Szabo defines smart contract as "a set of promises, specified in digital form, including protocols within which the parties perform on these promises" (Szabo, 1995). This definition is less technical and easy to understand. Another good definition can be found from the works done by the researchers from the National Institute of Standards and Technology, US Department of Commerce. Smart contract is defined by those researchers as "a collection of code and data (sometimes referred to as functions and state) that is deployed to a Blockchain (e.g. Ethereum)" (Yaga, Peter, Nik, & Scarfone, 2018).

In relation to smart contract's operation, the researchers from the National Institute of Standards and Technology, US Department of Commerce explain that "Future transactions sent to the blockchain can then send data to public methods offered by the smart contract. The contract executes the appropriate method with the user provided data to perform a service. The code, being on the blockchain, is immutable and therefore can be used (among other purposes) as a trusted third party for financial transactions that are more complex than simply sending funds between accounts" (Yaga et al., 2018). By applying smart contract in a blockchain, it seems that a secured online platform may be created and shared among the involved participants or parties only. Moreover, it automatically tracks or records the flow of the transaction and changes that happened within the secured online platform.

Smart contract versus traditional contract—Before the invention of smart contract, generally the traditional contract is created through the agreed exchanged terms between the concluded parties. The earliest trace of concluded contract under Common Law comes in the form of oral agreement between merchants in completing their trading for certain goods. In their agreement on quality and value of the goods, they orally agreed on the terms which are subsequently reduced into writing and recorded in a document or paper. They may bring their selected witness or more than two witnesses to observe the conclusion of the agreement. This is necessary, so in any occurrence of dispute, the witness or witnesses may be called upon regarding the concluded agreement.

The modern procedures relating to this traditional contract have become more complex in nature. With the existence of the transaction's collateral, the required legal fees, the taxation process by the government, and the involvement of legal representatives or legal counsel, the traditional contract has become more expensive and time consuming. Moreover, traditional contracts may depend on the existence of intermediaries. Based on a research done by Mohd. Zain (2018), majority of retail customers do not have bargaining power to negotiate terms with their Islamic financial institution. Thus, they are following the terms of traditional contracts as pre-prepared by Islamic financial institutions that they approached for financing. In the modern transaction, commerce is done in a centralized way where conventional or Islamic financial institutions stand as intermediaries that are responsible to interlink their customers to any possible investment that is carried out by a third party.

This centralized system of traditional contract opens a less space for a fair bargaining and negotiation between the concluded parties. Additionally, the involvement of intermediaries leads to the increase of costs and complexity of procedures. Such situation is different in the application of smart contract. As identified by Hsiao (2017: 685–686), the existence of intermediaries can be seen in commerce in three main ways which are: "(1) financial institutions that serve as a conduit for parties in financial transactions; (2) retailers that purchase goods from manufacturers and sell them to consumers; and (3) websites/mobile apps that facilitate the purchase of goods or engagement of services to be provided by third parties". Additionally, traditional contracts depend on the manual record process. Such records of legal documentation are usually done in writing. Later, the legal document is printed out by using a bundle of papers. This is only for one simple legal transaction. Majority of legal firms are flooded with pillars of papers by dealing with thousands of complex legal transactions daily. These printed legal documents are kept for years as evidential proofs for the concluded transactions. Even with the existence of e-filing system for documents, traditional legal practice is still persisting; thus, it warrants the so-called system of black-lettered law. Moreover, those legal documents are full with legal terminologies and concepts that only qualified advocates and solicitors or legal practitioners/lawyers have the ability to understand.

Contrast to the traditional contract, terms of the smart contract are prepared in codes. These codes basically are based on the computer algorithm. From the computer algorithm, a series of instructions are set to be executed in a chronological step by step. These steps will be executed automatically and immediately. These chronological steps are basically featured in the transaction cycle. The steps will continue to progress until the transaction cycle is completed. Different from the traditional contract, the smart contract can be executed faster. Depending on the automated execution of the agreed terms, the smart contract can be secured and automatically recorded by the blockchain-based system. In a matter of security, the concluded smart contract and its terms are stored in existing computers that are connected to the network. Thus, once the smart contract is concluded, it is difficult to erase its existence. It seems that the terms of smart contract are not opened for negotiation. Just like a pre-prepared agreement, the concluding parties are not opened to make any bargain with pre-prepared terms. If the concluding parties want to do so, the entire computer algorithm-based steps must be equally changed. This is rather difficult to be done since such changes are bound to influence the chronological steps as provided in the blockchain platform and the entire cycle of transaction. Unless, the computer algorithm-based steps are created to be flexible and complex enough to portray the changes of the terms made by the concluding parties.

When the concluding parties agree with the coded terms of the smart contract, their cryptographical signatures or digital signatures will eventually place in the system. Subsequently, the concluded smart contract will be recorded in the network through the distributed ledger of the blockchain. In comparison to the traditional contract, the smart contract has special features that depend on (1) recorded transactions and (2) automated ledger.

The Relationship of Common Law and *Sharīʿah*

Regardless of how smart is the contract or the way that it was drafted, a contract needs to be considered as valid and binding based on the regulated laws. If not, the contract cannot be enforced and can be considered as non-existence. In a situation where there is any exchange of money or transfer of property, such exchange or transfer may not be acceptable under the laws. Consequently, any claim can be made against the so-called concluded contract for any involved rights and ownership.

Common Law is one of the oldest collected unwritten laws that developed based on legal precedents that derived from legal decisions or judgement made by English courts (Plucknett, 2001). Nowadays, majority of these unwritten laws are legislated and codified under statues or acts by countries' parliaments. Common Law is spread, applied, and practiced in majority countries such as United Kingdom and Commonwealth countries. The legal principles of Common Law are the same in these countries. Subject to the rapid development of the laws, the uniqueness of Common Law's application in those countries may be varied and influenced by the countries' legal frameworks.

Instead of depending on court-made decisions, *Sharīʿah* is divinely revealed laws that codified through the verses of the holy Qur'an and the practices of the last Prophet Muhammad (bless and peace be upon him) or *Sunnah*. There are around 6348 verses of the holy Qur'an, and only approximately 500 verses are relating to legal principles. Through the strict methodologies of Islamic jurisprudence, the laws are extended to new cases and this continues the development of *Sharīʿah*'s principles in the modern time (Kamali, 2004).

There is a debate among legal scholars as to the origin of Common Law. There are many influences received by the Common Law since its first application during the reign of Henry II in England (Plucknett, 2001). While enriching the existing principles of Common Law, according to Makdisi (1999), there is a direct legal transplant and adoption of *Sharīʿah*'s principles towards the Common Law. In his research, Makdisi (1999) traces the history on how the Common Law received such legal transplant from *Sharīʿah's* principles. There are many striking similarities between the principles of Common Law and *Sharīʿah*. This can be traced from the principles of contract law, the principles of endowment or *Waqf*, and court procedures. Remarkably, the application of opinions from *Mālikī's Islamic schools of legal thought is apparent. Makdisi (*1999*: 1717) observed that:*

> In both structure and function, Islamic law and the Common Law demonstrated a remarkable kinship, while the civil law was a stranger to both. The similarity between the first two legal systems in their structure and function confirms the similarities that have been demonstrated above in the particular areas of contract, property, and procedure. One question still remains to be answered. How did Islam law and particularly Maliki Islamic law, which dominated the areas of North Africa in the twelfth century come to influence the England of King Henry II, which was dominated by the Normans in the twelfth century? The answer lies in Sicily, where the Normans had conquered the Muslims just a few short decades earlier.

Thus, it is not surprising if the implementation of the Common Law towards contract is consistent with the principles of Sharīʿah. Nevertheless, discussions as derived from Muslim scholars regarding formulation and conclusion of contracts are more comprehensive and in-depth.

Legality of Concluded Contract Under Common Law

In relation to smart contracts, the most relevant principles that can be referred to under Common Law is the principles of contract law. It is essential to evaluate the legality of the concluded contract, regardless if the concluded contract is done either orally, in writing, or electronically. When comes to smart contracts, even though without any specific legislation exists in any of the Commonwealth countries, such smart contracts may be recognized as legally binding contracts as long as they fulfil the conditions stipulated under the principles of contract law. Thus, regardless how advanced the smart contract may be or how old the traditional contract is, such concluded contracts are required to possess all main elements of contract law in order to be valid and binding upon both of the concluding parties.

Based on a normal process of transaction (for an example: the sale and purchase agreement) especially after the parties are agreed to the terms of the contract, a contract can be considered legally binding and enforceable when it fulfils certain elements. The elements are: (1) offer; (2) acceptance of the offer; (3) intention to create legal relations between the concluding parties; (4) consideration; (5) certainty; and (6) capacity. A brief elaboration of these elements is as the followings.

An offer: will take place when a person/party expresses to another his willingness to do or to restrain himself from doing something, where he gets agreement of that other party to such act. Decisions made in Goldsborough Mort and Co. Ltd. v Quiin [1910], and *Coelho v The Public Services Commission [1964]* indicated that offers made must be fulfilled accordingly through the required terms of the contracts. Thus, only by fulfilling the offer as given, then another party can be considered as making an acceptance. Moreover, offer is different from an option or an advertisement. It is also different from an invitation to treat where it is an offer to make an offer. In *Carlill v Carbolic Smoke Ball Co. Ltd. [1893]*, it was held that the company did not make an advertisement but rather an offer.

Since the defendant managed to fulfil the offer, then she was eligible to the promised price of £1000.

Acceptance of the offer: will take place when another person/party in which the offer is made expresses his agreement to such offer. Thus, an acceptance must be absolute and unqualified. It must be consistent with the offer made. Such acceptance must be expressed in reasonable manner which may be understood by the person/party that makes the offer. In *Lau Brothers & Co v China Pacific Navigation Co. Ltd. [1965]*, the parties were depending on exchanges of telegrams and letters in negotiating their terms of agreement. Later on, the Defendants withdrew while they were still doing the exchanges of letters. When they went to court, it was held that there was no contract concluded since there were no valid offer and acceptance since they were still in negotiation stage.

Intention to create legal relations between the parties: is an essential element for a valid contract. A transaction which involves special relationships (e.g. mother–child relationship or husband–wife relationship) usually will not involve a serious intention to create a legal consequence to each other. In making inference of the parties' intention to create a legal relation, normally the courts will deduce from the words used, the context in which those words are used, and the circumstances of the case. This intention can also be inferred from the seriousness of the parties in concluding the contract.

Consideration: can be easily understood as the exchange of promises/acts between the parties or between values with the goods (in the case of sale and purchase agreement) where the parties are committed to fulfil it. The nature of such exchange must have value before the laws. In Thomas v Thomas *[1842]*, it was held that a one-sided promise which was made without consideration cannot be considered as a legal contract. Instead, it should be treated as a gift. There is also a legal principle established in Tweddle v Atkinson *[1861]* concerning to consideration where an agreement cannot be enforced if a person other than the promise (the one that made the acceptance) is to provide the consideration.

Certainty: is related to the terms of an agreement where they cannot be ambiguous or vague. Such terms must be clear and understandable in ordinary use of words. In *Karuppan Chetty v Suah Thian [*1916*]*, the term used in this case was considered vague since the parties agreed to a lease "at RM35.00 per month for as long as he likes". Both parties must understand the terms of the concluded contract in their clear language.

Capacity: is relating to the parties themselves. They must be competent to enter into contract and possess legal capacity to do so. Under Common Law, the legal capacity covers the age of the parties that must reach the age of majority (which usually 18 years old across certain Commonwealth countries) and possess sound minds. In MohoriBibee v Dharmodas Ghose *[1903]*, it was held by the Privy Council that a minor can never execute a valid contract.

Thus, in order for a contract to be valid under Common Law, those elements as mentioned earlier must accordingly be fulfilled and followed. Only then, a contract is considered binding and enforceable to the involved parties.

In a traditional contract, it can be concluded either directly or indirectly. A direct traditional contract can take place when an exchange of offer and acceptance between the involved parties is made face-to-face (either orally or through sign language). With the existence of consideration such as through the exchange of money and goods, the traditional contract can be concluded. An indirect traditional contract can happen when it is concluded through the exchanges of letters or emails. Instead of negotiating, the parties express their offer and acceptance through such exchanges. This traditional contract normally will be reduced into writing depending on the complexity of the agreement. It will eventually be printed out and kept as records between the involved parties.

Different from traditional contracts, the smart contract that depends on a digital transaction can involve either *ex-parte* or *inter-parte* transaction. *Ex-parte* smart contract can be traced back to its earliest form through the operation of digital vending machine. Instead of dealing with a person/party, the customer has to deal with the vending machine by placing a coin to buy a tin of drink in the provided slot. Thus, the vending machine itself displays tins of drinks to the customers based on the concept of invitation to treat. When the customer places a coin in the provided slot, he not only makes an offer but also provides the consideration. When the vending machine releases the drink, it makes a valid acceptance, while concluding the smart contract through the chronological steps. In explaining such situation, Szabo (1995) said:

> The basic idea of smart contracts is that many kinds of contractual clauses (such as liens, bonding, delineation of property rights, etc.) can be embedded in the hardware and software we deal with, in such a way as to make breach of contract expensive (if desired, sometimes prohibitively so) for the

> breacher. A canonical real-life example, which we might consider to be the primitive ancestor of smart contracts, is the humble vending machine. Within a limited amount of potential loss (the amount in the till should be less than the cost of breaching the mechanism), the machine takes in coins, and via a simple mechanism, which makes a beginner's level problem in design with finite automata, dispense change and product fairly. Smart contracts go beyond the vending machine in proposing to embed contracts in all sorts of property that is valuable and controlled by digital means. (Szabo, 1995)

Nowadays, the nature of smart contract is more complex than before. With the increasing use of cryptocurrency and blockchain, the smart contract may involve two or more parties or ***inter-parte*** transaction. By a simple click, the parties may stipulate their offer and acceptance through the pre-prepared terms as provided in the online platform. Instead of depending on real currency, the parties may depend on the use of cryptocurrency as an exchange for the value of the asset or property. This can also be treated as a form of consideration. Ethereum is acknowledged as the first blockchain platform that ties down their cryptocurrency (Ether) and assets to the terms of their provided smart contracts. Moreover, this said platform is backed up by the Government of Switzerland. Moreover, this said platform can be easily regulated through the existing law.

Legality of Concluded Contract Under *Sharī'ah*

Contract or ***'aqad*** (in Arabic) literally means "ties, guarantee, or promise". Technically, it means a contract concluded on the basis of desire by two or more parties (Abdul Rahman, 2010). It derived its legality from verse no.1 of Surah Al-Maidah which means "O ye who believe! Fulfil (all) obligations (***'aqad*** in plural form)". When it comes to the elements for a valid contract, according to the majority of Islamic schools of legal thought, that is, *Mālikī's*, Ḥanafī's, and *Shāfiʿī's*, there are basically three pillars to a valid contract that stand with their own specific conditions. Here, it is traceable that the principles of contract law under *Sharīʿah* is more comprehensive in comparison to Common Law's. They are provided in brief as the followings.

Sighah: is an Arabic term that indicates the expression used by the involved parties in communicating an offer and an acceptance. The expressions that are used to indicate offer and acceptance must be clear and understandable. According to the majority of Islamic schools of legal thought, that is, Ḥanafī's, *Shāfiʿī's*, and Ḥanbal*ī's*, the words used must be expressive to avoid any confusion and misunderstanding. According to the opinion of *Mālikī, they allowed the use of customary words as long as the parties understand them. There is also no limitation as to the language used. Such clear and understandable words are also important to avoid delay between the involved parties. In absence of clear and understandable words, according to Mālikī*, Ḥanafī, and Ḥanbal*ī, such contract is permissible and valid as long as the parties are consented to such transaction. Shāfiʿī' takes a rather careful opinion here where they consider it as invalid contract. In completing offer and acceptance, the parties sustain their full capacity without fail. Additionally, offer and acceptance must be concluded within the same session of contract* (Abdul Rahman, 2010). *At the same time, the acceptance must fulfil the offer, without making any new condition.*

Contracting parties: are the involved parties that make the contract. They can be more than two parties. They must be legally competent persons/parties where they already reached their puberty or comes of age and have sufficient intellect in understanding the transaction. They must not be bankrupt. Furthermore, they must be able to give their valid consents without being force or coerce to agree to the contract. This said condition is agreed by all Islamic schools of legal thought.

Subject matter of the contract or '*aqad*: is the property or asset that involved in concluding the contract. Different from Common Law, the subject matter must be something that is legal and permissible under *Sharīʿah*. Any contract that is concluded based on a thing which is in contravention with *Sharīʿah* can be considered as null and void, thus making such contract to be unenforceable. The subject matter of a contract must be valuable according to *Sharīʿah*. Thus, selling of alcoholic drinks and drugs will be considered invaluable and illegal. Consequently, it will make the contract to be null and void. The subject matter of a contract must also be precise from the aspects of quantity, value, and types. The ownership of the subject matter must also be clear. The one that does not own it can never have a right to sell it. Thus, selling a stolen bag is considered illegal, null and void.

Besides having the abovementioned pillars and conditions of contract, the law of contract under *Sharīʿah* is governed under general rules and legal maxims. The general rules are relating to the prohibitions of certain elements such as interest (*riba*), speculation (*gharar*), and gambling (*maysir*).

Interest or *riba*: can be understood as unjustified excess that derived from the capital which may occurs in completing the transaction especially when it involves loans or an exchange of commodity or valued materials such as gold and silver (Yusof & Berhad, 2019). It is prohibited since it can cause negative effects towards the society, socially and economically. According to As-Syawkani, the presence of *riba* or interest in a contract can lead to its prohibition, as he said: "If the additional are stipulated or conditionalised at the time of the execution of the contract, unanimously the contract will be prohibited" (Ibnu Qudamah, 1984).

***Gharar* or speculation:** is defined by Al-Sharakhsi as "anything that the end result is hidden or the risk is equally uncommon, whether it exists or not" (Abdul Rahman, 2010: 72). *In tracing the application of gharar in contracts, gharar relates to uncertainty and ambiguity of the result of the contract regardless whether it is possible to be achieved or not. It is prohibited to protect interests and rights of both involved parties and stands for tangible results of the contract.*

Maysir or gambling*: is also known as qimar. It includes any kind of dealings that involve games of fate or chance. Different from daily risks of doing business or transaction, it is related to risks that undertaken by the parties to win in something (such as gaining profit) without any involvement of productive activities and may be based on other party's expenses. According to the opinion of the majority Muslim scholars, the existence of gharar* (speculation) and *maysir (gambling) may invalidate the concluded contract.*

Depending on the fulfilment of the contract's pillars and conditions, and avoidance of all the prohibited elements, legal maxims as derived from Sharīʿah are also important to be considered. When comes to the formulation of smart contract, it seems that there are not much different between legal principles as applicable in *Sharīʿah* and Common Law. As long as the smart contract fulfils all the required elements, such smart contract may be enforceable in both stipulated laws of *Sharīʿah* and Common Law. Thus, it is possible to apply smart contract which depends on the application of *Sharīʿah* and Common Law. Notably, many of the Commonwealth countries are not only subject to the principles of Common Law, but they are also Muslim majority's countries that depend on the application of *Sharīʿah* in their daily activities. By following *Sharīʿah*'s legal maxim of "the original status of things are their permissibility", the smart contract may be concluded by using the online platform and can be recorded through the blockchain as long as there is no indication as for its prohibition. Thus, *Sharīʿah* celebrates the progressive nature of innovation in smart contracts without any limitation as to the technical system or technological based features that they possess. As long as the pillars and conditions of the contract is fulfilled, the smart contract can be enforced legally through Common Law and *Sharīʿah*.

Best Practices of Smart Contract in Selected Commonwealth Countries

Up to now, there is no specific law legislated specifically on smart contracts. Majority of these Commonwealth countries are depending on either their e-commerce laws or Contract Acts that codify the principles of contract law as under Common Law. Under this discussion, the practices of smart contracts as done by only certain selected Commonwealth countries are presented. The selection of the countries depends on their regulators' acceptance towards implementing the smart contract within their existing legal system. These countries are (1) Malaysia; (2) Australia; and (3) England.

Malaysia: has the earliest exposure with the blockchain technology through its international participation in the global financial market. With the significant growth of their dual financial services, Malaysia has a place as one of the top countries that actively develop their Islamic banking and financing services. Due to the lack of regulations relating to smart contract, blockchain, and cryptocurrencies, the Central Bank of Malaysia takes cautious and gradual steps in catering the development of such technologies. Even though a strict space is opened for the establishment of FinTech companies in Malaysia, the Central Bank of Malaysia has a specific list on prohibited cryptocurrencies, such as Bitcoin (The Central Bank of Malaysia, 2014).

This does not mean that the Central Bank of Malaysia absolutely ignored the latest trend in using those mentioned technologies. On 18th of October 2016, they issued the Financial Technology Regulatory Sandbox Framework (The Central Bank of Malaysia, 2016). In their regulated legal framework, there are several laws that must be fulfilled along with the said Sandbox Framework. Among the stipulated laws are the Financial Services Act 2013, Islamic Financial Services Act 2013, and the

Development Financial Institutions Act 2002. Confined to their conventional banking sector, it is said that the draft for a regulation relating to cryptocurrencies was availably made by the Central Bank of Malaysia (BNM, 2018).

When it comes to the application of smart contract, Malaysia is equipped with e-commerce laws. Among those laws that are relevant are: (1) Digital Signature Act 1997; (2) Computer Crimes Act 1997; (3) Telemedicine Act 1997; (4) Communications and Multimedia Act 1998; and (5) Copyright (Amendment) Act 1997. Additionally, the Contract Act of 1950 remains as the general law that can be applicable in evaluating the smart contract's operation. Nonetheless, there is no reported legal case relating to smart contract that related to the blockchain technology in Malaysia. Moreover, with the establishment of Shariah Advisory Council of Malaysia, the principles of *Sharī'ah* are highly secured in the application of Islamic financial services business.

Australia: is actively involved as a member country of the Commonwealth. This country is also the founder member in establishing the Commonwealth in 1931. Depending on the principles of Common Law, they have a positive reaction towards the development of technologies relating to the formulation of the contract in their jurisdiction. In a report titled Blockchain Reaction, a legal firm called Allens identified challenges that Australian regulators may face in their adaptation of smart contract in their legal system (Allens, 2016). Generally, the smart contract must fulfil the required elements as according to the contract law. Even with the recorded ledger feature of blockchain, the legal firms tend to reduce the concluded smart contracts into the printed version.

United Kingdom: (or specifically England) is the birthplace of Common Law. In ensuring the English legal and regulatory framework is consistently in line with the latest trend in applying smart contracts, the Law Commission of United Kingdom was established (UK Law Commission, 2019). This said Law Commission has the responsibility to review the existing laws which include the law on electronic signature, digitalization of contract, and the interplay of the smart contract's terms with the established provisions of the laws. However, since March 2019, there seems that the research done on smart contract by the said Law Commission is placed at halt without known reason (UK Law Commission, 2019). The results of their research are most waited, especially to speed up the progress of adaptation of smart contract in the existing system both in the United Kingdom and in other Commonwealth countries.

Recommendations

The principles of contract under *Sharīʿah* and Common Law which are essential to be applied to smart contracts are almost similar without any huge difference. However, *Sharīʿah* provides more requirements when it is relating to the subject matter and consideration. Both of these conditions must be consistent with *Sharīʿah* without fail. Additionally, the prohibited elements that cover *riba*, *gharar*, and *maysir* must be avoided altogether without any excuses. It is a good practice to have an authoritative body to monitor or regulate the application of *Sharīʿah* in relation to smart contracts. The establishment of Shariah Advisory Council in Malaysia can be considered a good stepping stone; where instead of inventing the wheel, their roles can be extended in considering the application of smart contract. Furthermore, there is no serious debate among Muslim scholars relating to blockchain technology and smart contract. The only continuous debate that persists is relating to permissibility and legality of cryptocurrencies since there are existence of *gharar* and *maysir*.

Additionally, the Commonwealth countries need to scrutinise their security and criminal laws, especially in a situation when the smart contract is used for illegal purposes. Here, the laws such as anti-money laundering or anti-terrorism financing should be looked closely. The application of smart contract may also disturb the customer protection regime since the terms of the smart contract are majorly based on pre-prepared terms and most likely not opened for any negotiation. In the public blockchain, the data of the platform's users are opened for misused. Thus, the recorded smart contract may be exposed to other parties that not related to the contract. In this view, the law of personal data protection should be given a more serious consideration.

In certain jurisdictions, the laws relevant for establishments of FinTech companies are taken to be loose and easy. This is due to the motivation to increase the number of those FinTech companies and relevant to influence investors to have more active participations. Such kinds of establishments need to be controlled from competition laws' perspective. A popular online platform may have more monopoly over the digital market in comparison to the newly established online platform as provided by FinTech companies. Taxation and revenue laws also need to be looked at closely since the application of smart contract may reduce the dependency towards normal taxation and revenue fees.

Smart contract may reduce the function of advocates and solicitors in drafting the terms of the contracts. Thus, the dependency in creating the terms of smart contract is placed to computers' cryptologists. However, in a situation where a legal case is brought to courts, the parties are still in need of legal services that can only be provided by advocates and solicitors. Thus, advocates and solicitors need to equip themselves with new skills in understanding the operation of smart contracts and its underlined computerized operations. Same goes to modern *Sharīʿah* scholars where they have to upgrade their skills in understanding these new types of technological innovations.

Conclusion

Innovations of technology are changing the normal daily transactions concluded between the parties. Such changes cannot be stopped but they should be accepted and tolerated. Instead of treating this new form of contract, that is, the smart contract as a disturbance, it can be used positively in expanding the existing laws. While such appreciation is made, the value of legal principles from Common Law and *Sharīʿah* can be taken seriously.

References

Abdul Rahman, Z. (2010). *Contracts and the Products of Islamic Banking*. Kuala Lumpur: CERT Publications.

Agnikhotram, S., & Kouroutakis, K. (2019). Doctrinal Challenges for the Legality of Smart Contracts: Lex Cryptographia Or a New, Smart Way to Contract. *Journal of HighTechnology Law, 19*(2), 300–328.

Allens. (2016). *Allens Releases a Landmark Report on Blockchain*. Retrieved from https://www.allens.com.au/data/blockchain/index.htm

BNM. (2018, March 22). Deputy Governor's Opening Address at the Asian Banker Digital Finance Convention 2018, Kuala Lumpur. Retrieved June 18, 2018, from http://www.bnm.gov.my/index.php?ch=en_speech&pg=en_speech&ac=792.

Central Bank of Malaysia. (2014). *Statement on Bitcoin*. Retrieved from http://www.bnm.gov.my/index.php?ch=en_announcement&pg=en_announcement&ac=49&lang=en

Central Bank of Malaysia. (2016). *Digital Currencies*. Retrieved from http://www.bnm.gov.my/index.php?ch=en_policy&pg=en_policy_digitalcurr&lang=bm

Goldsborough Mort & Co. Ltd. V Quiin [1910] 10 CLR 674.

Hsiao, J. I.-H. (2017). Smart Contract on the Blockchain-Paradigm Shift for Contract Law. *US-China Law Review, 14*(10), 685–694.

Ibnu Qudamah. (1984). Muwaffaquddin, al-Mughni. Beirut: Dar al-Fikr.

ISRA. (2018). Shariah Compliance Via Blockchain and Smart Contract – The Case of Islamic Credit Card. Retrieved from https://ifikr.isra.my/news/post/shariah-compliance-credit-card

Kamali, M. H. (2004). *Principles of Islamic Jurisprudence*. Malaysia: Kuala Lumpur.

Karuppan Chetty v SuahThian [1916] FM SLR 300.

Makdisi, J. A. (1999). The Islamic Origins of the Common Law. 77 *N.C. L. Rev.* 1635.

Mohd. Zain, N. R. (2018). *Dispute Resolution Clauses in Islamic Finance Contracts in Malaysia: An Analytical Study*. Malaysia: IIUM.

Mohd. Zain, N. R., Engku Ali, E. R., Adewale, A., & Abdul Rahman, H. (2019). Smart Contract in Blockchain: An Exploration of Legal Framework in Malaysia. *Intellectual Discourse, 27*(2), 595–617.

MohoriBibee v Dharmodas Ghose [1903] 1 LR 30 Col. 539.

Nakamoto, S. (2018). *Bitcoin: A Peer-to-Peer Electronic Cash System*. Retrieved from https://bitcoin.org/bitcoin.pdf

Plucknett, T. F. T. (2001). *A Concise History of the Common Law*. The Lawbook Exchange, Ltd.

Statista. (2018). *Statista Report 2017: Blockchain Technology Market Size Worldwide 2016–2021*. Retrieved from https://www.statista.com/statistics/647231/worldwide-blockchain-technology-market-size/

Szabo, N. (1995). Smart Contracts: Building Blocks for Digital Free Markets. *Entropy Journal of Transhuman Thought*. Retrieved from http://www.alamut.com/subj/economics/nick_szabo/smartContracts.html

Thomas v Thomas [1842] 2 QB 851

Tweddle v Atkinson [1861] EWHC QB J57.

UK Law Commission. (2019). *Smart Contract*. Retrieved from https://www.lawcom.gov.uk/project/smart-contracts/

Williams, S. (2017). 5 Big Advantages of Blockchain, and 1 Reason to be very Worried. *Motley Fool LLC (US)*. Retrieved from https://www.fool.com/investing/2017/12/11/5-big-advantages-of-blockchain-and-1-reason-to-be.aspx

Yaga, D., Peter, M., Nik, R., & Scarfone, K. (2018). *Blockchain Technology Overview* (National Institute of Standards and Technology, US Department of Commerce). Retrieved from https://arxiv.org/ftp/arxiv/papers/1906/1906.11078.pdf

Yusof, A. Y. A. M., & Berhad, B. I. M. (2019). *The Concepts of Riba, Gharar and Maysir in Islamic Finance*. Chief Executive Officer Chairman Malaysian Institute of Accountants MIA Islamic Finance Committee, 5.

CHAPTER 7

Digital Smart Contracts: Legal and Shari'ah Issues

Ainul Azam bin Ahmad Khamal

Abstract This chapter seeks to examine recent issues that pervade digital contracts also known as smart contracts. Discussions and analysis will be made to understand smart contracts, its key features and applicability in modern commerce as well as its application in Islamic finance. Examples and reference will be made to contemporary smart contract and its symbiosis with blockchain technology and how smart contract has revolutionized the traditional concept of contract. Finally, the author will juxtapose the key legal characteristics of smart contract against the cardinal principles of Islamic finance governing Islamic commerce and the relevant Malaysian legislations and discuss the issues surrounding them.

Keywords Digital • Smart contract • Law • Shari'ah • Jurisdiction

Ainul Azam bin Ahmad Khamal (✉)
Ainul Azam & Co., Adcocates & Solicitors, Kuala Lumpur, Malaysia
e-mail: ainul@azamlaw.com

M. M. Billah (ed.), *Islamic FinTech*,
https://doi.org/10.1007/978-3-030-45827-0_7

Introduction

And it all began with Szabo. According to Szabo (1994), a smart contract is a computerized transaction algorithm, which performs the terms of the contract. In other words, it is but an agreement whose execution is automated. Alexander Savelyev (2016), a critique, was quick to quip that this definition hardly distinguishes a smart contract from a well-known device implementing automated performance, for example the ubiquitous vending machine.

Perhaps, to better understand the proper features of a smart contract, reference may be made to another definition by Greenspan (2016) that '[A] smart contract is a piece of code which is stored on a blockchain, triggered by blockchain transactions, and which reads and writes data in that blockchain database.'

By this definition, it implies that blockchain is the bedrock of a smart contract. It is one of the defining features of a smart contract. Alexander Savelyev (2016) opinions that blockchain is inherently significant in smart contract due to the fact that 'it allows to automate the process of performance contractual process of both parties', thus, debunking the vending machine analogy as it relates to automatic performance of only one party in the likes of coin insertion or application of a banking card.

In addition, Alexander Savelyev (2016) further notes that another important feature of blockchain based contract is that 'it allows not only to automate the performance of the contract but also a process of its conclusion; it can be concluded by electronic agents employed by the parties.'

Advantages and Characteristics

Efficiency

It is clear that the implementation of smart contracts would bring about greater efficiency in particular when the contract or agreement depends on big data with repeatable coding execution automated. As the codes are binaries, they will only be viewed by parties to the contract to the exclusion of others.

Transparency

It is also abundantly clear that since the terms of the agreement, they are to be mutually agreed and consented to in advance. In a way, there would not be any variations, amendments or supplements introduced subsequent to the consummation of the smart contract.

Distributable

Another salient feature of blockchain is that it is 'distributable', that is, the output of the contract is distributed to everyone in the network, and by consequent it promotes transparency. This is because the whole participants of the digital shared ledger are able to see all transactions recorded.

Immutable

It is also said that a smart contract is permanent or 'immutable' as it precludes the possibility of changes or tampering. The smart contract is thus cast in stone.

Application of Digital Contracts/Smart Contract

Smart contract presents a whole gamut of opportunity to support a spectrum of Islamic financial product ranging from sukuk, Islamic wealth management, for example, Islamic banking, crowdfunding and takaful industry (automated claims or renewal of general takaful products).

There are several notable examples where smart contract is used to underpin and support financial product transactions. For instance, in a crowdfunding scenario, smart contract may be utilized to create pool of resources and consequent to an agreed premise, allocate them accordingly.

Thus, in a crowdfunding exercise as alluded to earlier, smart contract serves to identify the flow of funds submitted to a specific crowdfunding project, and upon attaining the targeted threshold, the fund is transferred to the project promoter. Any amount exceeding the targeted threshold shall be remitted back to investors. And with all the terms of the agreement whose execution is automated.

In similar light, another crowdfunding platform to consider would be the Investment Account Platform (IAP), a platform to facilitate channelling funds from investors to finance viable ventures and projects which is backed by Islamic banking institutions via the offering of investment account (IA) to the investors. Through this platform, Islamic banking institutions will facilitate matching of investments by the investors with the identified ventures or projects that are in need of funding. The flow of funds to the Islamic banks and ultimately the channelling of the funds to identifiable ventures or projects may be executed via smart contract.

It is clear from the snapshot given further, the same sequences reflected in the chart earlier may be replicated in the IAP. In this context, the investors either individual, corporate or institutional investors would channel the funds to identified ventures via the conduits of Islamic banks based on pre-determined triggering events.

The Shariah and Legal Issues

As alluded to earlier, smart contract is used to describe a computer programme code capable of executing and ensuring the terms and performance of contract using blockchain technology. By way of iteration, the whole process is automated and enforceability.

Important Shariah Precepts Relevant to SMART Contract

Written Contract
Islam enjoins its followers to reduce contracts into writing in order to achieve fairness and accountability. It extols the virtues of ethical business practices—imbued with concepts of trust and fairness.

> O ye who believe! When ye deal with each other, in transactions involving future obligations in a fixed period of time, reduce them to writing. Let a scribe write down faithfully as between the parties: let not the scribe refuse to write: as Allah Has taught him, so let him write. (Al Baqarah: 282)

This principle sets out the paramount need for the terms of the contract to be exact and precise where fairness and accountability are being upheld. And in the context of a smart contract, nothing is more precise than a set of protocols specific triggering event(s) upon which both parties have agreed upon.

Free of Gharar
Gharar is an important precept in Islamic financial system. Gharar exist when there is element of uncertainty in a contract. The consequences of having Gharar or uncertainty element in the contract will be vitiated and thus renders it null and void.

> Narrated by Hakim ibn Hizam Hakim asked the Prophet: Apostle O Allah, a man comes to me and wants me to sell him something which is not in my

possession. Should I buy it for him from the market? He replied: Do not sell what you do not possess.

It is clear that *Gharar* is unjust as it leads to uncertainty in the contract and thus ipso facto renders the contract void.

(See: The Prohibition of Riba, Gharar & Maysir in Islamic Banking. Source: docuworks)

It is submitted that smart contract has features that preclude elements of uncertainty in regard to terms and/or execution of contracts. Smart contract negates elements of *gharar* not only in relation to the terms but also as to the implementation of the contract. For instance, in an Islamic crowdfunding structure, the smart contract is based on self-executing digital, with electronically coded contractual terms, such terms will only be executed only if conditions are fulfilled.

Islamic Fatwa on Smart Contract

At the time of writing neither the Shariah Advisory Council of Bank Negara Malaysia nor the Shariah Advisory Council of Securities Commission has issued any fatwa and or guidelines on smart contract.

The Mejella

It is interesting to note that maxims of Islamic Jurisprudence contained in the Mejella may be relevant in considering the status and validity of smart contracts. They include:

43. A matter recognised by custom is regarded as though it were a contractual obligation.
44. A matter recognised by merchants is regarded as being a contractual obligation between them.
45. A matter established by custom is like a matter established by law.

It is submitted that the Mejella has presciently provided the planks to consider and decide on the validity of smart contracts. As the practice of adopting smart contract continues to gain acceptance and increasingly accepted by the stakeholders in any Islamic financial product, for example by banks/financial institutions, takaful, venture capitals and the likes, smart contracts would invariably and consequently be held to be valid not only under the precepts of custom but also under the law.

Legal Issues and Challenges

Is smart contract a contract in a traditional contract law sense?

Raskin (2016, p. 13) argues that smart contract is a form of self-help because the absence of recourse to a court of law is needed for the machine to execute the agreement.

Alexander Savelyev (2016) further posits that the following features of smart contract are to be regarded as a legally binding agreement:

(a) It governs legal and commercial relations between parties similar to the traditional law of contract.[1]
(b) The transfer of digital blockchain-based asset either on chain asset, for example, digital currency or off chain asset, for example, stocks tantamounts to 'legal effect,' an inherent concept of a contract.
(c) Although smart contract's performance is automated, it still requires the presence of will of both parties—manifested by the fact when the parties decide to enter into such agreement as per the terms.
(d) It is reinforced by the (1) action of signifying consent[2] to the terms of the contract and (2) mode of the contract's execution, at the time of entering the contract.

He further crystallized and discussed the important features of smart contract to the following:

1. Solely electronic nature

   whilst traditional contract may be in oral or written form, smart contract exists only in electronic form.
2. Software centric

   smart contract computer code is the contractual terms. It is also possible to argue that smart contract vide its nature is also a com-

[1] See: Malaysian Contracts Act 1950 (Act 136) (Revised 1976), section 10: 'All agreements are contract if they are made by the free consent of parties competent to contract, for a lawful consideration and with a lawful object, and are not hereby expressly declared to be void.'

[2] See: Malaysian Contracts Act 1950, section 13: 'Two or more persons are said to consent when they agree upon the same thing in the same sense.'

puter programme as per intellectual property law.[3] Arguably, smart contract has a dual nature under the law, that is, as a 'document' governing the relationship of parties as well as being an object of IP law.

3. Enhanced certainty

   there is no room for interpretation under a smart contract as it is based on software codes or computer languages as compared to traditional contract which is subject to interpretation rules which bring in elements of uncertainty.

4. Conditional nature

   as alluded to above, smart contract is based on computer languages. It is based on conditional statements. For instance, 'if 'x' then 'y' which is in harmony with and akin to contractual terms and conditions.

   Raskin (2016) posits, 'the enforcement of contract is nothing more than the running of a circumstances through conditional statement.'

   In contrast, the Section 8 of the Malaysian Contracts Act 1950 provides 'Performance of the condition of a proposal, or the acceptance of any consideration for a reciprocal promise which may be offered with a proposal, is an acceptance of the proposal'.

5. Self-enforcement

   once smart contract is concluded, its further execution is no longer dependent on the will of its parties or third parties. It no longer requires approval or actions anymore. It thus binds the parties. There is no more room for human intervention.

6. Self-sufficiency

   Smart contract does not require any legal institution, legal enforcement or corpus of legal rules to supplement it; unlike the traditional contracts.

[3] See: Malaysian Copyrights Act 1987 (Act 332) section 3: 'computer program' means an expression, in any language, code or notation, of a set of instructions (whether with or without related information) intended to cause a device having an information processing capability to perform a particular function either directly or after either or both of the following:

(a) conversion to another language, code or notation; *(b)* reproduction in a different material form.

Can a Smart Contract Satisfy the Elements of a Contract Under the Malaysian Contracts Act 1950?

Offer or 'Proposal'

Generally, Salleh Abbas FJ in the Federal Court decision of *Preston Corporation Sdn Bhd v Edward Leong & Ors [1982] 2 MLJ*, FC held that '[A]n offer is an intimation or willingness by an offeror to enter into a legally binding contract. Its terms either expressly or impliedly must indicate that it is to become binding on the offeror as soon as it has been accepted by the offeree.'

The Malaysian Contracts Act 1950 (Act 136) (Revised 1976) ('CA') instead utilises the word 'proposal' which means:

1(a) when one person signifies to another his willingness to do or to abstain from doing anything, with a view to obtaining the assent of that other to the act or abstinence, he is said to make a proposal;

The effect proposal is only effective when it is communicated. Thus, Section 4 stipulates that an offer is only effective when it is communicated.

It is argued that the smart contract code made available on a distributed ledger may constitute an offer if the other counter party is able to interact and execute the code. By way of example, according to Scholz (2017) in the well-established context of algorithmic trading, parties use algorithms as 'negotiators' before contract is formed, allowing the parties to choose the order terms to the market.[4]

Acceptance

Another important element of a legally binding contract is acceptance. The context of 'acceptance' under the Contracts Act 1950 is clarified under section 2(b) thus:

[4] Scholz, L (2017). Algorithmic Contracts 20 Stanford Technology Law Review 128 (Smart Contract: Is the Law Ready, Chamber of Digital Alliance. Retrived from https://www.digitalchambers.org/smart contracts-white papers).

2(b) when the person to whom the proposal is made signifies his assent thereto, the proposal is said to be accepted: a proposal, when accepted, becomes a promise.

According to Sinnadurai (2011, p. 50), under the Contract Act 1950, the only person who can accept the offer is the person to whom the proposal was made. Thus, when the person signifies his assent to the proposal, the offeree is said to have accepted the offer, resulting with the offeror being bound by the contract proposed by him.

It is often observed that in the case of a smart contract, the offeree may signify acceptance through signing the transaction by a private key. Alternatively, parties may use computerized algorithms to negotiate the terms of a smart contract.

Consideration

Consideration is another fundamental element of a valid contract. Section 2(d) of Contracts Act 1950 defines 'consideration' to mean:

> when, at the desire of the promisor, the promisee or any other person has done or abstained from doing, or does or abstains from doing, or promises to do or to abstain from doing, something, such act or abstinence or promise is called a consideration for the promise.

In practice, a smart contract parlayed in the distributed ledger would constitute an offer. In consequence, the offeree may indicate acceptance by signing and signifying acceptance to the transaction by signing in the private key.

Consideration is reflected by the exchange of value or performance of the contract or a promise to pay or perform at a future time.

In addition, Section 26 of the Contracts Act 1950 amplifies the importance of consideration by emphasizing that an agreement without consideration is void unless it falls within the exceptions contained therein in the following terms.

It states:

> An agreement made without consideration is void, unless—
> it is in writing and registered

> (a) it is expressed in writing and registered under the law (if any) for the time being in force for the registration of such documents, and is made on account of natural love and affection between parties standing in a near relation to each other;
> or is a promise to compensate for something done
> (b) it is a promise to compensate, wholly or in part, a person who has already voluntarily done something for the promisor, or something which the promisor was legally compellable to do; or
> or is a promise to pay a debt barred by limitation law
> (c) it is a promise, made in writing and signed by the person to be charged therewith, or by his agent generally or specially authorized in that behalf, to pay wholly or in part a debt of which the creditor might have enforced payment but for the law for the limitation of suits.
> In any of these cases, such an agreement is a contract.

It is submitted that if and when each of all the elements are satisfied, that is, proposal/offer, acceptance, and consideration are satisfied them ipso facto, a smart contract is thus validly constituted and becomes legally binding under Malaysian law.

Contract by Electronic Means

Contracts Entered into by Electronic Means

Ancillary to the discussion given before of a smart contract, it is submitted that Malaysia has to a large extent made efforts to provide a legislative framework to govern contracts by electronic means. Arguably a smart contract fulfils the legal requirements of transactions using electronic means.

Recourse, discussion and guidance may be made to the Malaysian Electronic Commerce Act 2006 (ECA) which governs formation of contracts, communication of offer made through electronic means, and the place the contract is concluded.

Specifically, the Preamble reads:

> An Act to provide for legal recognition of electronic messages in commercial transactions, the use of the electronic messages to fulfill legal requirements and to enable and facilitate commercial transactions through the use of electronic means and other matters connected therewith.

Application of ECA

Section 2 provides:

(1) Subject to section 3, this Act shall apply to any commercial transaction conducted through electronic means including commercial transactions by the Federal and State Governments.
(2) This Act shall not apply to the transactions or documents specified in the Schedule.

Note that 'transactions' excluded are power of attorney, wills and codicils, creation of trusts, and negotiable instruments.

Consent Requirements Under the ECA

Consent as one of the cardinal elements of a commercial transaction or a contract is covered in section 3(2) of ECA. The section states:

(2) A person's consent to use, provide or accept any electronic message in any commercial transaction may be inferred from the person's conduct.

Note that 'commercial transactions' means a single communication or multiple communications of a commercial nature, whether contractual or not, which includes any matters relating to the supply or exchange of goods or services, agency, investments, financing, banking, and insurance.

Legal Recognition of Electronic Message

ECA expressly recognizes the legal effect of electronic message. Section 6 states:

(1) Any information shall not be denied legal effect, validity or enforceability on the ground that it is wholly or partly in an electronic form.
(2) Any information shall not be denied legal effect, validity or enforceability on the ground that the information is not contained in the electronic message that gives rise to such legal effect, but is merely referred to in that electronic message, provided that the information being referred to is accessible to the person against whom the referred information might be used.

Formation and Validity of Contract
The formation and validity of contract are reinforced by sections 7(1) and (2) of ECA:

(1) In the formation of a contract, the communication of proposals, acceptance of proposals, and revocation of proposals and acceptances or any related communication may be expressed by an electronic message.
(2) A contract shall not be denied legal effect, validity or enforceability on the ground that an electronic message is used in its formation.

In *Yam Kong Seng & Anor v Yee Weng Kai [2014] 4 MLJ 478,* the Federal Court of Malaysia considered Section 8 of the Electronic Commerce Act 2006 ('ECA').

> Section 8—Writing: 'Where any law requires information to be in writing, the requirement of the law is fulfilled if the information is contained in an electronic message that is accessible and intelligible so as to be usable for subsequent reference.'

Suriyadi Halim, FCJ (in delivering judgement of the court), held that where any law requires information to be in writing, the requirement of the law is fulfilled if the information is contained in an electronic message that is accessible and intelligible so as to be usable for subsequent reference. Accordingly, a message from an SMS, with all the attributes of Section 8 being present, viz, accessibility, intelligible and extractable for subsequent reference, such an electronic message is as good as in writing.

The Federal Court further held that signatures need not be written. Suffice if there be any mark, written or not, which identifies the act of the party, perhaps in the form of mark or by some distinguishing feature peculiar only to that person, then the acknowledgement has been signed. Analogically, the conventional paper is substituted by the mobile phone, which holds features that can preserve information or transmissions in the like of the SMS, with the telephone number representing the caller or the sender of some message. The legal requirement for a signature was fulfilled as the sender was adequately identified let alone admitted by him.

At the time of writing, there is no decided case yet discussing a smart contract transaction by the Malaysian courts.

The Way Forward: Conclusion

Whilst we wait for a deliberate discussion on smart contract, some viewpoints may be had as to the issues as to the validity of bitcoin (note that at the time of writing there has yet to be a deliberate discussion on the Islamic perspectives of smart contract).

This can be seen from the view offered by Dato' Seri Zulkifli bin Mohamad Al Bakri (2019). He is of the opinion that bitcoin does not fulfil Shariah requirements due to its inconsistency and the fear that this may harm the consumers in the future. Apart from that, the absence of any legal authorities to effectively regulate this digital transaction will muddle the official banking system of a country. He further emphasized that the banning of bitcoin is necessary on the principle of *Sadd al-Zarai* (to prevent harm).

It is clear at least from the 'bitcoin experience,' debates are still raging on the Shariah traditional front on the issue of Shariah compliance.

At the other end of spectrum, the civil and conventional laws appear to be more receptive and remains fluid as to the validity and enforceability of smart contracts albeit the absence of a comprehensive legislation governing such contracts. Some legal planks may be utilized to justify smart contract as having some semblance of legal characteristics often associated with common law jurisprudence.

As was alluded to earlier, some jurisprudential debates are still actively being carried out amongst scholars and practitioners alike although the writer is of the opinion that the sheer weight of usage, acceptance, and purpose of smart contract shall outweigh its legal and Shariah conundrum.

Conclusion

In sum, the writer has attempted to paint a broad-brush approach to discuss smart contract and its application and juxtapose them to Islamic Finance precepts and arrive to an unmistakable conclusion that contemporary smart contract legal characteristics are aligned with the cardinal principles of Islamic finance governing Islamic financial products.

References

Dato' Seri Zulkifli bin Mohamed al Bakri, Bayan Linnas Siri ke 153 (2019, August). Hukum Penggunaan Mata Wang Bitcoin. Retrived from https://muftiwp.gov.my/ms/artikel/bayan-linnas/2773-bayan-linnas-153-hukum-penggunaan-mata-wang-bitcoin

Greenspan G. (2016, April 12). Beware of the Impossible Smart Contract. *Blockchain News.* Retrieved from https://www.the blockchain.com/2016/04/12

Malaysian Contracts Act 1950 (Act 136) (Revised 1974).

Malaysian Copyrights Act 1987 (Act 332).

Malaysian Electronic Commerce Act (Act 658).

Raskin, M. (2016). The Law of Smart Contract, p. 31. Retrieved from http://ssrn.com/abstract

Savelyev, A. (2016). Contract Law 2.0; Smart Contracts as the Beginning of the End of Classic Contract Law.

Scholz, L. (2017). Algorithmic Contracts 20 *Stanford Technology Law Review* 128 (Smart Contract: Is the Law Ready, Chamber of Digital Alliance. Retrived from https://www.digitalchambers.org/smart contracts-white papers)

Sinnadurai. (2011). *Law of Contract* (4th ed.). LexisNexis.

Szabo N. (1994). Smart Contracts in Essays on Smart Contracts, Commercial Controls and Security. Retrieved from http://szabo.best.vmh.net/smartcontracts.html

The Mejella also known in Arabic as Majallah el-Ahkam-i-Adliya.

The Prohibition of Riba, Gharar & Maysir in Islamic Banking.

CHAPTER 8

Judicial Procedures in I-Fintech: The Malaysian Experience

Ainul Azam bin Ahmad Khamal

Abstract This chapter seeks to examine and discuss the vagaries of prevailing procedures relevant and available to e-commerce and/or I-fintech disputes. This brief would invariably entail discussions and analyses on dispute resolution mechanisms under the prevailing judicial—civil courts and other alternative dispute resolution ('ADR') legal—framework.

The chapter will also navigate, highlight and analyse models of ADR framework that offer fintech or I-fintech dispute resolutions and juxtapose them with ADR models and procedures available or potentially made available under the Shari'ah–Islamic financial system.

Finally, the author will highlight and argue that broader context of institutionalized Shari'ah–Islamic I-fintech judicial framework would not only be consistent and comparable with the rigours of existing modern dispute resolution legal framework demands but also underscore a viable case of an alternative judicial legal framework that not only is effective but also, more importantly, represents vibrant alternative judicial procedures to serve the needs and demands of any present and future I-fintech disputes.

Ainul Azam bin Ahmad Khamal (✉)
Ainul Azam & Co., Advocates & Solicitors, Kuala Lumpur, Malaysia
e-mail: ainul@azamlaw.com

M. M. Billah (ed.), *Islamic FinTech*,
https://doi.org/10.1007/978-3-030-45827-0_8

Keywords FinTech • Judicialcial procedures • Law • Application • Shari'ah • Malaysia

The Case for Litigation Before the Civil Courts

It is not uncommon for e-commerce litigants to canvass and ventilate their disputes before the courts. In Malaysia, disputes between litigants are, most often than not, brought before the Civil courts. The establishment of specialized courts is generally governed by Practice Directions. For example, *Practice Direction No. 5 of 2016 issued by the Chief Registrar of the Federal Court of Malaysia* sets out the establishment of Cyber Courts both Civil and Criminal in Malaysia whilst *Practice Direction No. 6 of 2013 issued by the Chief Registrar of the Federal Court of Malaysia* sets out the classification of codes for cases relating to Intellectual Property.

Groupon Sdn Bhd v Tribunal Pengguna & Anor [2016] *1 LNS 555* is a typical case involving e-commerce dispute and a case of judicial review. The facts are illustrated as follows:

> The Appellant ('Groupon') is a business agent connecting merchant partners ('Company') to consumers. The 2nd Respondent purchased an online voucher tour package deal from the Appellant for a total sum of RM999/- (with an exclusion clause contained in the Voucher of RM652/-). The sum of RM999/- was paid to Appellant whilst RM652/- was paid directly to the Company which was at all material time unlicensed and insolvent. The tour was eventually cancelled. The Appellant refunded RM999/- but not the RM652/- to the 2nd Respondent.

The main question was whether the Appellant is liable for the sum of RM 652 that was directly paid to the Company. The First Respondent argued that the Appellant was negligent for not ensuring the Company is reputable. It was held that the First Respondent had misconstrued the exclusion clause. The RM 652/- was not included in the tour and travel deal. Consequently, the Court held that it is not to be borne by the Appellant as the Second Respondent had paid directly to Company instead.

Groupon Sdn Bhd v Tribunal Pengguna & Anor [2017] 7 MLJ 354 is yet another case on e-commerce dispute and a case on judicial review. In this case, the Second Respondent purchased a package from the Appellant's (Groupon's) website for RM 999. Groupon also required the Second

Respondent to pay RM 450/- to a third party for flight and accommodation fees. The Appellant however failed to provide the services and the package was cancelled. As it was, the Appellant refunded RM 999/- but not the RM 450/-.

YA Dato' Hanipah binti Farikullah J (as her Ladyship then was) held that since the Second Respondent bought the package from the Appellant's website, the contract formed was between the Second Respondent and the Appellant. Further, the Appellant acted as agent that connects the merchant partner to consumers. Accordingly, the Appellant is responsible for the failure to provide the services and is thus responsible to refund the RM 450/-.

The author submits that these two cases established not only the readiness and willingness of litigants to refer to specialised Civil courts to decide disputes involving e-commerce but also the structure of time-tested dispute resolution legal framework at work. It is also important to note that the Civil courts occasionally employ Mediation process between litigants under *Practice Direction No. 5 of 2012 on Mediation*. However, before we embark and consider any novel judicial procedures to be adopted in I-fintech disputes, it will be instructive to observe and discuss existing ADR models outside courts in Malaysia.

Ombudsman: Ombudsman for Financial Services ('OFS')

OFS (formerly known as Financial Mediation Bureau) was incorporated on 30 August 2004 and commenced its operations on 20 January 2005. OFS is the operator of the Financial Ombudsman Scheme (FOS) approved by Bank Negara Malaysia (BNM) pursuant to the Financial Services Act 2013 and the Islamic Financial Services Act 2013.

The OFS is a non-profit organisation and functions as an alternative dispute resolution channel to resolve disputes between Members who are financial service providers (FSPs), licensed or approved by BNM and financial consumers. 'Financial consumers' refer to (1) individuals and (2) small and medium enterprise ('SME').

The term 'individuals' refers to:

(1) Insured person under group insurance, person(s) covered under a group takaful, (2) third party making a claim for property damage

involving motor insurance/takaful, (3) guarantor of a credit facility, (4) insured person and (5) beneficiary of the insured person under a group insurance.

Term 19 of Term of Reference for the Ombudsman for Financial Services empowers the OFS, in resolving a dispute, to employ any of the following methods during the entire resolution process, including the case management and adjudication stage, as the case may be:

(a) Negotiation
(b) Conciliation or mediation
(c) Adjudication

The writer submits that I-fintech disputes could potentially fall under the purview of OFS if and when such dispute involves Members offering fintech products.

Tribunal: Tribunal for Consumer Claim

More often than not, tribunals are bodies or fora established under administrative laws, set up to hear, decide and settle disputes independent from courts. Whilst courts in general are the creation of judiciary, tribunals are part of the administrative system. Both the courts and tribunals operate independently of each other. Decisions, findings or awards (as the case may be) are however subject to court's review only when such decisions, findings or awards are challenged based on their legality.

In Malaysia, the Tribunal for Consumer Claims Malaysia ('Tribunal') is an independent body established under the Consumer Protection Act 1999 ('CPA') with the primary function of hearing and determining claims lodged by consumers under and subject to the provisions of the Act and in particular section 107 of the CPA.

The Tribunal was established to provide an alternative channel apart from the civil courts for consumers to claim losses in respect of goods purchased or services acquired from traders or service providers where the claim does not exceed RM 25,000/-.

It is still uncertain whether parties to I-fintech disputes would avail themselves to the Tribunal's jurisdiction although theoretically, so long as the dispute does not exceed a claim of RM 25,000/- involving services provided by any fintech company, the claim may still be adjudicated by the Tribunal.

An example of an e-commerce website, that is, Shopee's Terms and Conditions [https://shopee.com.my] evidences a willingness to avail itself and buyer to the jurisdiction of claims tribunal. Paragraph 20 states:

20. Disputes

- *20.1 In the event a problem arises in a transaction, the Buyer and Seller agree to communicate with each other first to attempt to resolve such dispute by mutual discussions, which Shopee shall use reasonable commercial efforts to facilitate. If the matter cannot be resolved by mutual discussions, Users may approach the claims tribunal of their local jurisdiction to resolve any dispute arising from a transaction.*

It is apparently clear that by agreeing to Shopee's terms and conditions, e-commerce buyers would first be subjected to claims tribunal instead of courts. Another important feature of this provision also evinces an intention to pursue mutual discussions prior to submission to claims tribunal.

Mediation: Mediation Under the Asian International Arbitration Centre (AIAC)

Mediation is another method of ADR available to parties in disputes. Mediation is essentially a negotiation facilitated by a neutral third party. Unlike arbitration, which is a process of ADR somewhat similar to trial, mediation doesn't involve decision-making by the neutral third party. ADR procedures can be initiated by the parties or may be compelled by legislation, the courts, or contractual terms.

Section 4 of Mediation Act 2012 states:

(1) Subject to sec. 2, any person may, before commencing any civil action in court or arbitration, initiate mediation.

(2) A mediation under this Act shall not prevent the commencement of any civil action in court or arbitration nor shall it act as a stay of, or extensive of any proceedings, if the proceedings have been commenced.

Whilst this provision provides the jurisdictional legitimacy of mediation under the AIAC read together with Rule 1 of the Mediation Rules 2018, the process of mediation is by no means exclusive to AIAC. It is common to observe that mediation process are not only being utilised in courts but also employed in other ADR models.

Arbitration

The oft-quoted principles and objectives of arbitration as quoted in Mustill and Boyd (2001) rest on the following principles:

1. A fair, speedy and inexpensive trial. It seeks a fair resolution of disputes by an impartial tribunal without unnecessary delay or expense.
2. Party autonomy. An absolute doctrine of 'party autonomy' entitles the parties and their lawyers to control all aspects of proceedings.
3. Judicial minimalism. Arbitration seeks to marginalize court's intervention.

Two important arbitration models are discussed here, namely the Malaysian Institute of Arbitrators ('MIArb') and the Asian International Arbitration Centre (AIAC).

Arbitration Under the MIArb

MIArb was established in 1991 with the main aim of promoting the determination of disputes by arbitration in a variety of professional disciplines from industries such as building and construction, engineering, banking, finance, law, insurance, service and manufacturing industries. MIArb has widened its objectives to promoting and facilitating other forms of ADR such as mediation and adjudication.

Rule 1 of MIArb Arbitration Rules states:

> *Where any agreement, submission or reference provides for arbitration under or in accordance with the Arbitration Rules of the Malaysian Institute of Arbitrators ("the Institute"), the arbitration shall be conducted in accordance with these Rules or such amended Rules as the Institute may have adopted to take effect on or before the commencement of the arbitration.*

Presently, MIArb has developed and made available its Arbitration Rules and Mediation Rules for parties' adoption to govern the procedure of their arbitrations and mediations.

Arbitration Under AIAC

Another important model of arbitration is an arbitration under the auspices of AIAC which derives its jurisdictional basis from the Arbitration Act 2015.

Section 4 of Arbitration Act 2005 states:

(1) Any dispute which the parties have agreed to submit to arbitration under an arbitration agreement may be determined by arbitration unless the arbitration agreement is contrary to public policy.

The general framework of the arbitration process will be guided by the AIAC Arbitration Rules 2018. In addition, AIAC has also come out with the AIAC i-Arbitration Rules, the AIAC Fast Track Rules and the AIAC Mediation Rules.

Rule 1 of AIAC Arbitration Rules 2018 states:

Where Parties have agreed in writing to arbitrate their disputes in accordance with the AIAC Arbitration Rules, then:

(a) *such disputes shall be settled or resolved by arbitration in accordance with the AIAC Arbitration Rules;*
(b) *the arbitration shall be conducted and administered by the AIAC in accordance with the AIAC Arbitration Rules; and*
(c) *if the seat of arbitration is Malaysia, Section 41, Section 42, Section 43 and Section 46 of the Malaysian Arbitration Act 2005 (as amended) shall not apply.*

AIAC has also made available the AIAC-I Arbitration Rules effective 9 March 2018 to cater for Islamic financial disputes.

As alluded to earlier, another example of an e-commerce website, that is, Lazada's Terms and Conditions evidence a willingness to avail itself and buyer to submit to AIAC's jurisdiction. Lazada's Terms and Conditions [https://lazada.com.my] states:

8. Arbitration

- *8.1 Any controversy, claim or dispute arising out of or relating to these Terms of Use and/or other Lazada Terms and Conditions or the breach, termination or invalidity thereof shall be referred to and settled by arbitration in accordance with the Arbitration Rules of the Asian*

International Arbitration Centre ("AIAC") held in Kuala Lumpur, Malaysia. The arbitral tribunal shall consists of a sole arbitrator who is legally trained and who has experience in the information technology field in Malaysia and is independent of either party. The place of arbitration shall be Malaysia. Any award by the arbitration tribunal shall be final and binding upon the parties.

8.2 Notwithstanding the foregoing, Lazada reserves the right to pursue the protection of intellectual property rights and confidential information through injunctive or other equitable relief through the courts.

Arguably, we note examples of e-commerce websites deploying 'terms of use' to lead users to unwittingly agree on specific terms, and this invariably includes arbitration terms, or in the case of Lazada, it is the AIAC, whilst in the case of Shopee, it is the Consumer Claims Tribunal.

SIDREC

SIDREC was established by the Securities Commission under the Capital Markets and Services (Dispute Resolution) Regulations 2010 (P.U.(A) 437/2010) ('the Regulation'). Regulations 3(2)(a) states that SIDREC will be able to act as a dispute resolution body by receiving references in relation to disputes or claims and resolving such disputes or claims in an accessible, efficient and effective manner, based on the principle of fairness and reasonableness.

Key to SIDREC's role in the investor protection framework is the independence and impartiality to provide investors an independent and impartial ADR with capital market expertise, to resolve their monetary disputes with any SIDREC Member in a timely and cost effective manner. The process is informal and voluntary.

SIDREC's members comprise entities, who are either licensed or registered by Securities Commission (SC) pursuant to the Capital Market and Services Act 2007 (CMSA) and include investment banks, commercial banks, Islamic banks, stockbrokers, derivative brokers, fund management companies, unit trust management companies (UTMC), private retirement schemes (PRS) and fund managers (excluding Real Estate Investment Trusts [REITs] managers).

The SIDREC model is significant and interesting as it demonstrates that an industry-wide (in this context, capital market) dispute resolution model is not only workable but also proves that a specific fintech industry with wide judicial procedures may be considered as an alternative model.

It is submitted that potential I-fintech disputes involving the investors of capital markets and SIDREC members may fall under the SIDREC scheme. For example, hypothetically, an investor to the crowdfunding Investment Account Platform ('IAP') may avail itself to SIDREC to resolve their monetary disputes with any of the consortium of six Islamic bank institutions. IAP was launched in February 2016 is a bank-intermediated Fintech platform spearheaded by a consortium of six Malaysia's Islamic banking institutions.

World Intellectual Property Organization ('WIPO') Model

It will be a remiss if the WIPO IP disputes services specific to Fintech is not discussed in this chapter. Notably, the WIPO Arbitration and Mediation Center (see: https://www.wipo.int/) provides procedural advice and case administration to help parties resolve disputes arising in the area of financial technology ('Fintech') without the need for court litigation. It is stated that the 'WIPO International Alternative Dispute Resolution services enable parties to resolve IP disputes outside the courts, in a single neutral forum, saving significant time and money.'

Arbitration and Mediation

In so far as arbitration and mediation are concerned, 'WIPO fast, flexible and cost-effective services for settling IP and technology disputes outside the courts offers':

- Mediation where an impartial mediator helps two or more parties in dispute reach a mutually acceptable agreement between themselves.
- Arbitration where the parties agree to submit their dispute to an arbitrator, who then makes a final, binding decision (award).
- Expert determination where the parties agree to submit a specific issue (such as a technical question, or the valuation of an IP asset, or royalty rates) to one or more experts who make a determination on the matter.'

Arguably, the WIPO model represents and offers unique hybrid arb-med model to cater for IP and technology disputes (discussion on this subject is beyond the scope of this chapter although attempts will be made in the latter part of the chapter to highlight the Islamic ADR model using this concept). What we have seen from the foregoing paragraphs are but examples of existing ADR models ready to be used as alternative dispute resolution processes outside court.

A pertinent question that demands an answer is—what alternatives would the Islamic Shari'ah I-fintech judicial framework offer?

A Reformed Model: Arbitration in Islamic Law—A Traditional Perspective

A cursory look at the traditional application of Muslim laws reveals the existence of well-structured system of dispute resolution amongst many Islamic/Muslim countries.

For instance, OP Malhotra (2002) wrote that in India, where all Muslims were once governed by the Shari'ah, a compilation of Islamic laws and commentaries known as Hedaya, by Imam Abu Hanifa and his disciples Abu Yusof and Imam Mohammad, revealed the existence of provisions on arbitration for parties where the word used for arbitration is *Tahkeem* and the word used for arbitrator is *Hakam*. In Turkey and under the rule of the Ottoman caliphate, the *Mejella*, stood out as the first codified corpus of laws including those regulating Islamic financial transactions.

In Malaysia, N. Khalidah Dahlan (2018) observed that peaceful settlement of disputes has been practised widely since the era of the Melaka sultanate much in conformity with principles of *musyawarah*.

In addition to the litigation-based advocacy, the principles of *sulh* is widely practiced not only in family courts in Malaysia but also in civil disputes. Section 99 of the Syariah Court Civil Procedure (Federal Territories) Act 1998 (Act 585) states: 'The parties at any stage of the proceedings, hold sulh to settle their disputes in accordance with such rules as may be prescribed or, in the absence of such rules, in accordance with Hukum Syarak.'

The Malaysian Regulatory Regime

From the preceding paragraphs, the writer has argued that in addition to the two traditional main planks of legal framework governing disputes in Islamic banking, that is, litigation before the civil courts and arbitration, there are in existence parallel models represented by the ombudsman, tribunal and mediation.

It would also be pertinent to note that in the case of the in *JRI Resources Sdn Bhd v Kuwait Finance House (Malaysia) Berhad* [2019] MLJU 275 the Malaysian Federal Court held that findings on Islamic finance by Bank Negara Malaysia's Shariah Advisory Council (SAC) is binding on civil courts.

The SAC was set up in May 1997 as the highest Shariah authority in Islamic finance in Malaysia. Under the Central Bank of Malaysia Act 2009, the role and functions of the SAC was further reinforced—it was accorded the status of the sole authoritative body on shariah matters pertaining to Islamic banking, takaful and Islamic finance.

Section 56 of Central Bank Act 2009 vests an important jurisdiction to *Shari'ah* Advisory Council to refer to *Shari'ah* Advisory Council for ruling from court or arbitrator. It provides:

> *(1) Where in any proceedings relating to Islamic financial business before any court or arbitrator any question arises concerning a Shari'ah matter, the court or the arbitrator, as the case may be, shall-*
>
> *(a) Take into consideration any published rulings of the SAC; or*
> *(b) Refer such question to the SAC for its ruling*

A nine-member panel of judges, in a narrow majority 5-4 decision, however also ruled that the ascertainment of Islamic law by the SAC does not amount to a judicial decision.

The majority also held that the rulings by the SAC constitute an expert opinion in the matters of Islamic finance. 'The SAC members are highly qualified in the fields of shariah economics, banking, law and finance,' says Justice Zawawi, who wrote the majority judgement.

In the light of the earlier given judgement, the function and importance of SAC now cannot be over emphasized as the main point of binding-authoritative reference on issues relating to Islamic finance and it is submitted that it is a role that can be extended not only to disputes canvased before the courts and arbitration but also in all other ADR models.

However, in light of this case, it is important to observe that as the Federal Court's decision only binds lower courts, the only caveat to bear in mind is the binding effect of SAC on other ADR forums (in the absence of prior agreement of its binding nature upon referral) any SAC ruling on other ADR forum may be treated as of persuasive nature.

Some Key Shari'ah ADR Models

As can be seen in the foregoing discussions, by way of iterations, besides the court litigation procedures, the ADR models involving not only mediation and arbitration but also tribunal or ombudsman are often used in resolving financial disputes. And these models are not unlike existing and prevalent ADR models practiced in Shari'ah contexts which are discussed here:

(a) Tahkeem or arbitration

In the context of Shari'ah resolution of disputes models, it is noteworthy to observe that *tahkeem* or arbitration is a well-entrenched practice. Hence, it is noteworthy to observe that Samir Saleh (1984) wrote '[A]rbitration is a common and preferred method of settling commercial disputes in Islamic countries.' In fact, arguably, Abdul Hamid el-Ahbab (1987) cited that one of the most famous use of arbitration model was the arbitration agreement between Saidina Ali ibn Abi Talib (a.s.) and Muawiyah ibn Abi Sufian, the Governor of Syam over the succession of Caliphate, when two arbitrators were chosen to settle the dispute.

(b) *Sulh* or good faith negotiation

Another key dispute resolution mechanism is *sulh* or good faith negotiation. Aida Othman (2005) noted that 'in classical Islamic thought and tradition, sulh means the amicable settlement of disputes through good faith negotiation, conciliation/mediation, peacemaking, and even extends to compromise of action. This is an institutionalized method of dispute resolution recognized and prescribed by the primary sources of Shari'ah.'

(c) Mediation and Arbitration ('Med-Arb')

The Med-ARB model is a synthesis of both *sulh* (mediation) and *tahkim* (arbitration) models. The mechanism of Med-Arb in the context of Islamic law is succinctly explained by Umar A. Oseni (2009) thus:

> The Med-Arb process is a mechanism for dispute resolution enmeshed within the general framework of *Sulh* (amicable settlement) in Islamic jurisprudence...In most cases during the *Tahkim* proceedings, both *sulh* and *tahkim* are combined to facilitate the process of dispute resolution. (p. 19)

Hence, parties may still opt for mediation and reconciliation rather than continues to achieve an arbitral award even when proceedings are in place.

(d) *Muhtasib* or ombudsman

The institution of *Muhtasib* or ombudsman has existed in Islamic legal and political history. Athar Murtuza (2004) argues that one of the main general functions of a muhtasib is to 'regulate commercial activity within the state by protecting the interest of the consumers and the entrepreneurs alike, and guard public interest with much emphasis on administrative justice.'

(e) Fatāwa of Muftīs

In the modern context, Umar A. Oseni (2009, pp. 19–20) finds that this is best described as determination of experts or 'of a Muslim jurist[s] [which] represents three evaluative assessment of a dispute which may involve evaluative mediation, mini-trial or expert determination' and 'though the verdict or evaluation given by an expert is of persuasive nature and not considered binding, the significance of it is mostly felt in the area of dispute avoidance.'

It is submitted that determination of experts either persuasive or binding is extremely useful in dispute resolution in particular where the status of such determination is founded upon contractual undertakings or legislative sanctions.

The Way Forward: A Reformed Model(s)

Hybrid ADR Process

Umar A. Oseni (2009) proposed two hybrid ADR processes for the settlement of Islamic banking disputes which would and could be incorporated and institutionalized as 'Regional Sulh Centre for Islamic Banking and Finance.'

> The first is an amalgam of the triad consisting of mediation (sulh), expert determination (fatāwā) and ultimately, arbitration (tahkīm). On the other hand, parties may opt for the Med-Muh hybrid procedure which is more appropriate for the settlement of disputes between a customer and his/her financial service provider. (pp. 19–20)

The writer submits and associates himself to these two propositions and posits further that the schemes are equally valid and would apply to I-fintech judicial framework ecosystem. Both models are discussed in the foregoing paragraphs.

Mediation–Expert–Arbitration

Umar A. Oseni (2009) describes the process thus:

> the process starts with sulh and if such is not successful within a reasonable time, the dispute should proceed for binding Expert determination. This will be carried out by such expert who is learned in Islamic banking and financial services and has the requisite training-cum-expertise of dispute resolution. The same panel can conduct the sulh phase of the process and thereafter proceeds to Expert Determination. After an objective evaluation of the case, the experts give their opinion which is considered binding because the whole process will be based on a contractual agreement ab initio. Such expert opinion may assist in nipping the conflict in the bud. However, if the any of the parties to the dispute refuses to be guided by the opinion of the expert by accepting the decision, there is always the need for an enforceable procedure in form of tahkīm. (p. 20)

As alluded to earlier, the Malaysian Federal Court in *JRI Resources Sdn Bhd v Kuwait Finance House (Malaysia) Berhad (supra) in a majority decision* held that findings on Islamic finance by SAC is binding on civil courts. It is in this context, the writer submits that the SAC fulfils the functions of expert whose rulings constitute 'determination' which is binding both on the court and on arbitration.

The writer would posit further that in addition to court and arbitration, such a determination by SAC may be made binding on other ADR forums with parties' prior agreement of its binding nature upon referral.

Mediation–Muhtasib (Med–Muh)

On this model, Umar A. Oseni (2009) posits:

> Med-Muh is a mixture of mediation (sulh) and muhtasib. This amalgam is more relevant in the resolution of administrative-cum-financial disputes, claims or complaints which generally arise out of bank-customer relation-

> ship. As a preliminary step, such a hybrid process will begin by utilizing the sulh process before proceeding to the institution of ombudsman (muhtasib).

Further, he added:

> If the dispute, complaint or claim is not resolved or any of the parties is not satisfied, then, the muhtasib will decide the matter based on his assessment and applying the relevant laws from the Islamic perspective. The decision of the muhtasib is binding on the parties and no appeal can be made against such a decision. (pp. 19–20)

It is submitted that these descriptions aptly fit into the OFS, Consumers Tribunal and SIDREC models described and alluded to herein.

Conclusion

Clearly an institutionalized Shari'ah—Islamic I-fintech judicial framework is consistent and comparable with existing modern legal dispute resolution legal frameworks and technological demands. As was argued earlier, both these two hybrid models may be considered by I-fintech stakeholders including Bank Negara Malaysia, Securities Commission and Fintech Association of Malaysia, as newly reformed judicial ADR models, underpinning the perfect case of alternative judicial legal framework to cater to the needs and demands of any present and future I-fintech disputes.

Whilst any attempt to introduce and render binding submission to Mediation–Expert–Arbitration model may just require mere contractual arrangements and undertakings, attempts and efforts to have Med-Muh model as described earlier to be applicable would require legislative interventions as these models' legitimacy and application rests on legislative justifications. The introduction and application would inevitably require not only political will but also legislative interventions in order to carry through the proposed Mediation–Expert–Arbitration model into reality.

References

Abdul Hamid el-Ahbab. (1987, February 15–19). *Moslem Arbitration Law*. Proceedings of the International Bar Association First Arab Regional Conference, Cairo. Volume 1 at p. 337 cited by Sundra Rajoo at p. 8.

Khalidah Dahlan, N. (2018). Alternative Dispute Resolution for Islamic Finance in Malaysia. https://doi.org/10.1051/matecconf/201815005077

Malhotra, O. P. (2002). *The Law and Practice of Arbitration and Conciliation* (1st ed.). LexisNexisButterworths. Citing The Hedaya (Commentary on the Islamic Laws) at p. [1] 1–2.

Murtuza, A. (2004). *Muhtasib's Role: Safeguarding the Public Interest During the Islamic Middle Ages.* American Accounting Association 2004 Mid Atlantic Region Meeting Paper. Retrieved from http://ssrn.com/abstrac=488882. Cited by Umar A. Oseni.

Mustill and Boyd. (2001). *Commercial Arbitration: 2001 Companion Volume to the Second Edition.* LexisNexis.

Oseni, U. A. (2009, October 6–8). *Dispute Resolution in Islamic Banking and Finance; Current Trends and Future Perspectives.* Paper presented at the International Conference on Islamic Financial Services: Emerging Opportunities for Law/Economic Reforms of the Developing Nations, University of Ilorin, Kwara State, Nigeria Jointly Organised by the Department of Islamic Law, Faculty of Law, University of Ilorin-Nigeria & Islamic Research and Training Institute (IRTI), IDB Group, Jeddah, Saudi Arabia.

Othman, A. (2005). *And Sulh is Best: Amicable Settlement and Dispute Resolution in Islamic Law.* Ph.D Thesis, Harvard University, p. 1, cited by Umar A. Oseni.

Saleh, S. (1984). *Commercial Arbitration in the Arab Middle East.* London: Graham & Trotman, pp. 1–4, cited by Sundra Rajoo at p. 8.

PART III

Islamic FinTech: Its Mechanisms and Applications

CHAPTER 9

The Forms and Effects of Cryptocurrencies in a Dual Banking System

Khoutem Ben Jedidia and Hichem Hamza

Abstract This chapter examines the effects of private cryptocurrencies in dual system (conventional and Islamic), an area which has not been critically addressed in the literature. Despite the benefits of private cryptocurrencies, we highlight some challenges that private cryptocurrencies pose for financial stability. We show that the widespread use of private currencies causes a compromised payment system notably with the absence of guarantee mechanisms. Moreover, the impacts of cryptocurrencies on commercial bank activities may exacerbate financial stability risks. The loss of control over monetary policy and the lack of lender of last resort of Central Bank lead to higher exposition to systemic risk. Nevertheless, the cryptocurrency compatible with *sharia* can avoid many concerns and ensure better financial stability and social cohesion in a dual system.

K. Ben Jedidia (✉)
Higher Institute of Accountancy and Business Administration, University of Manouba, Manouba, Tunisia

Research Unit in Islamic Economics and Finance, University of Zitouna, Tunis, Tunisia

H. Hamza
Islamic Economics Institute, King Abdulaziz University, Jeddah, Saudi Arabia

M. M. Billah (ed.), *Islamic FinTech*,
https://doi.org/10.1007/978-3-030-45827-0_9

Keywords Banking Intermediation • Blockchain • Financial Stability • Sharia • Dual Banking • Central Banks • Islamic Bank • Cryptocurrency

Introduction

In recent years, innovations in the digitalisation of the financial and payment systems have led to the emergence and the proliferation of private digital currencies such as cryptocurrencies. The transactions linked to cryptocurrencies are based essentially on blockchain and cryptography technologies characterized by a higher degree of security, efficiency, and transparency. In this regard, the payment system is decentralized and the distributed ledger technology enables the transaction settlement to be peer-to-peer (P2P) without intermediary. Especially, innovations related to the Bitcoin and its underlying blockchain technology have attracted strong interest in cryptocurrencies (Fung & Halaburda, 2016). Virtual currencies and their associated technologies are rapidly evolving and the future landscape is difficult to predict (He et al., 2016).

In this context, regulatory authorities and public policy makers are dubious in the assessment of the risks and benefits of the private virtual currencies (Albahouth, 2018). Besides, due to their development and popularity, governments cannot simply forbid them (Spithoven, 2019). Even the Bitcoin, the most widespread among cryptocurrencies, causes scepticism (Urquhart, 2018). First, authorities wonder how to regulate this decentralized and relatively anonymous money. Second, important fluctuations in the value of cryptocurrencies result in important risks. Cryptocurrencies which are not associated with any tangible assets are characterized by astonishing price appreciation and pricing bubbles central (Corbet, Lucey, Urquhart, & Yarovaya, 2019). Glaser et al. (2014) specify that the majority of new users of virtual money are not interested in the mechanism of these currencies but use it as an investment tool in order to take advantage of fluctuations in their prices. Bitcoin and cryptocurrency markets illustrate a considerable speculative component and are extremely volatile (Fry & Cheah, 2016). Consequently, the speculative rationale of this money dominates the monetary one. Third, the inefficiency of cryptocurrency market is highlighted by many empirical researches. For example, Caporal, Gil-Alana, and Plastun (2018) demonstrate a positive correlation between past and future values of four main cryptocurrencies (Bitcoin, Litecoin, Ripple, Dash) with a change in the correlation degree over the period 2013–2017. They conclude to the inefficiency of these currencies since abnormal profits can be generated using trend trading strategies. Urquhart (2018) points out the evidence of informational market inefficiency of Bitcoin using a battery of robust tests and notes that the returns are significantly efficient in the latter period. Forth, cryptocurrencies are subject to potential illicit use and their infrastructural breaches are affected by the cyber-criminality development (Corbet et al., 2019). This debate of culminated recently following the closure of the black-market Silk Road[1] in October 2013.

Recent studies (Ali, Barrdear, Clews, & Southgate, 2014; Ammous, 2018; Bech & Garratt, 2017; Bordo & Levin, 2017; Fung & Halaburda, 2016; Prasad, 2018) have examined the money functions of the digital currencies (unit of account, medium exchange, and store of value) and results are not yet conclusive. All aspects of the new digital payment system require deep-thinking regarding challenges for the whole financial system, given both opportunities and threats. In fact, the cryptocurrencies challenge the traditional financial system. They are "alternative to the current financial system" (Geiger, 2017). Risks of financial stability may eventually emerge as the new virtual currencies become more widely used (He et al., 2016).

This chapter targets to study the effects of private cryptocurrencies in dual financial system characterized by the presence of Islamic banks, area which has not been critically addressed in the literature and tries consequently to contribute to fulfil this gap. As argued by Lietaer (2001), the usage of alternative monetary systems or complementary currencies is often motivated by feelings of inequity of fiat monetary systems. We focus on the impact of private cryptocurrencies on financial system notably on the payment system, banking, and financial stability. The novelty of this study is to discuss these issues in the dual framework as we investigate the cryptocurrency *sharia* compatible that meets the Islamic finance rules. In a dual banking system where Islamic banks coexist with the conventional banks, Islamic banking system might support the same consequences as the conventional system in term of financial stability. Given the development of private digital currencies, conventional and Islamic banks are

[1] It is a black market launched in January 2011 requiring Bitcoins for exchange of unlawful goods and services.

incited to face challenges to their business models mostly related to the payment system and their financial intermediation. The question is whether Islamic rules prevent many of macroeconomic perils caused by private cryptocurrencies.

The remainder of this chapter is organized as follows. The second section presents the features and the money functions of private cryptocurrencies. The third section examines the cryptocurrencies in view of *Sharia* considering the principles of Islamic finance. The fourth section discusses the implications of private cryptocurrencies on payment system and financial stability in a dual system. It is worth noting that insights from this study help regulators to understand the link between private cryptocurrencies and financial system stability in a dual system in a world increasingly invaded by Fintech.

Private Cryptocurrency Characteristics

According to the Merriam-Webster dictionary, cryptocurrency is "any form of currency that only exists digitally, that usually has no central issuing or regulating authority but instead uses a decentralized system to record transactions and manage the issuance of new units, and that relies on cryptography to prevent counterfeiting and fraudulent transactions".[2] In reference to this definition, we consider that the important aspects of the cryptocurrency are related to the digitization technology, regulation of competition, decentralization, and transaction purposes. In this perspective, it is important to analyse these principles' aspects and their effects on other forms of currencies and the financial system as a whole.

Emergence and Features of Cryptocurrencies

In recent years, digitalization and innovation technology in the financial and payment systems have led to the emergence of private digital currencies such as virtual currencies and cryptocurrencies. During the financial crisis, the pseudonym programmer Satoshi Nakamoto published in 2008 a paper on Proof of Work with description of a new currency: Bitcoin. The author suggests that the purely peer-to-peer version of electronic avoids the interposition of financial institutions. The first Bitcoins were created on January 3, 2009, through the P2P Foundation website. While Bitcoin

[2] https://www.merriam-webster.com/dictionary/cryptocurrency

has the greatest valuation, there were 2493 private cryptocurrencies of this type worldwide in August 2019.[3] The ten most important cryptocurrencies represent 80% of the total market, while the two most important, Bitcoin and Ethereum, represented around 64.29% of the market value in May 2019.[4]

As a new form of money or asset, private cryptocurrencies are based on cryptography using a decentralized ledger. In this regard, no central authority controls the transactions in the network. The realisation of transactions is based essentially on blockchain[5] and cryptography technologies characterized by their higher degree of security and transparency without financial intermediary.[6] Indeed, cryptocurrency is based on crypto proof and series of digital signatures. Their use is based on the distributed ledger technologies (DLT) which provide efficient and secure peer-to-peer transactions. In this view, there is no need to trust a third-party middleman such as Central Bank or Banks. For example, Bitcoin's technology relies on Open Source based on secured data exchange. The accuracy of blockchain is ensured by miners who solve a mathematical problem (Auer, 2019). This "proof-of-work" allows them to add a block of newly processed transactions to the blockchain and to receive Bitcoin as a reward of their participation.

Private cryptocurrencies are *electronic* (no physical form as they exist only in the network); are *not the liability of anyone*, convey *peer-to-peer* exchange and are *not backed by assets* (not redeemable for another commodity such as gold) (see Table 9.1). Cryptocurrencies have no intrinsic value and might be exchanged for goods or services at a later point in time (Bech & Garratt, 2017). Monetary and Financial Statistics Manual and Compilation Guide established by International Monetary Fund considers in paragraph 4.40 that "Internet-based currency such as Bitcoins is not electronic money because it does not meet the definition of currency, as it is not issued or authorized by a Central Bank or government, and

[3] https://coinmarketcap.com/

[4] https://coinmarketcap.com/

[5] The Blockchain is a decentralized and automatic database maintained by nodes that ensure the confirmation and storage of transactions.

[6] However, the absence of a financial intermediary in the transactions makes the traceability of the transactions more difficult.

Table 9.1 Features of private cryptocurrencies compared to cash and bank deposits

	Cash	**Bank deposits**	**Private crypto-currencies**
Peer to peer			
Electronic			
Not liability of any one			
Institution of emission/management	Central bank	Banks	Private firms

additionally it is not widely accepted as a medium of exchange. Bitcoins are classified as nonfinancial assets”.[7]

One can enumerate the advantage and inconvenient of cryptocurrencies compared to others money forms:

Cryptocurrency enjoys instantaneousness and flexibility. Unlike fiat and metal money, digital currencies cannot be altered, forged, or manipulated (Muedini, 2018) and people can access anywhere with private keys. It ensures low payment fees. Oubdi and Raghibi (2018) think that both virtual coin production system and transaction verification present a fair model for the remuneration of cryptocurrency community agents.

However, the exchange or gain of cryptocurrency usually escapes the tax authorities. Furthermore, as miners are privileged, users are not equal (Guegan, 2018). Many cryptocurrencies are opaque and operate outside of the conventional financial system, making it difficult to monitor their operations (He et al., 2016). Thus, virtual currencies can be considered as potential vehicles for money laundering, terrorist financing, tax evasion fraud, and criminal activities due to their anonymous nature. According to He (2018), cryptocurrencies do not enjoy the same degree of trust that citizens have in fiat currencies: they have been afflicted by notorious cases of fraud, security breaches, and operational failures and have been associated with illicit activities. Furthermore, there is sustainability issue due to huge energy notably electricity consumption used to mine cryptocurrencies. Indeed, Motherboard site indicates that a “single Bitcoin transaction

[7] Cited by IMF (2018), Treatment of crypto Assets in Macroeconomic statistics, Thirty-First Meeting of the IMF committee on Balance of Payments Statistics, Washington, DC, October, 24–26, 2018.

requires 215 kilowatt-hours of electricity to process, that is the equivalent of what an average American household consumes in one week".[8] Bitcoin is costly to produce compared to inexpensive paper currency (Amihud & Cukierman, 2018). Thus, mining of cryptocurrencies is expensive due to the large amounts of electricity and the increasingly dependency on highly specialized hardware of the computations (Berentsen & Schär, 2018). Besides, this energy wastage causes environmental cost.

Money Functions of Private Cryptocurrencies

It is widely considered that: "To be money, …currency should be a store of value, a unit of account, a medium of exchange, and also serves as a standard of deferred payment" (Bank of England, 2014). Central Banks make it clear that cryptocurrencies are generally not currencies but rather assets and high-risk investments (Ingves, 2018). Banque de France (2018) considered that cryptocurrencies are not currencies and that it is more correct to call them crypto-assets since they "do not meet, or only partially satisfy, the three functions of money". With the creation of Initial Coin Offerings (ICOs), cryptocurrencies are further used as investment or financing instruments. For instance, ICOs using cryptocurrencies replicate the concept of "crowdfunding" where the funders of projects have remuneration of their cryptocurrencies. What about the degree of fulfilment of the three money functions?

- **Unit of account**: In theory, cryptocurrencies can assume the function of unit of account as they can express the value of goods and services. Nevertheless, as they are not backed by some real commodities and their value fluctuates significantly, they cannot practically serve as a unit of account. For example, Bitcoin reached 19716 dollars in December 2017 and decreased to 6707 dollars in March 2018. The price of Bitcoin depends on both supply demand and so it is unstable. Ammous (2018) thinks that due to their inflexible supply and their wildly fluctuating demand and their instability;[9] digital currencies cannot fulfil the function of unit of account of money.

[8] Source: Motherboard site cited by Guegan (2018).

[9] The author notes that this instability constitutes "the Insurmountable hurdle" of the adoption of cryptocurrencies.

- **Instrument of exchange**: cryptocurrencies are instruments of exchange in the digital world.[10] They can be sold or bought against fiat currencies. But this medium exchange is restricted to online markets. Moreover, agents can refuse it as payment while fiat money has legal tender status. Bitcoin is an inefficient and poorly designed means of payment (Williamson, 2018). Besides, there are issues in filling this function, given important transaction cost for retail payments. Further, in the case of fraud or unauthorized payment, there is no guarantee of reimbursement at face value at any time due to the lack of legal guarantee (Banque de France, 2018). Berentsen and Schär (2018) highlight that price volatility and scaling issues tackle the suitability of Bitcoin as payment instrument.
- **Store of value**: Private digital currencies appear to be poor short-term stores of value given the significant volatility in exchange rates with traditional currencies (Ali et al., 2014). They suffer from a lack of relationship with trade or economic needs or any underlying fundamentals and so they are not very good stores of value (Claeys, Demertzis, & Efstathiou, 2018). Meera (2018) noted that due to its high volatility, the Bitcoin does not adhere well to the function of store of value. Also, it cannot survive as a safe haven asset (Williamson, 2018). Nevertheless, Ammous (2018) specifies that compared to other cryptocurrencies, Bitcoin is only serving as a long-term store of value thanks to its strict commitment to low supply growth and its credibly backed network distributed protocol.

It is true that what distinguishes the monetary economy from the barter economy is the existence of the intermediary function of exchange; however, this function is not sufficient in itself to consider that cryptocurrencies are effectively money because of the variance of their perceptions as a method of standard value and store value. So, they do not fulfil the three essential functions of money. Cryptocurrencies do not perform the role of money well, because their values are very volatile (Claeys et al., 2018). Cryptocurrencies do not "possess all the core attributes of money" (Andersen, 2018). Moreover, the speculative character of cryptocurrencies poses problems. There are two dimensions of this form of currency:

[10] For example, the Bitcoin "is a virtual asset stored electronically which allows a community of users that accept it as payment to carry out transactions without using fiat currency" (Banque de France, 2018, p. 1).

monetary (as unit of account and instrument of exchange) and speculative (as source of speculation gain). The fluctuations of private cryptocurrency exchange rates reinforce the speculative rationale. The primary use of Bitcoin is for speculation rather than for transaction (Guegan, 2018; Banque de France, 2018). Not only private cryptocurrencies do not meet the usual requirements for local money but also those of international reserve assets because of their unprecedented and exorbitant volatility (Clark & Mihailov, 2019).[11]

Sharia-Compliant Cryptocurrencies

The beginning of an Islamic digital currency including blockchain technologies and Islamic finance called OneGram was in May 2017 (Das, 2017; Maierbrugger, 2017). Recently, many scholars discuss the conformity of private digital to Islamic finance rules. In this section, we examine the cryptocurrencies in view of *sharia* considering the principles of Islamic finance. We ask whether there are additional conditions which must be fulfilled to establish Sharia-compliant cryptocurrencies?

The Money Sharia Compliant

Historically, at the time of prophet Muhammed (in the late 500s and early 600s), money was raw materials and coins from Byzantine. At the beginning, money was issued on silver (Dirhams) and after, at Muawiya's rule, money was gold (coins) (Muedini, 2018). However, coins which are subject to trade are weighted rather than counted (Siegfried, 2001). In 76 A H, Caliph Abdul Malik ibn Marwan introduced the first dinar and Islamic dirham. Besides, various forms of money circulated along the reign of Muslim empires such as the *Fulus* during the Mamluk period and the *Qaimah paper* currencies during the Ottoman period.

According to Adam (2017), the Holy Quran does not provide specific guidelines on what money must look like. In Islamic economics, the first attempt to conceptualize the notion of money was in XI century with Imam *Al-Ghazali* who asserts that money has no intrinsic value, it is a simple instrument of exchange and measurement of value. So, he doesn't

[11] Their study is based upon statistical analysis of measuring volatility compared to that of standard reserve assets and a counterfactual simulation.

consider money as a saving instrument.[12] Islamic scholars distinguished *al-istilah Money* (token money), that is, without the valued metal content of gold or silver from the *thamankhilqatan* money (real money).[13] In addition to the three functions, money is a standard in *sharia* legal requirement in *Zakat*, *jizya*, *Kharaj*, *Diyat*.

According to Mufti Faraz (2017), money is reposed on three conditions in Islamic rules:

- Tamawwul (التمول): consists of all things accepted as valuable as money by people
- Taqawwum (التقوم): limits money to *sharia*-compliant elements (*halal*);
- Thamaniyyah (الثمنية): is related to two important role of money as independent standard of exchange and unit of account.

We can then highlight the main principal features of money in Islamic rules:

- *Interest free currency*: In Islamic perspective, the forbidden of interest has implications on the nature of money and leads to no reward for time preference. With the payment of positive interest, money serves as store of value. The currency would be a potential capital requiring the association with another source to generate a productive activity. In other words, money must be channelled to the benefit of the real economy and not to the pure finance (speculation is prohibited).
- *A commodity money*: In Islamic law, money should have intrinsic value such as gold and silver. However, the fiat currency without intrinsic value is valid given the legal tender and it is *sharia* compliant according to the majority of the Islamic scholars. Almarzoqi,

[12] *Sharia* defines money as a means of exchange and a unit of account and does not consider money as a store of value (Ahmad & Hassan, 2006).

[13] *Mal* (مال) *in Arabic* refers to anything that can be acquired or possessed tangible or intangible (usufruct). According to the *hanafite* school, the two criteria of a currency are the desirability and the possibility of storage.

Mansour, and Krichen (2018) argue that a convertible paper money with 100% gold backing is *sharia* compliant.

- *Stability of the money value*: According to Meera (2018), money should have stable value to be a good "store of value" and protect the wealth in conformity with *Maqasid of Sharia*. Nevertheless, money is subject to the issue of value instability. The inflation target affects the value of currency over the time. If fiat money is used as policy tool to overcome government rigid laws such as minimum wage, impediments to trade, and this results in fraudulent inconvertible paper (Adam, 2017). Fiat Money is backed by debt denominated with a face value greater than the total amount of fiat in circulation. Consequently, fiat money can cause alterations of the measures of value, inflation tax, uncertainty in trade, unlimited supply, government abuse and forgery. Thus, gold reserves for fiat money are recommended by Islamic scholars to prevent inflation and excessive risk (Siegfried, 2001).

Private Cryptocurrencies and Sharia

The compatibility of current private cryptocurrencies to *sharia* is a controversial issue.

On one side, some authors such as Muedini (2018) consider that cryptocurrencies are "highly compatible" within Islamic finance and are preferred to "traditional money" in the Islamic law view. Oubdi and Raghibi (2018) argue that there is a convergence between the social justice, transparency, and general prosperity objectives carried by Islam and those carried by cryptocurrencies. Meera (2018) thinks that One-Gram, the gold-based cryptocurrency launched in Dubai, is acceptable as an "Islamic currency". Compared to fiat money, many arguments support the idea that private cryptocurrency is in line with *sharia* directives:

- Cryptocurrency is based on a proof of work and not on debt.
- Cryptocurrency is free of interest.
- The face value of the goodwill backing (Bitcoin) is equal to the value of the Bitcoin in circulation (Evans, 2015).
- In exchange for the expending of real resources, new units of cryptocurrencies come into circulation.
- Cryptocurrency is divisible, homogeneous, durable, mobile, and rare.

- If the supply of cryptocurrency is fixed, the problem of *gharar* is posed with fiat money is overcome (Muedini, 2018). For example, the quantity of Bitcoin in circulation increases at both predictable decelerating rate and should not exceed 21 million units in circulation-each divisible to the 1/100.
- Cryptocurrencies offer diversification benefits to investor with short investment horizons (Corbet, Meegan, Larkin, Lucey, & Yarovaya, 2018; Mensi, Mobeen, Khamis, Idries, & Sang, 2019).
- The cryptocurrency is considered as *MaalNaami* by scholars and it is subject to the zakat payment if it reaches the *nisab*.

On another side, some researches highlight that cryptocurrencies are far from *sharia* rules due to:

- The *absence of a central authority*: Sheikh Sulaiman Al-ruhayli[14] noted that the absence of a central authority that regulates this type of currency creates a risk (*gharar*) for the people who use it and caused its unstable and speculative character. The study of Benedetti and Kostovesky (2018) showed that more than 50% of initial cryptocurrency emissions fail after four months of the emission. According to Swielem (2018), this is explained by the lack of trust in the money issuer. *Fukaha* prohibit the issuance of money outside the State if this leads inevitably to damages to the society. Yet, if the damages are probable, some scholars such as *Abuhanifa* and Tawri accept the private issuer at a condition that currency has the same characteristics of those issued by the State. Oubdi and Raghibi (2018) indicate that the State monopoly of money issuer is supported by the jurisprudence of the stability that it provides, and it comes only from *ijtihad* (considering the realization of *maslahah*) and not explicitly from the Coran or Sunna.
- The *fraud and misuse of cryptocurrencies*: As the holder of cryptocurrency is anonymous, the track of the real holder of account is difficult and may results in suspicious activity. In this regard, the *Fatwa* of the Grand Mufti of Egypt, Chawki Allam, considered the Bitcoin as a game of chance. Meera (2018) argues alos that Bitcoin suffers from

[14] https://abutalhazahack.com/2017/12/07/bitcoin-islamic-ruling/

Gambling and *Maysir*. Further, a group of eight jurists[15] in *Sharia* constituting Wifaq Al-ulama conclude to the prohibition of the use of cryptocurrencies due to the motives of fraud and misuse of funds for mischievous purposes.

- The *excessive speculation*: As outlined by Oubdi and Raghibi (2018), the interdiction of cryptocurrencies is notably based on the excessive speculation and the anonymity of the transactions which emanate from purely Shari'atic jurisprudence.[16] As suggested by Clark and Mihailov (2019), the cryptocurrency markets generally function more like a speculative asset than strictly a currency market.[17] Albahouth (2018) concludes that private cryptocurrency suffers from a weak infrastructure causing them to be exposed to sharp fluctuations of their price. Following Ibn taymiya, Ibn Qaym, and Alghazali, it is forbidden to speculate with the currency. However, others scholars and AAOIFI (Standard n° 55) consider that trading money can be acceptable but subject to the compliance to many rules.
- The excessive *gharar*: Not only the inventor of Bitcoin is still unknown, but also it is difficult to track the real account holder. Due to its high volatility (Meera, 2018), the bitcoin value is subject to *gharar*. The main problem with private cryptocurrencies is the *gharar* in the Initial Coin Offering (Swielem, 2018). The author explains that the first issues of cryptocurrency by a company pose significant *gharar* problems.

Consequently, these problems can jeopardize the currency in the light of *Maqasid Al sharia* and cause some socioeconomics issues. We think that to be *sharia*-compliant, private cryptocurrencies should respected many constraints such as:

[15] Mufti Amjad Mohammed, Mufti Bil l Issak, Mufti Faisal al-Mahmudi (Canada), Qadhi Imran Sayed Falahi, Mufti Mohammed Ashfaq, Qari Muhammad ShoyaibNurgat, Mufti akariaAkudi et Mufti ubairDudha.

[16] For instance, some cryptocurrencies like Bitcoin have experienced excessive fluctuations ranging from a value of US$12 in 2013 to US$11,800 end 2017 with falls that exceed 10% in one month which compromises the element of preservation of value (Oubdi & Raghibi, 2018).

[17] However, the use of cryptocurrencies as speculative assets may promote the diversification (Gandal & Halaburda, 2016).

- *The prohibition of interest rate*: cryptocurrencies should be free from interest rate. Chapra (1996) notes that in Islamic finance, the value of money should be stable since the Islam advocates the honesty and fairness. Interest contributes to inflation which negatively affects the socio-economic justice and the general welfare.
- *The stability value*: Kahf (2014)[18] claims that cryptocurrencies and their exchange should undergo the same conditions of exchange of money in *Sharia*: a spot exchange and the prohibition of speculative transactions (Oziev & Yandiev, 2017). To be compatible with *Maqasid sharia* and promote socio-economic justice, Meera (2018) suggests that money should have intrinsic value.
- *The social role*: cryptocurrency can be used for social development-based projects (Dhaliwal, 2017) for microfinance and micro-takaful or cross-border crowdfunding. As suggested by Carstens (2018), even in the digital age, a good currency is likely to remain social rather than purely technological construct. While government seeks the maximization of national social welfare, private issuers of crypto-currency do not consider the impact of their actions for the rest of society and focus only on the maximization of profits (Amihud & Cukierman, 2018).

Effects of Private Cryptocurrencies on Dual Financial System

Cryptocurrencies may "transform the monetary system as a whole" (Papadopoulos, 2015, p. 128). The innovations in digital payment technologies and the development of private digital currencies have actively conducted Central Banks to study the potential implications on payment, monetary, and financial system. It is important for Central Banks to understand the impact of the cryptocurrencies on their monetary policy operations, the safety and efficiency of payments systems, and financial stability (Fung & Halaburda, 2016).

The issue of financial stability received increased attention particularly among government. However, the disparity in this area is quite pervasive. Although the blockchain and related technologies of cryptocurrencies

[18] http://lightuponlight.com/blog/fatwa-on-bitcoin-by-monzer-kahf/, retrieved on January 25, 2019.

offer a range of welfare-enhancing opportunities, they cause new risks and problems (Amihud & Cukierman, 2018).

Effects on Payment System

In recent years, the use of physical cash as a medium of exchange is decreasing which might allow cryptocurrencies to gain ground in the payment system. As demonstrated by Engert, Ben, and Fung (2017), the use of cash relative to others payment is declined in some developed countries notably in Sweden. In this country, only 13% of transactions are settled with cash as noted by the Central Bank's governor Stefan Ingves (Andersen, 2018). In the future, the widespread use of cryptocurrencies will reduce the demand for Central Bank money and the size of their balance sheets and could substantially reduce the demand for bank notes and even cheque' account deposits in banks (Fung & Halaburda, 2016).

Among the benefits of digital finance to customers, Ozili (2018) notes a greater control of customers' personal finance and the ability to make and receive payments within seconds. In addition, Amihud and Cukierman (2018) argue that the important gain is the reduction in the world transaction costs. Especially, distributed ledger technology may reduce the cost of international transfers including remittances (Bouveret & Haksar, 2018) and contributes to make transactions faster and more secure (Mühleisen, 2018). According to He (2018), crypto-assets performs many advantages as a medium of exchange: anonymity, more adequacy to long distancetransactions and more divisibility. Consequently, the cryptocurrency digital payment channels contribute to perform basic financial transactions and offer a reliable digital payment system.

In the next paragraph, we discuss the effect on the bank's role in the payment system, on the payment system cost, and on the payment incidents.

Since payments are at the centre of economic activity and exchange, commercial banks enjoy a pivotal role in society (Grym, Heikkinen, Kauko, & Takala, 2017). Banks have an effective monopoly on payment services. The payment-related income of commercial banks can be reduced, given the increased competition of cryptocurrencies. Muedini (2018) considers that private cryptocurrencies leading to peer-to-peer transactions will remove the need for any banking institution. However, the major role of banks in the provision and settlement of retail payments is currently secured since cryptocurrencies are not widely used. Moreover, unlike decentralized cryptocurrencies, the smooth operation of the payment system *via* bank deposits (both conventional and Islamic) is always supported by central authorities. So, these payments through the dual banking system have the benefit of this guarantee and the protection by a legal system compared to private cryptocurrency payment.

Regarding the payment system cost, Auer (2019) points out that to be unalterable and irrevocable, the final payment system of Bitcoin is extremely expensive. The author explains that proof-of-work can only achieve payment security if mining income is high. Yet, if the block rewards decrease, the security of payments decreases. Thereby, the proof-of-work requires high transaction costs (Budish, 2018). Especially, if the system is congested, that is, the newly added blocks are at the maximum size permitted by the protocol, fees are very high (see Easley, O'Hara, & Basu, 2019; Huberman, Leshno, & Moellemi, 2017). In this case, when users aim to have immediately skipped, fees are more than US$50 per transaction as in the crypto-hype in late 2017 (Auer, 2019). So, the decentralised blockchain system is more expansive than centralized one (Oubdi & Raghibi, 2018). While the centralized payment systems solve the double spending problem, each transaction with Bitcoin ought to point to the output of a previous transaction containing adequate funds in order to prevent this problem (Berentsen & Schär, 2018).

Moreover, with digital currencies, more payments are operated through virtual system and so potential technology failure may hamper the payment system. The uncertainty about the future technological progress may result in "digital runs". This may increase the liquidity risk within the system of payment. In this vein, Banque de France (2018) noted that the convertibility of cryptocurrencies into different fiat currencies is not guaranteed by regulation and so "the price of a crypto-asset may at any time collapse if investors wishing to unwind their positions cannot find purchasers and become holders of illiquid assets". Also, the transaction confirmation can take a significant time and sometimes several days or ends with no confirmation. Another issue is related to the loss of private key associated with the account of Bitcoin (e.g. in the case of formatting the hard disk where it is stored) which induces a definitive loss of associated Bitcoins.[19] In reality, the vulnerability and the high risk are illustrated by repeated incidents of major fraud such as the hacking of Coincheck in January 2018 (US$534 million were stolen), or the collapse in 2015 of

[19] Guegan (2018) noted that about 3 million bitcoins were lost.

MtGox (the first global Bitcoin exchange). Guegan (2018) enumerates many hackages notably this occurred February 2014 in the trading platform, MtGox, causing that over 70% of global Bitcoin transactions went bankrupt and a loss of the equivalent of more than $450 million. As "double-spending" attacks are profitable and no reputation loss in a decentralized system, the risk of counterfeiters is important (Auer, 2019). Moreover, if the block rewards of miners' income is eliminated progressively, the security of payments will be attenuated, and the Bitcoin's liquidity will fall substantially.

Putting the pieces of the aforementioned analysis together shows the absence of guarantee mechanisms, causing that the payment system has been compromised. As there is no insurance for deposit of private cryptocurrencies, users are not able to get their money back in the case of platform bankrupts, causing irreversible losses (Guegan, 2018).

These problems of payment system occur even in a dual banking system. In GCC countries, where Islamic finance is developed, Damak (2019) point out that Fintech may constitute a potential threat for money transfer as expatriates in these countries send more than $100 billion every year back home. At medium term, the author anticipates that this will causes some disruption in the payment services sector. We think that the development of cryptocurrencies in dual system will affect both conventional and Islamic banks. Nowadays, Islamic banks, for example, Emirates Islamic Bank, use the application of blockchain and quick response code technologies in order to reduce fraud, and enhance the security and traceability of transactions.

To sum up, to face payment system issues caused by private cryptocurrencies, it is advised, following Auer (2019),[20] to establish a semi-decentralized payment system (decentralized and coordination mechanisms tied to the legal system).

Effects of Private Cryptocurrencies on Banks' Activity

The distributed ledger technology may remove the need for an intermediary (Andersen, 2018). If there is a large flow from deposit accounts to private cryptocurrencies, this might significantly affect the commercial banks and all banking system. Consequently, deposit-related services offered by banks such as loans, wealth management and financial advice

[20] Auer (2019) recommended also the "proof-of-stake".

can be unbundled. Moreover, there is a change in the way money is created (He, 2018). In fact, unlike conventional banking system based on credit money, Crypto assets are not based on any credit relationship and are "more like commodity money in nature". Moreover, we highlight that due to the increased cost of their funding, commercial banks may raise their lending rate. They could increase the asset risk curve in order to earn more returns. Indeed, to face the reduced activity and maintain their profitability, commercial banks could engage riskier forms of lending to offset the higher cost of funding, this may cause financial stability risks (BIS, 2018). However, the net effect on credit supply by the bank is very difficult to quantify and other factors must be considered in the bank lending process: capital requirements, regulation, and the perspectives of economy. Nelson (2018) shows that leverage is low in digital investments and concludes that the effect of bursting bubbles on the banking system is small. Besides, one can anticipate that this contributes to the development of crypto banking.[21] In a white paper, EVOX coin report (2018, p. 4) highlights that as the cryptocurrency market grows "financial institutions will need to cater to these needs and give individuals a way to manage their money and store it in a safe and friendly environment".

According to Ben Dyson and Hodgson (2016), the peer-to-peer lending is simply a transfer of preexisting deposits and it is not created money. Thereby, the production is not elastic, and it does not depend on what the public is willing to hold. It is rather based on the principle of scarcity by which the number of virtual coins to be produced is capped (Oubdi & Raghibi, 2018).[22] For example, Bitcoin in circulation is scheduled to converge at its limit of 21 million units by 2035 (Berentsen & Schär, 2018). With cryptocurrencies, there is a guarantee with a mathematical certainty that the originator of the transfer owns the underlying assets. There is no possibility to create "fake" cryptocurrencies. Besides, regarding the withdrawing reserves from system banking, the multiplier of credit is reduced, and the money banking creation is limited. Nevertheless, Danielsson (2018) demonstrates that monetary system based on cryptocurrencies induces a persistent deflation and so prices falling combined with distributional and social consequences. It is worth noting that the mining controls

[21] Besides, banks take advantage from the cryptographic technologies allowing lower transaction costs, greater speed of transactions and higher security and transparence.

[22] The limited supply allows more credibility in considering them as money (Jenkinson, 2017).

only the crypto-base money but not the crypto credit. Thereby, the money creation is not under control and the money supply will be procyclical and causes financial crisis. Inevitably, coins would lead to the creation of crypto M1, M2, and M3.

In a dual system, conventional or Islamic financial institutions coexist under the unique financial and monetary authority. Similar to conventional banks, the intermediation activity of Islamic bank is basically reliant on the deposit fund for the assets financing and liquidity management. Thus, the competitive currency coming from cryptocurrency will be potentially added to the competition with conventional banks, leading so to more challenge for Islamic banks business model. Overall, Damak (2019) considers that Fintech presents both a potential threat and an opportunity for the Islamic finance industry. At the end of February 2018, the edition of "IFN Islamic Fintech Landscape" of Standard & Poor's 2018 highlights that there were around 100 Islamic Fintech companies. Especially, about 70% of these companies were active in financial services provision (money transfer, crowdfunding, and digital banking) while 30% operate in technical infrastructure (IT, artificial intelligence, and robotics among other things).

Nevertheless, Islamic banks cannot act on interest rate to face the competition of cryptocurrencies. Their ability of money creation is less than conventional ones. In Islamic view, Central Bank should ensure no sort of monetary inflation and should regulate the supply of money at the target stock of money (Chapra, 1996). In consequence, the effect of private cryptocurrencies on Islamic bank activity seems lower compared to conventional ones.

To judge how far cryptocurrencies have come to potentially affect Islamic bank activity, we here summarize the relative importance of cryptocurrencies against Islamic banking assets. We do so by comparing the market capitalization of cryptocurrencies[23] with the amount of Islamic banking assets.

A plot of cryptocurrency market capitalization for the period 2013–2019 is obtained from CoinMarketCap.com. After a period of relative tranquility, the total market capitalization of cryptocurrencies has been increasing since late 2015. In one year (from May 2016 to May 2017), the market capitalization doubled. On January 8, 2018, a peak is occurred with a

[23] The market capitalization is the product of the circulating supply of cryptocurrencies and their price.

market capitalization of US$814.2 billion, with a 24-hour transaction volume of US$43.6 billion. At the end of 2018, the top-10 cryptocurrencies represent almost 14.82% of US GDP (2017) (Clark & Mihailov, 2019). The cryptocurrency market capitalization reached about US$260 billion of capitalization in mid-2019. Over the period 2013–May 2019, the average annual growth rate was about 130.9%.

Bitcoin is by far the most important cryptocurrency but its market share has been steadily decreasing. It was responsible for about 68.9% of the capitalization on August 21, 2019.[24] Besides, Bitcoin is the most volatile cryptocurrency followed by Bitcoin Cash and Ethereum.[25]

Islamic banking is dominating the Islamic financing industry with a share of 71% of Islamic finance assets in 2017.[26] It has evolved in a remarkable way since the subprime crisis. In 2013, Islamic banking asset was about US$1.565 billion and increased to about US$1.72 trillion[27] in 2017. Islamic total assets increased by only 2% in 2018 and will continue to expand slowly in 2019–2020 (S&P Report, 2020).[28] Over the period 2013–May 2019, the average annual growth rate of Islamic banking assets was about 3.1% (S&P Report, 2019).

The effect of private cryptocurrencies on Islamic banking activity seems far away. First, the current volume of cryptocurrency market is smaller than the volume Islamic banking assets. In 2018, it was almost five times larger than the cryptocurrency market, which means that in terms of volume there is a significant difference. Second, the characteristics of evolution are not the same. For comparison, the average of evolution of Islamic banking assets over the period 2013–2019 was about 3.1% against 130.9% for cryptocurrency market capitalization. What is interesting is that the increasing evolution of Islamic banking is stable, while cryptocurrencies evolution is unstable with some turbulence. Third, the share of Islamic Banking Assets in the Global Banking Assets in 2017 for 43 countries was only 6%. This testifies that the effect of cryptocurrencies is more pronounced for conventional banks compared to Islamic ones. Except the Iran's banking system that has been fully Islamic since 1983, the top global Islamic banking markets—Saudi Arabia, Malaysia, the UAE, and

[24] https://coinmarketcap.com, retrieved on August 21, 2019.

[25] Yet, the lowest volatility among the cryptocurrencies is displayed by XRP, XLM and TRX (Clark & Mihailov, 2019).

[26] Rapport IFSB 2018.

[27] https://ceif.iba.edu.pk/pdf/Reuters-Islamic-finance-development-report2018.pdf

[28] In 2020, Islamic banking is reaching $2.6 trillion (Thomson Reuters' projections).

Qatar—are dual systems and they represent about 53.4% of the total of US$1.6 trillion in 2017. The largest Islamic banking share in total banking assets reached (51.5%) in Saudi Arabia, and it remains 24.9%, 20%, and 25.7% in Malaysia, the UAE, and Qatar, respectively (Islamic Financial Services Industry Stability Report, 2018—IFSB). Fourth, we think that the effect of cryptocurrency on Islamic bank activity is mainly related to the legal consideration of cryptocurrencies by monetary authorities in each country. As the Thomson Reuters report "Cryptocurrencies by Countries" (2017) outlined, Bitcoin is not recognized as legal tender in Malaysia, and Bank Negara Malaysia does not regulate the operations of Bitcoin. Besides, in many countries such as Saudi Arabia, Pakistan, and Bangladesh where Islamic banks coexist with conventional ones, the Bitcoin is forbidden.

Effects of Private Cryptocurrencies on Financial Stability

Cryptocurrencies pose a serious challenge to the business model of the established financial system (He et al., 2016).

Cryptocurrencies could be a challenge to the monopoly of official Central Bank-controlled currencies (Claeys et al., 2018), and the role of Central Bank may be reduced (Andersen, 2018). Thereby, Amihud and Cukierman (2018) indicate that the loss of seigniorage income from issuing its own currency leads to increased taxes which, in turn, hampers the welfare. Indeed, seigniorage constitutes an important source of income for sovereign governments. Furthermore, fairness concerns arise if cryptocurrencies replace fiat money. In this context, the expropriations of public goods (fiat money) result in the crypto-fortunes and precisely crypto-speculators (Danielsson, 2018). It is unfair that the power becomes in the hands of a small number of "shadowy and uncountable entities" and not the Central Banks which are democracy controlled. He (2018) notes that Central Banks could remain relevant by not only providing a more stable unit of account than cryptocurrencies but also by making Central Bank money attractive as a medium of exchange in the digital world.

Due to cryptocurrencies, the ability of Central banks to control issuing money or over the economy is altered as noted by both the Bank for International Settlements (BIS) and the world's leading Central Banks in November 2017. In this regard, in the absence of an important monetary policy instrument, there is a a concern of economy stabilization in the case of economic shocks (Amihud & Cukierman, 2018).[29] This loss of control over monetary policy is detrimental in normal and exceptional context.[30] In a context of single private world digital currency, there is no ability to affect the exchange rate by the instruments of monetary policy notably through short-term interest rates. The theoretical paper of Benigno (2019) investigates the effect of the coexistence of both monies in competition (fiat money and cryptocurrency) on monetary policy and demonstrates that the growth rate of cryptocurrency fixed a lower bound on the nominal interest rate and consequently Central Bank losses the control of target inflation rate and the overall macroeconomic variables. In addition, in economic crisis, the government has not the ability to temporarily suspend the interdiction on expanding the money due to the rigidity of the cryptocurrencies supply. In this view, He (2018) highlights three issues with crypto-assets: first, the protection against the risk of structural deflation, second the ability to smooth the business cycle by the response to temporary shocks of money demand and third, the capacity of the lender of last resort. If there is a crisis in crypto-system trust, the panic occurs notably due to the lack of central authority to provide the required liquidity assistance (Danielsson, 2018).

At macroeconomic level, given the scarcity of private cryptocurrencies and the high demand for speculative purposes, there are very large price fluctuations which, in turn, pose financial stability threats. The rigid predetermined supply of Bitcoin does not lead to a stable currency because the price of Bitcoin also depends on aggregate demand (Berentsen & Schär, 2018). This results in a complete detachment of the cryptocurrency supply growth to forecasted or estimated cryptocurrency demand growth (Clark & Mihailov, 2019). However, in fiat currency systems, the Central Bank seeks to stabilize the price level by adjusting the money supply in response to changes in aggregate demand for money. So, in the absence of a Central Bank with power to adjust the money supply, cryptocurrencies cannot offer stability (Ammous, 2018). Cryptocurrencies are governed by primarily anonymous groups of private agents without deep knowledge of monetary economics and policy. In this regard, risks of financial instability

[29] Yet, Nelson (2018) notes that digital currencies present minimal risks to monetary policy as they are unlikely to replace fiat paper currency.

[30] Amihud and Cukierman (2018) recommend that sovereign governments constraints the expansion of Bitcoin.

may eventually emerge as the new technologies become more widely used (He et al., 2016).

According to Danielsson (2018), the cryptocurrencies system presents additional forms of systemic risk which are not present in fiat system and, consequently, a higher systemic risk than both gold standard system and well-managed fiat monetary system. Moreover, the cryptosystem is notably vulnerable to endogenous systemic risk because of its presumed stability. However, the "stability is destabilizing" (Minsky, 1986) because in the case of stability, economic agents are encouraged to take more and more risks. The cryptocurrency market is becoming more integrated than the past and it shows an evidence of contagion effect between Bitcoin and the other cryptocurrencies, excepting Tether (Ferreira & Pereira, 2019). Authors conclude that cryptocurrencies are now more exposed to possible price shocks in the dominant cryptocurrency (Bitcoin). There is an evidence of the possible existence of bubbles in cryptocurrency markets (Corbet et al., 2018;[31] Chaim & Márcio, 2019). We think that cryptocurrencies which are internationally used help to propagate financial contagion during a crisis.

Furthermore, we believe that a *sharia*-compliant private cryptocurrency affects the financial stability differently. We argue that *sharia*-compatible cryptocurrencies could improve financial stability and contribute to reach the objectives of Islamic law. Indeed, if we avoid speculative rationale and agents feel their money is safe, *sharia*-compliant cryptocurrency is able to fulfil the three functions of money. Besides, the stability of the money value is guaranteed and so the financial stability is sustained. We discussed that cryptocurrency *sharia* compliance is controlled by authorities which may remove financial crisis and establish a stable environment. These arguments support the idea of a better financial stability in a dual banking system compared to conventional one.

Conclusion

The private cryptocurrencies are unregulated as they are issued and generally controlled by their developers. This chapter examines the impact of private cryptocurrencies on the payment system, bank activity, and the

[31] Corbet et al., 2018. Date stamping the Bitcoin and Ethereum bubbles. *Finance Research Letters, 26*, 81–88.

financial stability. Further, we discuss these issues for dual banking system while considering the *sharia*-compatible cryptocurrency.

The use of cryptocurrencies in the payment system through the distributed ledger technology enables the decentralization of the transaction settlement without a central authority which constitutes a revolution in the financial system controlled conventionally by monetary authorities. The rapid development of the digital technology constitutes the principal concern for the Central Banks to consider whether to regulate private digital currency, to conduct monetary policy or to issue and design their own digital currency. We show that the widespread use of private currencies causes a compromised payment system notably with the absence of guarantee mechanisms. The competition that comes from cryptocurrency will be potentially added to the competition with conventional banks, leading to more challenge for Islamic banks business model. Yet, the effect of private cryptocurrencies on Islamic banks seems nowadays far away. Moreover, the overall impact of cryptocurrencies on financial stability may depend on the behaviour of economic agents over time. However, the *sharia*-compatible cryptocurrency can avoid many concerns and ensure better financial stability and social cohesion in a dual system.

Government authorities should regulate the use of cryptocurrencies to prevent regulatory arbitrage and any unfair competitive advantage crypto assets that may derive from lighter regulation. That means rigorously applying measures to prevent money laundering and the financing of terrorism, strengthening consumer protection, and effectively taxing the crypto transactions (He, 2018). Spithoven (2019) considers that without strong external regulation, cryptocurrency may being like Veblenian (predatory) markets.

We recommend an adequate regulation of cryptocurrency and the adoption of *Sharia*-compliant cryptocurrency to guarantee the financial system stability.

References

Adam, M. F. (2017). *Bitcoin: Shariah Compliant?* Amanah Finance Consultancy, 1–54. Retrieved from http://darulfiqh.com/wp-content/uploads/2017/08/Research-Paper-on-Bitcoin-Mufti-Faraz-Adam.pdf

Ahmad, A. U. F., & Hassan, M. K. (2006). The Time Value of Money Concept in Islamic Finance. *American Journal of Islamic Social Sciences, 23*(1), 66.

Albahouth, A. S. A. (2018). Crypto-Currency: Concept, Typology and Economic Impacts. *Scientific Journal of Economics and Trade*, (1) (*in Arabic*).

Ali, R., Barrdear, J., Clews, R. M., & Southgate, J. (2014). The Economics of Digital Currencies. Bank of England. *Quarterly Bulletin, Q3.*

Almarzoqi, R. M., Mansour, W., & Krichen, N. (2018). *Islamic Macroeconomics: A Model for Efficient Government, Stability and Full Employment* (1st ed.). Routledge.

Amihud, Y., & Cukierman, A. (2018, October 9). The Macroeconomic Perils of a World with a Private Digital Currency and How to Address Them. *VoxEU.org.*

Ammous, S. (2018). Can Cryptocurrencies Fulfil the Functions of Money? *The Quarterly Review of Economics and Finance, 70*, 38–51.

Andersen, C. L. (2018, June). Our Digital Future, Editor's Letter, Finance & Development. *International Monetary Fund.*

Antonakakis, N., Chatziantoniou, I., & Gabauer, D. (2019). Cryptocurrency market contagion: Market uncertainty, market complexity, and dynamic portfolios. *Journal of International Financial Markets, Institutions and Money*, 61,37–51.

Auer R. (2019). *Beyond the Doomsday Economics of "Proof-of Work" in Cryptocurrencies.* BIS Working Papers No. 765.

Bank of England. (2014). *Quarterly Bulletin, Q1, 54*(1).

Banque de France. (2018, March 5). The Emergence of Bitcoin and Other Crypto-Assets: Challenges, Risks and Outlook. Banque de France. *Focus*, No. 16.

Bech, M., & Garratt, R. (2017, September). Central Bank Cryptocurrencies. *BIS Quarterly Review*, 55–70.

Benedetti, H., & Kostovesky, L. (2018, May 20). Digital Tulips? Returns to Investors in Initial Coin Offerings.

Benigno, P. (2019, February). *Monetary Policy in a World of Cryptocurrencies.* Centre for Economic Policy Research Discussion Paper 13517.

Berentsen, A., & Schär, F. (2018). A Short Introduction to the World of Cryptocurrencies. *Federal Reserve Bank of St. Louis Review, First Quarter 2018.*

BIS (Bank for International Settlements). (2018, March). *Central Bank Digital Currencies, Committee on Payments and Market Infrastructures.* Retrieved from https://www.bis.org/cpmi/publ/d174.pdf

Bordo, M. D., & Levin, A. T. (2017, August). *Central Bank Digital Currency and the Future of Monetary Policy.* NBER Working Paper No. 23711.

Bouveret, A., & Haksar, V. (2018, June). What Are Crypto-Currencies? *Finance & Development, International Monetary Fund*, 26–35.

Budish, E. (2018, June). *The Economic Limits of Bitcoin and the Blockchain.* NBER Working Papers, No. 24717.

Caporal, G. M., Gil-Alana, L., & Plastun, A. (2018). Long-Term Price Overreactions: Are Markets Inefficient? *Journal of Economics and Finance.* https://doi.org/10.1007/s12197-018-9464-8

Carstens, A. (2018, November 15). *Money in a Digital Age: 10 Thoughts, Speech at Lee Kuan Yew School of Public Policy, Singapore*. Retrieved from https://www.bis.org/speeches/sp181115a.pdf

Chaim, P., & Márcio, L. (2019). Is Bitcoin a Bubble? *Physica A, 517*, 222–232.

Chapra, M. U. (1996). Monetary Policy in an Islamic Economy. In Z. Ahmed, M. Iqbal, & M. Fahim Khan (Eds.), *Money and Banking in Islam* (pp. 27–46). Islamabad, Pakistan: Institute of Policy Studies.

Claeys, G., Demertzis, M., & Efstathiou, K. (2018). *Cryptocurrencies and Monetary Policy*. IPOL, Policy Department for Economic, Scientific and Quality of Life Policies.

Clark, A., & Mihailov, A. (2019). *Why Private Cryptocurrencies Cannot Serve as International Reserves but Central Bank Digital Currencies Can?* Discussion Paper No. 2019-09. Department of Economics, Henley Business School, Reading University.

Corbet, S., Meegan, A., Larkin, C., Lucey, B., & Yarovaya, L. (2018). Exploring the Dynamic Relationships Between Cryptocurrencies and Other Financial Assets. *Economics Letters, 165*, 28–34.

Corbet, S., Lucey, B., Urquhart, A., & Yarovaya, L. (2019). Cryptocurrencies as a Financial Asset: A Systematic Analysis. *International Review of Financial Analysis, 62*(C), 182–199.

Damak, M. (2019). The Future of Banking: Islamic Finance Needs Standardization and FinTech to Boost Growth. *Islamic Finance Outlook*, S&P 2019. Retrieved from https://ceif.iba.edu.pk/pdf/Islamic_Finance_201911.pdf

Danielsson, J. (2018). *Cryptocurrencies: Policy, Economics and Fairness*. Systemic Risk Centre Discussion Paper 86. Retrieved from SSRN: https://ssrn.com/abstract=3276606 or https://doi.org/10.2139/ssrn.3276606

Das, S. (2017, May 29). OneGram Launches $500 Million ICO for Sharia-Compliant Gold-Backed Digital Currency. *Crypto Coins News*. Retrieved from https://www.cryptocoinsnews.com/onegram-launches-500-million-ico-sharia-compliant-gold-backed-digital-currency/

Dhaliwal, S. (2017, February 23). Is Bitcoin Halal? How Cryptocurrency Conforms with Shariah. *Coin Telegraph*. Retrieved from https://cointelegraph.com/news/is-bitcoin-halal-how-cryptocurrency-conforms-with-islam-and-sharia

Dyson, B., & Hodgson, G. (2016). Digital Cash – Why Central Banks Should Start Issuing Electronic Money. *Positive Money*.

Engert, W., Ben, S. C., & Fung, B. S. (2017, November). *Central Bank Digital Currency: Motivations and Implications*. Bank of Canada Staff Discussion Paper 2017-16. Retrieved from https://www.bankofcanada.ca/wp-content/uploads/2017/11/sdp2017-16.pdf

Easley, D., O'Hara, M., & Basu, S. (2019). From mining to markets: The evolution of bitcoin transaction fees. *Journal of Financial Economics, 134*(1), 91–109.

Evans, C. W. (2015). Bitcoin in Islamic Banking and Finance. *Journal of Islamic Banking and Finance, 3*(1), 1–11.

EVOX Coin Report. (2018). *Evolution of Crypto Banking, Whitepaper, Version 1.0.2.* Retrieved from https://www.evoxcoin.io/wpcontent/uploads/2018/08/Evo_Whitepaper_v1.0.2.pdf

Ferreira, P., & Pereira, E. (2019). Contagion Effect in Cryptocurrency Market. *Journal of Risk and Financial Management, MDPI, Open Access Journal, 12*(3), 1–8.

Fry, J., & Cheah, E.-T. (2016). Negative Bubbles and Shocks in Cryptocurrency Markets. *International Review of Financial Analysis, 47*, 343–352.

Fung, B. S. C., & Halaburda, H., (2016, November). *Central Bank Digital Currencies: A Framework for Assessing Why and How.* Bank of Canada Staff Discussion Paper 2016-22.

Gandal, N., & Halaburda, H. (2016). Can We Predict the Winner in a Market with Network Effects? Competition in Cryptocurrency Market. *Games, 7*(3), 16.

Geiger, P. (2017, September 11). Get into Bitcoin Before the Next Financial Crisis. *Medium.* Retrieved from https://medium.com/@philgeiger/get-into-bitcoin-before-the-next-financial-crisis-f0707e2d56c1

Glaser, F., et al. (2014). *Bitcoin-Asset or Currency? Revealing Users' Hidden Intentions. Revealing Users' Hidden Intentions.* ECIS.

Grym, A., Heikkinen, P., Kauko, K., & Takala, K. (2017). Central Bank Digital Currency, Bank of Finland, 5. *BoF Economics Review.* Bank of Finland.

Guegan, D. (2018). *The Digital World: I – Bitcoin: From History to Real Live.* Documents de travail du Centre d'Economie de la Sorbonne 2018.11 – ISSN: 1955-611X. 2018. halshs-01822962.

He, D. (2018, June). Monetary Policy in the Digital Age. IMF. *Finance & Development*, 13–16.

He, D., Habermeier, K., Leckow, R., Haksar, V., Almeida, Y., Kashima, M., et al. (2016). *Virtual Currencies and Beyond: Initial Considerations.* IMF Staff Discussion Note. SDN/16/03.

Huberman, G., Leshno, J., & Moellemi, C. (2017). *Monopoly Without a Monopolist: An Economic Analysis of the Bitcoin Payment System.* Columbia Business School Research Papers, No. 17-92.

IMF. (2018, October 24–26). *Treatment of Crypto Assets in Macroeconomic Statistics.* Thirdy – First Meeting of the IMF Committee on Balance of Payments Statistics, Washington, DC.

Ingves, S. (2018, June). Going Cashless. IMF. *Finance & Development.*

Islamic Financial Services Industry Stability Report. (2018). *IFSB, Islamic Financial Services Industry Stability Report.* Retrieved from https://www.ifsb.org

Jenkinson, G. (2017, December 5). Keiser-Bitcoin Like 'Moses' for Gold. *Coin Telegraph*. Retrieved from https://cointelegraph.com/news/keiser-bitcoin-like-moses-forgold

Kahf, M. (2014). *Fatwa on Bitcoin*. Retrieved from http://lightuponlight.com/blog/fatwa-on-bitcoin-by-monzer-kahf/

Lietaer, B. A. (2001). *The future of money: Creating new wealth, work and a wiser world*. London: Random House Business.

Maierbrugger, A. (2017, June 27). Shariah-Compliant, Gold-Backed Digi-Coins Could Change Islamic Finance. *Gulf-Times*. Retrieved from http://www.gulf-times.com/story/554731/Shariah-compliant-gold-backed-digi-coins-could-cha

Meera, A. K. M. (2018). Cryptocurrencies from Islamic Perspectives: The Case of Bitcoin. *Bulletin of Monetary Economics and Banking, 20*(4), 475–492.

Mensi, W., Mobeen, R., Khamis, A., Idries, A., & Sang, K. (2019). Time Frequency Analysis of the Commonalities Between Bitcoin and Major Cryptocurrencies: Portfolio Risk Management Implications. *The North American Journal of Economics and Finance, 48*, 283–294.

Minsky, H. (1986). *Stabilizing an Unstable Economy*. Yale University Press.

Muedini, F. (2018). The Compatibility of Cryptocurrencies and Islamic Finance. *European Journal of Islamic Finance*, (10), 1–10.

Mufti Adam Faraz. (2017). *Bitcoin: Shari'ah-compliant?* Research Paper, Amanah Finance Consultancy.

Mühleisen, M. (2018, June). The Long and Short of the Digital Revolution, Finance & Development. *International Monetary Fund*, 4–10.

Nakamoto, S. (2008). *A Peer-to-Peer Electronic Cash System*. Retrieved from https://bitcoin.org/bitcoin.pdf

Nelson, B. (2018). Financial Stability and Monetary Policy Issues Associated with Digital Currencies. *Journal of Economics and Business, 100*, 76–78.

Oubdi, L., & Raghibi, A. (2018). La perception des cryptomonnaies selon la loi islamique: une analyse critique. *Recherches et Applications en Finance Islamique, 2*(2), 161–173.

Oziev, G., & Yandiev, M. (2017). *Cryptocurrency from Shari'ah Perspective*, 1–18.

Ozili, P. K. (2018). Impact of Digital Finance on Financial Inclusion and Stability. *Borsa Istanbul Review, 18*(4), 329–340.

Papadopoulos, G. (2015). Expanding on Ceremonial Encapsulation: The Case of Financial Innovation. *Journal of Economic Issues, 49*(1), 127–142.

Prasad, E. (2018, April). *Central Banking in a Digital Age: Stock-Taking and Preliminary Thoughts*. Hutchins Center on Fiscal & Monetary Policy at Brookings. Retrieved from https://www.brookings.edu/wp-content/uploads/2018/04/es_20180416_digitalcurrencies.pdf

Siegfried, N. A. (2001). Concepts of Paper Money in Islamic Legal Thought. *Arab Law Quarterly, 16*(4), 319–332.

Spithoven, A. (2019). Theory and Reality of Cryptocurrency Governance. *Journal of Economic Issues, 53*(2), 385–393.

Swielem, S. (2018, August 14). *About Crypto-Currencies.* Conference at University Mohamed Ben Saoud Al-Islamiya.

S&P Report. (2019). Islamic Finance Outlook 2019 Edition, available at https://ceif.iba.edu.pk/pdf/Islamic_Finance_201911.pdf

S&P Report. (2020). Islamic Finance Outlook, retrieved from https://www.spglobal.com/_assets/documents/ratings/research/islamic_finance_2020_screen.pdf

Thomsons Reuters. (2017, October 25). *Cryptocurrencies by Country, Answers for Fax Professional.* Retrieved from https://blogs.thomsonreuters.com/answerson/world-cryptocurrencies-country/

Urquhart, A. (2018). What Causes the Attention to Bitcoin? *Economics Letters, 166*, 40–44.

Williamson, S. (2018). Is Bitcoin a Waste of Resources? *Federal Reserve Bank of St. Louis Review, 200*(2), 107–115.

CHAPTER 10

Islamic FinTech and Financial Inclusion

Aishath Muneeza and Zakariya Mustapha

Abstract The modern Islamic finance as an offshoot of financial engineering is the product of permissible innovation as a manifestation of the dynamism of Islam which allows for permanence and continued relevance of Islam in any age to come. Using technology or any permissible means to bring about financial solutions in society that ease human life is an integral part of the overall objectives of Shariah. Speaking in economic terms, Sharia strives at individual prosperity as much as of the society on the ideal that prosperity of individuals that make up a society underlies the prosperity of the society. In this modern age and time, financial inclusion constitutes a fundamental component of most governmental policies and action plans aimed at ensuring prosperity of society via improved social welfare to eradicate poverty and enhance living standard. Financial inclusion constitutes a fundamental component of such policies and action plans. Accordingly, Islamic finance is said to be committed to the ideal of financial inclusion having regard to its ideal of bringing prosperity to individuals and society in such a way that will translate to and help

A. Muneeza
INCEIF, Lorong Universiti A, Kuala Lumpur, Malaysia
e-mail: muneeze@inceif.org

Z. Mustapha
University of Malaya, Jalan Universiti, Kuala Lumpur, Malaysia

M. M. Billah (ed.), *Islamic FinTech*,
https://doi.org/10.1007/978-3-030-45827-0_10

economies grow. This is to be pursued through every permissible means now available or to be invented in future, within the confines of Islamic values of financing.

Keywords FinTech • Islamic • Shari'ah • Finance • Financial Inclusion

Introduction

The emergence of Islamic finance in the modern finance scene has facilitated the development of alternative in the way banks and other financial institutions play their intermediation role. The Islamic alternative has enabled access to finance, investments and trading opportunities for growth, development and prosperity of society in a way that is not only cheaper but easier as well. Islamic finance has accordingly been recognized as a force to be reckoned with in the financial services industry globally. Often spoken in term of bringing banking services to the unbanked or non-banked and underbanked, financial inclusion is a way more than that given the context and dimension of financial services today where financial services are offered by non-bank financial services providers as well. Thus, financial inclusion is being enabled not by banks alone but by all other financial services companies that offer their services leveraging on technology that gives digital access and use of finance. Governments and corporate financial entities are turning attention to FinTech by investing in it in order to tap its potentials and improve their business. For corporate financial institutions, banks and non-banks alike, FinTech has already become the new normal. For government and regulators, is embraced with view to inclusion aimed at policy making for developmental projections. Thus, in the past few years, investments in FinTech has grown by over 201 per cent globally, in contrast to total investments in other segment of the finance industry, for example, venture capital, which grew by only about 63 per cent within the same period (Aldridge, and Krawciw, 2017; p.3).

In the face of the FinTech evolution, traditional financial institutions, banks in particular, are challenged by a new breed of non-bank, technology-driven entities that are fast spreading and developing all around the world. However, understanding the fact that FinTech has come to stay as the new normal for providing financial services, banks are doing away with all reservation against adopting the technology. Thus, financial institutions all around the world are doing all they can to jump on the FinTech bandwagon and partake in its ensuing revolution which is envisaged to phase out traditional financial intermediation and enable countless innovations for same purpose. The rate at which technologies generally evolve and develop today is so rapid and universal that every human endeavour can be potentially transformed. This explains why financial services providers resort to technology in their businesses with unprecedented reliance thereon. It is a gigantic revolution that disrupts the financial services industry through digitization, and so also everything about it, including regulation. Efforts at digitizing financial services provision has led to heavy investments in technology as well, aimed at surviving the revolution and remaining relevant within the financial services industry for all purposes. It is becoming a race against time, with billions of dollars expended to tap new opportunities that are ever unfolding and advancing in favour of FinTech companies with far-reaching returns. Regardless of all prospects, the FinTech phenomenon is both evolutionary and revolutionary in the sense that it is emerging while revolutionizing the financial services industry so much so that a corresponding new mechanism of regulation, known as regulatory technology or regtech, emerges with it, for regulators to prepare decisively and provide suitable regulation (Chakraborty, 2018).

The continuous change and improvement in technology has enabled financial inclusion in several ways that could not be imagined about two decades ago. Thanks to the internet, blockchain and artificial intelligence or machine learning facilitated by big data analytics. Employed in FinTech, these have collectively taken financial inclusion to an unprecedented level. Islamic finance as well, from broader perspective of its objective of ensuring a just society via equitable distribution of wealth, has naturally championed access to finance and thus leads a migration from exclusion to inclusion leveraging on FinTech. This is the reasoning behind the idea of Islamic FinTech and financial inclusion.

The Idea of FinTech and Financial Inclusion

'Fintech' is a portmanteau word that packs up two words—'financial' and 'technology'—which involves the use of computer software and other related technologies to provide support for and/or enable financial services by banks as well as non-bank financial institutions. In other words, FinTech involves a set of financial technologies that comprises, for instance, mobile computing, cloud computing, information and communication technology as well as internet ecosystems and platforms that render financial services and products not just accessible but efficient and affordable. The financial services under the said ecosystems and platforms include banking, funding, payment, lending, trading, investing and currencies (Chakraborty, 2018). FinTech presents a range of transformation to the global financial systems and process in such a way that disrupts incumbent institutions and their operations, though not entirely. As a wave of information transformation, FinTech is a promising phenomenon and is expected to reshape the industries and societies that deal with money, value and trust (Freedman, 2006: 1).

FinTech has made available several avenues and channels that facilitate its thrust and penetration into the financial services industry while leveraging on internet and smart mobile devices. FinTech manifests its presence in mobile wallets, payment apps, crowdfunding platforms, online lending platforms, chatbots and Robo-advisors among others that are trending and making wave in the world today (Chishti and Barberis, 2016).

Financial inclusion is a concept that gained its popularity from the early 2000s, as a common objective for many governments and central banks in developing nations. From the onset, the concept is used in relation to the delivery of financial services to low-income segments of society at affordable cost. However, in the past ten years or so, the concept has evolved to encompass four dimensions as follows: (a) easy access to finance for all households and enterprises, (b) sound institutions guided by prudential regulation and supervision, (c) financial and institutional sustainability of financial institutions, and (d) competition between service providers to bring alternatives to customers (Chishti and Barberis, 2016). Before the advent of FinTech, the financial inclusion of an economy is measured by the proportion of population covered by commercial bank branches and ATMs, sizes of deposits and loans made by low-income households and SMEs. However, it came to be realized that availability of financial services alone may not mean financial inclusion, because people may voluntarily exclude themselves from the financial services on cultural or religious reasons, despite the fact that they have access thereto and can afford the services (Demirguc-Kunt et.al. 2008). Therefore, the opportunity to be financially included has to be provided by taking into cognizance the cultural and the religious considerations of the people meant to be included. This is where Islamic FinTech becomes handy, particularly for Muslims' inclusion.

Financial inclusion is broader in scope. In furtherance of Maya Declaration 2011, which seeks to derive commitment of signatories to direct efforts at ensuring access to finance by those excluded therefrom, financial inclusion has been elaborated further by the Sasana Accord to mean more than just access to financial products and services but also usage of same in addition to quality dimension of the access (AFI, n.d.).

It encompasses not only accessing finance but also usage of finance by poor people in such a way that the access and use impact positively on the people lives. Financial inclusion in other words is doing away with exclusionary factors that hinder such access and use of finance. According to development economists, lack of access to finance by the poor people is a deterrent to key governmental policies and decisions regarding social investment, human and physical capital accumulation. In this regard, it is necessary to enable access and use of finance by the poor people (Demirguc-Kunt et.al. 2008). Poverty has entrapped these people where they are as they cannot save or borrow to survive starvation. Poverty has limited their opportunities and leading to persistent inequality and slower growth. The poor people, described as living on less a US dollar a day or live below poverty line, need to be empowered via financial inclusion for global inclusive growth and development. Financial inclusion is believed to blur the line between the poor and the rich to a certain standard that that would render life more meaningful.

Emergence of FinTech: Its Prospects and Potentials in Financing

FinTech has been described as the 'new normal' for the financial services industry following the global financial crisis just over a decade ago in 2008 and its attendant aftermath of global recession in 2008 to 2012 (Capgemini et.al., 2018). FinTech has been evolving and developing ever since and its influence over incumbent financial institutions and services has been growing. According to available statistics, 82 per cent of incumbent financial institutions were expected to increase FinTech partnership between 2020 and 2022. At the same time, 77 per cent of these institutions were expected to adopt blockchain as part of an in-production system or process by 2020. In terms of return on investment, not less than 20 per cent has been expected as annual rate on investment on FinTech-related projects globally (PwC, 2017). From inception, incumbent financial institutions have viewed FinTech as a threat that put their business at risk. Therefore, mainstream financial institutions having championed the financial services industry viewed FinTech as competitor. However, within a few years, FinTech gained popularity and widespread implantation, with utmost utility and trustworthy potentialities that prove to incumbent the need for adoption and synergy. Thus, FinTechs and financial services firms begin to compete less and come together more. FinTech and finance have become intertwined. Islamic finance has been part and parcel of this development and processes.

Global dimension of FinTech indicates that while FinTech firms and services are focusing more on online customers in developed countries, start-ups are addressing a broader market in developing countries through the use of cell phone and other mobile devices with a comparative advantage. An estimated 95.5 per cent of the world's population, according to the International Telecommunications Union, has access to a cell phone, in contrast to 51.2 per cent that was using the internet as at 2018 (International Telecommunications Union, 2018)—which gives short message service (SMS) an even greater impact than the internet (Chishti and Barberis, 2016). Therefore, the choice of internet or mobile device users as target for financial inclusion depends on region and the availability of either or both services therein. Thus, in Africa and other regions that lack internet access, several mobile money transfer services are being introduced by banks and non-banks financial services providers in taking this opportunity with view to inclusion and broader customer base.

State of Financial Inclusion in Muslim Countries

Financial inclusion measures are found to be low in Muslim majority countries. As it is illustrated in the earlier figure, 71 per cent of Muslims around the world do not have a bank account. One reason for the low rates is that in addition to the common contributors to financial inclusion such as geographical access, possession of necessary IDs and high costs of financial services, Muslims have a religious motive behind their choice of not using financial services under conventional system, as the services offered contain interest among other things that render such services non-Shariah-compliant. It is a part of the Shariah fundamentals to have a just society, with little inequalities, alongside greater social inclusion and equal opportunities to resources. Islamic financial system is designed to provide for these ideals through two ways. Firstly, through stimulating risk-sharing contracts to replace debt-based financing utilized by conventional financing institutions. Secondly, through redistribution of wealth in the society via instruments like Zakat, Waqf and Sadaqah. These ideals have been, to a certain extent, integrated into and provided by Islamic FinTech (Qatar Financial Centre, 2018).

Islamic FinTech and Perspective of Financial Inclusion

Islamic FinTech is at the very beginning of an exciting, transformative journey in Islamic finance industry. With assets expected to reach $3.9 trillion by 2023 according to Thomson Reuters, the Islamic finance industry holds much promise. Moreover, a young, digitally native Muslim demographic that is, on average, younger than the world's non-Muslim population, is the main force driving the growth of Islamic Finance (Dinar Standard and Dubai Islamic Economy Development Centre, 2018). The 'young digital natives', also known as generation Z, comprises young people that have been born and raised completely with the internet, and as such have very strong expectations of digital financial services. This is a strong base for FinTech in Islamic finance. Islamic FinTech has potential to disrupt all aspects of the Islamic finance industry, be it banking, takaful or Islamic Capital Market. Islamic financial institutions have already identified the potentials of FinTech and the opportunities it presents for the taking. Generational factors, including blockchain technology and artificial intelligence, already being applied in Islamic financial products and services development, have fuelled the development and sophistication of FinTech companies to challenge mainstream financial institutions. Islamic FinTechs have enhanced the making of competitive products and services among Islamic financial firms, increased their productivity and is fast overhauling the way they provide and offer such products and services. The outcome of all these has positively impacted not just in providing a widespread access and usage of finance to people hitherto excluded but the efficiency of such access and usage. As in all other spheres of activity where technology is involved, Islamic FinTech has significantly reduced the cost of intermediation for Islamic financial institutions regardless of the resulting expansion of access to large number of people. With view to inclusion, Islamic FinTech has facilitated attainment of other goals in Islamic finance, including poverty reduction and social empowerment.

Within the scope of inclusion as aimed by Islamic FinTech is the integration of Islamic social finance into Islamic financial services as well. Thus, Islamic social financing avenues of Sadaqah (charity), Waqf (endowment) and zakat (religious tax) have found expression and mobilization within the fold of Islamic FinTech for the purpose of financial inclusion. FinTech in general can be harnessed to offer relevant and sustainable financial services and products to serve the need of all while safeguarding Shariah ends (Moheildin et.al. 2012). The concept of zakat could be expanded to provide a sustainable source of income for the poor. Zakat has great potential as the main resource of social spending supporting poverty alleviation in Islamic society. It is seen as a significant tool for promoting financial inclusion and economic growth. Waqf is basically real properties that is voluntarily donated for philanthropic purposes. Although Waqf is dominated by fixed property mainly land or buildings, but can be applicable also to cash, shares, stocks and other assets. In modern Islamic economic, Waqf is disbursed to beneficiaries using FinTech, for the purpose of providing social services in addition to health, education and related services meant to improve welfare of the society. Importantly, all recipients and beneficiaries empowered through these mechanisms have been documented which provides official data for government financial interventions policies, besides serving inclusion purpose.

The operations of these means of social finance through Islamic FinTech has brought millions of Muslims access and usage of financial products and services by banks and non-banks financial institutions alike. The workability of Islamic social financing via Islamic FinTech has made possible the seamless distribution of wealth among Muslim societies and this has enabled the societies achieve significant balance between wealth creation and wealth sharing in line with Shariah objectives. Moreover, Islamic FinTech has enabled Islamic financial institutions to establish several start-ups as channels and avenues for payments, remittances, partnerships and crowdfunding investing through which wealth circulate and more people get access to finance in the process (Ali, 2018). In general, Islamic FinTech has been envisaged to enable Islamic finance attract more customers, increase its efficiency, reduce costs and offer a wider range of products that will help the sector become more competitive against conventional finance without compromising on profit margins (Qatar Financial Centre, 2018).

Financial Inclusion via Islamic FinTech

One of the Islamic FinTech key drivers that enhances financial inclusion is the young, digitally native Muslim demographic. With 24 years as the median age in Muslims countries worldwide, the Muslim demographic has rightly been described as young in comparison to 32 years globally. The Muslim consumers are young and demand digital change. In addition to this fact, 15 of the world's top-50 countries with smartphone penetration are Islamic countries. However, 72 per cent of Organisation of Islamic Cooperation (OIC) member countries' population which constitute the core Islamic finance market are unbanked, in contrast to 49 per cent worldwide. These parameters have set the pace for Islamic FinTech to bring in the desired financial inclusion. Therefore, this category of consumers otherwise referred to as the digitally native Muslim demographic is a major force in pushing for innovation in Islamic finance with governments, especially where governments with broader Islamic economy strategies are leading the response. Another key driver is government. Government initiatives towards Islamic FinTech propel financial inclusion. Accordingly, and fund wise, the Dubai International Financial Centre (DIFC) is to invest 100 million dollars in FinTech start-ups for Islamic finance in the country. In similar vein, Bahrain and Malaysian governments set up 'regulatory sandbox' to support FinTech growth. The governments drive change in the Islamic finance ecosystem through the establishment of digital Islamic economy based largely on FinTech. The digital Islamic economy is a broader area of strategic importance that several companies in OIC member countries are prioritising, with a particular focus on Islamic FinTech. Such governmental initiatives aimed at establishing digital Islamic economy include DIFC, Malaysia Digital Economy Corporation (MDEC), Bahrain FinTech Bay and Indonesia Financial Services Authority, among others. These organizations have undertaken and are in charge of various forms of Islamic start-ups for the purpose of inclusion. One more key driver of inclusion comprises FinTech start-ups themselves. As of 2018, there are globally over 93 Islamic FinTech players providing different kind of Islamic products and services that are made cheaply accessible (Dinar Standard and Dubai Islamic Economy Development Centre, 2018).

With a rapidly emerging ecosystem, the first effort in responding to the need for innovative digital Islamic finance solution is advanced by Islamic FinTech start-ups. In order to support these start-ups, notable corresponding incubators and accelerators are equally emerging which at the same time offer the potential of capable funding of business proposals. Such start-ups include Islamic FinTech Alliance (founding members are Blossom Finance, EasiUp, EthisCrowd, Narwi, FundingLab, KapitalBoost, Launchgood and SkolaFund), Goodforce Labs and Al Baraka Bank. See their description here.

Islamic FinTech Inclusion Avenues: Crowdfunding, P2P, IAP and Robo-Advisor

Islamic crowdfunding platforms are the early manifestation of Islamic FinTech as far back as 2016. Since then, several remarkable achievements have been recorded. Therefore, besides crowdfunding, there Islamic Robo-advisor, Islamic Account Platform (IAP), Islamic peer-to-peer (P2P) financing among other Islamic FinTechs initiatives aimed at inclusion that will provide access and usage of finance for empowerment and social as well as economic development of people. Islamic FinTechs leveraging on blockchain-based transactions, including P2P lending and crowdfunding, have been making inroads into Islamic finance.

A P2P is a network of computers wherein each computer and/or device works as a server for others in the network thereby enabling shared access to files and other resources without the intermediation of a central server. The P2P is a prominent FinTech innovation that makes possible a P2P lending that features and incorporates the blockchain technology (Ridza, 2017; Tapscott and Tapscott, 2016). Primarily, and in the spirit of Shariah-compliance, a Shariah-compliant P2P finance establishes a group of businesses and investors, and shares risks and channels resources into real economic activities that are beneficial to the group. For this purpose, the P2P is essentially designed to operate following the fundamental Islamic finance principles of profit and risk sharing. Crowdfunding refers to the sourcing of funds from small amounts of capital from a large number of individual contributors over the internet in order to finance a new business venture. Individual contributions represent their shares in a crowdfunded venture, usually via P2P. This development has resulted in an alliance, where eight Islamic Crowdfunding platform operators from across the globe come together and form the Islamic FinTech Alliance (IFT Alliance) which was launched on 1 April 2016 in Kuala Lumpur, Malaysia, the founding members are BlossomFinance (USA/Indonesia), EasiUp

(France), EthisCrowd (Singapore), Narwi (Qatar), FundingLab (Scotland/Palestine), KapitalBoost (Singapore), Launchgood (USA) and SkolaFund (Malaysia). It is an association of Islamic FinTech entities undertaking blockchain-based activities, with objectives that include serving as a self-regulating standards-setting body for Islamic FinTech.

IAP is multi-bank platform. Based in Malaysia, it is the first of its kind for financial intermediation in the Islamic financial system. Established in 2016, it is owned by a consortium of six Malaysian Islamic banks. The IAP functions as a central market place for the purpose of financing SMEs. The platform started operation with a total sum of Ringgit Malaysia 150 million (Global Islamic Finance Report, 2017).

Islamic Robo-advisor services were first offered for the Islamic financial services industry by Wahed Invest Inc. based in New York, USA. With its Robo-advisor services, Wahed aims to provide access to halal portfolio management for Muslims around the world. Shortly after Wahed, another company based in Kuala Lumpur, Malaysia, Faringdon Group, launched its Asia's first Shariah-compliant Robo-advisor known as Algebra, for online automated portfolio management advice (Global Islamic Finance Report, 2017).

Islamic FinTech for Financial Inclusion via Sukuk

Blockchain sukuk: Sukuk is roughly translated as Islamic bond. It is a major financial products of the Islamic capital market used as investment mechanism by corporations, governments and individuals. Blockchain technology is one of the means through which many FinTech products are developed. With the emergence of blockchain and linking same with the financial products and instruments, an invention was conceived known as blockchain sukuk. Simply put, blockchain sukuk is a financial instrument where the blockchain technology is used to structure sukuk using smart contracts to execute the transaction in a transparent and reliable manner. There is no much difference between the underlying Shariah contracts used to structure a blockchain-based sukuk and a classical sukuk. The difference lies in the use of technology to executing the former. A smart contract encodes business rules directly into the underlying payment currency itself—meanwhile the blockchain itself enforces the contract rules regarding payments and transfer of ownership. Matthew Joseph Martin, the founder and CEO of Blossom Finance Indonesia, initiated the idea of a blockchain sukuk which he called SmartSukuk. The name simply indicates that smart contracts are used to execute the transactions (IFN Fintech, 2018). In May 2018, Blossom Finance announced that SmartSukuk™ platform for issuing blockchain-powered Islamic financing instruments using Ethereum smart contracts was ready (Blossom Finance, 2018). The operation of the Smart Sukuk is explained as follows:

> An institution looking to raise funds can issue Blossom's Smart Sukuk, which collects funds from investors in exchange for Smart Sukuk Tokens representing an ownership portion of the sukuk. When the institution makes payments, the funds are automatically distributed back to the Smart Sukuk Token holders via the blockchain according to the rules of the smart contract—without the need of conventional banks or intermediaries. Smart Sukuk Tokens support an industry standard protocol, called ERC20. The standard allows tokens to be traded globally on a variety of public cryptocurrency exchanges. (Blossom Finance, 2018)

From the description of its structure, it is understood that there is no involvement of intermediaries for fund transfer in SmartSukuk and, as such, transaction cost has been reduced in this structure (Blossom Finance, 2018).

Mobile sukuk: Mobile sukuk is a sukuk that enables investors to invest to a sukuk using mobile phones. Normally, sukuk is considered as an investment suitable for corporate or institutional investors. In most parts of the world, sukuk is inaccessible for retail investors. This perception, taken after conventional bond, was changed in 2017 when the government of Kenya issued M-Akiba bond, a retail bond that seeks to enhance financial inclusion for economic development whereby the money received is used for new and ongoing infrastructural development projects. The unique feature of this bond is that it is a Mobile Traded Bond where all activities relating to registration, trading and settlement were done via mobile platform, dialling USSD code *889#. Maximum investment per account/per day was Kshs.140,000. Furthermore, the coupon of this bond shall be paid to the phone directly and automatically on the maturity date and this will be the case even if the coupon to be paid exceeds the Kshs.140,000 daily limit. It is also essential to note that M-Akiba bond is tax-free. Interest rate of the bond is 10 per cent per annum but will be payable semi-annually after every six months of which the maturity period is three years. Using the M-Akiba bond as a model, government of Indonesia issued a sovereign retail sukuk where mobile phones were used to subscribe. It was reported that the sukuk reached investors in all 34 provinces of the Republic, where 67 per cent of its 265 million-strong Muslim-majority population use mobile phones (Tan, 2018). This is an important initiative where Islamic FinTech is utilized for the purpose financial inclusion via sukuk.

Opportunities and Issues in Islamic FinTech

Generally, FinTech is an emerging or rather evolving phenomenon that is yet to attain its pinnacle in order for all opportunities it embodies be apparent. With Muslim population projected to rise over 2.2 billion by the next decade, Islamic FinTech inclusion will expand and the technology would be assuming an ever increasing prominence. The technology can play a critical role in the Islamic finance industry as well as governmental or public services involving money and payment in an Islamic digital economy. The potential of FinTech is generally so huge that many things, including banking and otherwise, that have to do with money and wealth now not yet envisaged, could come from it in the not too distant future. It presents tremendous opportunities for markets and individual institutions. As countries establish digital economies courtesy of FinTech, financial dealings become digitized (Blakstad and Allen, 2018). This is equally true of Islamic FinTech in an established Islamic digital economy.

However, the security and privacy of consumers and their data is a cause for concern as they remain in the hands of those digital banks and non-bank institutions or service providers. The internet, which is used as medium for the Islamic FinTech, is an unsafe space for certain data regarded as private and confidential. This is especially so in the event of unethical hacking to which data on the internet are susceptible. However, as genuine as this concern is, there would be no basis to express it in the face of the security assurances of consumers' data protection as championed by the immutability of blockchain. Such security assurance as blockchain transaction entails has made people transacting Islamic FinTech dealings on the blockchain to own and manage their personal data, to select where, when and with whomsoever to share same. In the same vein, other concerns like that of companies abusing or monetizing consumers' data in their custody will diminish and render regulation less relevant. However, the highly regulated financial services industry is at the moment dominated by banks which often resist disruption by technology. This makes uncertainties more obvious for both investors and innovators pertaining to FinTech and investing therein due to fear of data breach and regulatory risk. Nevertheless, specially tailored regulations are imperative to leverage on FinTech. Meanwhile incumbent financial institutions need to consider FinTech in the light of the disruption and the opportunities it brings and reconsider all reservations against it.

Challenges to Islamic FinTech Inclusion and Way Forward

Notwithstanding the successes recorded and the huge potentials of Islamic FinTech, there are challenges and obstacles facing it. This, in other words, is to say what is generally known in the FinTech scene that its advantages are often offset by bigger shortcomings. The success of Islamic FinTech would largely be determined by how these shortcomings are addressed. Foremost of the challenge is that of scaling-up and putting in place a business model that is financially viable. It is on record that while growth of FinTech firms keeps pace with the number of novel offerings by them, only a few of such FinTech companies have reached a significant scale. Moreover, as FinTech space fills up with new competitions, incumbent financial institutions are also catching up and replicating the successes recorded by FinTechs. So the FinTech business model has to be more disruptive (Paavola, 2018). Besides, leveraging on technology, there is no limit as to kind of financial products to be developed; anything can be established. It is, however, very complex to have that thing as a financial services company.

In essence, Islamic FinTech can scale-up successfully and become sustainable business model by addressing key challenges before them. These include bringing up a unique value proposition to resolve peculiar customer demands and issues that traditional companies are yet to address. This is to avoid being replicated by similar or larger companies. Such value proposition should be a unique solution that is hard to replicate and/or protected by such means as patent. Again, Islamic FinTech face distribution infrastructure deficit, unlike the incumbent Islamic financial services companies, which affects reaching out to a broader customer base. Customer trust is another constraint for Islamic FinTech as it takes time to become established in the financial services industry and create goodwill. Branding is another shortcoming for Islamic FinTechs. Branding plays a critical role in the marketing of Islamic products and services, particularly in the context of halal which by necessary implication applies to all Islamic products and services (Wilson and Liu, 2011). However, building a brand requires significant investment and time in marketing. Though due to size of the Islamic finance market generally, Islamic FinTech are relatively becoming popular but having a well-recognized brand name is mostly lacking among them. Economies of scale are one more issue that deserves consideration, as only low-cost FinTech offerings (as most Islamic FinTechs advocate to be) can be profitable with it; otherwise the challenge of new customer acquisition and expansion is too enormous.

One other thing, which can be the most important of all, is regulation. Without regulation, the whole disruptive innovation would be susceptible to abuse, misuse and devastating manipulations. FinTech would best be regulated by regtech (regulatory technology), a regulatory mechanism that emerges with technological innovations in not only the field of finance but also all endeavours leveraging on technology. Regulatory bodies are framing protocols across the world for FinTech (Capgemini et.al. 2018). While most FinTechs companies lack the expertise of navigating through complex regulatory mandates, in most cases cross-border, Islamic FinTech have to be abreast with Shariah governance as well which forms part of their responsibilities from the regulatory angle. Despite some progress in financial expansion and economic growth over the past decade or two in many Muslim countries, there is still low level of financial inclusion. This level of exclusion has been constraining the development of many Muslim countries (Moheildin et.al. 2012). To a certain extent, this can be remedied by regulation. Part of the measures needed to drive inclusion by regulation is encouraging Islamic FinTech start-ups by providing conducive regulatory regime and alongside Islamic finance literacy through training and certification. The regulatory regime should incentivize innovations via Islamic FinTech. Islamic FinTech operational guidelines should be developed for financial service providers, including requirements for Shariah compliance of the operations.

Conclusion and Recommendations

Obviously, several key players and stakeholders play different roles for the development of the Islamic FinTech ecosystem. In these regard, financial institutions, technology companies, start-ups, users/consumers, government and regulators as well as investors are all important (PwC, 2017). Each of these plays a vital role in accordance with the place it occupies in the FinTech ecosystem. Moreover, for the purpose of Islamic FinTech, experts in legal and Shariah matters are necessarily key players for scrutiny and consideration of applicable Shariah and legal rules. Shariah expertise, particularly in relation to Islamic finance, is imperative on government and regulators. As Islam is neutral about technology from permissibility standpoint. Technology is thus viewed as a phenomenon whose usage or application should determine the rules that govern it in line with the general objectives of Islamic law. Accordingly, Shariah scholars are required to be abreast, if not ahead, of the technologies underpinning the Islamic FinTech in order to ensure effective Shariah governance and regulation. This is necessary in order to understand and address such concern in the Islamic finance circle as the need to guard against Shariah non-compliance and protection of markets and consumers in the utilization of Islamic FinTech innovations. As key players in the Islamic FinTech ecosystem, this is where government and regulators are required to play decisive role in terms of governance, regulations and oversight on Islamic FinTech. A peculiar regulation, tailored to support Islamic FinTech and that does not stifle the underlying innovations of Islamic FinTech, needs to be devised and implemented to provide a framework for Islamic FinTech.

While access to finance by potential entrepreneurs is very important for economic growth, the private sector under conventional finance may not be willing to provide financing to some areas because of the high cost associated with credit assessment, credit monitoring and lack of acceptable collateral. Having done away with the strain of collateral or arduous guarantee by its methods and pattern of business, Islamic finance is known to be generally synonymous to inclusion of all and sundry (Oseni and Ali, 2019). This quality, leveraged by the technology, has given Islamic finance an edge to champion financial inclusion as it diminishes the wall of exclusion and brings people to access and use financial services in such a way that poverty is reduced. It is via this kind of access and usage of financing, Islamic FinTech brings economic empowerment among people that are thought of as ineligible for similar services under conventional finance. The versatility of FinTech and the rate of its development will certainly support a prediction that it will determine the future of Islamic finance practice. Nonetheless, FinTech is one technology that is at best a tool (Ardalan, n.d.) and how it is chosen to be applied in Islamic finance should dictate its impact therein in line Shariah governing principles. The bottom line is for Islamic financial businesses or any such service provider to focus on customer need while remaining aware and conscious of Shariah goal in relation to society in the pursuit of solving problems and making life easier. A synergy of FinTech stakeholders and Shariah scholars is required to guide and monitor Shariah compliance of the Islamic FinTech and directs its projection as it spearheads the future of Islamic finance practice. With that, FinTech unbundles limitless opportunities inherent in Islamic financing.

References

Aldridge, I., & Krawciw, S. (2017). *Real-time Risk: What Investors Should Know About FinTech, High-frequency Trading, and Flash Crashes.* New Jersey: John Wiley & Sons.

Ali, Mohammad Mahbub. (2018). Islamic Finance Promotes Inclusion. *New Straits Times*, October 19.

Ardalan, Valli. (n.d.). *Fintech'—Evolution or Revolution.* Retrieved June 30, 2019, from https://fintech.cioapplicationseurope.com/cxoinsights/-fintech-evolution-or-revolution-nid-932.html

Blakstad, S., & Allen, R. (2018). *FinTech Revolution: Universal Inclusion in the New FinancialEcosystem.* Cham: Palgrave Macmillan.

Blossom Finance. (2018, May 7). Islamic Finance Upgraded: Smarter Sukuk Using Blockchain. *Blossom Finance.* Retrieved June 20, 2019, from https://blossomfinance.com/press/islamic-finance-upgraded-smarter-sukuk-using-blockchain

Capgemini, LinkedIn, & Efma. (2018). *World Fintech Report 2018.* Retrieved June 30, 2019, from https://www.capgemini.com/wp-content/uploads/2018/02/world-fintech-report-wftr-2018.pdf

Chakraborty, Sumit. (2018). *Fintech: Evolution or Revolution*, 1st Edn. Retrieved June 26, 2019, from https://www.researchgate.net/profile/Sumit_Chakraborty/publication/328333395_FINTECH_Evolution_or_Revolution/links/5bc6c7e0a6fdcc03c78953b4/FINTECH-Evolution-or-Revolution.pdf

Chishti, S., & Barberis, J. (2016). *The Fintech Book: The Financial Technology Handbook for Investors, Entrepreneurs and Visionaries.* Chichester: John Wiley & Sons Ltd..

Demirguc-Kunt, A., Beck, T., & Honohan, P. (2008). *Finance for All?: Policies and Pitfalls in Expanding Access, A World Bank Policy Research Report.* Washington DC: The World Bank.

Dinar Standard and Dubai Islamic Economy Development Centre. (2018). *Islamic Fintech Report 2018.* Retrieved June 25, 2019, from https://www.dinarstandard.com/wp-content/uploads/2018/12/Islamic-Fintech-Report-2018.pdf

Freedman, R. (2006). *Introduction to Financial Technology.* London: Academic Press.

Global Islamic Finance Report (GIFR). (2017). *Islamic Finance in the Digital Age: Fintech Revolution*. Retrieved June 20, 2019, from http://www.gifr.net/gifr2017/ch_17.pdf

IFN Fintech. (2018, May 29). Blockchain Sukuk: The Smart Way of Doing It. *IFN Fintech*. Retrieved June 20, 2019, from http://ifnfintech.com/eng/article-detail.php?guid=0A2D0E40-C3B8-45D4-9F1C-3B69B2C02356

International Telecommunications Union, Statistics on Estimated ICT Usage. (2018). Retrieved June 22, 2019, from https://www.itu.int/en/ITU-D/Statistics/Pages/stat/default.aspx

Moheildin, M., Iqbal, Z., Rostom, A., & Xiaochen, F. (2012). The Role of Islamic Finance in Enhancing Financial Inclusion in Organization of Islamic Cooperation (OIC) Countries. *Islamic Economic Studies, 20*(2), 55–120.

Oseni, U. A., & Ali, S. N. (2019). Fintech in Islamic Finance. In U. A. Oseni & S. N. Ali (Eds.), *Fintech in Islamic Finance: Theory and Practice*. London: Routledge.

Paavola, Teppo. (2018). Agent of Change, *YouTube*, 11 January. Retrieved June 29, 2019, from https://buc.kim/d/6pqSAZdy8lff?pub=video

PricewaterhouseCoopers (PwC). (2017). *Global FinTech Report 2017*. Retrieved May 15, 2019, from https://www.pwc.com/gx/en/industries/financial-services/assets/pwc-global-fintech-report-2017.pdf

Qatar Financial Centre. (2018, October 5). Fintech—A Global Boost for Islamic Finance. *Reuters*. Retrieved June 27, 2019, from https://www.reuters.com/sponsored/article/Fintech-a-global-boost-for-Islamic-Finance

Ridza, M. A. (2017). *The Life and Law of Fintech*. Malaysia: Sweet & Maxwell Asia.

Tan, Vineeta. (2018). Indonesian Millennials Snap Up State Sukuk as Government Opens Digital Sales Channel. *IFN FinTech Hurdle Report 2018*. Retrieved June 30, 2019, from https://redmoneyevents.com/main/framework/assets/2018/reports/fintech.pdf

Tapscott, D., & Tapscott, A. (2016). *Blockchain Revolution: How the Technology Behind Bitcoin Is Changing Money, Business and the World*. New York: Penguin Random House.

Wilson, J. A. J., & Liu, J. (2011). The Challenges of Islamic Branding: Navigating Emotions and Halal. *Journal of Islamic Marketing, 2*(1), 28–42.

CHAPTER 11

Enhancing Financial Inclusion Using FinTech-Based Payment System

Mohamed Cherif El Amri, Mustafa Omar Mohammed, and Ayman Mohamad Bakr

Abstract Financial inclusion has gained a lot of attention in the recent years. In its simplest form, financial inclusion refers to a person having an account at an established financial institution (Zins, A., & Weill, L. (2016). The Determinants of Financial Inclusion in Africa. *Review of Development Finance*, *6*(1), 46–57. https://doi.org/10.1016/j.rdf.2016.05.001). Demirguc-Kunt *et al.* (2018). *The Global Findex Database 2017: Measuring Financial Inclusion and the Fintech Revolution*. Washington DC: The World Bank. https://doi.org/10.1596/978-1-4648-1259-0, define it as "access to and use of formal financial services." It is estimated that 1.7 billion adults do not have financial accounts around the world, where almost half of them are concentrated in seven developing economies, namely China, India, Pakistan, Indonesia, Nigeria, Bangladesh, and Mexico. Whereas the vast majority of adults in developed economies pay their utility bills through accounts, only about one in four adults in developing

M. C. El Amri (✉) • A. M. Bakr
Istanbul Sabahattin Zaim University, Istanbul, Turkey
e-mail: Mohamed.amri@izu.edu.tr

M. O. Mohammed
International Islamic University Malaysia, Kuala Lumpur, Malaysia

M. M. Billah (ed.), *Islamic FinTech*,
https://doi.org/10.1007/978-3-030-45827-0_11

countries do so using accounts (Demirguc-Kunt *et al.*, 2018: 50). The patterns of the unbanked vary with the different economies. In economies where half or more of the adults are unbanked, the unbanked from poor households have the same likelihood as those coming from rich households (Demirguc-Kunt *et al.*, 2018: 4). While in economies where 20–30 per cent of the adults are unbanked, the majority of the unbanked are most probably from poor (Demirguc-Kunt *et al.*, 2018: 4). An analysis of these numbers shows that most of the unbanked in developed countries come from poor households.

Keywords Enhancement • FinTech • Financial Inclusion • Payment System

Introduction

Most of the definitions on financial inclusion are in reference to established traditional financial institutions such as banks. Perhaps these definitions are narrow as one might be misled to think that a financially included person is one who has an account at a conventional bank. In reality a financial institution is not necessarily a bank; other institutions especially those FinTech related are rapidly evolving. These new disruptive institutions have dramatically enhanced financial inclusion, which has become important recipe for development and for improving people's standard of living. Take the simple case of mobile phones. Studies have shown that mobile money services can help people improve their potential of earning income and, in turn, help them in alleviating poverty (Demirguc-Kunt *et al.*, 2018: 1). For example, in Kenya, mobile money services allowed 185,000 women to leave farming and engage in business or retail activities, and these services also helped alleviate poverty among women-headed households by 22 per cent (Ibid., 2018: 1). The mobile money service is provided by the Kenyan mobile-network operator Safaricom through a service called M-Pesa which enables Kenyans to make payments and remittances through an SMS-enabled mobile. The availability of low-cost high-speed internet combined with the high penetration of mobile phones facilitated the mobile money services in developing countries. While mobile phones and the internet can drive financial inclusion, they have to be underpinned by the necessary infrastructure (Demirguc-Kunt *et al.*,

2018: 89). In fact, these key structural changes along with reduced reluctance to use online channels for financial transactions are what drives the developments in innovative financial services (Gomber, Koch and Siering, 2017: 538).

In summary, a broad definition of financial inclusion would rather be to support the reach of financial services to the people who never had access to them via the use of technology and its infrastructure. A financially excluded person is, therefore, someone who does not own a financial account and never had access to any financial services previously. Such people fulfil their financial needs using cash.

The primary objective of this chapter is to examine the extent to which FinTech-based payment systems continue to enhance financial inclusion. The chapter provides few cases of FinTech-based payment systems, such as M-Pesa in Kenya and Orange Money operating in 13 African countries, which have greatly enhanced financial inclusion. The chapter is structured into seven sections including the introduction. The second section reviews the extant works related to the subject. Section 3 provides overview of the FinTech industry, followed by discussion linking FinTech to the payment system in Sect. 4. The fifth section provides selected cases of applications of the FinTech-based payment systems. The subsequent text, Sect. 6, deliberates on the challenges facing the FinTech-based payment systems in enhancing financial inclusion. Finally, Sect. 7 concludes the chapter.

Review of Related Works

A cursory meta-analysis of the extant literature in the areas of FinTech and financial inclusion reveals a few research gaps. Firstly, works in these two areas are compartmentalized according to the different disciplines. Investigations on FinTech, payment, and financial inclusion are conducted from the lenses of individual researcher's specialization independent from each other. For example, researchers with engineering and technology backgrounds concentrate on studies related to customer adoption of technology, like the study of Jin, Seong and Khin (2019), while researchers from law schools focus their research on the regulation aspect of FinTech, such as the work of Buckley and Malady (2014), just to mention a few. As a result, there is hardly any work with a general framework or model that integrates FinTech, payment system and financial inclusion. Nevertheless, Kavuri and Milne (2019: 24) opine that variations of researches into different theoretical and analytical frameworks can become the bases for further studies.

Research gaps in the field of digital payment can be categorized into three main themes: behaviour of users towards digital payment systems, platforms of payments, and digital payments markets and competition (Gomber, Koch and Siering, 2017; Kavuri and Milne, 2019). But the following two themes are pertinent to this chapter: behaviour of users towards digital payment systems and the issue of trust.

While there have been a few studies on user's behaviour towards digital payment systems, they are limited to user's adoption of technology from an engineering perspective such as the work of Jin, Seong and Khin (2019). There is lack of studies on user's behaviour and adoption of FinTech related to factors other than technology such as those related to education, regulation and culture. Furthermore, there is lack of studies on financial inclusion in developed and developing countries (Kavuri & Milne, 2019). On the other hand, Gomber, Koch and Siering (2017) are of the view that identify there is underrepresentation of researches investigating merchant's adoption of FinTech in the field of digital payments. Merchants' adoption of FinTech is critical to the process of providing digital payment systems to users. This is also considered critical to enhancing financial inclusion. Gomber, Koch and Siering (2017) also opine that there is lack of researches on institutional, regulatory and monetary issues in addition to lack of papers covering standardization in the field. Recent developments in the digital payments industry provide promising research areas that include global peer-to-peer (P2P) money transfer systems, like TransferWise and Azimo, and the possibilities of integration of NFC solutions in devices beyond traditional credit cards, not only smartphones but also smart wearables like smartwatches, rings, or even biometric methods to payment (Gomber, Koch and Siering, 2017: 569). Such new areas of research can greatly enhance financial inclusion.

Developments in the promising research areas raise concerns about privacy and financial data security. Linking credit cards or recording financial data within the digital payments platforms has to be assured with high security measures. Otherwise, consumers will lose trust in these systems and FinTech will be doomed for failure and enhancing financial inclusion can become a dream. There are few studies on security like the study done by (Kang, 2018). But most of these studies do not go beyond describing the trends in FinTech and analysing the security challenges that arise from these technologies. Yet, there is lack of adequate research into fraud, financial crime, identity, and data infrastructure related to the transformation of payment mechanisms (Kavuri and Milne, 2019: 19). In fact, the subject of identity, biometric identification, and cyber security research with respect to financial service industry is almost unexplored (Kavuri & Milne, 2019). Hence there exists a research gap on the issue of trust. The last research gap for this study discussed below relates to the payment systems.

Progress in payments systems have proliferated over the past two or three decades. Advances in technology have created various methods and alternatives for people. Since digital payments are linked to the ever changing and developing technologies, it becomes very difficult to predict their future. Two issues come in mind. Firstly, the underlying infrastructures of traditional forms of payment are not sufficient for supporting new alternative forms of payment. The inability to predict the future, partly due to the rapid changes in technology, might cause delays in the transformation of the infrastructure required. Secondly, since payments have drawn great regulatory attention (Arner, Barberis and Buckley, 2015: 19), the constant innovation in payment systems puts great pressure on regulatory bodies to rapidly adapt and on financial institutions and FinTech companies to comply within acceptable timeframe.

Thus, understanding how technology transforms payments is quintessential. What is more important is to understand how such transformations in the developed countries differ from those happening in the developing countries. Yet, there exists large gap in research relating to changing mechanisms of payments including central bank digital currencies and the transformation to a cashless society (Kavuri and Milne, 2019). With that being said, perhaps extensive studies on cryptocurrencies and blockchain can help close such gap.

Another gap that faces payment systems is the challenge of integrating FinTech apps with the existing legacy systems (Lee and Shin, 2018: 44). Since there is a high degree of heterogeneity, payment between different payment schemes like, Apple Pay and Samsung Pay, cannot be established. The reason for this lies in the existing differences between their payment processes, transaction settlement methods, and software agents' deployment (Moon and Kim, 2017).

Overview of the FinTech Industry

The evolution of technology in finance and other fields from the past few decades is very fast with the rapid advancement in computer science and the hardware underpinning today's modern computers and machines. Today we see applications of computer algorithms and artificial intelligence (AI) that analyse big data to provide financial recommendations to customers instantly. Robo-advisors, for example, currently use algorithms to structure client's portfolio and wealth management without any human intervention (Arner, Barberis and Buckley, 2015; Gomber, Koch and Siering, 2017).

FinTech was first used by Citicorp in the early 1990s as the original name of its project "Financial Services Technology Consortium" (Hochstein, 2015). At the time there was a general perception that Citicorp was not sharing technology with others and therefore the objective of the project and its name was to change that perception and restore the reputation of Citicorp (Ibid., 2015). There are other views that the term "FinTech" had appeared much earlier in the names of several companies during the 1980s (Ibid., 2015). Nonetheless, whether it originated from the early 1990s or during the 1980s, the name had different connotations from what it is referred to currently.

Gomber, Koch and Siering (2017) define FinTech as the linkage between modern and internet-related technologies with established financial industry activities. Meanwhile Arner, Barberis and Buckley (2015) refer to it as "technology enabled financial solutions." The integration between finance and technology is the reason why the term "FinTech" is coined. Such integration is highlighted by Ryu (2018) saying, "Fintech is a portmanteau combining the words "financial" and "technology.""

The high interest in FinTech stems from the nature of FinTech startups that possess disruptive power combined with a high level of innovativeness (Gomber, Koch and Siering, 2017). "Fintech companies can directly provide their customers with standardized or customized financial services in the front office by disrupting and substituting the existing channel" (Ryu, 2018). Perhaps that is why the major source of revenue for FinTechs is individual customers and small and medium-sized enterprises (SMEs) (Lee and Shin, 2018). Traditional financial intermediaries have already started to discuss whether direct competition with FinTechs or acquisitions, adoption of co-operative approaches in return of gaining insights, or the use of these companies as service providers best cater to their business models (Gomber, Koch and Siering, 2017; Lee and Shin, 2018). In November 2012, for instance, the Commercial Bank of Africa partnered with the technology operator Safaricom to launch a financial service call M-Shwari (Buckley and Malady, 2014: 21). Furthermore, traditional financial intermediaries have already shifted to innovation, orienting themselves with using FinTech's new technologies and adopting new digital finance functions (Gomber, Koch and Siering, 2017).

There are key technological themes and concepts that underpin the innovation in the FinTech arena. According to Gomber, Koch and Siering (2017: 549), blockchain, Near Field Communication (NFC), P2P technologies, big data analytics, and social networks form key technology concepts that drive development in digital finance, while the enablers are mobile devices and security technologies. This list is not exhaustive, and added to it are artificial intelligence (AI) and its subset machine learning (ML). Figure 11.1 shows FinTech technologies and their enablers.

The importance of these technologies stem from the fact that they improve the way financial transactions are processed, remove some unnecessary stages in the interim such as manual and batch processing of payment claims, and enhance security. Blockchain technology, for instance, is revolutionary because it provides better transaction security and faster money exchange at lower costs (Lee and Shin, 2018). On the other hand, the way NFC-based payments work is by having an NFC-enabled smartphone brought next to an NFC-enabled cash desk. When communication happens, the payer is identified by the system, the transaction is initiated and the money is transferred from the payer's account to the payee's account (Gomber, Koch and Siering, 2017). Table 11.1 provides a brief description of each technology.

Due to the aforementioned technologies and technology enablers, FinTech has huge implication on people. Consumers now have a wide variety of alternative options to choose from. They are no more restricted to traditional financial institutions and banks to perform their payments or make payment remittances. A consumer may make his or her payment using PayPal, split a cab fare with a friend using Venmo mobile digital wallet, or use his or her local telecom company to make money remittance.

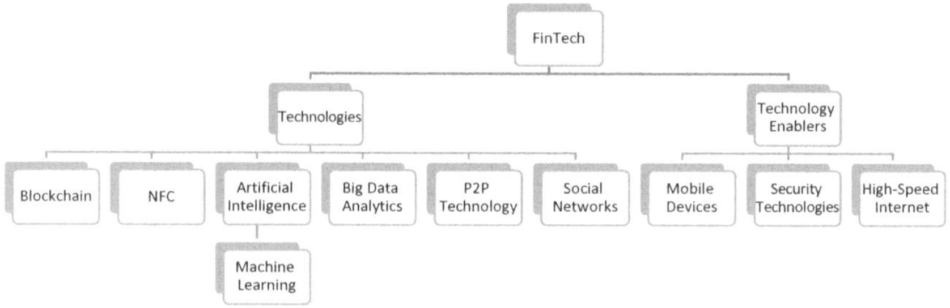

Fig. 11.1 FinTech technologies and technology enablers

Table 11.1 Technology list and their descriptions

Technology	*Description*
Big Data Analytics	A technology that automates queries and data aggregation on large and complex datasets using data mining techniques.
Blockchain	A system of ciphered blocks of data that store information (e.g. transactions, payments, and transaction history) across a network of personal computers. This approach makes information not only decentralized but also distributed. This way security is multiplied as it is not owned by one organization and it becomes almost impossible to be put down or hacked.
P2P	Peer-to-Peer technology refers to direct payments made by one individual to another without the need of a bank or financial institution. This technology is also used for lending purposes performed by peers.
NFC	Near Field Communication utilizes a technology whereby payments can be made immediately between an NFC-enabled smartphone placed in the proximity of another NFC-enabled device that accepts payments without the need for internet connection.
Machine Learning	A form of Artificial Intelligence system that utilises a training dataset to "learn" without being programmed and build models for prediction. It is used for automation.

Source: Authors' Illustration

FinTech and the Payment System

Payments have evolved dramatically over the years from barter system to using minted gold and silver coins, from fiat money to cheques and cards, and from digital electronic payments to QR codes, e-wallets, and cryptocurrencies. Each turning point in the history was a result of response to the real needs on the ground. The barter system was sufficient for individual exchanges; however, it was not convenient for big trades, let alone imports and exports. Salt seemed to be proper as a salary for Roman soldiers, yet it proved inconvenient by time and other means were sought. Later came the era of minted minerals (gold and silver) and so on.

The methods of payment have proliferated since the twentieth century. Obviously, the reason is the substantial advancement in technology and infrastructure supporting the development. FinTech companies are growing their scope of business to include services that are based not only on online platforms but also on mobile platforms like mobile payment and mobile remittance (Ryu, 2018). Moreover, payments are relatively simple as FinTech companies are able to attract customers rapidly at lower costs (Lee and Shin, 2018). With the advent of FinTech post the financial crisis, the advancement in payment methods have accelerated. Lee and Shin (2018) have argued that payments are one of the fastest-expanding financial services in terms of innovation, one of the most adopted and used retail financial services, as well as one of the least regulated. Figure 11.2 depicts how payments evolved since the second half of the twentieth century.

The forms of payments depicted in the figure and discussed are sometimes referred to as categories of payment. For instance, mobile payment and P2P are two categories of digital payment (Gomber, Koch and Siering, 2017). Digital Wallets fall under another category. Digital wallets and e-wallets are digital stores for money that carry out most of the functions of normal wallets like holding ID information, facilitating payments, and storing tokens like bus tickets (Gomber, Koch and Siering, 2017). Nonetheless, referring to them as forms or methods or categories of payment is not critical; what is important is identifying the different methods that exist today and those that we anticipate to see in the future.

Despite the fact that payments are characterized as relatively simple, a payment process involves a series of four steps. The conceptual steps are submission, validation, conditionality, and settlement (Mills *et al.*, 2016). The authors, Mills *et al.* outline the payment process as follows. First, the sender of payment submits a message that passes through the validation step. Depending on the payment framework, validation may include verification of the sender's identity. Then the system checks whether certain conditions for settlement, like availability of funds or credit, are satisfied. Once the message passes the conditionality test, the settlement step kicks in. In certain payment frameworks, settlement finality occurs when the receiver's account is credited.

Selected Applications of the FinTech-Based Payment Systems

People endure high costs and risk to make retail payments and remittances in developing countries. There is time cost, transportation cost, and transaction cost involved when a peasant travels to the city from a rural area to make a retail payment or remittance. A farmer experiences high risk carrying cash trying to settle some business of his own while roving over long distances. Resendiz (2018) has emphasized how digital payments at present promoted financial inclusion by eliminating barriers limiting the unbanked people's access to payment services. Currently, there are many applications of payment systems out there. What can be noticed is that the applications introduced in developed countries differ from those innovations that evolved in the developing countries. Nonetheless, through observation these applications can be classified into four main categories: mobile banking solutions, NFC-based mobile apps, P2P-based mobile apps, and mobile-network operator-based solutions.

Mobile banking solutions are those that are provided by traditional financial institutions and banks. Mobile banking allows clients who hold accounts at the financial provider to make their financial transactions virtually from anywhere without the need to meet a bank teller in person or use a bank's ATM. They can make utility payments, top-up their prepaid GSM mobile numbers, pay their children's school instalments, schedule tax payments, make remittances, exchange money, engage in a currency arbitrage, and make an investment, to mention a few. Mobile banking is the norm in developed countries. In developing countries, mobile banking serves only those who have bank accounts; consequently, the financially excluded do not enjoy such services. Moreover, due to lack of proper infrastructure, mobile banking is not as matured in the developing countries as those found in the developed ones.

Fig. 11.2 Steps of money transfer with Orange Money service

NFC-based mobile apps utilize Near Field Communication (NFC) technology, described earlier, for committing payments. The software of these apps use the NFC chip available in almost all current smartphones to send wireless payment messages to an NFC-enabled device in proximity. The essence of it is to eliminate the need of a bank's issued card and, instead, have one's own smartphone act like a credit or debit card. Obviously, such payment model requires an infrastructure in place that can process all these communications and be able to talk to the banks of both the payer and merchant. Examples of NFC-based mobile apps are Apple Pay, Samsung Pay, and Google Wallet (Lee and Shin, 2018). Again, due to lack of availability of proper infrastructure in the developing countries, these innovations have not reached out sufficiently and thus have not seen adequate adoption.

P2P-based mobile apps are those apps that allow a payment to be made directly from one peer to another without the need for a financial intermediary. In this model, an individual can transfer money to a family member, a friend, or a merchant with or without the need for an account at a financial institution. Examples of this model include PayPal and Venmo (Lee and Shin, 2018: 38). So Fi is another example of a P2P-based app, albeit it is not used for payments, but for managing loans between peers (Lee and Shin, 2018: 37). PayPal allows a person to make a payment against a purchase made through a merchant, like Amazon, from available balance within PayPal or using a bank's account attached to PayPal. Similarly, PayPal allows someone to make a remittance to a family member, friend, or any other individual who have a PayPal account. Venmo is a mobile app introduced in the US that can only link a US mobile number and US bank account. Consequently, Venmo peers can only transfer money to other peers who are physically located in the US.

On the other hand, mobile network operator-based solutions have seen a widespread burst in developing countries. One of the most successful stories is a solution named M-Pesa provided by the service provider Safaricom, an affiliate of Vodafone, in Kenya (Buckley and Webster, 2016: 17). A client registering with Safaricom for M-Pesa service and having an SMS-enabled phone can pay for utilities or send money to any other individual. A Kenyan can add money to his M-Pesa account by heading to one of the 40,000 Safaricom corner shop agents (T.S., 2015). He or she can also send money via his or her mobile through a menu choice to another individual. The latter either will have the money credited to his M-Pesa account if he is registered or can go to a nearby Safaricom agent and withdraw cash from there. More than two-thirds of the adult population, that is, over 17 million Kenyans, now use the service (T.S., 2015). Another similar example is EcoCash provided by EcoNet in Zimbabwe (Buckley and Malady, 2014: 20). Replicating the success of such cases, however, cannot be easily generalized. Vodafone attempted to carry the experience of M-Pesa Service to Tanzania, but it was slower to take off (Bourreau and Verdier, 2010). Figure 11.2 shows the modus operandi of M-Pesa in Kenya.

Another very interesting mobile network operator-based solution is Orange Money. The service is available in 13 African countries, allowing electronic money transfers between Orange customers within each country (*In Africa, Orange Money is making your life easier*, 2015). The way it works is more or less similar to M-Pesa service in Kenya. The only difference is that it uses a dialling code to initiate the service instead of utilizing an SMS-based menu choice. Figure 11.2 shows the steps used by a customer of Orange to commit a fund transfer to another using Orange Money service. Figure 11.2 shows the steps of money transfer using Orange Money service.

Orange has even gone further than Safaricom by providing international money transfer. Orange provides this service to three Western African markets, namely Côte d'Ivoire, Mali, and Senegal. Thus, Orange Money makes it possible for six distinct remittance corridors through direct bilateral agreements between these three countries (Scharwatt and Williamson, 2015). The amount of money exchanged is 30 million euros between these three big markets every year via Orange Money which accounts for 15 per cent of the total money circulating every year (*In Africa, Orange Money is making your life easier*, 2015). In Mali alone, Orange has more than 10,000 sales outlets, including 2000 Orange

Money kiosks specifically for this purpose (*In Africa, Orange Money is making your life easier*, 2015). With Orange Money, Orange reduced the transaction fees usually charged by formal money transfer organizations, which typically amount to 5 per cent of the transaction value, down to 2 per cent (Scharwatt and Williamson, 2015: 11–12). It is clear from the discussion how Orange Money has been effective in enhancing financial inclusion.

Challenges of the FinTech-Based Payment Systems in Enhancing Financial Inclusion

There are quite a number of challenges that the Fintech-based payment systems face in enhancing financial inclusion. Apart from insufficient number of financial institution branches in rural areas, where most financially excluded people live, culture, trust, security, infrastructure, and regulations are some of the challenges that can undermine financial inclusion.

Lack of understanding the culture and needs of people can be detrimental to financial inclusion as this may create a mismatch in the kind of products and services being offered to them. Buckley and Webster (2016) maintain that "Each economy presents a unique landscape of customer demand." With regard to regulations challenge, Ryu (2018) has found that legal risk is the most dominant factor perceived to negatively affect financial inclusion. In order to foster the environment for positive financial inclusion, poor countries need to be considerably developed in their regulatory institutions and laws. Another important challenge that hinders the adoption of FinTech is trust deficit. Buckley and Webster (2016) explained that the reason for a low number of Azerbaijanis above the age of 15 having a bank account was their mistrust in the banking system caused by currency devaluations. Building trust in the system is a very challenging mission. One way to significantly overcome this challenge is to provide a very secure environment for payments. According to Kang (2018), mobile FinTech payment service should ensure the following six security provisions are in order: availability, mutual authentication, authorization, integrity, Atomicity, and privacy. Atomicity means that a payment is only committed when the whole process is completed from start to finish. If at any point the system stops for any reason, payment is not committed at all (Kang, 2018).

The development of an efficient and secure payment solution cannot be attained without the availability of proper technology and infrastructure. Poor areas or countries are characterized by the underdeveloped state of their infrastructure, which pose a great challenge for enhancing financial inclusion. The extent of this challenge is exacerbated by the existence of poor technology operators. One of the major obstacles to payment development, and thus obstacles to financial inclusion, is the lack of Real-Time Gross Settlement (RTGS). RTGS is a system which works in real time where transactions are settled instantaneously as soon as payments are submitted in the system; also gross settlement can only occur if a bank has sufficient funds to transfer the full amount in central bank money (Galbiati and Soramäki, 2011). In developing countries, where there is lack of efficient market regulations or lack of clear regulatory frameworks, implementing RTGS poses a challenge. For example, Arner, Barberis, and Buckley (2015) found out that over 2000 peer-to-peer (P2P) lending platforms in China operate outside a clear regulatory framework. The issue is that RTGS is a critical infrastructure layer for supporting FinTech. For example, P2P payments such as Venmo smartphone app and P2P lending wouldn't have been successful in the developed countries without building around instantaneous payments/crediting. Of course, this would only be possible using RTGS systems.

Conclusion

The services of traditional financial institutions and banks have not largely reached to the poor, especially those who live in underdeveloped areas. It is estimated that 1.7 billion adults in the world do not have bank accounts, half of which concentrate in only seven developing economies. Remaining financially excluded and being unexposed to payment options, just add to the sufferings of the poor as they struggle to travel long distances for executing their financial needs at the opportunity cost of giving up their precious time, which they could have used to work and earn.

The rapid advancement in technologies has underpinned the innovation in financial services over the past century. However, the aftermath of the financial crisis in 2008 has witnessed a burst in FinTech start-ups that has changed the way financial services are provided. Utilizing new technologies, such as artificial intelligence, machine learning, big data analytics, and blockchain, coupled with negligible regulatory costs and lack of regulatory requirements for their business models, FinTech companies have posed stiff competition with the traditional institutions to the extent that their contributions are now characterized as disruptive.

Thus there are a lot of innovations too in the payment systems of many FinTech companies. These companies are able to reach the poor in rural areas and provide them financial payment services at very affordable costs. Such payment systems play a big role in enhancing financial inclusion and consequently in alleviating poverty. Over time these new FinTech-based payment systems face challenges in terms of availability of infrastructure underpinning these technologies, security of financial data, and the adoption of people to such technology.

There are a lot of research about FinTech and payments. However, these studies have been undertaken by researchers from different disciplines independently. It is clear that collaboration in this aspect is very important in order to reach a consensus on a common framework related to FinTech payment system. With this research gap, the present chapter sets a new direction for research on FinTech-based payment system and financial inclusion.

References

Arner, D. W., Barberis, J., & Buckley, R. P. (2015). The Evolution of Fintech: A New Post-Crisis Paradigm? *University of Hong Kong Faculty of Law, 2015*(047), 1–44.

Berlin Heidelberg, 87(5), pp. 537–580. https://doi.org/10.1007/s11573-017-0852-x.

In Africa, Orange Money is making your life easier. (2015). *Orange.com*. Retrieved June 10, 2019, from https://www.orange.com/en/Footer/Thematic-features/2015/SFM/In-Africa-Orange-Money-is-making-your-life-easier

Bourreau, M., & Verdier, M. (2010). Cooperation for Innovation in Payment Systems: The Case of Mobile Payments, *Ssrn*, (February). https://doi.org/10.2139/ssrn.1575036.

Buckley, R. P., & Webster, S. (2016). Fintech in Developing Countries: Charting New Customer Journeys. *Journal of Financial Transformation*, 44 (11.2016), pp. 151–159. http://ssrn.com/abstract=2850091%5Cn; http://www.law.

unsw.edu.au/research/faculty-publications%5Cn; http://www.austlii.edu.au/au/journals/UNSWLRS/%5Cn; http://www.ssrn.com/link/UNSW-LEG.html%5Cn; http://www.capco.com/institute

Buckley, R. P., & Malady, L. (2014). *Building Consumer Demand for Digital Financial Services : The New Regulatory Frontier.* E226.

Demirguc-Kunt, A. *et al.* (2018). *The Global Findex Database 2017: Measuring Financial Inclusion and the Fintech Revolution.* Washington DC: The World Bank. https://doi.org/10.1596/978-1-4648-1259-0.

Galbiati, M., & Soramäki, K. (2011). An Agent-based Model of Payment Systems. *Journal of Economic Dynamics and Control, 35*(6), 859–875. https://doi.org/10.1016/j.jedc.2010.11.001

Gomber, P., Koch, J. A., & Siering, M. (2017). Digital Finance and FinTech: Current Research and Future Research Directions. *Journal of Business Economics 87* (5), 537–580. https://doi.org/10.1007/s11573-017-0852-x.

Hochstein, M. (2015). https://www.americanbanker.com/opinion/fintech-the-word-that-is-evolves*Fintech (the Word, That Is) Evolves, American Banker.* Available at: https://www.americanbanker.com/opinion/fintech-the-word-that-is-evolves (Accessed 22 September 2020).

Jin, C. C., Seong, L. C., & Khin, A. A. (2019). Factors Affecting the Consumer Acceptance towards Fintech Products and Services in Malaysia. *International Journal of Asian Social Science, 9*(1), 59–65. https://doi.org/10.18488/journal.1.2019.91.59.65

Kang, J. (2018). Mobile Payment in Fintech Environment: Trends, Security Challenges, and Services. *Human-centric Computing and Information Sciences.* Springer Berlin Heidelberg, *8*(1). https://doi.org/10.1186/s13673-018-0155-4

Kavuri, A. S., & Milne, A. (2019). *FinTech and the Future of Financial Services: What Are the Research Gaps?* 18/2019.

Lee, I., & Shin, Y. J. (2018). Fintech: Ecosystem, Business Models, Investment Decisions, and Challenges. *Business Horizons.* Kelley School of Business, Indiana University, *61*(1), 35–46. https://doi.org/10.1016/j.bushor.2017.09.003

Mills, D. C. *et al.* (2016). *Distributed Ledger Technology in Payments, Clearing, and Settlement, Ssrn.* https://doi.org/10.17016/FEDS.2016.095.

Moon, W. Y., & Kim, S. D. (2017). A Payment Mediation Platform for heterogeneous FinTech schemes, *Proceedings of 2016 IEEE Advanced Information Management, Communicates, Electronic and Automation Control Conference, IMCEC 2016.* IEEE, pp. 511–516. https://doi.org/10.1109/IMCEC.2016.7867264.

Resendiz, R. M. (2018). The Role of Payment Systems and Services in Financial Inclusion – The Latin American and Caribbean Financial Inclusion. *IFC Bulletins Chapters, 47*, 1–27.

Ryu, H.-S. (2018). What Makes Users Willing or Hesitant to Use Fintech?: The Moderating Effect of User Type. *Industrial Management & Data Systems, 118*(3), 541–569. https://doi.org/10.1108/IMDS-07-2017-0325

Scharwatt, C., & Williamson, C. (2015). *Mobile Money Crosses Borders: New Remittance Models in West Africa.* Retrieved June 10, 2019, from www.gsma.com/mmu

Zins, A., & Weill, L. (2016). The Determinants of Financial Inclusion in Africa. *Review of Development Finance, 6*(1), 46–57. https://doi.org/10.1016/j.rdf.2016.05.001

CHAPTER 12

Islamic FinTech and Financial Inclusion

Ahmed Tahiri Jouti

Abstract Purpose—FinTech revolutionized financial services and created efficient solutions to target underserved people. This chapter aims at understanding the way Islamic FinTech can improve the Islamic finance industry in order to achieve economic inclusion.

Design/methodology/approach—The chapter presents a conceptual framework based on case studies and literature review describing the way Islamic FinTech can serve to upgrade economic inclusion efforts.

Findings—The chapter shows that Islamic FinTech can revolutionize the way Islamic financial services are provided and to ensure an integration between the Islamic social finance and the Islamic financial institutions.

Research limitations/implications—The chapter focused only on the implemented solutions without giving an insight about how new technologies such as blockchain can enhance the efforts and the results.

Practical implications—The chapter demonstrates that Islamic FinTech should be seen as a fundamental pillar of any financial inclusion policy. The latter should target economic inclusion.

A. T. Jouti (✉)
Al Maali Institute, Casablanca, Morocco
e-mail: a.tahiri@almaaligroup.com

M. M. Billah (ed.), *Islamic FinTech*,
https://doi.org/10.1007/978-3-030-45827-0_12

Social implications—In general, any financial inclusion policy drafted by Islamic financial institutions shall target economic inclusion and adopt Islamic FinTech.

Originality/value—Financial inclusion literature focuses mainly on the access to financial services. This chapter upgrades the initiatives and efforts to achieve economic inclusion.

Keywords Islamic FinTech • Financial inclusion • Economic inclusion

Introduction

Most of the definitions related to *financial inclusion* are focusing on the process of bringing different segments of people under a single roof of the financial system (Sethi & Acharya, 2018) especially the very low-income population. Nevertheless, financial inclusion could be an efficient instrument to achieve economic inclusion and growth if it is perceived as a part of an integrated approach and strategy.

Indeed, economic inclusion (Bettcher & Teodora, 2015) refers to equality of opportunity for all members of society to participate in the economic life of their country as employees, entrepreneurs, consumers and citizens. This means that people from different segments of society would have suitable opportunities to be part of the formal economic system and share the benefits. Otherwise, people would move to the informal economy or even worse to the criminal economy because of economic exclusion.

The informal economy (Williams et al., 2017) is composed of all the monetary exchanges of legal goods and services that are unregistered by or hidden from the state, for tax, social security and/or labour law purposes while the criminal economy is related to the exchange of goods and services that are illegal. Thus, fostering economic inclusion would help bringing people from the informal and the criminal economies to the formal economy.

If the financial authorities are overseeing the monetary flows and exchanges in order to eliminate the criminal and informal activities, they are also supposed to contribute actively in reducing the proportion of people excluded in a way that encourages the formal economy.

From this perspective, financial inclusion is not only about giving access to financial services, it must focus on the way it can connect people to adequate opportunities in the formal economy. Indeed, financial inclusion starts with a bank account but it should not stop here.

On the other hand, from a theoretical perspective, Islamic finance seems to be the right answer for self-excluded people with religious concern (The World Bank, 2018). Nevertheless, the impact of introducing Islamic finance in terms of financial inclusion varies according to several parameters (Jouti, 2018). Therefore, the contribution of the Islamic finance industry players in terms of financial inclusion should not be limited to self-excluded people with religious concern but extended to include people regardless of the reasons behind their exclusion.

During the past decade, adopting FinTech solutions gave a new impulse to the financial inclusion efforts in different countries. It enlarged the scope of the population to serve, the services to provide and the partnerships to conclude. It also inspired a new generation of start-uppers and investors to innovate in terms of technology, business models and products. The Islamic FinTech industry has the potential to disrupt all the aspects of the Islamic finance industry (Dinar Standard, 2018) and to enhance its contribution in terms of financial inclusion.

This chapter tries to identify the way Islamic FinTech can enhance economic inclusion through efficient and adapted financial inclusion efforts and innovations. The first part defines the way financial inclusion can lead to economic inclusion while the second part presents the way Islamic FinTech can enhance a financial inclusion that achieves economic inclusion.

Financial Inclusion to Achieve Economic Inclusion

The Sustainability Development Goals (SDGs)[1] defined by the United Nations promote economic inclusion. Indeed, the target n° 10.2 consists of '*empowering and promoting the social, economic and political inclusion of all, irrespective of age, sex, disability, race, ethnicity, origin, religion or economic or other status*'. Moreover, other Sustainability Development Goals target directly or indirectly economic inclusion.

From an Islamic law (Shari'ah) perspective, the sustainability Development Goals are in line with the Shari'ah principles and objectives

[1] For further details, please visit : https://www.un.org/sustainabledevelopment/sustainable-development-goals/

and should be endorsed by all countries for the good of humanity and the world (Mukhtar, Ashiqin, & Jusoh, 2018).

This part will identify the Sustainability Development Goals (SDGs) that focus on economic inclusion. Then, it will present the main objectives and challenges facing both conventional and Islamic financial institutions when targeting economic inclusion.

Economic Inclusion and Sustainability Development Goals

The Sustainability Development Goals (SDGs) pay particular attention to economic inclusion of people in order to access welfare and wealth creation. Indeed, Islam promotes the equal distribution of wealth among people as a way to widespread fairness and justice:

> '7. Whatever God restored to His Messenger from the inhabitants of the villages belongs to God, and to the Messenger, and to the relatives, and to the orphans, and to the poor, and to the wayfarer; **so that it may not circulate solely between the wealthy among you**. Whatever the Messenger gives you, accept it; and whatever he forbids you, abstain from it. And fear God. God is severe in punishment'. —(Surate Al Hashr, 7)

Moreover, these goals aim at promoting the formal economy and fighting against criminal and illicit transactions. Islam also promotes the fair exchange of wealth among people:

> '29. O you who believe! Do not consume each other's wealth illicitly, but trade by mutual consent. And do not kill yourselves, for God is Merciful towards you'.—(Surate an-nisa', 29)

Economic Inclusion to Access Welfare

Economic inclusion to improve welfare is giving access for all to healthcare services, to quality education, to affordable housing, to low-cost and clean energy as well as to water and sanitation.

- *Health Goal*

The target 3.8 aims at achieving universal coverage including financial risk protection and health care services to access safe, effective, quality and affordable essential medicines and vaccines for all.

The financial institutions, especially insurance companies, shall find out new solutions to provide an efficient healthcare system with an optimal cost.

Bundled Payments System (Kaplan & Porter, 2011)

At a global scale, the cost of healthcare is increasing due to the aging populations and the development of new treatments but also to the healthcare business models adopted. In this context, the bundled payments model can contribute in improving the cost of the healthcare system. It is a value-based reimbursement that rewards providers who deliver the best overall care at the lowest cost and who minimize complications. Indeed, this model would reward hospitals for reducing the cost of care and penalize them for overruns. In some aspects, the bundled payments model achieved clear savings with no increase in emergency department visits readmissions, or 30-day mortality (Maddox & Epstein, 2018).

- *Education Goal*

The targets 4.1, 4.2, 4.3 and 4.6 aim at ensuring access to free, equitable and quality education for kids while ensuring access to affordable and quality technical vocational and tertiary education, including university for adults (men and women).

The financial sector shall provide adequate instruments to finance the education sector and enhance the quality as well as the access to education.

Sukuk IHSAN Initiative (Khazanah Nasional Berhad, 2017)

Sukuk IHSAN in Malaysia is the first Sukuk issuance oriented to the education sector to improve the access to high-quality education in the public sector schools. Depending on the key performance indicators (KPI) defined by the Malaysian government, the profit rate would change. If the KPI are met, the rate would be equal to 4.2%. Otherwise, the rate goes up to 4.6%.

- *Sustainable cities and communities*

The target 11.1 aims at ensuring access, for all, to adequate, safe and affordable housing that provides basic services and contributes in upgrading slums.

Credit Guarantee Institutions

Financial institutions shall dedicate a part of their resources to finance housing for the vulnerable. Indeed, Credit Guarantee institutions offer adequate Guarantee schemes for housing loans and financing serving the vulnerable populations. From the Islamic finance perspective, the Credit Guarantee Corporation (CGC) in Malaysia and the 'CCG' in Morocco implemented Shari'ah compliant schemes to help people with religious concern access housing and other services.

- *Affordable and clean energy*

The target 7.1 consists of ensuring universal access to affordable, reliable and modern energy services.

Climate Bonds Initiative

Climate bonds initiative is an international not-for-profit organization aiming at mobilizing $100 trillion bond market for climate change solutions. Its strategy consists of developing a large liquid green and climate bonds market that will lead to decreasing the cost of capital for climate projects in developed and emerging markets.

The organization certified 166 Climate bonds all over the world with an outstanding volume as of 1 May 2019 of US$67 billion (using exchange rates of date of issuance).

Moreover, the Climate bonds initiative established the Green Sukuk and Working Party (GSWP) in association with the Gulf bond and Sukuk Association and the Clean Energy Business Council in order to promote and develop Shari'ah Compliant financial products to invest in climate change solutions.

- *Clean water and sanitation*

Targets 6.1 and 6.2 aim at achieving universal and equitable access to safe drinking water for all. The climate bonds initiative includes the financing of clear water infrastructure.

Economic Inclusion to Access Wealth Creation

Economic inclusion for wealth creation is giving access for all to different forms of ownership and property, to economic resources, to financial services and technology while fighting against informal and criminal economies.

- *No poverty goal*

The target 1.4 stipulates that '*all men and women—especially the poor and the vulnerable—must have equal access to economic resources and to basic services, ownership and control over land and other forms of property, inheritance, natural resources, appropriate new technology and financial services including microfinance*'.

This target aims at ensuring equal access to resources in order to include more people in the economic cycle. Indeed, financial institutions shall play an important role to achieve this target through dedicating a part of their resources to grant adequate financing to the poor and vulnerable to access to different forms of ownership (land, buildings, technology, etc.)

- *No hunger goal*

The target 2.3 aims at increasing the agricultural productivity as well as the incomes of small-scale food producers through secure and equal access to land, other productive resources and inputs, knowledge, financial services, markets and opportunities for value addition and non-farm employment.

This target aims at developing the agricultural production and productivity by encouraging small farmers to access the necessary resources to develop their outputs. Therefore, financial institutions shall dedicate a part of their resources to grant adequate financing to small farmers.

The SAGCOT Initiative (Southern Agricultural Growth Corridor of Tanzania) (Kramer & Pfitzer, 2016) is a successful experience that improved the life of hundreds of thousands of small farmers as well as their productivity. The initiative consisted of building a fully developed agricultural corridor in Tanzania including the investment in the necessary infrastructure (port, roads, rail, electricity, fertilizer terminal) and involving agro-dealers and microfinance services to facilitate the access to fertilizers.

- *Life below water*

Target 14.B aims at providing access for small-scale artisanal fishers to marine resources and markets.

For this purpose, financial institutions shall dedicate a part of their resources to grant adequate financing products to small-scale fishers to access to modern equipment that would enhance their productivity and wealth.

- *Industry innovation and infrastructure*

Target 9.3 aims at increasing the access of small-scale industrial and other enterprises to financial services, including affordable credit, and their integration into value chains and markets.

For this purpose, governments set up specialized institutions in guarantee schemes for loans and financing granted to small and medium businesses. These institutions can also grant direct financing and offer a credible incentive for financial institutions to serve small businesses.

- *Peace, Justice and strong institutions*

Target 16.4 aims at reducing illicit financial and arms flows. Indeed, financial institutions are required to fight against both the criminal and the informal economy in order to encourage the formal economy.

Anti-money Laundering Regulations (FATF, 2017)

Global and local regulations are focusing on the illicit financial transactions in terms of detection, prevention and control. Indeed, facilitating the economic inclusion could not be sufficient without fighting against the criminal economy and the rule here is that the cost of dealing in the criminal economy should be much higher than dealing in the formal economy.

Islamic Financial Institutions and Economic Inclusion: Objectives and Challenges

Why Should Islamic Financial Institutions Target Economic Inclusion?
Targeting Economic inclusion and adopting Sustainability Development Goals are ways to contribute in achieving a better and more sustainable future for all including the institutions that take part or take the lead on different initiatives.

Even from a pure business perspective, targeting economic inclusion would have positive impacts on financial institutions, including the following:

- *The strengthening of their brand image*

Targeting economic inclusion and sustainability development goals would help positioning the financial institution as being sensitive to the welfare of the community and enriching the features of its services in a way that helps their customers to achieve what they want to accomplish through buying these services (Christensen, Hall, Dillon, & Duncan, 2016) and to serve the community.

- *The enlargement of the customers' base*

Targeting economic inclusion and sustainability development goals enables the financial institution to implement convenient schemes and products in terms of risk and profitability profile to serve the vulnerable and the poor. These schemes and products target new segments of customers in collaboration with different stakeholders such as government agencies and third party guarantors.

Moreover, including economically these new segments of people would help them to improve their financial and economic situation and thus join gradually the middle class. Indeed, it would enable the financial institutions, in the medium term, to enlarge the middle-class customers' base.

- *The opportunity to reduce the cost of financing or/and refinancing*

In order to serve correctly the population targeted by sustainability development and economic inclusion initiatives, social and sustainability bonds (and Sukuk) are generally used to attract investors who are sensitive to the community welfare. Moreover, issuing social bonds (or Sukuk) would mean adding a feature to bonds that would make investors accept to waive a part of their benefits as a counterparty of the social performance.

How Should Islamic Financial Institutions Target Economic Inclusion?
To target economic inclusion, Islamic financial institutions need to take into account the following elements:

- *Tackling the lack of access and self-exclusion issues*

The concept of financial inclusion covers both the lack of access and the self-exclusion issues. In order to improve the access to financial services and to target underserved populations, there were many initiatives in this direction.

First, microfinance institutions (both conventional and Islamic) were created to serve exclusively the poor and the vulnerable. Nevertheless, their cost of financing is still high.

Second, to ensure more proximity to people, some financial institutions collaborated with existing networks of nonbank retailers such as gas stations and post offices.

Third, financial institutions started offering Shari'ah compliant solutions through specialized entities or windows in order to attract self-excluded people with religious concern.

Finally, digital financial services were successful in terms of reducing the cost as well as improving the proximity to customers.

- *Integrating or initiating sustainable ecosystems*

All the sustainability development initiatives require funding that could take different forms and serve different targets. In this context, financial institutions shall be part of the sustainable ecosystems and initiatives and provide appropriate financing products oriented to achieve the target of sustainability development goals.

From an Islamic finance perspective, Islamic financial institutions can cope with Zakat and Waqf institutions to target economic inclusion. Indeed, Islamic banks can contribute in the efforts of the collection of Zakat or/and Waqf funds as per the Indonesian Islamic banking law (UU n° 21 2008). Moreover, Islamic financial institutions can finance social projects initiated by Islamic social finance organizations.

- *Developing adequate financial services, instruments and business models*

Islamic financial institutions need to develop appropriate financial services, instruments and business models to respond in an efficient way to the different sustainability development initiatives and needs. Indeed, targeting underserved populations would require different business models and products. Therefore, endorsing sustainability development goals for Islamic financial institutions assumes the continuous review of their business models and instruments.

The Challenges of the Islamic Financial Institutions in Terms of Economic Inclusion

Islamic financial institutions looking forward to achieving economic inclusion would face several challenges that can be summarized as follow:

- *Absence of government global initiatives*

The Islamic financial institutions contribution to achieve economic inclusion is limited to providing adequate Shari'ah compliant financial services to the targeted population. In the absence of global initiatives lead or at least supported by the government, the contribution of Islamic financial institutions in this field would have a limited impact.

Let us take the example of the SDG target 11.1 related to giving access to affordable, safe and adequate housing for all. In the absence of a governmental policy that promotes social housing projects or any other similar form of initiatives, the Islamic financial institutions cannot contribute effectively in achieving this target.

Therefore, the absence of global initiatives would impact the ability of Islamic financial institutions to contribute effectively in achieving economic inclusion.

- *Absence of an adequate business model*

Targeting a new population would not require solely the conception of new products; it would involve the adoption of new business models and schemes that would contribute in achieving correctly the economic inclusion goals.

For instance, the *2017 Global Findex Report* (The World Bank, 2018) enumerated the reasons behind the financial exclusion phenomenon. Indeed, the high cost of financial services, the lack of sufficient resources, the limited geographical availability, the lack of trust in financial institutions and the religious beliefs seem to be the most relevant reasons leading to financial exclusion.

Therefore, including more people in the financial system would require tackling the issues listed earlier and thus adopting new business models. Indeed, offering affordable financial services while improving their geographical availability necessitates the creation of a less expensive and wide distribution channel such as tobacconists,[2] advanced automated teller machines (ATMs)[3] and telecom operators' network. However, the downside of this model is that the possibility to offer customizable financial services would be reduced -if not eliminated-.

Moreover, targeting self-excluded people with religious concern would require the development of a Shari'ah Compliant financial offer that would require the creation of a new subsidiary or window.

- *The cost of transaction*

Generally, providing financial services on a large scale is time consuming and labour intensive while the financing amounts are small. This is to explain the high rates applied to microfinance products. Moreover, in practice, microfinance showed its limited impact on customers since it has been often used to cover the cash gaps of household spending and thus cannot be transformative (Robet & Johnathan, 2017).

Hence, tackling the cost of transaction issue seems to be a challenge to target underserved populations for both conventional and Islamic microfinance.

Islamic FinTech to Achieve Economic Inclusion

Islamic FinTech Adoption: Impacts and Success Factors

What Is the Impact of Adopting Islamic FinTech?

Introducing technology to the Islamic financial sector can bring three important advantages starting with a lower cost of transaction and a wider geographical coverage and finishing with newcomers adopting new rules and business models but more than that, Islamic FinTech solutions can facilitate the access to social services and economic benefits for the poor and the vulnerable.

- *Lowering the cost*

[2] The Nickel Account is a payment account that can be opened at any tobacconist in France. For further details, Check the website : https://compte-nickel.fr/

[3] The XTM solution provided by Kuveyt Turk Participation bank in Turkey. For further details, Check the website : https://www.kuveytturk.com.tr/en/branchless-banking/digital-xtm-branch/general-features

Lowering the cost would enable Islamic financial institutions and Islamic FinTech startups to target underserved population that finds the access to financial services expensive. Moreover, it would lead to lowering the cost of financing when it comes to large-scale financial services.

- *Widening the geographical coverage*

Through Islamic FinTech, users can execute their operations without the need to physical branches or locations. Indeed, it helps serving more people without the need to invest in enlarging the physical network or to collaborate with external retail non-financial networks that would have an impact on the cost of financial services.

- *Collaborative business models*

In general, FinTech startups (in conventional and Islamic finance) are facing two main challenges that are regulation and customers trust. Indeed, regulators are often pro-incumbents because they fear financial instability or they have been captured by lobby groups (The Economist, 2019) while that the absence of a physical network limits the trust of customers in FinTechs to renounce totally to the financial services offered by incumbents.[4]

Therefore, collaborating would help incumbents to reinforce their operational efficiency and enable FinTechs to attract more customers to use their services and platforms.

From a practical perspective, FinTechs are getting the customer relationship and the data to create value while passing the regulated part to banks (The Economist, 2019).

What Are the Success Factors for Adopting Islamic FinTech?

For the introduction of a new technology, it is necessary to identify its impact on the existing stakeholders and identify the new players as well as the necessary infrastructure required to make the implementation process smooth and successful (Ron & Kapoor, 2016).

[4] Let us take the example of BNP PARIBAS. The bank has more than 30 million of clients (in France, Italy, Luxembourg and Belgium) while its digital bank (HELLO BANK) has reached only 3 million of customers in Europe. Indeed, the threat is here but not as estimated.

When it comes to Islamic FinTech, the main elements that would contribute deeply in its enhancement and its potential impact on economic inclusion are the wide use of smartphones and the high-speed internet connection.

- *Mobile subscriptions*

According to the World Bank Data, the total of mobile subscriptions from 1980 to 2018 in the different regions of the world is as follow (Table 12.1):

- *Smartphone global sales*

According to statista.com, the global annual smartphone unit sales to end users in 2018 reached 1.56 billion with a total number of 2.1 billion smartphone users worldwide representing 32.3% of the global population.

From another perspective, in the top-50 countries/markets by smartphone users and penetration, 10 countries are African with China leading the ranking (55.3% as the penetration rate).

- *Internet users worldwide*

According to statista.com, the number of worldwide internet users in 2018 was 3.9 billion with China having the highest number of internet users worldwide (772 million). Moreover, the mobile internet traffic as a share of total global online traffic was about 48%.

Table 12.1 Total subscriptions to mobile services for the period 1980–2018

Region	*Number of subscriptions*
Arab World	4,134,845,240
East Asia & Pacific	25,777,318,462
Europe & Central Asia	15,984,901,658
European Union	9,899,629,901
Least developed countries: UN classification	4,765,869,211
Sub-Saharan Africa	6,118,396,091

Source: Worldbank.org

Indeed, enhancing Islamic FinTech starts with the development of mobile subscriptions, smartphone penetration and mobile internet penetration.

Islamic FinTech Initiatives for Economic Inclusion

As discussed earlier, implementing the necessary infrastructure contributed in the development of Islamic FinTech solutions in a way that lowered the cost of transactions and enlarged the targeted population while initiating new business models.

In this context, adopting Islamic FinTech could lead to economic inclusion brining more impact to different initiatives. In this part, successful initiatives and experiences based on both conventional and Islamic FinTech would be presented.

Islamic FinTech Solutions to Access Economic Resources

Successful initiatives and experiences of introducing FinTech solutions showed their high potential to achieve economic inclusion and sustainability development goals. From clean energy, risk coverage to health, FinTech solutions contribute in enhancing the quality of life of people at a lower cost and with high benefits.

From the Islamic FinTech perspective, successful experiences in conventional FinTech can be easily duplicated while complying with Shari'ah principles. In parallel, Islamic FinTech can contribute in improving the economic inclusion efforts.

- *Mobile payments to access smartphones*

In the technology era, the smartphone is the main pillar of the revolution that many sectors and industries witness today. Indeed, to improve the access to financial services and to platforms and economic resources, it is necessary to facilitate the access to smartphones. Indeed, Easypaisa[5] in Pakistan provides an opportunity to its customers to own a 3G smartphone (Easypaisa) by paying in easy instalments.

[5] Easypaisa is an initiative launched by Telenor Pakistan in collaboration with Tameer Microfinance Bank with the approval of State Bank of Pakistan.

Providing such a product aims at enlarging the customers' base of Easypaisa who can pay the instalments through their mobile money accounts and benefit from other services.

Islamic financial institutions can contribute in improving the accessibility to smartphones and therefore to all the financial services and technological platforms.

- *Mobile payments to prevent health crisis* (The Economist, 2018)

In the EBOLA crisis that was devastating the western part of Africa in 2014, SIERRA LEONE faced a particular issue related to its emergency workers that were covering the territory but had problems in getting their wage. Sometimes, they had to cross a long distance to collect the money, in cash and not fully and sometimes, they would find their money disbursed to impostors.

Indeed, this situation could lead to a catastrophic result if the workers decide to resign. Thus, the government decided to move to digital payments since 95% of the country was covered by a mobile phone signal and 90% of the emergency workers had mobile phones. Nevertheless, only 15% of workers had mobile money accounts and the identification issue was raised. At the end, the government decided to use the facial recognition technology to solve the identification issue.

- *Mobile payments and M-KOPA for accessible clean energy* (The Economist, 2017)

M-Kopa is the largest firm in Africa (eastern Africa) providing mini rooftop solar panels in connection with mobile phone network, enabling the provider to switch off or on the panels remotely. Moreover, instead of paying US$250 in one shot for such installations, M-KOPA offer them to pay 50 cents daily through mobile money accounts, otherwise, the panels would be switched off.

Such initiatives can improve the quality of life of people in terms of food preservation and health. Indeed, mobile money accounts serve as a way to facilitate the access to clean and cheap energy in many east African countries.

The M-KOPA experience can easily be duplicated by Islamic FinTech solutions to provide underserved population with appropriate equipment and services.

- *Mobile payments to access risk coverage and insurance products*

Mobile payments solutions can provide customers with appropriate insurance products with a lower price. Generally, an insurance premium is composed of three components: the pure premium, the management fees and the acquisition costs. If the insurance operators move to a digital business model, the management fees and the acquisition costs would get lower and thus the total premium would become accessible to the vulnerable and the poor.

Easypaisa is commercializing insurance products underwritten by insurance companies and takaful operators through its mobile accounts solutions providing significant benefits with a minimum annual premium and a flexibility of treatment.

A full digital Takaful operator would contribute effectively in reducing the amount of contributions through decreasing the management fees of the operator and enlarging the size of the takaful funds.

FinTech Solutions to Assist Help Producers and Entrepreneurs

For small businesses, FinTech solutions can enable them to access to cheap economic resources, to appropriate funding and to the market in a way that can help them develop their business and thus move from small businesses to medium businesses.

- *Nano-loans*

FinTech enables financial institutions to reduce the underwriting and infrastructure costs. Therefore, targeting underserved population becomes possible and profitable. Indeed, Digital nano-loans become more common in Africa with operators like EcoCashLoan, Timiza, KCG M-PESA, and M-Shwari.

In practice, nano-loans are based on low amounts starting with US$5 or US$10 granted through simple mobile user interfaces that provide funds in real time.

Islamic financial institutions cannot provide cash financing but they can identify marketplaces offering low-cost products and grant adequate financing on that basis.

- *Electricity*

According to a study about rural electrification in India and its impact on customer behavior and demand (Rockefeller foundation, 2019), enterprises that have better access to reliable electricity (relying less on diesel) can offer better services and have longer opening hours that help them to increase their income.

Solutions such as the one provided by M-KOPA can help enterprises and merchants to open for more hours with an acceptable cost of energy and to increase their income and their investments.

Indeed, the access to electricity through financial services can help them to include more people from the economic perspective.

- *Takaful coverage for farmers*

From another perspective, financial inclusion through mobile money accounts can enable producers to get access to insurance services. For instance, Econet in Zimbabwe offers farmers an index insurance product to receive an income in case the rainfall index drops below a certain level. Farmers would get the amount automatically without need to claim it (The Economist, 2018).

Takaful operators shall adopt Islamic Fintech solutions in order to have the necessary capacity to target new segments of population.

- *Multi-sided platforms*

Small businesses cannot grow without a low-cost access to large markets. Multi-sided platforms represent a real opportunity to small-scale producers to access to large communities and markets.

A multi-sided platform (Hagiu, 2007) provides a support that facilitates transactions among the two or more constituents that it serves, such that members of one side are more likely to get on board the multi-sided platform when more members of another side do so.

Many marketplaces and platforms offer financing for their customers in order to conclude deals. Nevertheless, when adhering to a marketplace, a small business is exposed to the risk of getting lost on a sea of similar products.

Indeed, consumers are loyal to the marketplace (amazon as an example), not the brands they are buying on it (Teixeira, 2019).

In this context, creating fairly regulated marketplaces and platforms oriented to small-scale producers would enhance their economic inclusion. Moreover, Islamic financial institutions can grant adequate financing for customers of small-scale producers when it is relevant.

Conclusion

Achieving financial inclusion is not an end in itself. It should be seen as a way leading to economic inclusion. Indeed, most of the technological innovations in the financial sphere constitute a real opportunity to find efficient ways to target underserved people.

Lowering the cost of transactions while simplifying the processes lead to creating a new range of products more adapted to the needs of the vulnerable and the poor. This change in the business model of financial services and institutions fosters the launch of new initiatives and high social impact businesses.

Financial services can contribute in improving the access of underserved population to economic resources such as land, equipment, housing, clean energy and funding. Nevertheless, financial institutions are just part of an ecosystem that requires global and local initiatives under the supervision of governments and international organizations to achieve the predefined targets. These initiatives include regulations, policies, frameworks, funding and guarantee schemes to foster the creation of efficient ecosystems.

All in all, financial inclusion is not only about creating more accounts or making accessible the different services provided by financial institutions, but also about linking the underserved population to economic opportunities in a transformative way. The experiences presented in this chapter can be inspiring for other initiatives and projects.

References

Amena, S. et al. (2016). Journal of Marketing Management and Consumer Behavior, 1: 2.

Bettcher, K. E., & Teodora, M. (2015, May 26). Economic Inclusion: Leveraging Markets and Entrepreneurship to Extend Opportunity, Center for International Private Enterprise. Retrieved May 26, 2019, from https://www.cipe.org/wp-content/uploads/2015/05/FS_05262015-Economic-Inclusion.pdf

Christensen, C. M., Hall, T., Dillon, K., & Duncan, D. S. (2016). 'Know Your Customers' 'Jobs To Be Done'. *Harvard Business Review, 94*, 7.

Dinar standard. (2018). Islamic Fintech Report 2018: Current Landscape & Path Forward. Retrieved July 7, 2018, from https://www.dinarstandard.com/wp-content/uploads/2018/12/Islamic-Fintech-Report-2018.pdf

FATF (Financial Action Task Force). (2017, November). Anti-money Laundering and Terrorist Financing Measures and Financial Inclusion. Retrieved June 6, 2019, from http://www.fatf-gafi.org/media/fatf/content/images/Updated-2017-FATF-2013-Guidance.pdf

Hagiu, A. (2007). Multi-sided Platforms: From Microfoundations to Design and Expansion Strategies. Retrieved September 12, 2007, from https://www.hbs.edu/faculty/Publication%20Files/07-094.pdf.

Jouti, A. T. (2018). Islamic Finance: Financial Inclusion or Migration? *ISRA International Journal of Islamic Finance, 10*(2), 277–288. https://doi.org/10.1108/IJIF-07-2018-0074

Kaplan, R. S., & Porter, M. E. (2011). The Big Idea: How to Solve the Cost Crisis in Health Care. *Harvard Business Review, 89*, 7.

Khazanah Nasional Berhad. (2017). Sukuk ihsan - sustainable and responsible investment sukuk. Retrieved June 6, 2019, from http://www.khazanah.com.my/About-Khazanah/Our-Case-Studies/Khazanah-360/Sukuk-Ihsan-Sustainable and-Responsible-Investment

Kramer, M., & Pfitzer, M. W. (2016). The Ecosystem of Shared Value. *Harvard Business Review, 94*, 10.

Maddox, K. J., & Epstein, A. M. (2018, October 29). Using Bundled Payments to Improve the Patient Experience, Digital Article, Harvard Business Review. Retrieved June 6, 2019, from https://hbr.org/2018/10/using-bundled-payments-to-improve-the-patient experience

Mukhtar, S., Ashiqin, Z. Z., & Jusoh, S. (2018). Islamic Law and Sustainable Development Goals. *Tazkia Islamic Finance and Business Review, 12*, 1.

Robert, C., & Johnathan, M. Microfinance and Economic Development (2017). World Bank Policy Research Working Paper No. 8252. SSRN. Retrieved August 18, 2018, from https://ssrn.com/abstract=3076231

Ron, A., & Kapoor, R. (2016). Right Tech, Wrong Time: How to Make Sure Your Ecosystem Is Ready for the Newest Technologies. *Harvard Business Review*, 94(9), 61–67.

RURAL ELECTRIFICATION IN INDIA CUSTOMER BEHAVIOUR AND DEMAND, Rockefeller foundation. (2019). Retrieved June 5, 2019, from https://assets.rockefellerfoundation.org/app/uploads/20190219123625/Rural-Electrification-in-India-Customer-Behaviour-and-Demand.pdf.

Sethi, D., & Acharya, D. (2018). Financial Inclusion and Economic Growth Linkage: Some Cross Country Evidence. *Journal of Financial Economic Policy*, 10(3), 369–385. https://doi.org/10.1108/JFEP-11-2016-0073

Teixeira, T. (2019). Case Study – Sell Direct to Consumer of Through Amazon. *HBR, 97*, 2.

The Economist. (2017). Special Report: Technology in Africa, November 11th–17th.

The Economist. (2018a). Special Report: Financial Inclusion. May 5th.

The Economist. (2018b). Special Report: Financial Inclusion Is Making Great Strides, 3 May.

The Economist. (2019). Special Report: A Bank in Your Pocket. May 4th–10th.

The World Bank. (2018). The 2017 Global Findex and the Fintech Revolution. Retrieved June 6, 2018, from www.worldbank.org/en/events/2018/04/23/global-findex-fintech-inclusion

Williams, C. C., Horodnic, I. A., & Windebank, J. (2017). Explaining Participation in the Informal Economy: A Purchaser Perspective. *International Journal of Social Economics, 44*(11), 1421–1436. https://doi.org/10.1108/IJSE-03-2016-0099

Websites

Climate bonds initiative: https://www.climatebonds.net

Credit Guarantee Corporation (CGC) in Malaysia - https://www.cgc.com.my/

Caisse Centrale de Garantie (CCG) in Morocco –http://www.ccg.ma/

https://www.easypaisa.com.pk/easypaisa-handset-financing

Fonds de garantie des crédits aux PME (FGAR) in Algeria - https://www.fgar.dz/portal/fr

Kuveyt Turk Bank : https://www.kuveytturk.com.tr/en/branchless-banking/digital-xtm-branch/general-features

Compte nickel in France : https://compte-nickel.fr/

https://newzoo.com/insights/rankings/top-50-countries-by-smartphone-penetration-and-users/

https://www.statista.com/topics/840/smartphones/

United nations: https://www.un.org/sustainabledevelopment/sustainable-development-goals/

CHAPTER 13

Utilization of Digital Technology for Zakat Development

Irfan Syauqi Beik, Randi Swandaru, and Priyesta Rizkiningsih

Abstract The nature of digital technology, which can induce efficiency, transparency, and access widening, is basically in line with the objective of zakat in enlarging the impact of zakat for poverty alleviation and public welfare. However, lack of advancement on the use of digital technology may lead to a failure in addressing poverty and equality problems. This emphasizes the importance of digital technology which is able to tackle the entire process of zakat management in terms of operation, collection, and distribution. This study analyzes the endeavor of the National Board of Zakat of Indonesia (BAZNAS) in applying digital technology to create muzakki and mustahik identification number in order to establish a structured database. On the fundraising side, BAZNAS collects zakat fund

I. S. Beik (✉)
IPB University, Bogor, Indonesia

The National Zakat Board of Indonesia (BAZNAS), Jakarta, Indonesia
e-mail: irfan_beik@apps.ipb.ac.id

R. Swandaru • P. Rizkiningsih
The National Zakat Board of Indonesia (BAZNAS), Jakarta, Indonesia

M. M. Billah (ed.), *Islamic FinTech*,
https://doi.org/10.1007/978-3-030-45827-0_13

through website, mobile application, artificial intelligence, e-pay, as well as e-wallet to ease muzakki in paying zakat. In the case of zakat distribution, BAZNAS utilizes the technology to create ATM Beras (Rice Automatic Telling Machine) that is designed for the poor to get easy access to rice using their identification card on the machine.

Keywords Utilization • Digital • FinTech • Technology • Zakat • Social fund

Introduction

The emergence of revolution industry 4.0 becomes a game changer in the business world. This is not merely to cut the time used within the process, but also to innovate the way current businesses run. To succeed in this interconnected world, it needs integrated cooperation from technological field. For instance, there has been a success story from the vast coffee chain Starbucks. Looking back in 2009, its stock price was 8 USD, but with a touch of technology in its operational activities which increased its consumer engagement, the price skyrocketed to 73 USD in 2012. This is simply because technology connects the world; the transformation needs to be linked to technology if we do not want to be far behind with the innovations. Further, it has been said by George Westerman, a research scientist at MIT's Center for Digital Business, that the changes made by technology have been impacting every industry rapidly (Fitzgerald, et al., 2013), not to forget social sectors as well. In the social sector, the utilization of digital technology also has brought a massive change. For example, the existence of crowdfunding platform for social project transforms donator behavior in donating their fund. Crowdfunding establishes a borderless environment; hence wherever the donator is, they can directly donate via the platform by using, for instance, fund transfer, e-wallet, mobile payment, and the other payment channels. Further, as crowdfunding provides all the data about the project campaign, it makes easier for donator to know the details of the project, and they can monitor the project or in other words it increases the program transparency.

For the purpose of explaining the utilization of digital technology for zakat development, it is crucial to define what digital technology is, as there are various definitions for this term. According to the OECD (2018), new and emerging digital technologies which are applied in financial services are known as financial technology. However, there are no specific definitions about what financial technology is. In some cases, financial technology refers to companies that provide services based on technologies. Further, this terminology can be misleading as it only assumes start-up companies and forgone well-established companies using digital technologies. Hence, by adopting OECD definition, FinTech definition in this section involves not only the application of new digital technologies to financial services but also the development of business models and products which rely on these technologies and more generally on digital platforms and processes.

To be more specific, digitalization that happens in financial industry is presented in Table 13.1.

Several relations among digital technologies mentioned above result in financial technology where it involves additional in development of business models and product designs that used technology, particularly digital platform, as its fundamental media to operate. By mentioning relations, it means that there is interrelation between AI, big data, and cloud computing. From ledger technology, DLT takes part in financial transactions like payment (OECD, 2018).

As transformation leads the financial activities, the way social movements operate must change as well, in this case about raising money through *zakat* for the social purpose. In addition, applying digital technology able to broaden the coverage, both in terms of the recipient (*mustahiq*) and the payer (*muzakki*). In the end, the impact will be well-spread to those who are indeed classified into eight groups (*asnaf*), not just merely to certain groups or just to abort the responsibility of *muzakki* to pay *zakat*.

Digital Technology and the Objective of Zakat Management Act: The Case of Indonesia

Zakat purpose is to eradicate inequality as well as to reduce the social gap within society. *Zakat* has been part of five worshiping actions in Islam. Respectively, they are declaration of faith, prayer, *zakat*, fasting, and pilgrimage. Obligation in paying *zakat* classified into two, the first for *zakat fitrah* (zakat collection during *Ramadhan*, the deadline is the night before

Table 13.1 Application of new technologies to financial services

Digital technology	*Financial activities and services*							
	Payment services	*Advisory and agency services planning*	*Investment and trading*	*Lending and funding*	*Insurance*	*Security*	*Operations*	*Communications*
Distributed ledger technology (DLT) or blockchain	x	x	x	x	x	x	x	x
Big data		x	x	x	x	x	x	x
Internet of Things					x			x
Cloud computing				x			x	
Artificial Intelligence		x	x		x			x
Biometric technology					x	x		
Augmented/virtual reality		x	x					x

Source: OECD (2018)

ied prayer) and the second for *zakat mal*, where it becomes the act of wealth management for Muslim. *Zakat fitrah* is zakat type where it should be delivered in the form of staple food of each region like rice, wheat, and bread. Even so, people can pay *zakat fitrah* in the form of cash; later *amil* (people who manage *zakat collection and distribution*) can buy the staple food from it.

Zakat is a unique feature in Islamic Moral Economy (IME) as it is endogenously embedded as a socio-economic mechanism that can redistribute wealth among the society, which is also one of the foundational worships in Islam. It is also directly linked to the concept of moral economy that emphasizes norms and sentiment that inspires individual or institution to conduct their rights and responsibilities in an economic system in respect to others in developing a moral economy based on sharing principles (Sayer, 2000, 2004, 2007). In this regard, *zakat* embodies Islamic values that essentialize the welfare of the individual alongside the public interest. Moreover, *zakat* as the moral economy instruments is an essential tool in articulating and practicing social justice without curbing the motivation of people to achieve worldly success along with success in hereafter or *falah* which aligns to what Tripp (2006) defines as the ideal concept of Islamic economics.

Zakat represents the idea of moral economy, where economic activity is submerged into the social formation in a society and is determined by non-economic factors, or as the well-known concept of embeddedness that was brought upon by Booth (1993), Granovetter (1985), Polanyi (1945), and Thompson (1971). Under this assertion, the obligatory of *zakat* that was derived from Divine source (Quran and Sunnah) determines the wealth redistribution from the rich to the poor and strengthens the social cohesion among society by emphasizing kinship, neighborhood, and reciprocity as opposed to the notion of market economy that merely focused on creating economic value regardless of the consequences. Likewise, the *zakat* institution endogenously aligns with IME, which aims at creating a just ambience whereby the less fortunate can be elevated, can be functioned, and has a space to grow as *ihsani* behavioral norms suggest (Zaman & Asutay, 2009).

Lastly, *zakat* inherently embodied the objectives of *shari'ah* (*maqasidshari'ah*) in its operation by achieving the ultimate human well-being both in material and spiritual (Asutay, 2007a, 2007b, 2012). In the micro level, *zakat* operation redistributes wealth among the society and emancipates the less fortunate parallel with the intention of Islamic law, which is safeguarding and essentializing human faith, self, intellect, progeny, and wealth (Chapra, 2000). Nonetheless, Siddiqi (2004) argues that the objectives of *Shari'ah* should not merely be confined into the five notions but beyond that to achieve justice and equity. Under this assertion, *zakat* is a valid and reliable mechanism to present a just and equitable growth in a society.

In relation to the aforementioned, the application of digital technology is aligned with the objective and principles of zakat act in Indonesia. The nature of digital technology that can induce efficiency, transparency, redundancy avoidance, and access widening, is symmetrical with the objective of zakat act that aims to increase efficiency and effectivity of zakat operation and services as well as enlarge the impact of zakat for poverty alleviation and public welfare.

Moreover, the application of digital technology also emphasizes the principle of zakat act in Indonesia on zakat operation. For example, a robust database mustahik is a baseline for a disbursement activity that is sharia compliance, trustworthy, expedience, and fair. Moreover, the national zakat management system assures accountability, legal certainty, and integrated reporting.

In addition, the zakat act induces to the unified and integrated *zakat* management system whereby *zakat* institutions conduct their activities under a standard regulation and integrate their report into an agreed platform to create a national report and database. *Mustahik* database integration is one of the benefits of a unified and integrated *zakat* management system that can avoid redundant distribution, prevent inequality disbursement between regions, and become a baseline of performance measurement or policy-making (Beik, 2014). This aligns with Ahmed's (2004) statement that the performance of *zakat* institution to combat poverty hinges on the information exchange in which the *zakat* institution can gain trust from the customer and increase its credibility.

The zakat act in Indonesia assigns BAZNAS (the National Board of Zakat) as the leader of national *zakat* management. Having this role, BAZNAS is charged with several tasks as identified below that will be impossible to conduct without a robust national *zakat* information system or abbreviated as SIMBA in Bahasa:

1. To implement the principles of *zakat* act, that is, sharia-compliant, trust, expedience, justice, legal certainty, integrated, and accountable to the national *zakat* management system.

2. To increase the service effectiveness and efficiency of national *zakat* management.
3. To eradicate poverty by optimizing the *zakat* fund utilization and consider some principles such as equity and fairness in each region.
4. To provide a *zakat* transaction receipt for payers that can be used as tax deduction.
5. To conduct national *zakat* hierarchical reporting system.

On October 2012, with the help of Bank Rakyat Indonesia Syariah under its CSR scheme, BAZNAS launched SIMBA as the national *zakat* management information system (Republika, 2012). SIMBA has two main functions: recording collection and disbursement of *zakat* and creating a report based on the submitted data which works under the *zakat* information management system. In addition, SIMBA also consists of supporting organizational information system that maintains several information systems such as finance, human resource, logistic, and public affairs. It is a web-based system that connects each BAZNAS office in every region to BAZNAS headquarter in Jakarta. Therefore, this feature allows SIMBA to create a real-time online report of national *zakat* activities in each level in every region. This model is even more suitable to produce the national *zakat* hierarchical report as mandated by the *zakat* act.

Indisputable Benefit of Digital Technology for Zakat Development

Studies on the *zakat* management system, especially on utilization of digital technology for zakat development, are quite limited if not scarce. One can expect the reason is that this particular type of study needs a stronger involvement and attachment to operational activities of *zakat* in the sense of assembling primary data. Nonetheless, there are some studies that scrutinize Wahab and Rahman's (2013) emphasis on the importance of information and communication technology as well as the computerized zakat system to improve zakat institutions' efficiency. There are several findings on how *zakat* institutions do not successfully address the poverty and equality problem because of the lack of advancement of digital technology (Embong & Nor, 2013; Mahamod, 2011). Inaccurate database of *asnaf*, under-identification of *asnaf*, bureaucracy, and geographical challenge are some hindrances on the effective use of *zakat* for poverty alleviation (Othman & Noor, 2012) that can be resolved by optimizing the *zakat* management information system.

This emphasizes the importance of digital technology which is able to tackle the entire process of zakat giving, such as an information system benefiting from the latest technology that can robustly conduct such identification and ease the *zakat* management in modern time. This identification is important both for *muzaki* and *mustahiq*. For muzaki, the identification may be relevant for deducting or reducing the amount of tax payment. On the distribution side, such identification is important to avoid redundant disbursement so that it can attain equitable and fair *zakat* distribution. Such identification is also important to monitor the progress of *zakat* recipient and the effectiveness of the *zakat* program.

Several studies also have revealed the importance of management information system (MIS) in the non-profit organization (NGO) such as *zakat* institution. Dash and Mishra (2014) argue that MIS can ease NGO in data documentation and analysis, performance monitoring, and strategic decision-making. Moreover, MIS will help NGO to increase credibility and accountability by presenting their activities to the public. It might also help in safeguarding the four pillars of ethics in NGO, namely, disclosure, transparency, avoidance of conflict of interest, and oversight as elaborated by White (1952).

Moreover, digital technology can ease the *zakat* administrator to run the operation efficiently as it can lower the cost of dissemination of information (O'Connor & Martinsons, 2006). In this regard, management information system can reduce unnecessary cost by enlarging the usage of internet and online transaction system. This is absolutely relevant to the fact that the amount of *zakat* that can be utilized to organize *zakat* is limited to one-eighth in accordance with Hanafi's ruling. Therefore, integrating management information system to the *zakat* operation is essential to enhance the *zakat* management system.

The Digital Technology Advancement for Zakat Collection, Disbursement, and Operation

Zakat collection used to be traditional where *muzakki* will come to the mosque where *amil* will reside, out of their daily activities, temporarily during *zakat fitrah* collection. Most of the time, *muzakki* will bring the staple food or cash to the *amil*. The food collected will be delivered to the needy people who live around it. But in case there is no one needy on the neighborhood, the *zakat* is permitted to be delivered to the other needy person. The key of delivery is to put the closest needy people live near the area. Even, if there is no one worth-giving, it may be delivered to the needy people across country.

Currently, with the evolving technology, new payment systems are developed almost in every facet of life, including social fund start-up which already initiated through crowdfunding, namely, EthisCrowd. For example, in banking they already facilitate the customer to pay zakat by using mobile banking or ATM machine. But, specifically, start-ups about Islamic social fund are rarely to be found. As minority Muslim country life in the region, Russia and the USA have started to begin by launching start-ups catering the Muslim need to pay *zakat* by establishing PayZakat in Russia and Zakatify in the USA (Dubai Islamic Economy Development Center, 2018).

In the case of Indonesia, the most populous Muslim country, even though a specific platform for zakat or social fund is still limited, the National Board of Zakat (BAZNAS) in Indonesia continues to occupy digital technology for fundraising. There are five strategies which are developed by BAZNAS in the digital era: (1) BAZNAS Platform, (2) Commercial Platform, (3) Artificial Intelligent Platform, (4) Social Media Platform, and (5) Innovative Platform. Those five strategies can be categorized into two main groups which are platforms that are built by BAZNAS and those that are channeled with existing platform.

The former includes zakat payment through BAZNAS's website and an application named Muzaki corner for mobile phone, while channeling with existing digital technology platform involving commercial platform such as crowdfunding and e-commerce platform. For instance, muzaki could pay their zakat through an Indonesian crowdfunding platform named kitabisa.com. By utilizing this crowdfunding platform, BAZNAS can engage with muzaki by communicating the story of the program. Further, muzaki could know the progress of the program through this platform. Thus far, BAZNAS has engaged with several e-commerce and banks such as Kaskus, Kitabisa.com, Bukalapak.com, ATM Bersama, MatahariMall.com, CIMB Niaga, Mandiri E Cash, and E Pay BRi to set up host-to-host data interchange with SIMBA. By having this system, *muzakki* will get direct notification whenever they give donation. In parallel, our finance system will automatically record the transaction in the ledger.

Moreover, BAZNAS also occupy artificial intelligence (AI) in its digital fundraising by cooperating with current existing platforms. For examples, BAZNAS has an AI in LINE application that will help muzaki in paying their zakat. Besides that, in order to increase zakat fund collected, BAZNAS also maximizes social media platforms, as 56% of Indonesian population are active internet users particularly in social media, according to We Are Social (2019). As innovation in today's world cannot be avoided, BAZNAS also facilitates muzaki to pay zakat through e-wallet, which is easier for muzaki as they only scan BAZNAS's barcode to pay zakat to BAZNAS.

Utilizing digital technology in *zakat* development might be a challenge as what is familiarly used maximally is for profit purpose. In fact, there is only some who utilize digital technology for developing religious social fund, *zakat*. Regarding the fact that from 7.697 billion people in the world, 66% have become unique mobile users, 58% are internet users, 45% are active social media users, and 45% are mobile social media users, there is still huge potential to maximize the resources (WeAreSocial, 2019).

In another case, looking at the number of *Muslim* population in the world might be a surprise that it has huge potential to be an incredible source of *zakat* from all over the world. We help people from different parts of the world to help their sisters and brothers who live in other parts of the world through *zakat*. We can collect money in a short time just like a start-up, for instance, kickstarter and kitabisa but in a form of Islamic social finance. Basically, such a thing has been initially started by Islamic relief in collecting money for *iedqurban*. They collect money to facilitate people from all over the world to buy animal for *iedqurban* for people who live in the other side of the world. It is inevitably ease people who live in a country where Muslim is minority and there is no *zakat* Centre provided or by distance it is quite far.

The use of digital technology improves transparency through DLT; thus the institutions are able to control the transaction records, about from where the fund was sent or about to where the fund is transferred. It is kind of providing double-checking services. By doing so, we can control whether the fund is received by the right parties or not. Hence, *muzakki* does not feel betrayed as there is a proof that the fund they gave was received by the right person. Whilst Internet of Things (IoT) provides information about each individual where it can be used to tailoring product, it has been understood that there is huge opportunity to be explored. But it is impossible to be actualized, to gain maximum purpose of *zakat*, if there is no demand met by *zakat* institutions. *Zakat* is indeed an obligation, and it has various types, from *zakatmaal* (for purifying wealth based on the *nisab*) and *zakatfitrah*. For Muslim, it is a must to pay it, both for *zakatmaal* and *zakat fitrah*. In fact, there are just few percentages who understand on how to count how much should they pay for *zakatmaal*. By using digital technology, we might be able to read what kind of services they need, what kind of interface they are comfortable with, what kind of payment they prefer to use.

Despite the risks it inherits like cybercrimes, realized it or not, digital finance helps increasing financial inclusion. It improves efficiency; hence operational cost is low along with the quicker speed and more convenient services offered (World Bank, 2016). It avoids trauma that happens because of fake news that is currently spreading; there is supposed to be an institution which is able to bridge its news authenticity, for instance, legal institution for *zakat* collection from a country representative. People are supposed to be aware about fake news, but anticipating those who are traumatized because of being led by certain party for doing good deeds is also part of the effort to gain more *zakat* fund to help more people who are in need.

On the disbursement side, digital technology has been implemented on several zakat programs. For instance, BAZNAS in Indonesia creates ATM Beras (Rice Automatic Telling Machine) that is designed for easing the poor to get access for rice by taping their identification card on the machine. It will identify the amount of rice that is dedicated for the identified mustahik who has priorly been assessed by amil. By having this machine, it can protect the dignity of mustahik for not begging publicly for rice. They can go to the ATM Beras secretly and get their right. Secondly, on the last enormous earthquake in Sulawesi, BAZNAS launched Cari Temu Apps to ease people in finding their relatives after the disaster. As we all know, traditionally, after the tragedy victims are looking for their relatives in several hospitals by asking the nurse or reading the announcement letter that is stuck on the huge board or wall. They hope that their family will be found and alive. However, this method is exhausting and inefficient. Having said that, BAZNAS creates Cari Temu Apps that allows everybody to submit information about the family that they have lost or anybody who they found after the calamity.

Moreover, to emancipate traditional stall in the middle of the giants of retail store chain, BAZNAS emancipates mustahik in the urban area through ZMART. In this program, mustahik get several intervention programs such stall renovation, branding, additional cash capital, intensive assistance, and ZMART system installation. By this system mustahik can have modern retail transaction record system. They can scan the barcode of each product to calculate the amount of sale for each transaction. This system allows mustahik to count and check their stock and sales. Other than these three examples, BAZNAS is now enlarging the usage of digital technology for helping farmers, cattleman, and micro entrepreneurs.

On the operation side, BAZNAS has utilized digital technology in several divisions including human resources, finance, and legal. Amil BAZNAS can proof their absence digitally through an app that internally build. Moreover, they can claim their day off, healthcare services, insurance, and so on. Every legal document issuance also can be produced and monitored using the internal network system. Obviously, every finance transaction both collection and disbursement can be recorded using SIMBA. It can be accessed through desktop unit or using mobile applications.

Challenges, Opportunities, and Threats

In efforts to raise the involvement of people to evolve *zakat* collection is by making Islamic wealth management more automated to cater the need of stakeholders. According to Dubai Islamic Economy Development Center, the growth was still in the low level (Dubai Islamic Economy Development Center, 2018).

According to Dubai Islamic Economy Development Center (2018), the development of financial technology might be successfully utilized if it has well cooperation among the crucial parties as below:

1. Governments as the regulator.

   In the establishment of regulations, government has provided direct supports. It disciplines citizens as well as the *zakat* organization in terms of channeling the fund to parties in need. For instance, we have Financial Services Authority of Indonesia (OJK) in Indonesia, Financial Conduct Authority in the UK, and Central Bank of Russia in Russia.
2. Investors in support of giving capital and analyzing the market of conducting *zakat* services through financial technology.

3. Start-ups in providing media to make the scheme run well. Create engagement with the venture builders.
4. Consumers as the *muzakki* and *mustahiq* are the wheel of this system.
   Indirectly, consumers help to acknowledge the targeted society about the information through word of mouth or rather we call it as word of fingers since the information spreads through fingertips. This action will result in the raise of consumer awareness. In broader scope, the consumers are the adult, who already have an obligation to pay *zakat maal* and *zakat fitrah*.

Challenges

Some aspects to put into consideration about improving *zakat* collection through digital technology are about the market targeted. Currently, according to Dubai Islamic Economy Development Center (2018), the Muslim consumers are dominated by youth, and they are tech-savvy in which they demand for changes in digital reformation. In other words, they demand for changing the traditional way to the automated way just like their day-to-day activities from doing payment and commute.

According to Pew Research Center (2015), there will be a tremendous domination of Muslim population starting from 2010 to 2050. It is expected that Muslim majority will fulfill 73% of world population. This is a great news and also a challenge at the same time on how to improve the quality of life with *zakat* along with the growing number of Muslim population.

The questions arise on how many people are using the technology wisely and maximally in terms of using it for social purpose, in this case for paying *zakat*, both for *zakat fitrah* and for *zakat maal*: how many people are aware of the obligation to pay *zakatmaal* and *zakat fitrah*? These are problems from each individual as a Muslim. But then, in a broader scope the concern revolves around how many independent *zakat* institutions are already established. Through the digitalization technology, it is expected to detect on how much an individual should pay for *zakat fitrah* and also *zakat maal*. By providing ease, it will trigger people to fulfill their obligations.

Indonesia as one of the countries with the largest Muslim population has many independent *zakat* institutions; further it is followed by independent *zakat* group collection in the level of sub-district, even in a smaller scope to bridge the need of Muslim to fulfill their obligations. Even some Islamic bank has been providing platform for its customer to distribute some of the money for *zakat*. This is in fact a good thing. But, the development is not integrated and not well-recorded by the *zakat* representative institution. On the other hand, the targeted *mustahiq* might have received *zakat* from different sub-districts if they rely on the "circle" principle.

There will be "C" parties who received double fund from the *amil*. But, this circle principle will not happen if each independent institution does the recording and have transparent system that can be accessed publicly. In fact, as this is not their expertise to do so, thus it remains traditional and not updated, only for the sake of doing it to abort their responsibility.

To cope with the circle principle, an integrated filing system is in demand, a national filing system from the application or start-up about who is the *mustahik* as well as the *muzakki*. Why is *muzakki* data needed as well? It is as a mapping about the *zakat* payers; thus national zakat collection organization is able to allocate the fund to the nearest people in need.

Further, another question pops up on how to integrate those institutions with the *zakat* center in each country. This is in relation between consumers and institutions in the world. These institutions are needed for the sake of outreaching those beyond reach of the *zakat* center of each country. There are people in need in spread all over the world: certain place might have surplus in receiving *zakat* donation, and certain place might be in scarcity of *zakat* donation.

If we notice in social media, some people who have huge care will make a movement in the internet to collect fund to help people from another world. They do it individually, organizing the mass to donate and distribute the fund directly to the region or groups of people who need help. The operational cost is rising as they do individually, but when the cause is organized by the representative, it might save some pennies. By doing this, the excess money for operational cost can be donated as *zakat* payment.

As some countries have thousand islands, some targeted market of *mustahiq* are not well-addressed. Thus, they remain live under poverty line, whilst actually they can get the best care if we can address it well. By utilizing technology, it can overcome these problems. Through the satellite, we can map the people who live in certain island. By rechecking it to the government, we gain information, whether the people are having a standard of proper life or not. Then, we can execute them whether or not to be a *mustahiq*.

Another challenge to be focused on is that not every area in every country is under the radar of having proper electricity and signal to connect to the system. In Indonesia, some regions do not have access to the communication signal. For having the access, they need to go to the city center, which is miles away.

Opportunities

Considering the future population of Muslim in the world, according to Pew Research Center's Forum on Religion and Public, there will be a rise from 1.7 billion in 2014 to 2.2 billion in 2030, or in other words there is 26.4% rise in population. It means there are billions of people who are potential to be *muzakki*.

This huge potential should be maximized by providing an online platform to be a media of sending *zakat* online, considering the development of revolution industry 4.0. Other platforms for donating money for social causes have been mushrooming tremendously, but not for Islamic social funds. Taking a closer look at the development of FinTech to bridge the need of paying *zakat*, based on Dubai Islamic Economy Development Center (2018) in Islamic Fintech Report 2018, a number of FinTech in *zakat* in this world are coming from two countries that established it, Russia and the USA. These two countries are the place of Muslim who live as minority. It stressed the need of *zakat* platform to cater the need of Muslim needs no matter where they live.

It occurs that those Muslim who live as minority somehow find difficulty to circulate the *zakat* fund. While so, in another part of the world, there are people who are in urgent need of help from their brothers and sisters.

As the establishment of *zakat* center, it is expected that they will be able to give a valid information in the whole world about the update of the recipients' (*mustahiq*) life. Whether or not they still need help, for instance, Muslim who live in Palestine are in struggle to free their country.

The Muslim familiarity of *zakat*, particularly for *zakat maal*, is by utilizing Internet of Things (IoT) to customize the user feed based on the region. The application of digital technology is also as a media for introducing Muslim who are not familiar to *zakatmaal* to put their attention on it and apply it as the information is all over the page of their screen.

People might be Muslim, but the awareness toward the *zakat maal* might be low as people are faced to the hassle to count their income and wealth which is varied from time to time. In short, they somehow do not do bookkeeping for their wealth.

The benefits transferred to the *amil* for utilizing the digital technology are the efficiency improvement. *Amil* no longer face the hassle to make a report one by one as everything is automatically reported by the system. For example, if muzakki transfers zakat funds, amil no longer need to do the bookkeeping right away, as the data will be updated in a real time basis by the system.

Further, the use of digital technology can increase the transparency of zakat institution and everyone can monitor from whom and to where zakat is allocated. *Zakat* practice is to give the money collected to the closest circle who need help. *Muzakki* has all the right to witness in which area or which person is their money being transferred to. To make a difference between the *zakat* practice in the past and in the present, the real-time update about the targeted *mustahiq* can be a relief. We cannot deny that the social gap that happens in our life somehow leads the tears brimming from our eyes. Through the things that the least people can do, it can make a change. It might trigger people to help more people to be freed from this poverty, inequality.

Threats

By implementing the digital technology in *zakat* to collect the fund from all over the world, it means a risk behind the technology is threatening. Cybersecurity is highly threatening the sustainability of the Islamic social fund. But, through the data encryption, the data stored will be protected and will get improved with the technology. The data analytics also can detect the unusual activities that happen in the system. Even the DLT helps increase the transactions transparency where it eases to track and control (OECD, 2018).

On the other hand, as the transparency improved, once the *muzakki* witnessing inappropriate things occurred, this will impact their behavior. Whether they will not trust the *zakat* institution anymore, from the national level or even international level, they will move to another non-Muslim social fund institution without spreading the news or they will not trust the *zakat* institution by spreading the news. This latter might create a domino effect. Through this case, it is not only the name of *zakat* institution who get crossed but also the name of Islam as religion. Thus, the system should be well maintained, and there will be no error that cost the public trust toward Muslim and Islam as a religion.

References

Ahmed, H. (2004). *Role of Zakah and Awqaf in Poverty Alleviation*. Jeddah: IRTI, IDB.

Asutay, M. (2007a). A Political Economy Approach to Islamic Economics: Systemic Understanding for an Alternative Economic System. *Kyoto Bulletin of Islamic Area Studies*, 3–18.

Asutay, M. (2007b). Conceptualisation of the Second Best Solution in Overcoming the Social Failure of Islamic Banking and Finance: Examining the Overpowering of Homoislamicus by Homoeconomicus. *IIUM Journal of Economics and Management, 15*(2), 167–195.

Asutay, M. (2012). Conceptualising and Locating the Social Failure of Islamic Finance: Aspirations of Islamic Moral Economy vs the Realities of Islamic Finance. *Asian and African Area Studies, 11*(2), 93–113.

Beik, I. S. (2014). *http://irfansb.blogdetik.com* [Online]. Retrieved August 5, 2017, from http://irfansb.blogdetik.com/2014/02/03/integrasi-database-mustahik

Booth, W. J. (1993). A Note on the Idea of the Moral Economy. *American Political Science Review, 87*(4), 949–954.

Chapra, M. U. (2000). *The Future of Economics: an Islamic Perspective*. Leicester: Islamic Foundation.

Dash, K. C., & Mishra, U. (2014). Critical Considerations for Developing MIS for NGOs. *SSRN Electronic Journal*, 1–12.

Dubai Islamic Economy Development Center. (2018). *Islamic Fintech Report 2018: Current Landscape and Path Forward*. s.l.: DIEDC.

Embong, M. R., & Nor, M. N. M. (2013). Role of Zakat to Eradicate Poverty in Malaysia. *Jurnal Pengurusan, 39*, 141–150.

Fitzgerald, M., Kruschwitz, N., Bonnet, D., & Welch, M. (2013). *Embracing Digital Technology*. Massachusetts: Massachusetts Institute of Technology.

Granovetter, M. (1985). Economic Action and Social Structure: The Problem of Embeddedness. *American Journal of Sociology, 91*(3), 481–510.

Mahamod, L. H. (2011). *Alleviation of Rural Poverty in Malaysia: The Role of Zakat, A Case Study*, PhD Thesis. Edinbrugh University, Edinbrugh.

O'Connor, N. G., & Martinsons, M. G. (2006). Management of Information Systems: Insights from Accounting Research. *Information and Management, 43*(8), 1014–1024.

OECD. (2018). *Financial Markets, Insurance and Private Pensions: Digitalisation and Finance*. s.l.: OECD.

Othman, A. B., & Noor, A. H. M. (2012). Role of Zakat in Minimizing Economic Inequalities Among Muslim: A Preliminary Study on Non-Recipients of Zakat Fund. In *The 3rd International Conference on Business and Economic Research Proceeding* (pp. 1–14).

Pew Research Center. (2015). *Why Muslims Are the World's Fastest-Growing Religious Group*. Washington, DC: Pew Research Center.

Polanyi, K. (1945). *Origins of Our Time: The Great Transformation*. London: s.n.

Republika. (2012). *BRIS Serahkan Sistem IT Zakat* [Online]. Retrieved August 10, 2017, from http://www.republika.co.id/berita/ekonomi/syariah-ekonomi/12/07/09/m6wieo-bris-serahkan-sistem-it-zakat

Sayer, A. (2000). Moral Economy and Political Economy. *Studies in Political Economy, 61*, 79–104.

Sayer, A. (2004). *Moral Economy* (pp. 1–15). Department of Sociology, Lancaster University.

Sayer, A. (2007). Moral Economy as Critique. *New Political Economy, 12*(2), 261–270.

Siddiqi, M. N. (2004). *What Went Wrong with Islamic Economics*. Jeddah: s.n.

Thompson, E. P. (1971). The Moral Economy of the English Crowd in the Eighteenth Century. *The Past and Present Society*, 76–136.

Tripp, C. (2006). *Islam and the Moral Economy: The Challenge of Capitalism*. Cambridge: Cambridge University Press.

Wahab, N. A., & Rahman, A. R. A. (2013). Determinants of Efficiency of Zakat Institutions in Malaysia: A Non-Parametric Approach. *Asian Journal of Business and Accounting, 6*(2), 33–64.

WeAreSocial. (2019). *Digital 2019*. s.l.: WeAreSocial.

White, D. E. (1952). *The Nonprofit Challenge: Integrating Ethics into the Purpose and Promise of Our Nation's Charities*. New York: Palgrave Macmillan.

World Bank. (2016). *Digital Dividends*. Washington, DC: World Bank.

Zaman, N., & Asutay, M. (2009). Divergence Between Aspirations and Realities of Islamic Economics: A Political Economy Approach to Bridging the Divide. *IIUM Journal of Economics and Management, 17*(1), 73–96.

CHAPTER 14

I-FinTech and Its Value Proposition for Islamic Asset and Wealth Management

Hazik Mohamed

Abstract Artificial Intelligence (AI) is a highly evolved area of computer science that strives to create intelligent machines that can replicate certain human behaviour without its irrationalities for better predictability and consistency. Advanced AI that utilizes machine learning makes it possible for machines to learn from previous data (experience), adjust to new inputs (instructions) and perform tasks through updated algorithms. Through sophisticated algorithms, modern AI systems can be trained to accomplish specific tasks by processing large amounts of data, obtaining insights and recognizable patterns in the data to act upon. As such AI has become a hot topic, with much interest on its advantages to the highly regulated financial services industry.

Similarly, blockchain technology also has the potential to both enrich and improve financial processes and asset management systems, and progressive corporations have invested and devoted resources to utilize and incorporate blockchain into their businesses. The use of distributed ledgers or blockchain has been explored in areas such as compliance and

H. Mohamed (✉)
Stellar Consulting Group, Singapore, Singapore
e-mail: hazik@stellarcg.com

M. M. Billah (ed.), *Islamic FinTech*,
https://doi.org/10.1007/978-3-030-45827-0_14

securities settlement, and these technologies could also be used to improve efficiencies in asset management.

In this chapter, we provide a short discussion of AI and blockchain applications in asset management and understand the benefits and the shift in processes, as well as the challenges that need to be overcome for practical applications for AI and blockchain and how to approach such innovations.

Keywords Islamic • FinTech • Value • Asset • Wealth • Management

Introduction: Explosive Artificial Intelligence (AI) Growth Around the World

In the last 60 years the AI field has experienced curious interest, but in the last five years, it has turned into explosive growth where governments around the world are competing to create superior AI facilities and research with a view to AI being a lever for greater economic power and influence. According to the Wuzhen Institute Report (2017), 5154 AI start-ups have been established globally during the past five years, representing a 175% increase relative to the previous 12 years. There are two explanations for this impressive growth. First, exponential advances in computing power have led to declining processing and data storage costs, and secondly, the immense data availability has increased, creating more possibilities in the AI field.

Historically, the USA has dominated the AI industry, with 3033 AI start-up between 2000 and 2016, accounting for 37.41% of the worldwide total (Buchanan, 2019). Between 2012 and 2016 the USA invested $18.2 billion into AI compared with $2.6 billion in China and $850 million in the UK.[1] However, the proportion has been decreasing and in 2016 dropped to under 30% for the first time. During the same period, the USA received $20.7 billion in funding, accounting for 71.78% of the world's total funding (Wuzhen Institute Report, 2017). In 2017, China surpassed the USA for the first time in terms of AI start-up funding. In

[1] "Britain Urged to Take Ethical Advantage in Artificial Intelligence," John Thornhill, Financial Times. 16 April 2018. Available at: https://www.ft.com/content/b21d1fb8-3f3e-11e8-b9f9-de94fa33a81e

2012, China accounted for 48% of global AI start-up funding, and in 2017 the total global AI funding was $15.2 billion. AI equity deals increased 141% relative to the previous year, and since 2016 more than 1100 new AI companies have raised their first round of equity financing. However, the US global AI equity deal share has fallen significantly, from 77% to 50% during the last five years. China leads the Asian market in terms of AI growth. During the past five years China accounted for 68.67% of Asian AI start-ups, dominating with 60.22% of corresponding the total Asian AI funding.

With the help of AI, blockchain not only benefits wealth managers but also works on making returns for their clients. AI in return gets more information and that helps the system's evolutionary process. Furthermore, the more sophisticated the AI becomes efficient. The innovation of technology and the susceptibility to work in harmony with AI will also improve machine to machine interactions. These machines were made to facilitate human actions; thus, clustering computer systems together will make processes quicker and simplify complex processes. In fact, the Japanese Government Pension Investment Fund (the world's biggest manager of retirement savings) is considering AI to ultimately replace human fund managers.

The integration of blockchain and AI into a decentralized intelligence system has profound possibilities to employ data in innovative ways. An effective amalgamation of both technologies will enable faster and seamless data management, validation of transactions, detection of illegal documents, amongst others. For the asset and wealth management industry, blockchain will simplify transaction-tracking and reduce costs, as well as produce novel asset structures that can possibly maximize returns to the investor. AI has the ability to update and optimize investment strategies by diligently digesting new market data and consequently using them as inputs to project returns and risks for much attuned advisory and customer-centric service.

AI Applications in Asset Management

The term AI was coined in 1955 by the American computer scientist John McCarthy, based on the idea that "every aspect of learning or any other feature of intelligence can in principle be so precisely described that a machine can be made to simulate it" (McCarthy, Minsky, Rochester, & Shannon, 1955). Other terms—like machine learning (ML), smart automation, cognitive computing, self-service analytics—are all closely related to AI. Within the financial services industry, AI applications include algorithmic trading, portfolio composition and optimization, model validation, back testing, Robo-advising, virtual customer assistants, market impact analysis, regulatory compliance and stress testing.

Much of AI in the 1950s and 1960s did not focus on finance applications. In the 1960s, a substantial body of work on Bayesian statistics was being developed that would later be used in ML (Buchanan, 2019). Neural networks (which would become a cornerstone of deep learning) were developed in the 1960s and grew rapidly. However, due to a lack of sufficiently available electronic data and computing power, it did not progress much further (FSB, 2017). During the 1980s, however, AI made a revival when Japan, the UK and the USA competed heavily in AI funding. Japan invested $400 million through the Japanese Fifth Generation Computer Project (Kaplan, 2016). The UK invested £350 million in the Alvey Program and DARPA spent over $1 billion on its Strategic Computing Initiative. In 1982, AI made inroads into the financial services industry when James Simons founded quantitative investment firm Renaissance Technologies. Chase Lincoln First Bank and Arthur D. Little Inc. developed AI systems to carry out investment planning, debt planning, retirement planning, education planning, life-insurance planning, budget recommendations and income tax planning. And institutional investors used programme trading to capitalize on pricing disparities in the market.

The late 1980s witnessed the rise of IBM and Apple desktop computers, but specialized expert systems became more expensive to maintain. While probabilistic reasoning models dominated the 1960s and 1970s, Bayesian networks gained more acceptance by combining classical AI and neural nets which allowed for learning from experience (Buchanan, 2019). In the 2000s and 2010s, the development of machine learning, deep learning technology, bots and intelligent agents on a powerful cloud computing platform has ushered in a new era of computing. Although there are initial fears of AI taking over human activities, more awareness will shift these perceptions that AI harnesses humanity's collective knowledge and experiences to make better decisions and enrich communications across institutional or consumer omni-channels. For example, large firms like BlackRock, Deutsche Bank, UBS and Wells Fargo are already using AI engines to analyse consumer digital footprints[2] via their online behaviours, to understand and subsequently predict the products and services most likely to be embraced and used.

Personalization of Services

With increasingly high levels of client expectations, the need for quick, secure and highly personalized solutions is vital. High-net-worth individuals (HNWIs) and wealth management clients have become accustomed to highly personalized services by their wealth managers, who do so through a support network of connected channels and integrated systems. Contextual insights from massive data analytics can be distributed to wealth managers to help them schedule their daily activities—engage clients in a timely manner and identify opportunities for them whilst all the time remaining compliant to regulations. Peers (2018) believes that this enables them to keep up with the "increasing speed, complexity and scale of the financial services industry". As such, they are still able to make every interaction personal and relevant, while being able to "build long-term rapport and trust by confidently helping clients solve their most important financial challenges".

Some possible situations where Peers suggests that AI can help achieve these are:

- Attaining a holistic evaluation of the client's portfolio and using automated recommendations to advance engagement for further improvements. What can make this possible is through leveraging advanced machine learning algorithms that utilizes client's actions and behaviours from customer relationship management (CRM) systems to better understand unspoken client sentiment whilst generating targeted engagements and relevant conversations across all the channels with full orchestration from these customer insights.
- Retrieving instantaneous client relationships status, preferences and needs through tools such as sentiments, market analyses and sector alerts will enable real-time solutions, and they can produce insights that help to assess timely opportunities for a wealth manager to give

[2] FinTech—How Exponential Technological Progress will affect Asset & Wealth Management https://finlantern.com/fundforum/wp-content/uploads/2017/12/FACTSET_FinTech-how-exponential-technological-progress-will-affect-Wealth-Mana…pdf

their clients a call or visit. Customized engagements delight clients with pertinent information that are relevant to them.
- AI-driven services for wealth management have the capacity to craft new business models, provide incredible insights and spin off value-added products and services through massive data that can inform decisions better and quickly. This generates quality advice at a much lower cost through an optimal combination of intelligence from data analytics from technology and human assessment.

Certain facets of client engagement within financial services that can increase client relations and meaningful exchange without escalating fees are:

- Chatbots are programmed to answer clients' FAQs (frequently asked questions) or direct them to appropriate channels like appointment bookings, or lead clients to the best resources for further assistance—be it to check portfolio status, or find updates on order status or submissions, new financial reports and market events.
- Secure authentication bots that handle automated verification through reliable channels to conclude financial transactions.
- Transactional bots that answer simple queries and flag events to trigger alerts, such as when a transaction exceeds trigger limits, a deduction is due or when trading authorizations close.

Portfolio Management

Asset and wealth management firms are studying and testing prospective AI solutions to better their investment decisions through insights gleaned from mammon of historical data.[3] Digital asset management (like an investment portfolio) is ripe for automation through AI where copious amounts of data about the assets (like the historical performance of a particular fund and market movements) are already being monitored.

> More and more investors are turning to advisory services augmented with Robo-advisors for essential investment needs because of their convenience, ease of use, affordability and transparency. They can provide a range of advi-

[3] https://emerj.com/ai-sector-overviews/machine-learning-in-investment-management-and-asset-management/

> sory services, from personalized, automated, algorithm-based portfolio management to sophisticated tax strategies and risk management, all at a markedly lower cost than the traditional advisory model. (Peers, 2018)

Applying cognitive technologies and AI to various advisory utilities across the industry value chain[4] can be done by analyzing historical data, market patterns and market dependencies. While there have been debates like fundamental vs. macro, and passive vs. active investing in the past, it may be about AI enhancing (or replacing?) modern portfolio theory with drastically better projections.

Chatbots and Robo-Advisory

Robo-advisors and chatbots are "emerging across the financial services sector, helping consumers choose investments, banking products and insurance policies" (Buchanan, 2019). A "bot" is a software application created to automate certain tasks using AI technology (Future Today Institute, 2017). A Robo-advisor is an algorithm-based digital platform that offers automated financial advice or investment management services. Robo-advisors have the potential to lower costs and increase the quality and transparency of financial advice for consumers. Rohner and Uhl (2017) see Robo-advisory services in three ways: "(1) access to and rebalancing of passive and rule-based investment strategies, (2) cost-efficient implementation of a diversified asset allocation and (3) overcoming behavioural biases". They find that compared to traditional investment advice, Robo-advisors can save costs of up to 4.4% per year.

Banks are also engaging chatbots to improve their self-service interfaces. The Bank of America has launched its AI chatbot *Erica*, and it is available through voice or message chat on the bank's mobile app. *Erica*'s AI engine also leverages analytics to assist in managing personal finance. JP Morgan has invested in *COiN*, which is an AI technology that reviews documents and extracts data in far less time than a human. *COiN* can review approximately 12,000 documents in a matter of seconds, whereas a human would spend more than 360,000 hours of work on the same documents (Brummer & Yadav, 2019).

[4] "Artificial intelligence: The Next Frontier for Investment Management Firms," Deloitte, 2019.

Chatbots and conversational interfaces are a rapidly expanding area of venture investment and customer service budget. Such chatbots have had to be built with robust natural language processing engines as well as reams of finance-specific customer interactions. Natural language processing is making it increasingly difficult for bank customers to tell whether they are talking to an AI interface or a human. Japan's three megabanks are using AI and robotics to streamline customer questions.[5] For example, the Mizuho Group has a robot that helps answer asset management questions and compiles documents.

Financial Prediction

Advances in technology have been the vanguard of financial services, especially if these solutions can provide strong and viable economic advantages to them. In portfolio management, AI and machine learning tools are being used to recognize new signals on price movements and to generate effective use of vast available data to improve market assessment and decision acumen than with current models. "The key task is to identify signals from data on which predictions relating to price level or volatility can be made, over various time horizons, to generate higher and uncorrelated returns" (FSB, 2017). Portfolio construction with probabilistic (risk) calculations, stochastic modelling and scenario testing are some of the mathematical models (including option-related calculations) that are computationally intensive. Technology again will provide that leap forward with

> cloud computing streamlining existing infrastructure and at the same time enabling many new, previously unimaginable or un-implementable, applications. In addition to the currently available near-unlimited, on-demand cloud computing, recent progress in quantum computers could soon provide the next disruptive chapter in humanity's unbounded appetite for computational processing. (Buchanan, 2019)

Black swans or extreme events in financial markets have been impossible to predict or time, but historically most of the profits have been made

[5] "Megabanks in Japan Embrace Artificial Intelligence", Robot Technology. 30 October 2017. Available at: https://business.inquirer.net/239571/megabanks-japan-embrace-artificial-intelligence-robot-technology

or lost during these extreme events.[6] It is now possible to not depend on predictive analytics based on existing models and past events. Newer technologies, for example, those that use forward-looking directional market risk forecasting instead of being limited to historical data, are beginning to be adopted by asset managers and other financial institutions globally. Concepts like the efficient market hypothesis (EMH) and portfolio diversification may still applicable, but these concepts will give birth to new ones as the financial data gets increasingly processed by the improved algorithm types in the enhanced AI systems for better projections and predictions.

Algorithm Trading

Algorithmic trading (AT) has become a dominant force in global financial markets. Also called "Automated Trading Systems", AT's origins date back to the 1970s. Kirilenko and Lo (2013) provide a brief survey of the evolution of the AT field. Chakravorty (2016) defines AT as: "Algorithmic trading is about implementing trading rules into a program and using the program to trade, [and AI trading] can be defined as an approach to machine learning that learns the structure of the data, and then tries to predict what will happen". Algorithmic trading now involves the use of complex AI systems to make extremely fast trading decisions. Computers generate 50–70% of equity market trades, 60% of futures trades and 50% of treasuries (Brummer & Yadav, 2019). Aldridge and Krawciw (2017) estimate the share of market AT to be between 10 and 40%. The benefits of AT include (1) the ability of trades to be executed at the best possible prices, (2) increased accuracy and a reduced likelihood of mistakes, (3) the ability to automatically and simultaneously check multiple market conditions and (4) human errors caused by psychological or emotional conditions are likely to be reduced.

Algorithmic trading's target clientele is hedge funds, proprietary trading houses, bank proprietary trading desks, corporates and the next-generation market makers. AT includes making certain trading decisions, submitting orders and managing those orders after submission. Martinez and Rosu (2013) argue that algorithmic speed should have a positive effect on the informativeness of prices. Hendershott and Riordan (2013)

[6] http://mebfaber.com/2011/08/12/where-the-black-swans-hide-andthe-ten-best-days-myth

find that AT improves liquidity and enhances the informational content of quotes. On the other hand, AT may also impose higher adverse selection costs on slower trades.

Algorithmic systems often make thousands or millions of trades per day. The term given to this is HFT. HFT is the most recognizable form of AT and uses high-speed communications and algorithms in financial market transactions. HFT has both its supporters and detractors. Since 2013, two-thirds of the top 30 cited papers on HFTs show positive market effects from HFTs (Das, 2017). There are supporting arguments that HFT helps with price discovery and efficiency by trading in the direction of permanent price changes and in the opposite direction of transitory pricing errors (Brogaard, Hendershott, & Riordan, 2014). These types of trading improve market liquidity. Hendershott and Riordan (2013) find that HFT can provide market stability, and Menkveld (2016) finds that HFT reduces trading costs. Hasbrouck and Saar (2013) provide evidence that HFT improves market quality and reduces bid-ask spreads. In fact, HFT is changing the traditional field of market microstructure and will continue to be reinvented through new AI and DL techniques.

Most hedge funds and financial institutions do not openly disclose their AI approaches to trading (for proprietary reasons), but it is believed that ML and DL play an important role in calibrating real-time trading decisions. It also involves neural networks, fuzzy logic and pattern recognition.

Blockchain Applications in Asset Management

Many blockchain experts believe that "distributed ledgers are highly flexible; once implemented, they can be used to remove friction from the client onboarding process, streamline management of model portfolios, speed the clearing and settlement of trades, and ease compliance burdens associated with anti-money laundering (AML) and KYC" (EY, 2017). Blockchain applications bring efficiencies in eliminating redundant functions, reducing operational expenses and increasing client ease-of-use experience. It may be used to reconcile information across current legacy systems and subsequently enable new infrastructure for potentially new markets and novel products.

Blockchain experts are sure that it can be used to develop client profiles more efficiently and reliably. "Storing client profile data on a blockchain allows for data points—profile data, behavioural preferences, wealth net worth, personal account information, social media profiles—to be shared as needed, with each individual block of data being stored securely, but permissioned for access by the individual (read, write, edit) as needed" (EY, 2017).

Client Onboarding Process

In the current system, prospective patrons are required to show identification and residency documents and prove marital status, sources of wealth, pronounced business interests and official occupation (and even declare political ties in order to set up certain accounts) for financial transactions. Going through this process, financial institutions may take days or weeks to verify information and conduct due diligence with reliable accuracy. In such cases, the blockchain presents a strong use case for client onboarding in wealth management.

Utilizing the blockchain, it would enable profiles of customers to be stored on a blockchain/distributed ledger where assigned groups can be granted access to selected information or entire profile based on issuing cryptographic access keys. The system intrinsically embeds an audit trail for tracking any change along the chain of information blocks (hence the blockchain). As a result, processes requiring information-verification and fact-checking, such as those employed in AML or KYC, can be very much streamlined. In addition, blockchain technologies can be integrated into onboarding and "automated clearinghouse (ACH) and automated customer account transfer (ACAT) systems that traditionally takes multiple days and involve manual processes using multiple systems and databases" (EY, 2017). The blockchain can also enhance transfers of assets between financial institutions with verified derivation of tracked changes.

Management of Model Portfolios

The propagation of open architecture investment offerings and the availability of third-party investment vehicles have presented significant hurdles for wealth managers. "Distributed ledger technology would allow portfolio managers to instantly communicate portfolio changes to all clients 'subscribed' to the model, as well as enable real-time views of individual account performance, drift outside of tolerances and cash flows" (EY, 2017). Also, smart contracts built on the blockchain would execute trade terms and conditions, including management of fees to be paid by the sponsors, if programmed to take proprietary fees every time the model is used.

Currently, asset managers use legacy platforms operating on archaic data architectures which inhibit ease of distribution, interfacing and updating newer third-party models. In some cases, corporations may end up supporting redundant model management systems and remain stuck in time-consuming processes and frustrating users. However, with the blockchain, investment EY notes that managers can create and maintain a model which "could be transmitted through a blockchain to various subscribed brokers where individual accounts can be invested according to the model". Other account-level constraints or restriction customizations can be implemented conveniently.

Trade Clearing and Settlement

The last few decades have seen the asset management industry grow remarkably in both size and complexity. The range of fund structures and coverage of underlying asset classes has expanded to meet the investor's demands for a distinct set of products. To service this global set of products, "the industry makes significant use of service companies that act as intermediaries between them and the clearing and settlement infrastructure, currently a complex network of brokers, custodian banks, stock transfer agents, regulators, and depositories" (BIS, 1997). A single transfer can require multiple liaising transactions and usually takes three days to settle, of which about 20% generate errors, which has to be corrected manually (Mohamed & Ali, 2019).

With a blockchain, two trading parties can read and write to a shared, trusted and error-free platform.[7] "The transaction could be written in legal language as well as in computer code, so that the data exchange itself is the settlement" (BCG, 2016), which can be made to be visible to regulators where necessary. "The brokers (as agents of the buyer and seller) could trade on a larger blockchain to remove custodians as intermediaries, thereby reducing total transaction costs. Institutions issuing securities, such as corporations, cities and municipalities, could issue them directly onto the blockchain", thereby removing the need for share registry agents.

[7] https://www.bcg.com/en-sea/publications/2016/blockchain-thinking-outside-the-blocks.aspx

The "ability of blockchain distributed ledgers to replace intermediary centralised systems of record has attracted real interest in investment firms given the potential to cut cost, reduce delays, provide more timely and accurate data and enhance reporting accuracy".[8] The blockchain can have a deep bearing on the settlement of securities transactions and offer massive reduction in transactional costs leading to reduced charges for investors.

Regulatory Compliance to Shariah Observance

Blockchainized platforms can be used to address the administration and coordination of identity, privacy and security across millions of devices by making them autonomous. These decentralized platforms give integrated systems an identity, make and receive payments, enter into complex agreements and transact without an intermediary (Mohamed & Ali, 2019).

One way to help ease compliance burdens is to build and deploy identity management solutions using blockchain. A blockchain consists of a node and any transaction comprises a chain of blocks that have been accepted by the participating node through a consensus mechanism. One of the most important elements in the blockchain is the identity of a node, and once the node has been identified flawlessly, the entire transaction becomes trustworthy.

An identity management system based on verification cryptography can be built using AML, CTF and KYC[9] requirements according to the country-specific regulations. The same is stored virtually, and a part of this information is released to the counterparty at the time of transaction to suffice the counterparty's requirement. The entire solution is built on the distributed ledger where an enterprise is a node and the platforms developed by asset management companies provide a cryptographic code for each node based on AML, CTF and KYC requirements.

Islamic asset and wealth investment funds are similar to conventional funds in terms of the common objectives that they share, such as pooled investment, capital preservation and returns optimization. The distinguishing feature between the two types of funds is that Islamic funds must

[8] https://sokodirectory.com/2018/01/blockchain-and-its-impact-to-the-investment-industry/

[9] AML refers to anti-money laundering, CTF is counter-terrorism funding and KYC is know-your-client.

always comply with Shariah rules and laws in terms of their operations, activities and investments. Islamic fund management is therefore about the professional management of investors' money in Shariah-compliant securities and assets, in line with Shariah principles to achieve set financial goals. Elements such as the contractual relationship between fund managers and investors, Shariah screening of investments, the role of Shariah boards, Shariah governance mechanisms involving Shariah reviews and audits, purification of impure income and alms-giving (zakat) calculation are important in the adherence of Islamic funds' activities to Shariah requirements.

Automated reporting, automated audits and process streamlining are other benefits offered by such blockchainized platforms to address regulatory compliance, where technology is bridging the gap between regulators and the asset management industry.

Openness to Adoption and Regulations

While many technologists are able to grasp the decentralized ledger concept and the complex Bayesian algorithms, many business leaders are still fuzzy on how it can benefit their business in a profound way, or where it can disrupt current models for competitive advantage. Because blockchain applications may be complicated to understand, determining a good business strategy for using it becomes even more difficult.

Establishing an effective framework to identify real business value is critical especially when there are many potential blockchain opportunities. "Firms should focus on those use cases that have the greatest opportunity with minimal risk, and use a framework to properly allocate time and resources" (EY, 2017). In the short-term, there are use cases that can be developed quickly to drive results to win support for long-term solutions that may be slow to show returns. In addition to creating blockchain-specific business solutions, blockchain should be seen as an enabling technology to improve business operations in the areas of data management through transparency and revenue-generating opportunities captured through ease of use.

AI and ML are moving faster than policy-makers can understand to the extent it is almost outstripping the current legal and regulatory framework. Technology is opaque and fast moving, and regulators find it hard to keep pace, for both the cumulative impact and risks of contagion. Athey and Imbens (2017) and Mullainathan and Spiess (2017) argue that ML methods hold great promise for improving the credibility of policy evaluation. The technology underpinning Fintech is also fuelling a spinoff field known as RegTech which aims to make compliance and regulatory activities easier, faster and more efficient. RegTech utilizes Big Data and ML. RegTech is an emerging field to reduce costs and increase effectiveness. Alarie, Niblett and Yoon (2016) explore how ML technology can improve regulation of human behaviour. They argue that ML techniques can provide fast, accurate and consistent judgements and streamline operations with reduced error.

Financial regulators are also exploring the use of AI for better monitoring of financial institutions. The UK Financial Conduct Authority (FCA) is examining "the possibility of making its handbook machine-readable and then fully machine-executable. This would mean that machines can interpret and implement the rules directly" (Citi, 2018). "The Division of Economic and Risk Analysis (DERA) at the SEC is exploring ML to extract actionable insights from massive datasets, helping examiners find cases of potential fraud or misconduct" (Bauguess, 2017). "As institutions find algorithms that create uncorrelated profits or returns, there are concerns that these will be manipulated on a suitably wide scale that correlations actually increase, which will only become clear as such advanced technologies are actually adopted". More generally, "greater interconnectedness in the financial system may help to share risks and act as a safety net to potential shocks or contagion effects" (FSB, 2017).

International regulators utilize "AI-supported analytical methods to recognise vulnerability patterns, scan lengthy reports or analyse incoming data" (Buchanan, 2019). In 2017, the Bank of England (BoE) joined forces with MindBridge to use an AI auditor to help detect anomalies in transactions and reports. In 2018, Chancellor Angela Merkel announced that the German government would spend €3 billion to boost AI capabilities. The Deutsche Bundesbank is already using AI in its risk management area and uses neural networks (NN) to assess financial market soundness.

The European MIFID II50 (which also came into effect in 2018) requires that "firms applying algorithmic models based on AI and ML should have a robust development plan in place. Firms need to ensure that potential risks are included at every stage of the process" (Wuermaling, 2018). In February 2018, the FCA and Prudential Regulatory Authority released consultation papers on algorithmic trading which lists key areas of supervisory focus in relation to MIFID II.

Conclusion

Along with Big Data, AI is viewed in the financial services sector as a technique that has the potential to deliver huge analytical power. Yet many risks still need to be addressed. Many AI + blockchain techniques remain untested in financial crisis scenarios. There have been several instances in which the algorithms implemented by financial firms appeared to act in ways quite unforeseen by their developers, leading to errors and flash crashes (notably the pound's flash crash following the Brexit referendum in 2016). Technology needs to be more robust to be capable of adapting to human idiosyncrasies so that users can employ these tools safely, effectively and effortlessly.

In the asset management industry, advanced AI technology supported by blockchain applications will help us automate existing processes and realize new revenue streams and business models. In the distributions space, we use AI + blockchain technology to help us predict customer journeys throughout the life cycle of their engagement with the company—from onboarding to redemption—and explore ways consumers can be better served by offering products better suited to their investment style at certain stages in their customer journey. On the product management front, AI + blockchain technology help our portfolio managers make the smartest possible investment decisions at a given point in time using sophisticated analytics. Other emerging technologies and approaches to be adopted in the financial space—such as virtual reality (VR) and integrating the Internet of Things (IoT) to create holistic solutions.

References

Alarie, B., Niblett, A., & Yoon, A. H. (2016). Using Machine Learning to Predict Outcomes in Tax Law. *Canadian Business Law Journal, 58*, 231.

Aldridge, I., & Krawciw, S. (2017). *Real-Time Risk: What Investors Should Know About FinTech, in High-Frequency Trading, and Flash Crashes*. Hoboken, NJ: John Wiley & Sons, Inc.

Athey, S., & Imbens, G. W. (2017). The State of Applied Econometrics: Causality and Policy Evaluation. *Journal of Economic Perspectives, 31*(2), 3–32.

Bank for International Settlements. (1997, March). *Real-Time Gross Settlement Systems*. Basel.

Bauguess, S. W. (2017). *The Role of Big Data, Machine Learning, and AI in Assessing Risks: A Regulatory Perspective*. Keynote Address: OpRisk North America.

BCG. (2016). A Strategic Perspective on Blockchain and Digital Tokens. https://www.bcg.com/en-sea/publications/2016/blockchain-thinking-outside-the-blocks.aspx.

Brogaard, J., Hendershott, T., & Riordan, R. (2014). High-Frequency Trading and Price Discovery. *The Review of Financial Studies, 27*(8), 2267–2306.

Brummer, C., & Yadav, Y. (2019). The Fintech Trilemma. *Georgetown Law Journal, 107*, 235–307.

Buchanan, B. (2019). *Artificial Intelligence in Finance*. Seattle University with Funding from The Alan Turing Institute. https://doi.org/10.5281/zenodo.2612537

Chakravorty, G. (2016). What Is the Difference Between AI and AlgoTrading? Retrieved from https://www.quora.com/What-is-the-difference-between-AI-trading-and-algo-trading

Citi. (2018, March). *Bank of the Future: The ABCs of Digital Disruption in Finance*. CitiReport.

Das, S. R. (2017). The Future of FinTech. Retrieved from https://srdas.github.io/Papers/fintech.pdf

Ernst and Young. (2017). Blockchain Innovation in Wealth and Asset Management: Benefits and Key Challenges to Adopting This Technology.

FSB. (2017). Artificial intelligence and machine learning in financial services: Market developments and financial stability implications. https://www.fsb.org/wpcontent/uploads/P011117.pdf

Future Today Institute. (2017). *Tech Trends Annual Report*. Retrieved from https://futuretodayinstitute.com/2017-tech-trends/

Hasbrouck, J., & Saar, G. (2013). Low Latency Trading. *Journal of Financial Markets, 16*, 646–679.

Hendershott, T., & Riordan, R. (2013). Algorithmic Trading and the Market for Liquidity. *Journal of Financial and Quantitative Analysis, 48*(4), 1001–1024.

Kaplan, J. (2016). *Artificial Intelligence: What Everyone Needs to Know*. Oxford University Press.

Kirilenko, A. A., & Lo, A. W. (2013). Moore's Law Versus Murphy's Law: Algorithmic Trading and Its Discontents. *Journal of Economic Perspectives, 27*(2), 51–72.

Martinez, V. H., & Rosu, I. (2013). *High Frequency Traders, News and Volatility*. In AFA 2013 San Diego Meetings Paper.

McCarthy, J., Minsky, M., Rochester, N., & Shannon, C. (1955). A Proposal for the Dartmouth Summer Research Project on Artificial Intelligence.

Menkveld, A. J. (2016). The Economics of High-Frequency Trading: Taking Stock. *Annual Review of Financial Economics, 8*, 1–24.

Mohamed, H., & Ali, H. (2019). *Blockchain, Fintech and Islamic Finance—Building the Future of the New Islamic Digital Economy*. Boston/Berlin: De|G Press.

Mullainathan, S., & Spiess, J. (2017). Machine Learning: An Applied Econometric Approach. *Journal of Economic Perspectives, 31*(2), 87–106.

Peers, R. (2018). Digital Super Powers – The Role of Artificial Intelligence in Wealth Management. In S. Chishti & T. Puschmann (Eds.), *The WEALTHTECH Book: The Fintech Handbook for Investors, Entrepreneurs and Finance Visionaries*. Hoboken: Wiley.

Rohner, P., & Uhl, M. (2017). Robo-Advisors vs. Traditional Investment Advisors – An Unequal Game. *Journal of Wealth Management, 21*(1), 44–50.

Wuermaling, J. (2018). *Artificial Intelligence in Finance: Six Warnings from a Central Banker*. Intervention at the 2nd Annual Fintech Conference, Brussels.

Wuzhen Institute. (2017, August). *Global AI Development Report*. Retrieved from http://sike.news.cn/hot/pdf/25.pdf, www.iwuzhen.org

CHAPTER 15

The Opportunities of Digital Wallets from an Islamic Perspective

Mezbah Uddin Ahmed and Kazi Md Tarique

Abstract Digital wallets are gaining popularity in recent years. Besides convenience, the promotional offers provided by these wallets are among the primary reasons for people to be attracted to use the wallets. This chapter explores Shariah permissibility of these promotional offers. The chapter finds that the money kept in digital wallets can be looked at from two different perspectives, and the Shariah opinion on the permissibility of promotional offers will vary according to the perspective. The chapter argues that if the money kept in digital wallets is considered as a loan-based deposit (*qard*), then the promotional offers or additional benefits provided by the wallets are not permissible, unless the benefits are fully discretionary. However, the chapter also argues that the money does not hold its original form as soon as it is credited to digital wallets, that is, money transforms into a new form of digital currency. In this case there may not be any Shariah issue on the additional benefits received. The

M. U. Ahmed (✉)
International Shari'ah Research Academy for Islamic Finance (ISRA), Kuala Lumpur, Malaysia
e-mail: mezbah@isra.my

K. Md. Tarique
University of Liberal Arts Bangladesh (ULAB), Dhaka, Bangladesh

M. M. Billah (ed.), *Islamic FinTech*,
https://doi.org/10.1007/978-3-030-45827-0_15

paper also identifies several issues related to digital wallets that require further research.

Keywords Digital wallet • Shariah • Islamic finance • FinTech

Introduction

Similar to a physical wallet, digital wallets store an amount of money that can be used to buy goods and services. PriceWaterhouseCoopers (PwC, 2018) has identified an array of use cases for digital wallets. This includes retail, food and beverage, e-commerce, peer-to-peer transfer, transportation, prepaid top-up, and bill payments. An increasing number of retailers are now accepting payment via digital wallets. The number of users is also increasing. The top three reasons for using digital wallets identified by PwC are promotions, convenience, and digital receipts.

Digital wallets bring convenience to the daily lifestyle of users, as they need not carry cash or worry about small change to pay for goods and services. The transactions can also be executed faster than in physical currencies. The digital wallets also keep records of transactions that allow the users to keep track of their expenditures.

Users are also attracted to the promotional offers and additional benefits provided by digital wallets. These wallets currently provide a wide range of promotional offers and additional benefits to the users. These include discounts, rebates or cashback, redeemable points, coupon codes, loyalty points, and other freebies. As a consumer-oriented technology-based service, these offers are attracting more and more people to subscribe to digital wallets.

Studies conducted in the UK and the US have shown that customers are attracted to promotions and offers (Madan & Yadav, 2016). Accordingly, Madan and Yadav (2016) have also identified promotional benefits as among the factors that significantly influence digital wallet use decisions. Bagla and Sancheti (2018) also found similar factors as responsible for the growing popularity of digital wallets in India. They found that attractive cashback and rewards, ease of use, instant money transfer without using cash, relatively higher transaction security as compared to credit/debit cards, and absence of transaction fees are the factors responsible for the growing use of digital wallets.

Shariah prohibits receiving any benefit over a lent amount, as that is considered *riba* or interest. It has been unequivocally established that a Muslim is prohibited from receiving or paying interest. Therefore, to meet the needs of Muslim users, it is important to analyse digital wallets in the context of Shariah, that is, to identify whether the digital wallets are Shariah compliant as a whole and there are any elements that are objectionable. If there is any objectionable element, then the remedial actions also need to be identified.

Given the growing demand for Shariah-compliant alternatives to conventional financial solutions, there is also a need to develop Shariah-compliant digital wallets. Alternatively, existing digital wallets should get Shariah endorsements to assure the Muslim users about their Shariah compliance.

With the above background, this chapter attempts to address the following questions: (1) What is the contractual relationship between digital wallet and its user? (2) What is the Shariah view on money kept in digital wallets and the benefits it provides? (3) What is the zakat status of the balance remaining in a digital wallet? The research also identifies the scope of future research pertaining to digital wallets and related Shariah issues.

Adoption and Prospect

A digital wallet is not simply a wallet that holds digital money. It also provides a wide range of services. For instance, Agarwal and Tuteja (2018) reported that Paytm in India is used to transfer funds through mobile numbers, the online payment of utility bills, payment for taxies and other services, and payment to offline merchants. Grab in Malaysia also provides similar services.

The listing of merchants in the digital wallet app brings the customers closer to the merchants and results in a more active market. Umeokeke, Okoruwa, and Adeyemo (2017) have identified digital wallets as an important tool for small farmers to increase agricultural income and escape poverty. David-West and Nwagwu (2018) identified digital financial services as an enabler of an inclusive economy. Greater access to financial services is also the key to achieving many of the Sustainable Development Goals (SDGs) of the United Nations (UN). Accordingly, Umeokeke et al. (2017) found that the users of digital wallet are well off in the society than the non-users. They have observed that poverty incidence, its depth, and severity are higher among non-users of digital wallets than the users.

Fintech News (2019) found that 40 per cent of digital wallet users are high earners.

Digital wallet is seen as a lifestyle necessity in China, which is the global leader in digital wallet market. Thirty-six per cent of all transactions in China are now done by digital wallets (Fintech News, 2019). In Malaysia, 11 per cent of total payments now involve digital wallets Yuen (2019), although its digital wallet market still is in infancy. Zion Market Research (2019) estimates that by 2022 the global digital wallet market will cross the USD three trillion mark, achieving a 32 per cent cumulative annual growth rate (CAGR) from 2017.

The use of digital wallets is common among younger professionals. In 2018, PwC surveyed around 200 individuals in Malaysia. Most of these individuals were working professionals and age 44 or below. The survey has identified that 22 per cent of the respondents are digital wallet users. Of them, 91 per cent intend to use digital wallets up to five times a week, and the remaining 9 per cent intend to use six times or more (PwC, 2018). At a global level, a similar trend was identified by Fintech News (2019), who found that 35 per cent of digital wallet users are millennials.

The increased use of digital wallets has become possible with the increase of mobile phone users, particularly the increase in smart phone users with internet connections. As mobile phones have evolved into a necessity in daily life, they are used as the perfect platform to host digital wallets. A person may not have a bank account but may still be a mobile phone user. It is estimated that there are more mobile phone users than there are bank account holders in the world. With the increase in mobile phone users, particularly those with smart phones with internet connections, it is natural to use these devices for financial transactions. Hence, digital wallets can also serve as an ideal opportunity for financial inclusion and create a vibrant economy.

According to the Malaysian Communications and Multimedia Commission (MCMC, 2017), the mobile-cellular subscription in Malaysia reached a penetration rate of 131.2 per cent in 2017, that is, 42.3 million subscriptions for 32.3 million people. About 75.9 per cent of mobile phone users are using smartphones. A survey conducted by MCMC (2018) found that 93.1 per cent of smartphone users have an internet connection, and more than half of these internet users use internet banking. Even though a lot more progress is yet to be made, digital payments are seen by the MCMC Chairman Tan Sri Dr. Halim Shafie as a key factor in achieving Malaysia's vision of the digital economy (The Star Online,

2018). In fact, demonstrating the great prospects of the digital wallet market, there are around 40 digital wallet service providers currently in Malaysia (Kana, 2019). A similar trend and prospect may also be observed in other countries as well.

An Analysis from Islamic Perspective

Is It a Loan?

Money credited in a digital wallet by top-up or reload bears a resemblance to deposits made in a bank account. The credited amount is secured, and the user can spend it at any time. This is similar to maintaining a current account in a bank and spending the deposited money using a debit card. Hence, from an Islamic finance perspective, the credited amount in a digital wallet can be considered a deposit based on a loan (*qard*) contract. Hence, an important concern arises on Shariah permissibility of the promotional offers or additional benefits provided in a loan contract. This is because a well-established rule in a loan contract is that there cannot be additional benefits to the lender (in this case, the digital wallet user).

Based on AAOIFI Shariah Standards No. 19, Para 5/1, the fundamental requirements of a *qard* contract includes the following: "It is not permissible to the borrower to offer tangible property or extend a benefit to the lender during the period of the qard when this is done for the sake of qard." Therefore, it appears that the additional benefits (discount, rebate, or redeemable points) provided by digital wallets are not allowable by Shariah.

However, it should be noted that in a loan contract, the borrower (in this case, digital wallet) is free to offer additional benefits at its full discretion. In this regard, AAOIFI in its Shariah Standards No. 19, Para 5/2, states that "an excess over *qard* is permissible in terms of quantity or quality, or offering of tangible property or extending of a benefit, at the time of satisfaction when it is not stipulated or is part of custom, irrespective of the subject-matter of *qard* being cash or kind." With this evidence, it can be argued that the additional benefits provided by digital wallets are solely at its discretion and hence allowable by Shariah.

Is It Digital Money?

Money is a means of exchange, a store of value, and a unit of account. Money is something we can use to buy things and the value of which does not change much. Governments and central banks work hard to ensure that fiat currency is guaranteed as an acceptable form of money and that the supply of money into the economy is neither inflationary nor deflationary.

According to Dandapani (2017), digital currency or electronic money is an alternative form of currency used for digital or online transactions. One may argue that the money deposited in a digital wallet is not a deposit or a loan, rather a form of digital currency. This is because once an amount of money is credited to a digital wallet, it cannot be withdrawn by the user in the form of cash or be transferred to his bank account. The user may only be able to use the balance available in the digital wallets to purchase goods and services from listed merchants. Hence, it can be argued that the Shariah rules and prohibitions of a loan contract does not apply here.

It can be argued that the money changes its form from one currency to another as soon as the user tops up an amount in his digital wallet. The balance in a digital wallet is a digital currency or a digital token, even if it is denominated or referred to as the same as the original form of money (i.e. dollar, ringgit, etc.). The user subsequently uses the digital token to purchase goods and services. Hence, any discount he gets at the time of purchase is perfectly acceptable, as the amount is known and agreed upon between the parties (i.e. between user and digital wallet) at the time of transaction. Any rebate, redeemable point, or other benefits are part of the agreed price at the time of transaction and thus acceptable.

Zakat on Amount Kept in a Digital Wallet

Zakat is obligatory for every affluent Muslim, that is, whoever has a certain amount of wealth (*nisab*). Cash and cash equivalents are included in measuring this wealth. If the digital wallet balance is considered as a form of digital currency, then how that shall be measured in the calculation of zakat payer's wealth? Shall the balance be equated at par, that is, one digital currency unit will be measured as one unit of national currency? Is there a need for formulating a valuation mechanism in calculating national currency equivalent of the digital currency?

For an asset to be zakatable, the zakat payer must have ownership and control over the asset. Does the balance in a digital wallet fulfil these two conditions, particularly the condition of having control? It might be argued that the user has full control over it, as he can use it to purchase goods and services. However, the opposite argument could be that the user cannot withdraw the digital wallet balance or convert it into other currencies as it wishes. The user cannot use the digital wallet balance outside the designated purposes or listed merchants. There are restrictions in using digital wallet balance during an overseas trip. These limitations deplete the user's control over the digital wallet balance.

If the money kept in a digital wallet is considered a loan, then which zakat rule will apply here? Shall there be zakat on the balance as of the zakat calculation day or a different rule shall apply? These issues have yet to be sufficiently deliberated on.

Ensuring End-to-End Shariah Compliance

The issue of Shariah compliance is broader than mere avoidance of Shariah prohibited elements in transactions with digital wallets. A digital wallet itself needs to ensure Shariah compliance in its activities. For instance, prior to listing merchants in digital wallet app, the merchants must be validated as Shariah compliant. A restaurant that serves alcohol or pork may not be eligible to be listed in a Shariah-compliant digital wallet app.

More importantly, the money collected from users must be deposited in Islamic bank accounts or be invested in Shariah-compliant instruments or activities. Otherwise, there is a risk that the digital wallet service provider will be using customers' money to earn Shariah non-permissible income, for example interest. Further studies need to be conducted to identify Shariah parameters of digital wallets to determine those as Shariah compliant.

Other Issues

Regulating Digital Wallet Service Providers

The role of cryptocurrencies and methods to regulate these have been debated globally. While a few countries have adopted a welcoming approach, many others have been cautious and adopted a very restrictive approach. These new forms of currencies have unique challenges for the regulators (Simser, 2015). Among the greatest concerns for the regulators have been using these digital currencies for terrorism financings. Many have raised this concern, including Teichmann (2018), who examined the use of cryptocurrencies in terrorism financing and found that the terrorists could use Bitcoin to receive donations from their supporters.

Accordingly, questions have arisen about digital wallets. Shall the digital wallets be subjected to the same level of caution and restrictive approach? Is there any risk of breaking the laws by using digital wallets? For example, could they be involved in terrorism financing or money laundering activities?

Digital currencies, which lack centralized monetary authority and mostly comprise anonymous users, are difficult to regulate and control. However, in the case of digital wallets, users can be easily tracked. It is possible that some users may provide false information at the point of account registration. However, by way of tracing the phone number or GPS location of the phone, it may not be too difficult for law enforcement agencies to track an offending user. Furthermore, while the other crypto or non-cryptocurrencies can be used for any form of transaction, digital wallets can be used only for an approved set of purposes and at an approved set of merchants.

The regulation of digital currency is still at its infancy. Authorities around the world are still trying to figure out its mechanics, impacts, and the best methods of regulation. This is a challenge where the pace of legal development does not sync congruently with the rapid progress of technology (Hanafi & Rahman, 2019). Achieving greater financing inclusion with lagging financial literacy is also a challenge. Ajwani-Ramchandani (2017) has identified that in countries like India a large segment of the population is not conversant with the usage of electronic transaction options.

Chawla and Joshi (2019) identified a lack of robust, reliable, and secure infrastructure for digital wallets. They proposed establishing a think tank involving key stakeholders (financial institutions, mobile wallet providers, government, security experts, etc.) to propose guidelines to ensure safe and secure transactions. A sound regulatory framework will help the digital wallet industry to flourish. The regulations need to address issues like:

- Shall the digital wallet service providers be subject to capital adequacy requirements like a bank?
- Shall they have a certain liquidity at all times?

- Shall they be subject to other restrictions like a bank, for example, maintaining a reserve?

Addressing Any Grievances of the Users

As the digital wallet is a new phenomenon, a clear and transparent regulatory framework is essential to safeguard the interests of all parties involved. The issue is not only terrorism financing, money laundering, or fraud. As it is a consumer-oriented service, there must also be an established mechanism to settle any disputes arising at any stage during the usage of digital wallets and regulations about it.

Proper procedures need to be stipulated for any grievances of the transacting parties. Digital wallet service providers normally do not have physical customer service centres. The only option available for an aggrieved customer or user is to make phone calls or write complaints. However, solving problems by calling the service provider also costs money and time. Communicating through writing may not be an easy option for many due to their lack of education or just being not used to it. Hence, the impact of financial inclusion while financial literacy is low must be studied and necessary steps to be formulated. Furthermore, user protection schemes in the case of bankruptcy or dissolution of the digital service provider also need to be formulated and communicated with the users.

Protection of Users' Data

When creating a digital wallet account, the user compulsorily provides personal information. This may include but is not limited to name, date of birth, email address, affiliation, phone number, address, and so on. In some cases, the users also provide their debit or credit card details while linking the card with digital wallet account for top-up or reload.

There is no doubt that digital wallet operators develop a database of the users' transaction behaviours. The collected information allows the entity to identify the target market to sell their products or sell the personal data of the users to the third parties.

The Shariah view of giving consent in installing apps for digital wallets also needs to be scrutinized. While installing a mobile application or software, users almost always give consent without reading the terms and conditions. It can be argued that the users bear the responsibility of reading the terms and conditions and holds the absolute right to give or not to give consent. However, in reality, terms and conditions are often very long and ambiguous. The users might be in a rush or lazy to read all the terms and conditions. However, a common user may also do not have the competence to understand the consequences or impact of agreeing with those terms and conditions. Furthermore, if the user does not agree, he cannot use that application or software. If the application or software is essential for his work or daily needs, then he may not see any option but to agree with all the terms and conditions.

The same applies when the user gives permissions while installing a mobile application. Some applications want permission to take pictures, record audio, manage calls, access to device location, access to media and files, and so on. In this context, two important Shariah issues need to be discussed:

- For a developer of application or software: What is the Shariah standing on compulsorily requiring a potential user to agreeing with terms and conditions? While formulating terms and conditions, what is the Shariah parameter in terms of clarity? Does Shariah allow using of the users' data or transaction behaviour without their clear consent? Does Shariah allow selling of users' data or transaction behaviour to a third party without their clear consent?
- For a user: Does Shariah recognize consent to terms and conditions or permitting which are not carefully read or clearly understood? Does the giving of consent without reading all terms and conditions or understanding them still constitutes a valid contract?

Security of the System

Cases of hacking IT systems and databases are not uncommon. In countries where many are living only on a little or hovering around the poverty line, even a small loss of money due to technical glitches or hacking may cause great frustrations. Hence, it is of paramount importance that the security systems of digital wallets are up to mark.

As hackers find new ways and techniques such as phishing, water holing, ransomware, and scanning, it remains a constant challenge in regularly upgrading the cybersecurity of the system. While some of these attacks are random, the most damaging attacks are targeted, where attackers focus on a specific entity spending months to plan and focus on the vulnerabilities of the entity.

Globally, cyber-attacks are on the rise. These affect millions of people worldwide. However, the challenge is that the cost of taking protective measures may outweigh the benefits. For instance, Zurich and the Atlantic Council explored four possible scenarios and discovered a startling USD 120 trillion gap between the best and worst outcome for the global economy. Such attacks could cost the world USD 120 trillion by 2030. The report argues that the annual cost of managing cyber risks could begin to outweigh the annual economic benefits globally by 2019.

In such a scenario, digital wallet service providers need to assure its users that their cybersecurity is up to the standard to prevent any fraud, theft, or security breach. Regulators also have an important role to play in the oversight measures taken by these service providers. Further research needs to be conducted in identifying the cybersecurity measures taken by the digital wallet service providers and their sufficiency in tackling the cyber threats.

Conclusion

Due to a lack of confidence or skill, some may still prefer cash-based transactions. However, over time these limitations will be overcome, and cashless transactions will be preferred. As the use of smartphones is on the increase, this is undeniable that the use of digital wallet will increase as well. However, users must be provided with necessary awareness and financial literacy on the risks of digital wallets and their rights and responsibilities in the case of any dispute. Hence, training and educating the masses will enable customers to understand the features, risks, and protection measures fully.

The security infrastructure required to protect the users and vendors is still evolving. Customer protection laws in many developing countries are also outdated and need to be revised in light of the latest developments.

Shariah issues related to existing digital wallets also need to be sufficiently deliberated on so that the Muslim users can identify the Shariah-prohibited elements and stay away from those elements. Furthermore, digital wallet operators may also consider receiving an endorsement from Shariah scholars to assure Muslim users that there are no Shariah-prohibited elements in the wallet or its services. A digital wallet app may also require merchants be endorsed for Shariah compliance if they wish to be listed.

References

Agarwal, R., & Tuteja, S. (2018). Paytm's Wallet Business: On a Growth Trajectory or Suicide Mission? *The CASE Journal, 14*(1), 112–138.

Ajwani-Ramchandani, R. (2017). Less Cash or Cashless: What About the Common Man? In *The Role of Microfinance in Women's Empowerment* (pp. 275–281). Emerald Publishing Limited.

Bagla, R., & Sancheti, V. (2018). Gaps in Customer Satisfaction with Digital Wallets: Challenge for Sustainability. *Journal of Management Development, 37*(6), 442–451.

Chawla, D., & Joshi, H. (2019). Consumer Attitude and Intention to Adopt Mobile Wallet in India – An Empirical Study. *International Journal of Bank Marketing* (Ahead-of-Print).

Dandapani, K. (2017). Electronic Finance – Recent Developments. *Managerial Finance, 43*(5), 614–626.

David-West, O., & Nwagwu, I. (2018). SDGs and Digital Financial Services (DFS) Entrepreneurship: Challenges and Opportunities in Africa's Largest Economy. *Entrepreneurship and the Sustainable Development Goals, 8*, 103–117.

Fintech News. (2019, July 23). *The Number of Mobile Wallet Users Grows by 140 Million per Year.* Retrieved September 12, 2019, from Fintech News: https://www.fintechnews.org/the-number-of-mobile-wallet-users-grows-by-140-million-per-year/

Hanafi, S., & Rahman, S. (2019). Regulating Digital Currency: Taming the Unruly. In *Emerging Issues in Islamic Finance Law and Practice in Malaysia* (pp. 265–280). Emerald Publishing Limited.

Kana, G. (2019, June 19). *CEO: Time for e-Wallet Environment to Consolidate.* Retrieved September 12, 2019, from The Star Online: https://www.thestar.com.my/business/business-news/2019/06/19/ceo-time-for-ewallet-environment-to-consolidate

Madan, K., & Yadav, R. (2016). Behavioural Intention to Adopt Mobile Wallet: A Developing Country Perspective. *Journal of Indian Business Research, 8*(3), 227–244.

MCMC. (2017). *Hand Phone User Survey 2017.* Selangor Darul Ehsan: Malaysian Communicaitons and Multimedia Commission. Retrieved September 12, 2019, from https://www.skmm.gov.my/skmmgovmy/media/General/pdf/HPUS2017.pdf

MCMC. (2018). *Internet Users Survey 2018.* Selangor Darul Ehsan: Malaysian Communications and Multimedia Commission. Retrieved September 12, 2019, from https://www.mcmc.gov.my/skmmgovmy/media/General/pdf/Internet-Users-Survey-2018.pdf

PwC. (2018). *Banking on the e-Wallet in Malaysia.* PricewaterhouseCoopers Advisory Services Sdn Bhd. Retrieved September 12, 2019, from https://

www.pwc.com/my/en/assets/blog/pwc-my-deals-strategy-banking-on-the-ewallet-in-malaysia.pdf

Simser, J. (2015). Bitcoin and Modern Alchemy: in Code We Trust. *Journal of Financial Crime, 22*(2), 156–169.

Teichmann, F. (2018). Financing Terrorism Through Cryptocurrencies – A Danger for Europe? *Journal of Money Laundering Control, 21*(4), 513–519.

The Star Online. (2018, February 14). *Mobile Cellular Penetration Reaches 131.8%.* Retrieved September 12, 2019, from The Star Online: https://www.thestar.com.my/business/business-news/2018/02/14/mobile-cellular-penetration-reaches-1318

Umeokeke, N., Okoruwa, V., & Adeyemo, T. (2017). Impact of Electronic-Wallet System on Farmer's Welfare in Oyo State, Nigeria. *International Journal of Social Economics, 44*(4), 474–490.

Yuen, M. (2019, February 3). *Cashing in on e-Wallets.* Retrieved September 12, 2019, from The Star Online: https://www.thestar.com.my/news/nation/2019/02/03/cashing-in-on-ewallets-its-a-growing-trend-more-people-are-using-ewallets-in-their-phones-these-days

Zion Market Research. (2019, July 10). *Global Share of Mobile Wallet Market to Surpass $3,142.17 Billion by 2022: Zion Market Research.* Retrieved October 26, 2019, from Zion Market Research: https://www.globenewswire.com/news-release/2019/07/10/1880730/0/en/Global-Share-of-Mobile-Wallet-Market-to-Surpass-3-142-17-Billion-by-2022-Zion-Market-Research.html

CHAPTER 16

The Optimization of Blockchain for Greater Transparency in Zakat Management

Irfan Syauqi Beik, Muhammad Hasbi Zaenal, and Abdul Aziz Yahya Saoqi

Abstract Technology has developed rapidly in the last decade. Many business sectors have been affected by technological changes. They are required to adapt their business process to the latest technology. The digitalization of financial services became proof that technological changes have shifted the traditional services in financial institutions. One of the innovations developed in digital services today is blockchain technology, which was first developed in 2008 by someone with a pseudonym Satoshi Nakamoto. The uniqueness and advancement of the blockchain technology may be utilized and adopted by any institution, including zakat institution in managing zakat funds more accountable, effective, efficient, and transparent. Hence, the blockchain technology could assist zakat institution in improving its sound amil governance. Thus, the paper aims to

I. S. Beik (✉)
IPB University, Bogor, Indonesia

BAZNAS, Jakarta, Indonesia
e-mail: irfan_beik@apps.ipb.ac.id

M. H. Zaenal • A. A. Y. Saoqi
BAZNAS, Jakarta, Indonesia

M. M. Billah (ed.), *Islamic FinTech*,
https://doi.org/10.1007/978-3-030-45827-0_16

elaborate further on the possibility, challenges, and opportunities for zakat institutions in adopting blockchain technology in their zakat administration.

Keywords Optimization • Zakat • Blockchain • Technology • Transparency

Introduction

In the last decade, technology has developed rapidly. Many business sectors have been affected significantly by technological changes. Therefore, they are required to adapt their business process to the latest technology. The digitalization of many financial services became evidence that technology has shifted the conventional services in the industry. One of the innovations that has developed in digital services today is the existence of blockchain technology which was first developed in 2008 by someone with a pseudonym Satoshi Nakamoto. Through his article entitled ***Bitcoin: a Peer-to-Peer Electronic Cash System***, he proposed a new electronic payment system without third-party involvement that will lead to the greater efficiency. At the first time, blockchain technology was initially adopted by digital currency users to facilitate the exchange of their currency among its users without the involvement of the middle man (financial institution) in their transaction activities. Essentially, blockchain is a system that consists of a set of data records where this data (block) is tied to other data in a network (chain) and each block is bound and secured by the code that has been elaborately encrypted.[1]

In blockchain technology, all computers in the network can see each activity of these transactions without knowing each other because the records of these transactions have been encrypted into a hash or code that is quite complicated. Furthermore, this technology also allows all computers in the network to validate every transaction that has been done, so that

[1] Imran Bashir, *Mastering Blockchain*, Birmingham, Packt Publishing, 2018, page 16.

each computer can correct each transaction that occurs in order to prevent fraud or other errors in recording transactions.[2]

Principally, blockchain technology carries three very unique things: first, decentralization where the peer-to-peer connection system eliminates third-party involvement in each transaction; second, transparency where all computers in the network can know all transactions; and third, it is permanent in the sense that each previous transaction cannot be changed to prevent actions that lead to fraud.

The uniqueness and advancement of the blockchain technology may be utilized and adopted by any institution including financial institutions both commercial and social so that the technology could help the institution in managing public fund more in an accountable, effective, efficient and transparent manner. Hence, the blockchain technology could assist the institution including zakat institution in improving their good management and governance in managing zakat fund. But it is important for the readers to understand firstly regarding the fundamental concept of zakat and its management in Islamic perspective. Moreover, the chapter also will discuss the current practice of zakat management in several Muslim countries. The current practice of transparency process in zakat management will be explained as well. At the end of the chapter, the discussion will be focused on the challenges and opportunities for zakat institution in adopting blockchain technology in zakat management and the examples of best practice model of blockchain implementation in Islamic social finance sector.

The Concept of Zakat and Its Management

As the third pillar of Islam, zakat has a great position in Islam, because for a Muslim, zakat is not just vertical worship to Allah, but zakat is also part of social worship among humans, so it is not surprising that Allah SWT calls zakat 30 times in the Qur'an and the word zakat is often juxtaposed with the word prayer at many verses. This is because zakat has a very important role in human life. Zakat is also a form of love for Allah among fellow human beings because those who have excess wealth are

[2] Barantum, *Pengertian dan Panduan Lengkap Blockchain*, https://www.barantum.com/blog/blockchain-adalah/, 2 July 2019, 08:30.

encouraged to set aside part of their wealth for those who need it, so that affection between their fellow people is established.[3]

Qardhawi (1973) defines zakat into two aspects which are terminology aspect and sharia law aspect. In the aspect of its terminology of zakat, it can be interpreted as something that grows, increases, blessings and purifies. Furthermore in the aspect of sharia law, zakat is defined as a part of the assets which required to be given to the eight classes that have been set by Allah in the Holy Quran.

Not all Muslims are required to pay zakat; only certain people called muzaki or certain donors are obliged to pay zakat. To be said as muzaki, the assets owned or the income generated has reached certain conditions set by sharia law such as the wealth or income should achieve zakat minimum nishab and haul or zakat's term. Then, the object of the zakat property and the amount of zakat issued have also been determined in sharia law. Furthermore, sharia also regulates that the beneficiaries of zakat also have specific criteria which is included in the criteria of the eight groups that have been stipulated in the Holy Quran.

As for who has the right to manage zakat, many of Islamic scholars agreed that as described by Allah in the Holy Quran and from what the Prophet exemplified, the management of zakat funds starting from the collection of zakat funds from the donors and distribution to the eight groups of beneficiaries was carried out by the zakat institutions.[4] There are several lessons from the role of the zakat institution in the management of zakat funds. First, zakat institutions play a role in maintaining the discipline of the donors in paying zakat. Second, zakat institutions play a role in maintaining the dignity and inferiority feelings of the beneficiaries. Third, zakat institutions play a role in drawing up strategic steps so that zakat fund distribution will reach the rightful eight beneficiaries.[5]

Hence, from the above explanation we can conclude that the management of zakat funds is regulated and stipulated by sharia law, so that who pays zakat, the object of zakat, who has the right to manage zakat funds and who has the right to receive zakat funds has special provisions and is

[3] Sri Nurhayati et al., *Akuntansi dan Manajemen Zakat*, Jakarta, SalembaEmpat, 2019, Page 17.

[4] Didin Hafidhuddin, *Zakat dalamPerekonomian Modern*, Depok, GemaInsani, 2008, Page 53.

[5] Ibid., Page 126.

limited in sharia law. Thus in managing zakat funds sensitivity and a very high level of transparency are needed to avoid mistakes that violate sharia rules.

Current Practice of Zakat Management in Muslim Countries

The practice of managing zakat funds among Muslim countries has differences between one another. This is due to several factors such as regulation, government format, geographical location and different Muslim population numbers. This chapter will explain the current practice of zakat management in several Muslim countries such as Indonesia, Malaysia, Saudi Arabia and Sudan.

Indonesia

As a country with the largest Muslim population in the world, the practice of zakat management in Indonesia began in a structured and systematic manner after the reformation phase in 1999. In that year the new Indonesian government issued regulation number 38 of 1999 governing the management of zakat funds in Indonesia.[6] In 2011, the government issued a new regulation on national zakat number 23, which regulates the management of zakat more specifically in the territory of Indonesia region. In the regulation number 23, zakat management arrangements are carried out centrally by the state institutions assisted also by the private sector, and the supervision is carried out by the ministry of religion. In general, the management of zakat in Indonesia can be seen in Fig. 16.1.

Zakat institutions established by the state are called the National Board of Zakat (BAZNAS). BAZNAS has the authority to collect, manage and distribute zakat funds to eligible groups at the national level.[7] Given the vast territory of Indonesia, the Indonesian government also formed BAZNAS in every province, district and city to help the central BAZNAS in collecting zakat funds in all regions of Indonesia. In addition to accommodating zakat payments by employees in state companies, BAZNAS forms a Collection of Zakat Unit (UPZ) in every state company. The UPZ

[6] Sri Nurhayati et al., op. cit., page 8.

[7] Republic of Indonesia, *Indonesian Zakat Act Number 23 Year 2011*, Chapter 2, Article 7.

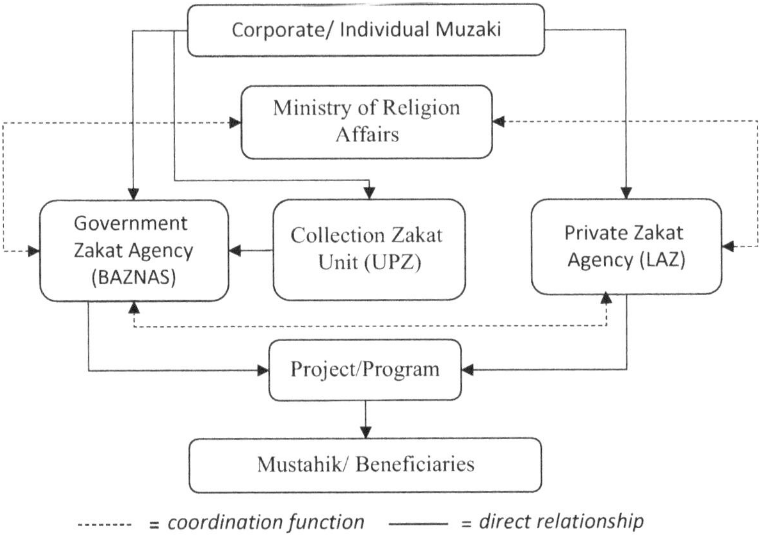

Fig. 16.1 The model of zakat management in Indonesia. (Source: Adapted from National Zakat Act of the Republic of Indonesia, 2011)

only helps BAZNAS in collecting zakat funds and does not have the authority to distribute zakat.

Then, regulations in Indonesia also allow private institutions to establish zakat institutions called the private zakat agency (LAZ). LAZ is a zakat institution formed independently by the community. According to the applicable regulations, LAZ has the duty to assist BAZNAS in collecting, managing and distributing zakat funds to eligible groups.[8] Like BAZNAS, LAZ also has representative offices at the provincial, district and city levels throughout Indonesia. So that we can conclude that the management of zakat in Indonesia has been arranged in a structured and systematic manner as stated in the legal law where the collection, management and distribution is carried out centrally by the state assisted by private zakat institutions.

[8] Ibid., Chapter 4, Article 17.

Malaysia

Systematic management of zakat in Malaysia is fairly long compared to Indonesia. The Malaysian government officially began regulating the management of zakat in 1991 by issuing regulations related to the management of zakat. As we can see in Fig. 16.2, the management of zakat in Malaysia is decentralized in that the management authority is given in full to each state but remains under one supervision under the State Islamic Council in each region of the federal government of Malaysia.[9]

On this basis, each federal government in Malaysia forms a zakat institution in each of them, called the zakat collection center (PPZ). Private zakat institutions are also permitted to assist federal state zakat institutions in collecting, managing and distributing zakat funds. Each of these zakat institutions, whether owned by the federal government or the private

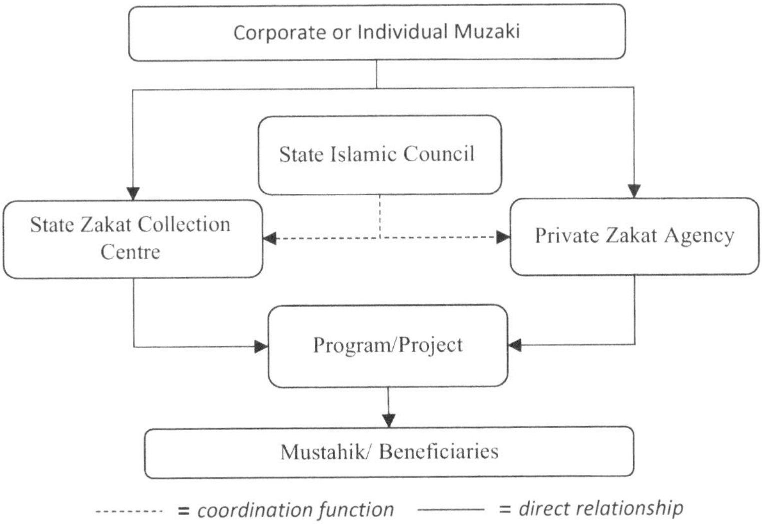

Fig. 16.2 The model of zakat management in Malaysia. (Source: Adapted from Mhd Shahril et al., 2016)

[9] Mhd Shahril et al., *Zakat Management in Malaysia: A Review*, American-Eurasian Journal of Scientific Research Volume XI, Issue 6, 2016.

sector, is only authorized to collect, manage and distribute zakat funds in their respective federation areas and is not permitted to do so outside the federation's territory except in certain circumstances.[10]

Saudi Arabia

Saudi Arabia is known as a country that implements sharia rules as a whole in all aspects including regulations in the management of zakat funds. Under the government system of the monarchical kingdom, the King of Saudi Arabia issued a decree of the King (Royal Court) with number 17/2/28/8634 dated 29/6/1370 H concerning the obligation to carry out Islamic sharia law including the obligation to pay zakat in the Saudi royal jurisdiction Arabia.[11] The management of zakat in Saudi Arabia is carried out progressively and centrally under the direct control of the finance ministry through a special department, namely, the General Authority of Zakat and Tax (GAZT).[12]

GAZT was formed by the government of Saudi Arabia in 1951. GAZT has special authority to collect zakat as well as taxes from all Saudis and bay residents living in Saudi Arabia. The majority of zakat donors in Saudi Arabia are private donors or pure government joint venture corporations. Meanwhile, government-owned companies are not subject to zakat because all profits are intended for the public interest. Foreign companies are only required to pay taxes.[13]

What is unique about the management of zakat in Saudi Arabia is the management of zakat funds having a system similar to tax management. Saudi Arabians who have paid zakat are exempt from paying taxes. Unlike in Indonesia or Malaysia, the results of zakat funds collected by GAZT are not directly distributed to residents in need. The authority to distribute zakat funds is in the Ministry of Social Affairs and Labor under the Directorate of General of Social Security. In summary, the management of Saudi zakat funds can be seen in Fig. 16.3.

[10] Amiruddin, *Model-model Pengelolaan Zakat di Dunia Muslim*, Ahkam Journal Volume 3 Number 1, July 2015.

[11] Uswatun Hasanah, *Zakat Management in Saudi Arabia, Sudan and Indonesia*, Indonesian Management and Accounting Research Journal Volume 13 Issue 1, January 2014.

[12] Muhamad Fuad Nasar, "Zakat Management in Saudi Arabia", retrieved from http://abumujahidah.blogspot.com/2012/11/pengelolaan-zakat-di-arab-saudi-sebuah.html

[13] Ibid.

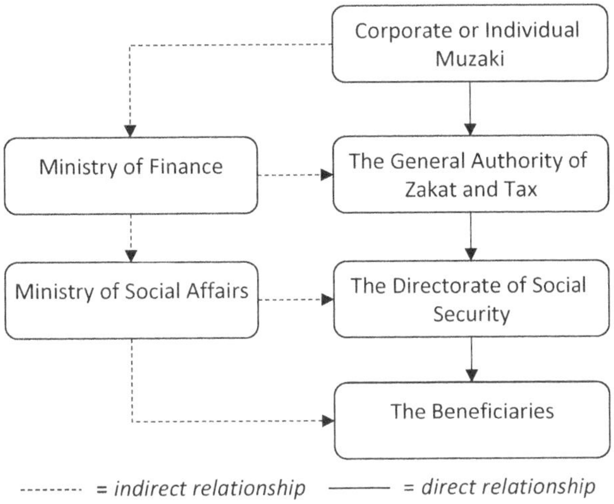

Fig. 16.3 The model of zakat management in Saudi Arabia. (Source: Adapted from Nasar 2012; Hasanah, 2014; Amiruddin, 2015)

Sudan

Sudan is a country in parts of North Africa that declares its country as an Islamic state. Structured management of zakat in Sudan has been started since 1984 with the issuance of zakat management laws which were later renewed by a new law in 2001. Management of zakat in Sudan is carried out centrally by the Zakat Chamber of Sudan with supervision from the Higher Council of Zakat Management.[14] Practically, the management of zakat in Sudan is described in Fig. 16.4.

Figure 16.4 depicts the flow of zakat management in Sudan. The unique thing about managing zakat in Sudan is that the Zakat Chamber delegates its authority in collecting zakat funds through the tax department of the finance ministry because indeed zakat management in Sudan has similarities in tax management. Then, in the distribution activities, the Zakat Chamber also delegated its role to the Ministry of Finance's Economic and Financial Planning Department. This is because the management of zakat in Sudan is equated with tax management.[15]

[14] Aulia Candra Sari, *Zakat Management in Sudan*, ZISWAF Journal Volume 4 Issue 1, 2017.

[15] Uswatun Hasanah, op.cit.

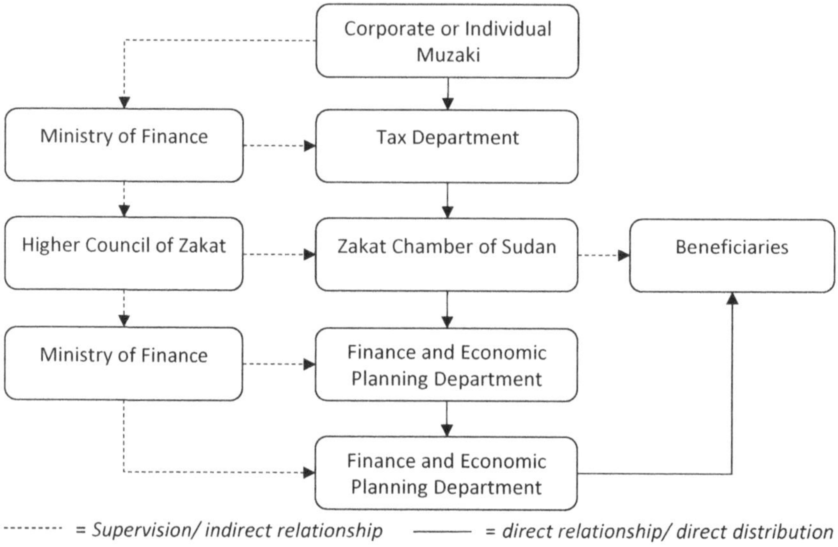

Fig. 16.4 The model of zakat management in Sudan. (Source: Adapted from Hasanah, 2014)

As in Indonesia, the Sudanese government also formed Zakat Chamber in every province in Sudan. However, the difference is that the law does not allow private institutions in Sudan to establish zakat institutions. The management of zakat in Sudan is entirely carried out by the state centrally from the collection, management and distribution of zakat funds.

Transparency in Zakat Management

Transparency can be interpreted as an openness of an organization in terms of its financial position, governance of organization and organization's performance where the three things can be easily accessed by both internal and external parties.[16] Transparency in every non-profit organization is part of the fundamental thing that must be done because it becomes a measure of their level of professionalism and credibility in managing

[16] BKC, "Transparency in Non Profit Organizations", retrieved from https://www.bkc-cpa.com/transparency-in-non-profit-organizations/

public funds.[17] There are many advantages, especially by non-profit organizations from the implementation of a high level of transparency, including increasing trust in donors, increasing opportunities for collaboration with other non-profit institutions, increasing reputation and improving the ethic work of the organization.[18]

In terms of zakat management, openness or transparency is very crucial. Because basically zakat is a mandatory order in Islam. So, in terms of transparency, zakat managers are responsible to two parties. First, in this world zakat managers must be responsible horizontally to the donors. Second, in the hereafter, the zakat manager must also be responsible to God.[19] Thus, in the management process starting from the collection of zakat funds from the donors, zakat management until the zakat distribution stage to beneficiaries must be managed in a greater accountable and transparent manner.

The efforts to implement the principles of transparency in the management of zakat funds have been carried out either by the government or zakat authorities or by the zakat institution itself. The joint efforts that have been made on a global scale by the government and authorities of various countries have been done by issuing the Zakat Core Principle (ZCP) document in Istanbul in 2016. The ZCP is a document which containing 18 minimum standards of zakat management that must be owned by zakat institutions so that in the future governance in zakat institutions will get better.[20]

As can be seen from Fig. 16.5, the ZCP is generally classified into six aspects, namely, aspect legal foundation which consists of ZCP 1–3, supervisory approach aspects collected in ZCP 4–6, aspects of Zakat Governance accommodated in standard ZCP 7–8, the intermediary function aspect contained in the ZCP 9–10 standard, the risk management aspect contained in the ZCP 11–14 standard and the Sharia Governance aspect contained in the ZCP standard 15–18. One of the principles relating to this topic is the 17th ZCP standard, the Disclosure and Transparency

[17] Ari Khusuma, "MenjadiOrganisasiNirlaba yang Akuntabel dan Transparan", retrieved from http://www.integrasi-edukasi.org/menjadi-organisasi-nirlaba-yang-akuntabel-dan-transparan/

[18] Ibid.

[19] Saad et al., *Islamic Accountability Framework in the Zakat Funds Management*, Procedia Social and Behavioral Science Journal Number 164, 2014.

[20] BI, BAZNAS & IRTI-IsDB, *Core Principles for Effective Zakat Operation and Supervision*, May 2016.

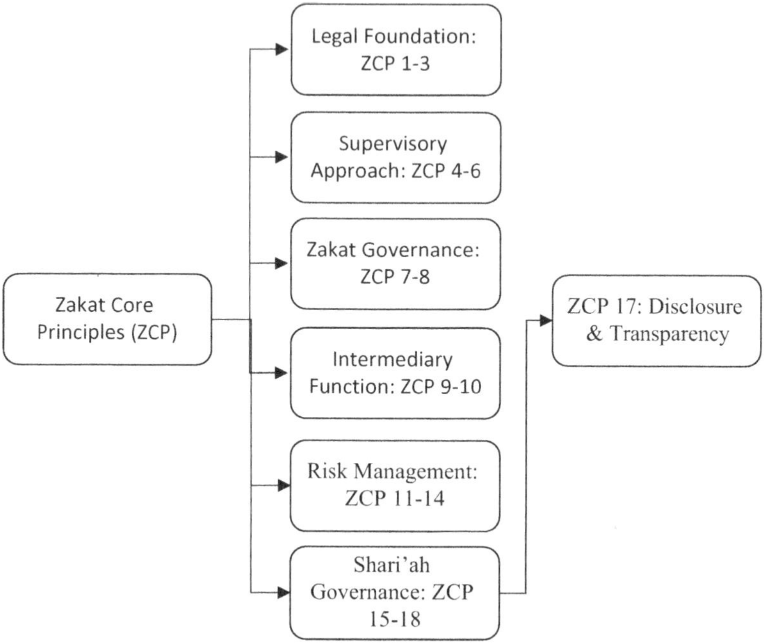

Fig. 16.5 The standard of Zakat Core Principles. (Source: Adapted from Bank Indonesia, BAZNAS & IRTI-IsDB, 2016)

standard, where the ZCP gives encouragement to zakat supervisors to ensure that zakat institutions regularly publish financial reports and the conditions of their organization's performance to the public.[21]

In addition, many zakat institutions are currently trying to maintain and implement the principles of transparency in the management of zakat funds. For example in Indonesia, the zakat law regulates each zakat institution in Indonesian jurisdiction to periodically conduct conventional and sharia audit. In general, the audit process in Indonesia is carried out by an external auditor. Furthermore, zakat institutions continue to be committed to safeguarding the values of transparency through regular reporting to donors through annual reports and e-mail, news letters and phone numbers, so donors can get information about the utilization of zakat funds that they have been provided. In addition, some Muslim countries

[21] Ibid., page 17.

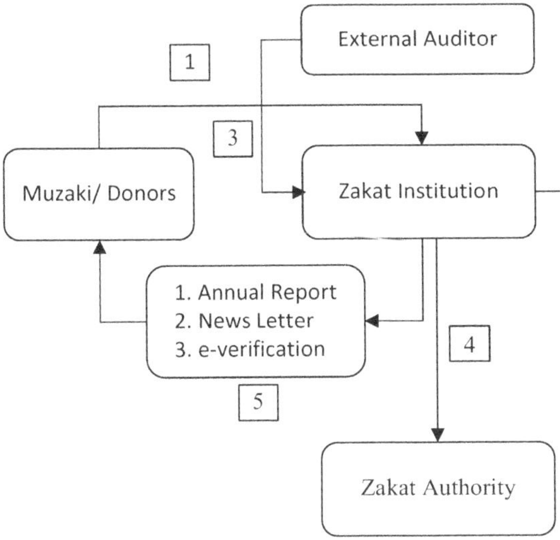

Fig. 16.6 The current practice of transparency process at zakat management

also require zakat institutions to report the results of the collection and distribution of zakat funds to zakat authorities on a regular basis. The process of transparency in zakat management can be seen in Fig. 16.6.

Indeed we need to appreciate the various efforts that have been made by the zakat institutions in maintaining the principles of transparency in managing zakat funds; however, these traditional efforts still have some weaknesses in various matters, especially the presence of vulnerability in falsifying reports in the annual report and financial statement. Hence, the preventive action is needed to minimize these risks. So as a concrete step, zakat institutions can make maximum use of blockchain technology to preserve the management of zakat funds to be more transparent and accountable.

The Implementation of Blockchain in Zakat Management for Greater Transparency

It cannot be denied that the existence of technology, especially the use of blockchain, has such a huge impact on all aspects of the industry, including zakat institutions. As a financial service-based institution, blockchain technology is very helpful in increasing effectiveness, efficiency, accountability and transparency in organizations. However, at present, there is no zakat institution in the world that utilizes blockchain technology in managing zakat funds. However, within the scope of Islamic social finance, namely, waqf has been implemented this technology in managing waqf funds.

The best practice is coming from Finterra company in managing fund by using blockchain technology. Finterra is one of the tech startup companies headquartered in Singapore; they have been developing blockchain technology for managing waqf funds based on crowdfunding system.[22] In utilizing blockchain technology, Finterra creates a Waqf Chain platform where there are several parties involved in the ecosystem of the chain, namely, platform providers, waqf institutions, waqf authority and donors. All parties must be registered and have access to the platform.

In raising waqf funds on the blockchain system, waqf institutions will issue a smart contract containing documents about waqf projects to be carried out. The smart contract must be approved in advance by the waqf authority. Once approved, the smart contract will be placed in the wakafchain system. Donors who have registered in the wakafchain ecosystem can choose the smart contract they want and then the waqf money will be returned to the waqf institution through a fund manager to be managed. All stages in the wakafchain can be seen by anyone in the ecosystem,[23] so that the implementation of the principles of accountability and transparency will be better maintained.

Zakat and waqf have similarities in several aspects. Both waqf and zakat are in detail regulated by sharia law, but the thing that distinguishes between them is that the waqf is a voluntary charity that targeted at anyone who needs it, and conversely, zakat is an obligation that must be fulfilled by a Muslim, and the parties involved in zakat have been determined in sharia law, starting from the category of the donors, zakat managers and its beneficiaries that are strictly regulated by sharia law. With a fairly strict arrangement in the management of zakat funds, logically, the management of zakat funds must be done far more transparently than the

[22] Emha S. Ashor, "*Fintech di Singapura Kembangkan Platform Wakaf Blockchain*", retrieved from https://sharianews.com/posts/fintech-di-singapura-kembangkan-platform-wakaf-blockchain

[23] Rich Management, "FInterra Waqf Chain", retrieved from https://www.youtube.com/watch?v=XipYn2ATt7Q

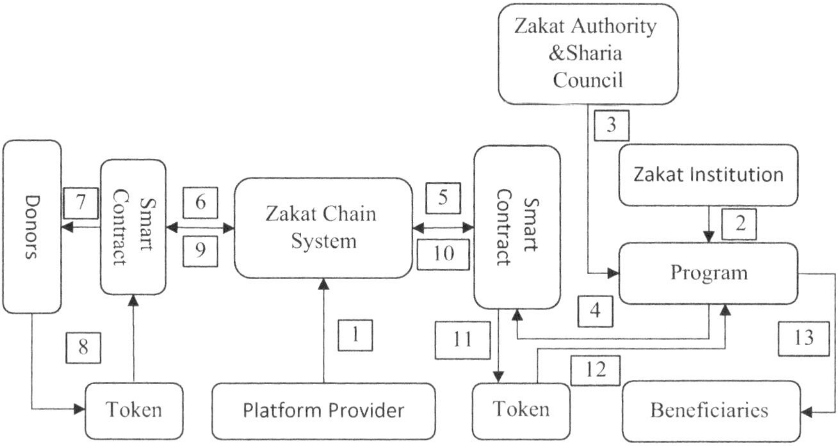

Fig. 16.7 The proposed model of Zakat-Blockchain (Zakat Chain) system

management of waqf funds. The utilization of blockchain technology in waqf management can be adopted by zakat institutions to do the same in order to increase the level of transparency in the management of zakat funds; the system on wakafchain can be adopted in managing zakat funds as can be seen in Fig. 16.7.

Figure 16.7 describes the proposed model of Zakat-Blockchain (Zakatchain). The figure shows how the flow of managing zakat funds by using blockchain technology. In the first stage, zakat institutions were required to collaborate with the platform provider to form a blockchain system for zakat. In the next stage, before offering empowerment programs whether consumptive or productive zakat programs, zakat institutions are required to have a plan to use zakat funds.

Furthermore, in the next stage, the program that has been set by zakat institution will first be examined by the zakat authority or sharia council which has the authority to conduct an assessment of that program. After getting permission, the program will be entered into the zakat chain system and converted into a blockchain product called smart contract. When the zakat smart contract is entered into the system, donors who have joined the zakat chain can choose the smart contract that suits their desires and goals. After agreeing, donors will convert their zakat funds to tokens in order to enter the zakat chain system.

Aftermath, at the next stage, the zakat institution will receive tokens from donors and convert the tokens into currencies which will then be channeled to the programs described in the smart contract. In the final stage, all zakat funds collected in the form of empowerment programs will be allocated to the beneficiaries of zakat funds. If in a conventional system, donors, zakat authorities or all parties involved in zakat cannot know the position of their zakat funds and must wait for the official report from the zakat institution. This time lag will open up fraudulent practices in the management of zakat funds, so in the zakat chain system that utilizes blockchain technology, all zakat stakeholders can find out all the stages and position of their zakat fund whether they are in collecting stage or managing stage, or even whether their fund has been distributed. This will certainly provide enormous benefits in managing zakat funds, so that the risks of human error and fraud can be minimized or even eliminated.

Conclusion

As part of the third pillar of Islam, zakat is one of the obligatory worships in sharia law. Zakat does not only contain vertical worship values, but zakat also has such a large economic and social mission, so that Islam regulates in detail and strictly in managing zakat funds. Islam regulates who is obliged to fulfill zakat funds, Islam also regulates who has the authority to manage zakat funds and Islam regulates who has the right to receive zakat funds. For this reason, the management of zakat funds requires a very high level of accountability and transparency.

The utilization of blockchain technology had a considerable effect on all industrial sectors. Better efficiency, effectiveness and transparency make financial institutions, both commercial and social, try to implement blockchain technology, including zakat institution. The advantages of blockchain technology can provide benefits for the management of zakat which consequently the zakat institution would manage zakat funds in greater transparency. Several social Islamic financial institutions such as waqf have utilized blockchain technology. Nonetheless, this technology is very possible to be applied in the management of zakat funds.

The proposed model of zakat chain can be one of the solutions, benchmarks and references for zakat institutions to implement blockchain technology in managing zakat funds to further increase their level of accountability and transparency which will ultimately lead to the inclining of the level of public trust in zakat institutions. The application of this technology is certainly facing several challenges. The lack of the relevant regulations, infrastructure and financial limitation become the current challenges for the zakat institution to develop this kind of technology. Thus, it is important to all related parties to support zakat institutions in adopting blockchain technology to achieve a greater transparency in zakat fund management.

References

Amiruddin. (2015). Model-Model Pengelolaan Zakat di Dunia Muslim. *Ahkam Journal, III*(1), 139–166.

Ashor, E. S. (2018). *Shariah News* [Online]. Retrieved July 15, 2019, from https://sharianews.com/posts/fintech-di-singapura-kembangkan-platform-wakaf-blockchain

Barantum. (2019). *Barantum.com* [Online]. Retrieved July 2, 2019, from https://www.barantum.com/blog/blockchain-adalah/

Bashir, I. (2018). *Mastering Blockchain*. Birmingham: Packt Publishing Ltd.

Bank Indonesia, BAZNAS & IRTI-IsDB. (2016). *Core Principles for Effective Zakat Operation and Principles*. Jakarta: s.n.

BKC. (2017). *Bedard, Kurowicki & Co* [Online]. Retrieved July 9, 2019, from https://www.bkc-cpa.com/transparency-in-non-profit-organizations/

Hafidhuddin, D. (2008). *Zakat dalam Perekonomian Modern* (1st ed.). Depok: Gema Insani.

Hasanah, U. (2014). Zakat Management in Saudi Arabia, Sudan and Indonesia. *Indonesian Management & Accounting Research Journal, XIII*(1), 40–61.

Khusuma, A. (2018). *Bina Integrasi Edukasi* [Online]. Retrieved July 9, 2019, from http://www.integrasi-edukasi.org/menjadi-organisasi-nirlaba-yang-akuntabel-dan-transparan/

Nasar, M. F. (2012). *Abu Mujahidah Al-Ghifari* [Online]. Retrieved July 5, 2019, from http://abumujahidah.blogspot.com/2012/11/pengelolaan-zakat-di-arab-saudi-sebuah.html

Nurhayati, S., Siswantoro, D., & Rahman, T. (2019). *Akuntansi dan Manajemen Zakat* (1st ed.). Jakarta: Salemba Empat Publisher.

Qardhawi, Y. (1973). *Fiqh Zakat: Dirasatu Muqaranatu al-Ahkamiha wa falsafatuha fi daifil Quran was Sunnah*. Beirut: Ar-risalah Foundation.

Republic of Indonesia. (2011). *Indonesian National Zakat Act Number 23*. Jakarta: Indonesia Government.

Saad, R. A., Marina, N., & Sawandi, N. (2014). Islamic Accountability Framework in The Zakat Funds Management. *Procedia-Social and Behavioral Sciences*, (164), 508–515.

Sari, A. C. (2017). Zakat Management in Sudan. *ZISWAF Journal, IV*(1), 347–364.

Shahril, M., Rahim, A., & Farid, M. (2016). Zakat Management in Malaysia: A Review. *American-Eurasian Journal of Scientific Research, XI*(6), 453–457.

CHAPTER 17

Zakat Digital Management Techniques

Mustafa Omar Mohammed, Aroua Robbana, and Houssemeddine Bedoui

Abstract Today, poverty is one of the biggest challenges that exist in the world [Kuzudisli, Fight Against Poverty From the Islamic Point of View: The Wealth Distribution and Share. 5(1), 9–15 (2017). https://doi.org/10.17265/2328-7144/2017.01.002]; it is regarded as the most crucial and the most significant social problem of the modern age [Saifee, Islamic Strategies for the Elimination of Poverty from the Society (June 2012), 2018. https://doi.org/10.13140/RG.2.2.28281.16486], a danger to belief, to morality, to safety, to family, to society, a plague and

Disclaimer The views and opinions expressed in this chapter are those of the authors and do not necessarily reflect the official policy or position of their institutions.

M. O. Mohammed
International Islamic University Malaysia, Kuala Lumpur, Malaysia

A. Robbana (✉)
Department of Economics, International Islamic University Malaysia (IIUM), Kuala Lumpur, Malaysia

H. Bedoui
Chez Dr. Zaim Bedoui, Teboulba, Tunisia

M. M. Billah (ed.), *Islamic FinTech*,
https://doi.org/10.1007/978-3-030-45827-0_17

a misfortune [Qaradawi, Fekeh Al Zakat, 1123 (1973)], a destructive force from all aspects [Salleh, Contemporary Vision of Poverty and Islamic Strategy for Poverty Alleviation (2017). https://doi.org/10.1177/2158244017697153], a curse at individual as well as at a community level and a threat to humanity [Mian Akram and Afza. Dynamic Role of Zakat in Alleviating Poverty: A Case Study of Pakistan (56013), 2014]. According to UNDP, more than 3 billion people representing approximately half of the world's population, live on less than $2.50 a day. Moreover, more than 1.3 billion people live with less than $1.25 a day. Half of the global poverty is located in the Muslim majority countries. Definitions of poverty are varied. However, the UNDP adopted a few years ago in the Human Development Report the Multidimensional Poverty Index (MPI). The MPI tries to capture some human deprivations at the household level across the same three dimensions as the HDI (health, education, and living standards). MPI covers ten deprivation indicators, including school attainment and attendance, nutrition, child mortality, assets, and access to some essential services. Currently, 26.5% of adults who are employed are part of the working poor representing less than $3.10 a day in purchasing power parity terms. If poverty is not controlled soon then it will be alarming.

Keywords Digital • Management • Zakat • Technique • Mechanisms

Introduction

Zakat: An Islamic Approach to Poverty Alleviation

Islam is a religion of justice and fairness that has no tolerance for a community that remains idle when there exists among them people who cannot afford necessities such as the daily bread, a cloth to cover their back, or a dwelling to shelter them. In fact, it is an obligation upon every Muslim to dedicate their blood, sweat, and tears to fulfill their basic needs. However, in case a Muslim is confronted by circumstances that restrict him from earning his necessities, it falls within the responsibility of the Muslim community to sponsor him and ensure that he does not fall prey to hunger, nudity, and misery. Abu Musa (May Allah be pleased with him) reported:

Messenger of Allah (□) said, "The relationship of the believer with another believer is like (the bricks of) a building, each strengthens the other." He (□) illustrated this by interlacing the fingers of both his hands.[1]

In a similar vein, "Islam denies a community where there is accumulation of wealth in a few hands, where no hoarding and no profiteering; a society in which there will be none slums nor multi-millionaires, neither the exploited proletariat nor the exploiting bourgeoisie" (Bello, 2010).

In order to bridge the gap between the rich and the poor, to alleviate poverty to the extent of eradicating it, to eliminate inequality and to achieve socioeconomic justice, Islam provides a compelling social security instrument that guarantees a permanent, smooth, and uninterrupted flow of wealth from the haves to the have nots. This effective tool for wealth distribution is called Zakat.

The meaning of the word Zakat linguistically varies from being purified to being guiltless, to being referred to as a mandatory payment of charity, to justify and to praise oneself, depending on the verse it is mentioned in, in the Quran. While technically, it refers to the act of a part of the wealth of a Muslim being given away for distribution in the cause of eight specifically mentioned groups of beneficiaries. In a nutshell, Zakat is defined as the right of the poor.

Allah has made Zakat compulsory upon every Muslim who meets specific criteria, to give a predetermined portion of his wealth. In fact, Hayeeharasah, Sehvises, and Ropha (2013) have said: 'Paying zakah is an obligation for Muslim when possessing assets that cover a specific amount according to Islamic rule (nisab) and reach the time period of a year (haol).'

The benefits of Zakat are manifold from both social and economic aspects cannot be neglected. At a social level, it helps the community at large by instilling values of collectivism through the teachings of assisting and supporting the less privileged in their community. It spreads social cohesion and mutual solidarity, which minimizes social disparities and social frictions between classes. Ibrahim (2014) believes that 'apart from what Zakat produces in giving out to poor and helping them to sustain their basic necessities of life, it also serves as a means of creating equality and reducing poverty in the society at large.' Hence, it is seen as social leverage for Muslim communities.

[1] Al-Bukhari and Muslim. Arabic/English book reference: Book 1, Hadith 222.

At the economic level, Zakat is ordained to create and maintain an economic balance within the Muslim society to redistribute wealth from the wealthy to the less fortunate. According to Sheikh Yusuf al Qaradawi in his book *Fiqh al zakah* (Volume I), Zakat has been described as 'a way to regain balance and equilibrium in social and economic life.' This redistribution of wealth will accelerate poverty alleviation both with social justice and social security. In a similar vein, Zakat payment has the power to speed up the velocity of money, which will consequently help the economy to grow faster.

Zakat has dual-fold impact on society, wherein the rich are cleansed off the feelings of greed and acquisitiveness while the poor are liberated from the misfortune or bondage of unsatisfied needs. While the rich experience purification of the soul and mind from thoughts of selfishness and stinginess by detaching from materialism, the poor are provided the opportunity to venture into living outside the dimensions of poverty, ensuring dignity within society. This will consequently make the poor feel respected in a decent human society that cares about them and their necessities. This will strengthen the community ties, prevent one from feeling ignored, rejected, outcast, abandoned, deficient, and lost, which may cause one to engage in criminal activities such as robbery, looting, and sometimes murder.

History of the Zakat Management Techniques

In the earlier days, at the time of the advent of Islam, a majority of people in Arabia lived in poverty, including our Prophet and most of his companions. There was widespread inequality in the quality of life, wealth, provisions, and skills, and absence of social services made matters worse. (Bashir, 2018)

> Yahya related to me from Malik that he heard that the Messenger of Allah, may Allah bless him and grant him peace, entered the mosque and found Abu Bakr as-Siddiq and Umar Ibn al-Khattab there. He questioned them and they said, "Hunger has driven us out." The Messenger of Allah, may Allah bless him and grant him peace, said, "And hunger has brought me out." They went to Abu'l-Haytham ibn at- Tayyihan al-Ansari. He ordered that some barley that was in the house be prepared and he got up to slaughter a sheep for them. The Messenger of Allah, may Allah bless him and grant him peace, said, "Leave the one with milk." He slaughtered a sheep for

them and brought them sweet water and it was hung on a palm-tree. Then they were brought the food and ate it and drank the water. The Messenger of Allah, may Allah bless him and grant him peace, recited, "Then, on that day, you will be asked concerning pleasure." (Sura 102 ayat 8)[2]

The concept of Zakat was first implemented and practiced in that early Muslim community in Mecca in 9H[3] by the Prophet (peace be upon him) with the core objective of enhancing poor people's life to facilitate for them the worship of Allah by all means. Although Zakat became compulsory after the Hijrah to Medina according to the majority of scholars some of which (Shawkani, 1834) (Al-Nawawi) (Imam Malik), the practice of the same had begun years earlier in Mecca (Damilola & Nassir, 2015). When it was first imposed in Mecca, the amount of money given away as Zakat was left to the discretion of the believers. The terms *hawel, nisab, Zakat* rate and types of properties subject to Zakat, the individuals entitled to receive Zakat, and the Zakat payment procedure were all determined only after the Hijrah to Medina. (Kahf, 1999)

The Zakat system was a centralized structure managed by the state that involved the Zakat managers, who were known as *Amils*. These were individuals personally designated to collect the Zakat by the Prophet (peace be upon him), at a prescribed rate, on fair terms from the fortunate to disburse it amongst the less fortunate in the same area (Wahid & Ahmad, 2017).

As narrated by Mu'adh (May Allah be pleased with him) when reported:

> The Messenger of Allah (□) sent me as a governor to Yemen and (at the time of departure) he instructed me thus: "You will go to people of the Scripture (i.e., the Jews and the Christians). First of all invite them to testify that La ilaha ill Allah (There is no true god except Allah) and that Muhammad (□) is His slave and Messenger; and if they accept this, then tell them that Allah has enjoined upon them five Salat (prayers) during the day and night; and if they accept it, then tell them that Allah has made the payment of Zakat obligatory upon them. It should be collected from their rich and distributed among their poor; and if they agree to it, don't take (as a share of Zakat) the

[2] English reference: Book 49, Hadith 28/Arabic reference: Book 49, Hadith 1701.

[3] 9H refers to the 9th year of the Hijra of Prophet Muhammed from Mecca to Medina in year 622G (Gregorian).

best of their properties. Beware of the supplications of the oppressed, for there is no barrier between it and Allah."[4]

"The whole Zakat Management System managed to live up to the standards of modern principles while maintaining simplicity" (Arif, 2017). The appointed Zakat administration officers were in every country (Masyita, 2018). Qaradawi stated that more than twenty-five companions were appointed by our Prophet (peace be upon him) as Zakat officers throughout the Arabian Gulf. The primary function of these officers was to collect Zakat from the rich, register, and audit the Zakat funds collected, look after the Zakat property and distribute it to the eligible recipient.

The Prophet (peace be upon him) had succeeded in laying down a strong foundation to administer Zakat through his wisdom and leadership by introducing principles of division of labor, distribution of authority, and maintaining records or logs of the Zakat funds being managed. The successful implementation of an effective Zakat management and distribution system by the Prophet (peace be upon him) resulted in the elevation of the standard of living of Muslims, which in turn increased the passion for upholding Islam (Saad, Sawandi, & Mohammad, 2016).

After the death of Prophet Muhammed (peace be upon him), during the time of the first Caliph Abu Bakar Siddique (R.A.), the rules, regulations, and management system devised by Prophet Muhammed (peace be upon him) remained the same without any modification. However, the major incident that occurred during his reign was the refusal of the peninsula to continue paying Zakat after the Prophet's death. Abu Bakar Siddique (R.A) sent armies that subdued these rebels in large-scale battles as he considered Zakat as the right of the needy (Micheal Bonner).

The Era of the 2nd caliph Umar Ibn al-Khattab (R.A.) is considered very significant as a Zakat management system, and laws had encountered several substantial changes and modifications through Ijtihad to coup with the social reality. The administration of Zakat was strengthened through the establishment of *Bayt Al-Mal* for the management of Zakat. (Akbar) *Bayt Al-Mal* constitutes a place where the wealth was administered and recorded through its storage, accumulation, and distribution. This wealth includes *Zakat, kharaj, jizya, usyr, booty, fay'*, and many others.

[4] Narrated by Al-Bukhari and Muslim/Grade: Mtafakunalayh.Arabic/English book reference: Book 9, Hadith 1077.

Besides, Umar Ibn al-Khattab (R.A.) formalized the system for the management of Zakat through proper distribution of power and responsibilities. Medina was made the center of administration while other branches were open across Muslim cities to help establish the formal system for the effective collection and distribution of Zakat. Managers (*Amil*) and other staff of Zakat were instated as permanent government employees, qualifying them to receive a continuous flow of wages, thus, motivating them to become more committed to performing their assigned responsibilities. Furthermore, efficient checks and balance were placed in the form of officers who audited/monitored the tasks related to Zakat, and its property.

Umar Ibn al-Khattab introduced the concept of metamorphosing the lives of Zakat recipients to become eligible Zakat payers too. This was carried forward by transforming the lives of the poor who were eligible to receive Zakat through sustainable and overall development of the same using the Zakat funds. Umar Ibn al-Khattab (R.A.) ensured that all the money in the *Bayt Al-Mal* was spent in the cause of Zakat at the end of the year to avoid embezzlement or exploitative activities of the Zakat funds. To prevent exploitation activities and misappropriation of Zakat funds, Umar Ibn al-Khattab spent all the money in *Bayt Al-Mal* at the end of the year (Saad et al. 2016).

The management of the Zakat system was very efficient during the time of Umar Ibn al-Khattab to the extent that certain provinces of the Islamic State were able to overcome poverty. It was reported that Mua'dh Ibn Jabal had sent the proceedings from Yemen, for three consecutive years, after satisfying the needs of the province, in quantities of one-third, one-half and full, respectively, to Medina for further disbursement (Kahf, 1999).

During the time of the 3rd caliph Othman (R.A), Zakat management system as regarded as similar to the previous during Umar Ibn al-Khattab's reign with a little difference in practice whereby he divided property in two types: apparent property and non-apparent property. He made Zakat on the apparent property, which are agriculture crops, livestock, etc., to be paid through *Bayt Al-Mal*, while the non-apparent property was left to the individual desire (Wahab, Rahim, & Rahman, 2014). However, if he learned that some people were not paying Zakat, he would take it from them by force.

This practice remained the same later on during the Umayyah's Empire, and people were paying the Zakat of their non-apparent assets by themselves as they did not trust the rulers. However, during the time of Caliph

Umar Ibn Abd Al Aziz, who was known for his trustiness, righteousness, straightness, rectitude, and probity, things evolved. In fact, people rushed to pay their Zakat to the state and Zakat management became fully centralized as it was before the reign of Caliph Othman, whereby Zakat collection and distribution was assessed, controlled, and managed by *Bayt Al-Mal*. During his leadership, there was a surplus of Zakat fund in *Bayt Al-Mal* as Zakat eligible receivers could not be found (Faisal, 2011). On the attribution of Suhail bin Abi Salih, Abu Ubaid narrated that a man from the Ansar said: Umar ibn Abdul-Aziz wrote to 'Abd al-Hamid bin' Abd al-Rahman in Iraq: Give people their Zakat. Abd al-Hamid wrote back to him: I gave people their Zakat and remained in *Bayt Al-Mal*. Umar wrote to him: Check everyone indebted not in luxury, and not in profusion and give him to pay back his loan. He said 'I have spent them and remained in *Bayt Al-Mal*." He wrote to him: "Help every young man wants to marry." He wrote to him: He remained in the *Bayt Al-Mal*, and wrote to him after the exit of this: to see who was a tribute to the weak of his land, lend him what strengthens the work of his land, we do not want them for a year or two. Also, Caliph Umar Ibn Abd Al Aziz directed Zakat fund to be distributed to the unfortunate in Africa. However, Yahya could not find the needy there; so then, he used the Zakat funds to free slaves (Saad et al. 2016). Zakat surplus was also used to build houses that were given to the homeless, to buy horses and animals that are suitable to transport people who did not have a vehicle at the time and to fund young people who wanted to get married.

These channels of Zakat distribution were employed by Caliph Umar Abdul Aziz to evade the accumulation of undistributed funds of Zakat. The diversification of Zakat distribution channels had benefitted the Muslim community back then. Thus, it can be concluded that under a centralized and fully controlled non-corrupt government, the management of Zakat becomes increasingly efficient.

This system prevailed until the downfall of the Islamic rule during the eighteenth and nineteenth centuries when the Islamic lands were colonized. During that period, Zakat as an institution collapsed and was abandoned in favor of secular strategies enforced by the colonizers. As a result, the Muslim world, postcolonization, witnessed poverty; an increase in income inequality; social insecurity, and so on. These postcolonial new strategies showed their inefficiencies, increasing poverty and wealth inequalities.

Various Islamic countries, later, replaced the Zakat system with elements or institutions of almsgiving that funded and delivered humanitarian support. However, they have been ineffective and unsustainable when compared to the potential that the Zakat system has to offer, which is the tools employed to empower the poor and destitute with only the essential means of livelihood.

Modern Management Techniques of Zakat and Its Challenges

The recent decades have witnessed serious efforts from organizations, institutions, and states toward the institutionalization of Zakat and the implementation of an efficient system. Even though due to some factors, namely, technology and privatization of Zakat institutions, Zakat collection has witnessed a significant rise. However, results are a mirage and Zakat institutions worldwide still suffer from several obstacles and imperfections, which have been generally managed informally. Zakat administration in most jurisdictions has been based on traditional methods with inherent challenges in the calculation, inadequate collection mechanisms and inefficient distribution channels, and so on. This often results in skepticism on the part of both Zakat payers and recipients.

One of the most supported suggestions to overcome this widely widespread skepticism that surrounds the collection and distribution of Zakat is the institutionalization of this system to derive the optimum benefit from its vast potential for society. According to Mutmainah (2015), institutionalizing the Zakat system while creating a suitable governance procedure is one of the earliest propositions recommended to reinforce Zakat and overcome its cited deficiencies. In fact, the role of government institutions to take over the systematization of this pillar is considered imperative. Only six countries in the world have made the governmental collection of Zakat compulsory according to the 2017 report produced by BAZNAS and the UNDP. The report further noted that in most Muslim-majority countries, there did not exist any form of a governmental system that governed the collection and distribution of the Zakat (Beik, Buana, & Pickup, 2018).

A glimpse back into our history throws light on the unmistakably crucial role the State played in governing, supervising and controlling Zakat implementation especially at the time of the Prophet (peace be upon him), wherein the *Amils* overlooked the smooth functioning of the collection and distribution of Zakat. The State is even entitled to modify the rules of Zakat in the matters of its detailed implementation, provided the alteration remains within the spirit of Quranic precepts (Kasiam, 2009)

To revive the Zakat system in its traditional form is neither feasible nor efficient for our current times. Thus, this has to be managed by embracing the use of the ever-advancing technology of our times. Indeed, the emergence of the latter that seeks to improve and enhance the design and delivery of financial services, the traditional Zakat system seems to have found its misfortune. However, governmental bodies, today, are at a better position to harness the power of technology to realize and attain better the goals and the objectives of Zakat.

Disruptive innovation must be sought after and adopted while executing the collection as well as the distribution of Zakat.

Calculation Challenge

The various issues that the existing Zakat system are explained further; one of the core reasons that explain Muslims' abstinence toward paying Zakat is the accounting problem. Gambling, Kareem (1986) contended that one of the primary objectives of accounting in an Islamic society is to provide information to enable the individual to determine his Zakat liabilities as specified in the Shari'ah. At the time of the Prophet (peace be upon him) and the Caliphas, *Amils* were appointed to fulfill the duty of Zakat accounting, collection, and distribution. This discharged the Zakat payers from the responsibilities of carrying out most of the tedious work. However, due to the gap in information that is widely prevalent today, Muslims are encountering the problem of Zakat accounting, which prevents them from paying their dues. Thus, the government should undertake suitable financial technology strategies that are dedicated to increasing the awareness of Muslims to enable them to determine their Zakat obligations.

There have been numerous attempts by non-governmental institutions to assist Muslims in the calculation of their Zakat through various applications and software. These are mainly website or phone application calculators that help to calculate the total amount needed to be paid according to the type of Zakat such as Zakat on income, Zakat on business, Zakat on gold and silvers and others. (Ahmad, 2018) Some examples of such devices are ZakatPay, Zakat calculator by the National Zakat Foundation, Zakat calculator by Islamic Relief Worldwide and so on.

However, clarifying the intention behind the acquisition of an asset precedes calculation of the amount to be paid in Zakat. This is because the intention that resulted in the acquiring of the asset is a decisive factor that determines whether Zakat should be paid on that property or not. For instance, if a woman bought jewelry with the intention of adornment, according to Imam Malik, she is not required to pay Zakat; however, if she intended to trade with it or save it or rent it, then, it becomes required to have Zakat paid upon it. The drawback with the applications mentioned above is that, the intention for the acquiring of an asset that makes the same required to be paid Zakat upon is neither investigated nor clarified. As a result, the amounts calculated through these apps do not necessarily be authentic. Also, there are differences of opinion amongst the juristic schools with regards to Zakat calculation. For example, in a similar vein with the previous example, when Imam Malik, Imam Shafii and Imam Ibn Hanbal agreed that jewelry intended for adornment is not Zakatable, Imam Hanafi said it is. Such differences usually add on to the confusion of the Zakat payer whom we witness regularly depending on scholars for clarification. These deficiencies are yet to be addressed, and the government must pay attention to finding an effective solution.

Collection Challenge

Another challenge that exists in setting up an effective Zakat system is the failure to realize the full potential of Zakat amount in its collection. Indeed, some researchers claim that, of the existing Zakat systems, not one has been able to achieve more than 25% of the Zakat potential in its form of collection (Haq, Binti, & Wahab, 2017) This could be explained by the unwillingness amongst Zakat payers to pay their Zakat due to the lack of trust that exists amongst people in paying their Zakat to third parties, and from the government side collection is costly and the methods adopted are not effective the reason why Zakat collection is yet to be effective.

Fortunately, the emergence of digital technology (Internet and mobile application) created vast opportunities to develop smooth and thrifty tools for the direct collection of Zakat. Rachman and Salam (2018), divided these tools into two main categories: crowdfunding and information technology media.

The rise of charity-based crowdfunding platforms in the recent years have shown platforms being set by the creator, who is either an individual or an institution, calling for collection of funds to support campaigns through the acceptance of donations. These campaigns often contain detailed information that explains the flow of disbursement of these funds and the various usages of the same. A Zakat distribution can adopt a similar program, wherein the proposed campaign is based on principles that prioritize the interests, justice, and welfare of the Mustahiq.

Processing transactions payments through information technology media, on the other hand, takes the form of a Zakat payer proceeding to make a payment through e-commerce channels or marketplaces. For instance, Zakat payer shops online and then proceeds to pay his Zakat through one of those websites, which are in collaboration with governmental bodies or NGOs. There are different Zakat payment channels like Zakat mobile applications, Islamic banking tools such as mobile banking that facilitates transactions and other online systems that are unlike crowdfunding; as these are only the tools that enable Zakat payment transactions. For instance, in Malaysia, according to (Lubis, Yaacob, Omar, & Dahlan, 2011) most Zakat institutions are in the process of making Zakat information electronically available to the public through the development of E-Zakat platforms

The use of the above-cited digital devices and financial technology by some countries such as Malaysia and Indonesia have helped to slightly increase the amount collected in Zakat relative to its potential. However, the impact of the same falls very short from justifying its actual potential. For instance, the potential of Zakat in Indonesia is considered quite immense. However, according to (Canggih, Fikriyah, & Surabaya, 2017) the realization of Zakat collection compared to its potential is as low as 0.09% (Friantoro & Zaki, 2018). In Malaysia, the Zakat amount realized is only 19.4% in the collection (Payers & Selangor, 2018) This could be explained by the increasing concerns over online fraud, cybercrime, data security and some other issues related to the internet of things (IoT).

To achieve the optimum level of Zakat collection, it is immensely crucial that the concerns as mentioned earlier are addressed and tackled with the use of blockchain technology to facilitate a safer and more secure passageway for transactions and payments.

Without a doubt, Zakat collection methods have been evolving from year to year, but unfortunately, the mediums for Zakat distribution have failed to meet the improvement that Zakat collection has undergone over the years. Thus, much work and innovation are still needed to improve and benefit the *Asnaf*. (Lubis et al., 2011). The gap between Zakat distribution and collection is a result of non-transparent and unreliable distributors, which has resulted in the lack of trust amongst the Zakat givers. Zakat payers are interested to know where and to whom has their Zakat contributions been channeled to (Ahmad, 2018). Moreover, high costs of distribution further fuel this, besides the non-confirmation of the authenticity of the recipients of Zakat, the arduous processing of Zakat and disturbing level of involvement of bureaucracy that hinders the speed of disbursement (Lubis & Azizah, 2018) has resulted in the failure to distribute Zakat most efficiently and effectively (Haq et al., 2017).

Transparency and Trust Challenges

Zakat in Muslim countries is lacking transparency and reliability in the distribution process, which incidentally was the same reason that prevented Muslims from paying their Zakat during the reign of *Banu Umayyah*. The information on the collection and distribution of Zakat is, in most cases, inaccessible to the public, suggesting a low level of transparency in the Zakat institutions (Taha et al., 2017).

Several factors lead to the trust problem that occurs when payer want to pay Zakat to *Amil*. These factors are the reputation of the institution that plays a significant role, the contact person who has a strong positive influence on the corporate image of service firms in the hospitality industry.

The fulfilment of the principle of transparency may be achieved through the embracement of Blockchain technology that is designed to be an open tamper-proof ledger that provides all information about the amount of Zakat collected, the disbursement flow, the official financial reports and the operational accountability which will consequently increase the effectiveness and responsibility of service in Zakat management.

The Islamic Social Financing App is the first of its kind to have leveraged the blockchain technology mentioned above, initiated by the International Centre for Education in Islamic Finance (INCEIF) in partnership with AidTech, a Dublin-based FinTech company; and the International Federation of Red Cross and Red Crescent Societies. This application was both well received and awarded accolades by the Islamic Development Bank Group as well as the IE Business School in Madrid in 2018.

This app provides its users to choose from an array of projects such as water irrigation, sanitation, poverty, etc. to direct their contributions. Upon the selection of the project, users fulfill their payment through a secured gateway. The payers are notified with notes of thanks through the sophisticated features of blockchain once all the money donated by the user is completely utilized. Governmental Zakat Institutions must establish a similar rigorous governance structure that corresponds with the functionality of the Islamic Social Financing App to enhance transparency and operating efficiency.

According to some empirical studies (Hakim, 2014); (Mutmainah, 2015), variables of accountability, financial transparency, and independence contribute to the Zakat payer's awareness and willingness to pay Zakat. Thus, the eventual generalization of such governance principles among Zakat institutions would undoubtedly increase their efficiency and contribution to poverty alleviation and social development. As a result, the community's trust and confidence are restored through the establishment of good governance and the transparency of Zakat management (Rachman & Salam, 2018).***

Distribution Challenge

Another major hindrance in the process of establishing an efficient Zakat system is the discrepancy that exists between the amount of Zakat that is collected and the amount distributed. According to Azman, Mohammad and Syed Mohd Najib (2012), what is collected is unfortunately not appropriately and effectively distributed. In other words, it is not put to the right use. This misuse factor is explained by Ali et al. (2017) as to how Zakat institutions handle and play their role as a medium of distributing the fund collected from Zakat payers to those entitled to receive Zakat.

The Zakat funds collected are supposed to be dedicated to the use of empowering *Asnaf* to increase the quality of their life at the micro as well as the macro levels. The *Asnaf* are supposed to be transformed from being the receivers of Zakat to becoming the payers of Zakat in the long run. This can only be achieved when the Zakat funds are specifically directed toward developing opportunities for the education, skills, and training of the *Asnaf*, which would eventually allow him/her to have access to employability or to start a business in the future. Unfortunately, the current practices entail the *Asnaf* being directly handed over the sum of money required to fulfill their short-term needs. As a result, the Zakat money goes through the vicious circle of invoking no sustainable value in the long run for its receivers.

A recent example is the Zakat funds' use in Kenya that benefits more than 1.2 million people through the purchase of seeds and farming packets. This successful project, which is managed by the International Federation of the Red Crescent (IFRC), has actually witnessed the transformation of the communities involved from the subsistence and need-based category (*daruriyyat*) to the level of *hajiyyat* (complementary-based category). Thus, the net effect of the project was the movement of groups of people from poverty to become Zakat payers for those of lesser fortune, until poverty is eventually eradicated (Umar, Abdul, & Alchaar, 2018).

However, with the increase in the trend to defraud authorities amongst the public to enjoy the benefits of being Zakat beneficiary, there exists a confusion problem arises to determine who deserves Zakat payments as the growing trend to defraud authorities can no longer be debated. In the time of the Prophet (peace be upon him), he did not want to give Zakat to people who ask for Zakat but created a fact-finding group that finds and determines who is entitled to receive Zakat. As a good Muslim, many of them feel that they are not allowed to be paid Zakat money (Masyita, 2018). This is in stark contrast to the present circumstances where identifying and locating the rightful *Asnafs* of all eight categories have become tedious.

Despite most Zakat institutions and NGOs possessing a comprehensive database and access to information technology, these institutions still struggle to obtain useful information on *Asnafs* and identify potential *Asnafs* in a region.

In a similar vein, proving to Zakat payers that the recipients selected are rightful *Asnafs* and determining that their Zakat is directly utilized for the needs of those who are eligible is another issue that most institutions and NGOs face. Some of these institutions have successfully overcome the tracking issue with the utilization of the blockchain tracking system.

Bureaucracy is yet another significant barrier that exists to the establishment of a systematic and effective Zakat distribution system, which reduces the efficiency of operations and is time-consuming.

The speed of disbursement of Zakat funds is different from one country to another, depending on the method adopted for the distribution and the spread of the IoT in it.

For instance, in Malaysia, there are mainly three methods of disbursement (monetary), namely, cash, check, and internet banking. According to the Zakat officers, the most popular way to distribute funds amongst the recipients is through internet banking, as more than 80% of the *Asnaf* today hold bank accounts. However, in certain instances such as the application of an *Asnaf* to purchase a bicycle, the Zakat funds are distributed in the form of a check to ensure the proper exercise of the funds provided. Thus, the type or method of distribution differs according to the circumstances (Ahmad, 2018). These methods help to increase the velocity and acceleration of distribution.

In some countries, in stark contrast to Malaysia, the mode of distribution that is adopted is still very traditional in nature. It is important to note that the speed of disbursement becomes a significant concern in cases where the *Asnaf* requires financial help on an immediate basis, such as in the case of emergencies. In such circumstances, the process and procedures adopted by the Zakat institutions can prove to be cumbersome and even fatal. With the advancement of technology nowadays, Zakat institutions can generate a spot system that fulfills the need for such cases.

Blockchain can potentially improve efficiency, streamline the process, decrease audit burden, and ensure quick delivery by significantly reducing bureaucracy and paperwork as well as reducing cost. This is usually done with the help of smart contracts built on the blockchain. A smart contract is a computer program envisioned to digitally facilitate, verify, or enforce the negotiation or performance of a contract. Smart contracts allow the execution of transactions without third parties. These transactions are trackable and irreversible.[5]

All the aforementioned issues need to be tackled to ensure that the Zakat is moving on the right track. Today, with the emergence of financial technology that seeks to improve and enhance the design and delivery of financial services, we can say that Zakat traditional system has found its misfortune. The financial technology can help to address all the deficiencies of Zakat and replace the classical approach by a new, more sophisticated, efficient, effective, and transparent one. There have been several tentative to tackle different problems of Zakat process, but none of them attempted to create a whole new technological design that solves the deficiencies all along the Zakat process.

[5] https://medium.com/@abhibvp003/smart-contracts-on-the-blockchain-a-deep-dive-in-to-smart-contracts-9616ad26428c

Conclusion

This chapter dealt with the digital management techniques of Zakat, highlighting at the beginning how the Zakat could be the Islamic approach to alleviate poverty challenges. The chapter further outlined the Zakat management techniques throughout history and later tackled the current and modern Zakat management techniques. In fact, the innovate Zakat management has few challenges that the blockchain and new technologies fixed like the Calculation, collection, Distribution, Transparency and Trust Challenges.

References

Ahmad, K. (2018). Financial Inclusion through Efficient Zakat Distribution for Poverty Alleviation in Malaysia: Using FinTech & Mobile Banking. *Proceding of the 5 International Conference on Mangement and Muamalah* (September 2000), pp. 15–31.

Ali, M. A. M., Tazilah, M. D. A. B. K., Shamsudin, A. I. B., Shukri, F. R. B. F., Adelin, N. M. F. A. B. N., & Zaman, W. M. S. B. W. Z. (2017, August). Factors That Influence the Zakat Collection Funds: A Case in Kuantan.

Arif, M. (2017). Zakat as a Mode of Poverty Alleviation. *International Journal of Economics & Management Sciences, 6*, 6. https://doi.org/10.4172/2162-6359.1000473

Azman, A. R., Mohammad, A., & Syed Mohd Najib, S. O. (2012). Zakat Institution in Malaysia: Problems and Issues. *Gjat, 2*(1), 35–41.

Bashir, A. H. (2018). Reducing Poverty and Income Inequalities: Current Approaches and Islamic Perspective. *Journal of King Abdulaziz University, Islamic Economics, 31*(1), 93–104. https://doi.org/10.4197/Islec.31-1.5

Beik, I. S., Buana, G. K., & Pickup, F. (2018). Unlocking to Achieve the SDGs in Indonesia. *United Nations Development Programme*, p. 23.

Bello, D. A. (2010). Islamic Social Welfare and the Role of Zakah in the Family System (23192).

Canggih, C., Fikriyah, K., & Surabaya, U. N. (2017). Potensi dan realisasi dana zakat Indonesia. *1*, 14–26.

Damilola, W., & Nassir, A. (2015). The Role of Zakat as a Poverty Alleviation Strategy and a Tool for Sustainable Development: Insights from the Perspectives of the Holy Prophet (PBUH). *5*(3), 8–17.

Faisal. (2011). Sejarah Pengelolaan Zakat Di Dunia Muslim Dan Indonesia. *XI*, 241–273.

Friantoro, D., & Zaki, K. (2018). Do We Need Financial Technology for Collecting Zakat?

Gambling, K. (1986). Islam and 'Social Accounting. *13*(June 1985).

Hakim, M. M. (2014). Pengaruh Transparansi Dan Akuntabilitas Pengelolaan Zakat Terhadap Minat Muzakki Di Rumah Zakat Cabang Semarang.

Haq, M. A. Al, Binti, N., & Wahab, A. (2017). Effective Zakah Distribution: Highlighting Few Issues and Gaps in Kedah, Malaysia, *9*(July), 259–288. https://doi.org/10.15408/aiq.v9i2.4002

Hayeeharasah, F., Sehvises, S., & Ropha, H. (2013). The Timeline of Zakah. *Procedia—Social and Behavioral Sciences, 88*, 2–7. https://doi.org/10.1016/j.sbspro.2013.08.474

Ibrahim, P. (2014). Pembangunan ekonomi melalui agihan zakat: tinjauan empirikal, (January 2008).

Kahf, M. (1999). The Performance of the Institution of Zakah in Theory and Practice.

Kasiam, S. (2009). Governing Zakat as a Social Institution: The Malaysian Perspective.

Kuzudisli, A. (2017). Fight Against Poverty From the Islamic Point of View: The Wealth Distribution and Share. *5*(1), 9–15. https://doi.org/10.17265/2328-7144/2017.01.002

Lubis, M., & Azizah, A. H. (2018). *Towards Achieving the Efficiency in Zakat Management System: Interaction Design for Optimization in Indonesia Towards Achieving the Ef fi ciency in Zakat Management System: Interaction Design for Optimization in Indonesia*. Springer Singapore. https://doi.org/10.1007/978-981-13-1628-9

Lubis, M., Yaacob, N. I., Omar, Y., & Dahlan, A. A. (2011). Enhancement of Zakat Distribution Management System: Case Study in Malaysia. *International Management Conference 2011 Proceedings*, pp. 1–10.

Masyita, D. (2018). Lessons Learned of Zakah Management from Different Era and Countries. *Journal of Islamic Economics, 10*(2), 441–456.

Mian Akram and Afza. (2014). Dynamic Role of Zakat in Alleviating Poverty: A Case Study of Pakistan (56013).

Mutmainah, L. (2015). The Influence of Accountability, Transparency, and Responsibility of Zakat Institution on Intention to Pay Zakat. *Global Review of Islamic Economics and Business, 3*(2), 108–119.

Payers, Z., & Selangor, I. N. (2018). Social & Behavioural Sciences. *IEBMC 2017 8th International Economics and Business Management Conference Challenges in Zakah Collection: In Case of Business.*

Qaradawi, Y. al. (2001). دور الزكاة في علاج المشكلات الإقتصادية وشروط نجاحها.

Rachman, M. A., & Salam, A. N. (2018). The Reinforcement of Zakat Management through Financial Technology Systems. *3*(1), 57–69.

Saad, R. A. J., Sawandi, N., & Mohammad, R. (2016). Zakat Surplus Funds Management. *International Journal of Economics and Financial Issues, 6*(S7), 171–176.

Saifee, A. (2018). Islamic Strategies for the Elimination of Poverty from the Society (June 2012). https://doi.org/10.13140/RG.2.2.28281.16486

Salleh, M. S. (2017). Contemporary Vision of Poverty and Islamic Strategy for Poverty Alleviation. https://doi.org/10.1177/2158244017697153

Shawkani, I. (1834). نيل الأوطار شرح منتقى الأخبار.

Taha, R., Adam, F., Sultan, U., Abidin, Z., Nurhidayatie, N., Ali, M., & Ariff, A. M. (2017). Religiosity and Transparency in the Management of Zakat Institutions. *20*(1), 1–9.

Umar, F., Abdul, B. I. N., & Alchaar, O. (2018). Classical Zakat Modelling for the Blockchain Age Inspiration from Umar Ibn Abd Al Aziz.

Wahab, N. A., Rahim, A., & Rahman, A. (2014). A Framework to Analyse the Efficiency and Governance of Zakat Institutions. https://doi.org/10.1108/17590811111129508

Wahid, H. S., & Ahmad, R. A. K. (2017). The Acceptance of Amil and Zakat Recipient Toward Localization of Zakat Distribution in Malaysia (June 2016).

CHAPTER 18

Zakat Calculation Software for Corporate Entities

Mezbah Uddin Ahmed and Noor Suhaida binti Kasri

Abstract Ensuring socio-economic justice, eradication of poverty and equitable distribution of wealth are among the primary objectives of Islam. Even so, a significant number of Muslims around the world are deprived of their basic needs. The scenario only worsens in times of financial and political turbulence. There is a desperate need to find sources of funding to rescue people from their miseries and offer sustainable solutions. Zakat has great potential to meet the funding needs. This chapter argues that zakat contributions will be amplified if corporate entities pay zakat as legal persons or on behalf of their Muslim shareholders. This chapter proposes development of a zakat calculation software to facilitate corporate entities and Islamic financial institutions calculating their zakat obligations reliably. Development of such software requires Islamic finance research entities to team up with information technology experts. Prominent Shariah scholars

M. U. Ahmed (✉) • N. S. b. Kasri
International Shari'ah Research Academy for Islamic Finance (ISRA), Kuala Lumpur, Malaysia
e-mail: mezbah@isra.my

M. M. Billah (ed.), *Islamic FinTech*,
https://doi.org/10.1007/978-3-030-45827-0_18

will play the essential role of validating and endorsing the Shariah compliance of the software.

Keywords Zakat • Corporates • IFIs • Accounting • IFRS • Technology • FinTech

Introduction

Islamic economic principles propagate socio-economic justice, poverty eradication and equitable wealth distribution. Yet there are many Muslims who are living in poverty, deprived of their basic needs. Many are facing exacerbated hardships due to prolong armed conflicts in their home countries that have resulted in their internal displacement or in becoming refugees in other countries. Hence, there is an urgent need to find sources of funding to provide them with food, shelter, healthcare, education and other essentials of life. The World Bank (2018) and Pew Research Center (2015) data show that three-fourths of the world's Muslim population are living in low-income and lower-middle-income economies. It is estimated that 11% of the world's Muslim population reside in low-income economies, 65% in lower-middle-income economies, 20% in upper-middle-income economies, and a mere 4% in high-income economies. The economic state of the Muslim population worsens during times of financial and political turbulence. According to the statistics of the United Nations High Commissioner for Refugees (UNHCR, 2017), it is estimated that six Muslim majority countries together host nearly nine million refugees. These countries are Turkey, Pakistan, Lebanon, Iran, Bangladesh and Sudan. The bulk of these refugees also come from Muslim majority countries or are Muslim minorities. For instance, more than half of the world refugees are from Syria, Afghanistan, Myanmar (Rohingya) and Somalia. In this regard, zakat can act as a major source of funding in addressing the pressing needs of this large and increasing number of people. While Muslims are primarily targeted as beneficiaries of zakat distribution, people of other faiths may also benefit from it.

Zakat is one of the five pillars of Islam. It is a mandatory financial obligation on every Muslim who meets certain wealth requirements. While the Shariah rule is explicit on Muslim individuals to remit zakat, it is herein argued that the zakat obligation ought to be extended to legal persons like corporate entities. The implication is enormous as zakat collection can be amplified if corporate entities are included as payers of zakat, either as separate legal entities or on behalf of their Muslim shareholders. The credibility of the argument above is substantiated by the fact that Islamic financial institutions (IFIs) in several jurisdictions are currently paying zakat. However, unlike IFIs, the other corporate entities do not have human resources or facilities to calculate zakat. Thus, an easy-to-use zakat calculation software could save the entities from this limitation. Against this backdrop, this chapter aims to highlight the need for zakat calculation software for corporate entities and accordingly proposes a model for developing such software.

Literature Review

Organized Efforts to Collect and Distribute Zakat

There have been numerous initiatives to manage zakat through formal channels. Several countries have established specific institutions to collect and distribute zakat. Many non-government institutions have also been set up for this purpose. Every year Muslims around the world contribute tens of billions of dollars as zakat through these formal channels (Bremer, 2013; UNHCR, 2019). However, this represents only a fraction of the total zakat contribution as many donors still prefer to pay their zakat through informal channels.

Kashif, Jamal and Rehman (2018) found that direct payment of zakat to beneficiaries has intrinsic satisfaction for the donor. However, lack of trust in the formal channels, particularly entities established by governments, is the main reason for donors preferring informal channels. Kashif et al. (2018) have identified that, in the case of Pakistan, people in general do not trust their government to manage zakat. Bremer (2013) has also identified the reason donors prefer to pay zakat directly to the zakat beneficiaries is that they consider the government system to be unreliable. Nonetheless, several countries are providing tax incentives for donors who pay zakat to designated zakat bodies. These countries include, but are not limited to, Bangladesh, Indonesia, Malaysia and Sudan. In Saudi Arabia and Kuwait, zakat is fully integrated with income tax.

Different non-governmental zakat entities have been set up with their unique sets of value propositions. Their main objectives are to fully optimize zakat collection and distribute it to serve specific funding needs. These entities mainly operate online, allowing anyone to easily contribute zakat via an online transfer, using a debit card, PayPal account, and so on. They also generate reports to show the impact of their zakat activities. Examples of such initiatives include the UNHCR zakat fund and Global Sadaqah—an online platform based in Malaysia.

The UNHCR launched their zakat fund in September 2016 and officially unveiled their online zakat platform on 1 May 2018. Anyone can donate zakat using this online platform. The donor only needs to have a valid debit card, credit card or PayPal account. The donor can also use traditional bank transfers to donate their zakat. Even though UNHCR has received endorsements from five reputed Shariah authorities regarding their zakat fund, the accuracy of the zakat calculation remains the sole responsibility of the donor (UNHCR, n.d.).

Global Sadaqah is an online crowdfunding platform for zakat as well as sadaqah. It was launched in July 2018. The platform hosts different fund collection campaigns and invites the public to donate their charity in the form of zakat or sadaqah. The donors can choose any campaign according to their individual preferences. The contributions of many toward specifically targeted campaigns assure that the funding requirements will be met and that the campaigns will be a success. Vetting of each campaign prior to its being hosted on the platform, and disclosures made by the platform regarding funding status and other matters provide high assurance to the donors (Global Sadaqah, n.d.).

While the UNHCR and Global Sadaqah merely mobilize zakat from donor to receiver, the Center for Zakat Management (CZM) in Bangladesh does more than that. They utilize their zakat collection to undertake various programs. These include healthcare, livelihood development, scholarships, training, awareness building, emergency humanitarian assistance, microenterprise development, and so on (CZM, 2018). There are many other entities in different countries that undertake various initiatives to achieve socioeconomic impact through collection and distribution of zakat.

Payment of Zakat by Corporate Entities

Whether or not corporate entities should pay zakat, is debatable. There are some who argue that zakat is not payable by corporate entities while some argue the opposite (Hasan, 2008; Hasan, 2018). The chapter does not iterate the debate on zakat by corporate entities as the matter is well discussed in the literature. The chapter is developed based on the assumption that zakat is an obligation on Muslim shareholders. They are obligated to pay zakat if their respective corporate entities do not pay zakat on their behalf. Hence, there is a need for the shareholders to reliably calculate their zakat obligation if the zakat obligation is not calculated by their corporate entities.

In a few countries like Saudi Arabia, Pakistan and Sudan, zakat laws have explicitly covered the issue of business zakat. Recognizing the importance of zakat calculation by corporate entities, several international and national bodies have also issued standards on corporate zakat calculation. The notable ones include:

- Standards issued by the Accounting and Auditing Organization for Islamic Financial Institutions (AAOIFI)
- Guidelines issued by Zakat House Kuwait
- A technical release issued by the Malaysian Accounting Standards Board (MASB)
- Guidelines issued by the Department of Waqf, Zakat and Hajj (JAWHAR) in Malaysia

One of AAOIFI's early initiatives was to issue standards on zakat. Their first standard on zakat—Financial Accounting Standard (FAS) No. 9—was issued in 1995. They also issued Shariah Standard No. 35 on zakat in 2008. Even though these standards are primarily intended for IFIs (i.e., Islamic banks and takaful operators), they can be equally applied to other types of corporate entities.

AAOIFI in its Shariah Standard No. 35, Item 2/2/1 has identified the following circumstances in which a company is committed to pay zakat: (a) if local regulations require the company to pay zakat; (b) if the articles of association stipulate commitment of the company to pay zakat; or (c) if in a general assembly of the company, a resolution is passed for the company to pay zakat. If such a circumstance is absent in the case of a company, AAOIFI requires the company to at least disclose the amount of zakat payable per share (Shariah Standard No. 35, Item 2/2/5).

In Kuwait, since 10 December 2007, a zakat tax is enforced on all public and closed joint-stock companies (KPMG, n.d.). Many of the IFIs around the world also currently pay corporate zakat or zakat on behalf of their shareholders.

Nonetheless, in the context of Nigeria, Saad and Farouk (2019) argued that the absence of zakat law and zakat accounting standards are among the major barriers for a functional zakat management system. Meanwhile, Cokrohadisumarto, Zaenudin, Santoso and Sumiati (2019) argued that in Indonesia the absence of government regulations relating to zakat obligation necessitates enhanced disclosures on zakat collection.

However, the existence of zakat accounting standards has still not sufficed to gain the confidence of the community. Adnan and Abu Bakar (2009) argued that the existing standards and guidelines on zakat contain general misconceptions about zakat that result in inappropriate zakat accounting and reporting. Therefore, they argued that the current zakat calculation practices fail to capture the spirit of Shariah. Obaidullah (2016) cited Khan (2013), who commented that the existing zakat standards do not comprehensively cover business zakat.

Divergence in Zakat Calculation Practices

In Malaysia, the calculation of business or corporate zakat is subject to diverse calculation methods. Obaidullah (2016) cited Abdul Wahab (1995), who found that three different methods have been practiced by various states and institutions in Malaysia calculating zakat on business. These methods are: (1) current assets only; (2) current assets plus profits from investments; and (3) net working capital plus current profits. Nasir and Hassan (2005) found that zakat centers have recommended at least five methods for corporate zakat calculation. These are: (1) net assets (or working capital); (2) net equity (growth model); (3) net profit after tax; (4) combined methods; and (5) dividend methods.

Nonetheless, recent studies have found that IFIs are applying only three different methodologies for zakat calculation. These are: (1) net profit method; (2) working capital method; and (3) capital growth method. The latter two are argued to render the same amount of zakat obligation (AAOIFI, 2015; Lukman, Hussain, & Ahmed, 2018).

The competencies of the standard setters and zakat authorities play an important role in developing appropriate and applicable zakat standards. For example, Abdul Rahman and Awang (2003) have identified that improved competencies in Shariah and accounting on the part of the zakat administration staff at Pusat Zakat Selangor were a driving factor for it to move from a simple profit-based method of zakat calculation to more advanced working capital and capital growth methods.

The differences in the methodologies used are one matter, but the differences in details are a far wider issue. There are different opinions regarding zakat of different items. One classic example is zakat on debt; that is, who shall pay zakat on debt—the debtor or the creditor? What are the parameters for determining the ownership and control conditions of debts? Abdul Rahman and Awang (2003) and Obaidullah (2016) have identified issues pertaining to valuation of inventory; that is, whether it shall be valued at cost or current value. The classification of financial assets (e.g., financial assets at fair value through profit or loss, or at fair value through other comprehensive income and amortized cost) and their status as *zakatable* items are debatable among the Shariah fraternity.

Some have called for harmonization of zakat practices (Abu Bakar, 2007). However, this chapter recognizes the fact that the current industry practices are diverse. Therefore, any proposed solution needs to accommodate these diverse practices. The corporate entities need to be afforded the flexibility to adopt their own interpretation of Shariah and zakat rules. Hamat (2009) and Tajuddin (2017) found that different assessment methods for business zakat are necessary in order to fit with the particular characteristics of different businesses. Hence, this chapter argues that the corporate entities should be given enough flexibility to calculate their zakat obligations. The individual payers of zakat must also have the privilege of adopting their own preferences. There must be freedom of choice to adopt any opinion as long as it is supported by sound Shariah justification.

Zakat Deducted at Source (ZDS)

Traditionally, zakat has been contributed individually by Muslims based on their *zakatable* assets. The contribution could be amplified if corporate entities are also included as payers of zakat on behalf of their Muslim shareholders. In fact, many IFIs are currently paying zakat. Abbas, Sulaiman and Bakar (2018) have identified that 12 out of 16 Islamic banks in Malaysia pay zakat. The same could be replicated by other types of corporate entities. Similar to tax deducted at source (TDS)—which aims to maximize tax collection and minimize tax evasion, zakat deducted at source (ZDS) could be made compulsory by national authorities.

Kashif et al. (2018) have observed that the banks in Pakistan are required to deduct zakat at source. There the government nominates banks to collect zakat directly from the donor's bank account(s) during the month of Ramadan. However, to evade this deduction at source, the bank account holders withdraw their money only to deposit it back once the zakat deduction deadline has passed. This creates a disturbance in banks' operations.

Nonetheless, this scenario of Pakistan is unlikely to be replicated in the case of corporate entities. This is because investment in shares is not as liquid as bank deposits. Due to regular fluctuations in share price, exit and reentry might be costly for a shareholder. Regulatory restrictions could also be put in place to prevent actions that may disrupt the market. Hence, unlike a depositor in a bank, a shareholder is unlikely to liquidate his shareholding just to evade his zakat obligation. Furthermore, no research has found such zakat evasion behavior among the shareholders of zakat-paying entities, particularly zakat-paying IFIs.

Discussion

Even though companies are artificial persons, the ultimate obligation of zakat remains with the shareholders. Listing status is irrelevant to determine the zakat obligation of a company (Wahab, 2016). If a company pays business zakat, the shareholders do not have a further obligation to pay zakat on their shareholding. Hence, if a company pays zakat, it is very important to assure the shareholders that the zakat is paid in accordance with the Shariah.

However, there is no easy-to-adopt zakat calculation system that can be used by an entity that does not have the requisite Shariah and accounting expertise. Moreover, the system needs to provide transparency so that it can be subjected to public scrutiny, continuous monitoring and adaptation to the continuous changes in the financial reporting world. The system also needs to respect the different schools of Islamic jurisprudence so that it remains acceptable and relevant in the Muslim community at large.

There are several mobile applications and online platforms currently available on the market, but they allow only a basic zakat calculation option for individuals. They are in a very basic form that does not accommodate the unique financial reporting dimensions of different business types. They also do not allow for user choice between the different schools of Islamic jurisprudence. These limitations make them unsuitable for corporate entities in practice.

In overcoming these limitations, this chapter proposes a zakat calculation software that embodies more advanced and comprehensive features. The software would allow its users to calculate the zakat of different types of corporate entities and customize zakat calculation based on the user's preference in Islamic jurisprudence.

The Proposed Zakat Calculation Software

Features of the Software

The proposed software could be used by any corporate entity to calculate zakat for their Muslim shareholders. The users of this software would not need to know the requirements of zakat calculation. They would only need to insert financial data in the required fields. The application would then automatically generate the zakat obligation amount.

The proposed software would provide a comprehensive range of features for calculation of the zakat of corporate entities. The software would be designed taking into account the needs of different business types; for example, financial institutions and manufacturing, trading, construction, property development, technology and service-providing entities. The layout of the installed software and financial reporting terms used will be business-type-specific. This will allow users to recognize the required fields easily. To avoid any omission or error, the software algorithm will automatically reconcile the inserted amounts.

Similar to the calculation of a company's tax liability, financial statements will be used as the basis for calculation of zakat. The amounts reported in financial statements will be adjusted in deriving the zakat base of the company. The applicable zakat rate will be multiplied times the zakat base to determine the zakat liability.

The financial statement items will be identified based on the International Financial Reporting Standards (IFRS), which have been adopted in 144 jurisdictions as the basis for financial reporting (IFRS Foundation, 2018). The accountants of the corporate entities need not have knowledge about the different schools of Islamic jurisprudence for zakat calculation as the major opinions are already configured into the application. There will be a default setting based on the opinions of the majority of scholars, but there will also be customizable options.

The software will be configured with the requirements of different zakat accounting standards and schools of Islamic jurisprudence. The users will have the option to select their preferred standard and school in the calculation of zakat. The software can be installed with default settings or advanced settings.

The default settings will give results based on the majority or most acceptable opinion of the selected school. In the absence of such an opinion on a matter, the default settings will assume the requirement that provides the highest zakat obligation. This is to be on the safer side in terms of performing religious obligations. Each of the items will be linked to further description and Shariah basis for inclusion or exclusion in zakat calculation.

While the advanced settings (i.e., fully configured installation) will contain the same features as the default settings, it will also present different opinions on a single matter and allow the users to select any of the opinions presented. The opinions presented will be from within the same school as well as other schools. The users will immediately see the impact of their selection on the zakat obligation amount. Figure 18.1 shows the installation flow of the proposed zakat software.

If the corporate entity is calculating zakat on behalf of its shareholders, then the opinion selected must be subjected to the approval of its board of directors and conform to any stipulation imposed by the state authorities. Whichever opinion the user selects, it must be applied consistently in the subsequent periods, unless a change of opinion increases the zakat obligation. Shifting between different opinions to reduce zakat obligation in the subsequent periods must not be allowed.

To ensure accountability and transparency, the corporate entities must make disclosures in their financial statements on the settings they have

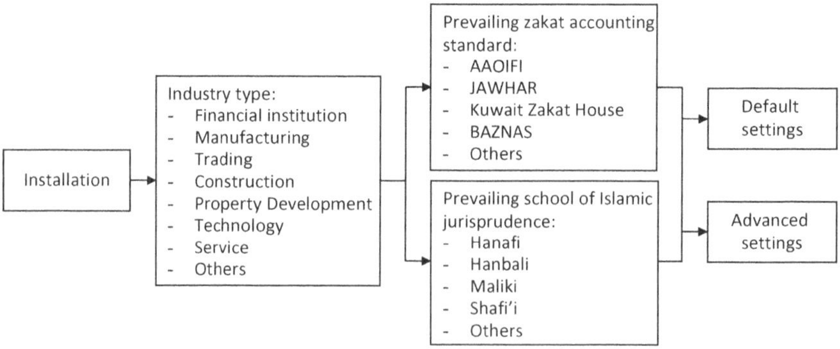

Fig. 18.1 Installation flow of zakat calculation software

selected and the basis of their selection. They must also disclose the alternate zakat obligation amount in different settings, so that their Muslim shareholders can easily decide whether or not the zakat obligation has been duly discharged based on their individual preference.

Development Process

The zakat software will be developed in two stages. The first stage will involve the zakat calculation methodology, and the second stage will develop the software.

Stage 1: Development of a Zakat Calculation Methodology for Corporate Entities

An expert research team will be engaged at this stage to develop the zakat calculation methodology for the corporate entities. The team will comprise experts in financial reporting and Shariah. The work done by the team will be critically evaluated by a council of Shariah scholars.

The research team will examine the financial reporting standards and financial reporting practices of different types of corporate entities. The research team will further examine different schools of Islamic jurisprudence in establishing items that are: (1) subject to zakat obligation, (2) deductible in calculation of zakat obligation, and (3) excluded from zakat calculation.

The research team will gather sufficient evidence and arguments from different schools of Islamic jurisprudence in establishing the zakat status of individual financial statement items. The majority or most acceptable opinion will be identified while other opinions will also be noted.

The chapter does not propose unification of zakat practices as it is not easily achievable. It proposes to accommodate different interpretations of zakat rules as long as they are supported by strong Shariah justifications. Hence, the software is proposed with the belief that the users have freedom of preference for zakat rules as long as those have acceptable justifications and are supported by reputed scholars.

Stage 2: Development of the Zakat Calculation Software

The zakat calculation methodology developed by the research team will be used in developing the software. This will be done by a team of software developers. The research team will closely oversee the software development process. At the end of development, the software will go through several trial runs. The marketing of the software will commence only after receiving approval by the council of Shariah scholars. The zakat calculation software development process flow is illustrated in Fig. 18.2.

Potential Usage

The ease of calculation will motivate the corporate entities to calculate zakat on behalf of their shareholders. The calculated zakat amount may eventually be paid by the entities or by the shareholders based on the disclosures made by the entities. The software will also enable the state authorities to impose and monitor zakat payments by the corporate entities under their jurisdiction. The software will overcome the possibility of miscalculation of the zakat obligation and bring transparency in the calculation method adopted, which is relevant to the IFIs as well. The derived zakat calculation methodology or software could also be integrated into zakat management platforms.

The software would have the potential to grow in the future. It could be further developed into an online zakat management platform that would facilitate transparent and efficient transnational flows of zakat funds. In disbursing the zakat funds, the recipients can be prioritized based on priorities of the time. The zakat recipients will also be categorized based on their sector and social impact. The developed methodology and software could be easily integrated with this platform.

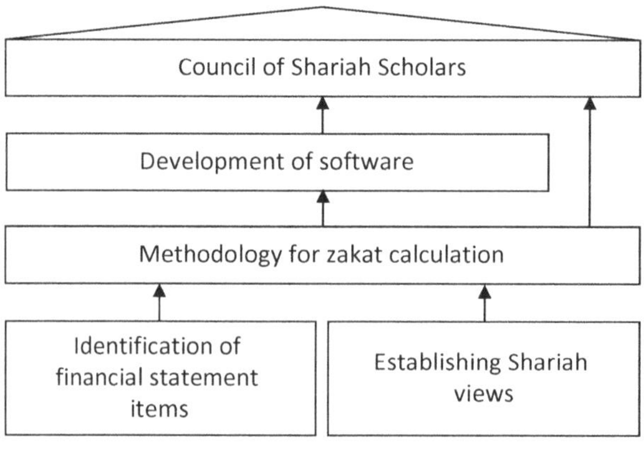

Fig. 18.2 Zakat calculation software development process. (*Source*: Author's own)

The methodology and the software will be patented and protected under intellectual property rights. Any entity that wishes to use any of these would be subjected to royalty agreements and licensing. A software license fee could be imposed on its users or could be provided for free, depending on the financial needs of the developer. A differentiated fee structure can be adopted, with one fee for only the default setting and additional fees for the customizable options. The mobile application can also be developed, and its subscription can be subject to a fee payment.

Conclusion

Contribution of zakat by corporate entities will amplify global zakat collection. A well-developed software will make the zakat calculation easy and bring transparency. Reliable calculation of zakat will also make the concept of ZDS acceptable to the public. Another benefit of this might be a successful negotiation with the tax authorities in securing tax rebates for the amounts paid as zakat. With the continuous enhancement of the system, disclosures on zakat obligation by corporate entities can eventually be included as one of the criteria they would have to fulfill in order to be considered Shariah-compliant.

References

AAOIFI. (2015). Shari'ah Standard No. (35) Zakah. In AAOIFI (Ed.), *Shari'ah Standards* (pp. 865–904). Manama: AAOIFI.

Abbas, S., Sulaiman, S., & Bakar, N. (2018). A Review on Zakat Payments by Islamic Banks in Malaysia. *International Journal of Zakat* (Special Issue on Zakat Conference 2018), 71–82.

Abdul Rahman, R., & Awang, R. (2003). Assessing Business Zakat at Pusat Zakat Selangor: Between Theory and Practice. *Journal of Financial Reporting and Accounting, 1*(1), 33–48.

Abdul Wahab, M. (1995). Malaysia: A Case Study of Zakat Management. In A. El-Ashker & S. Haq (Eds.), *Institutional Framework of Zakat: Dimensions and Implications.* Jeddah: Islamic Research and Training Institute, Islamic Development Bank.

Abu Bakar, N. (2007). A Zakat Accounting Standard (ZAS) for Malaysian companies. *American Journal of Islamic Social Sciences, 24*(4), 74–92.

Adnan, M., & Abu Bakar, N. (2009). Accounting Treatment for Corporate Zakat: A Critical Review. *International Journal of Islamic and Middle Eastern Finance and Management, 2*(1), 32–45.

Bremer, J. (2013). Zakat and Economic Justice: Emerging International Models and their Relevance for Egypt. *Third Annual Conference on Arab Philanthropy and Civic Engagement*, Tunis, pp. 51–74. Retrieved August 16, 2019, from https://pdfs.semanticscholar.org/317d/3df7f444b91dbac7e762e60bc3d82500e31a.pdf

Cokrohadisumarto, W., Zaenudin, Z., Santoso, B., & Sumiati, S. (2019). A Study of Indonesian Community's Behaviour in Paying Zakat. *Journal of Islamic Marketing, 11*, 961–976.

CZM. (2018). *Exploring Zakat Potential*. Dhaka: Center Potential of Zakat. Retrieved August 18, 2019, from http://czm-bd.org/wp-content/uploads/2018/10/CZM-Brocheure-2018.pdf

Global Sadaqah. (n.d.). *About Us*. Retrieved August 18, 2019, from Global Sadaqah: https://www.globalsadaqah.com/about-us/

Hamat, Z. (2009). Business Zakat Accounting and Taxation in Malaysia. In *Islamic Perspectives on Management and Finance* (pp. 13–18). Leicester: School of Management, University of Leicester.

Hasan, A. (2018). Zakat on Legal Entities (Shakhsiyyah I'Tibariyyah): A Shari'ah Analysis. *Al-Shajarah: Journal of the International Institute of Islamic Thought and Civilization (ISTAC)* (Special Issue), 255–282.

Hasan, Z. (2008, May). *Does Islamic Financial Institutions Need to Pay Zakat?* Retrieved August 18, 2019, from http://www.zulkiflihasan.com/wp-content/uploads/2008/05/Does-Islamic-Bank-Need-to-Pay-Zakat.pdf

IFRS Foundation. (2018, April 25). *Who uses IFRS Standards?* Retrieved August 18, 2019, from IFRS Foundation: https://www.ifrs.org/use-around-the-world/use-of-ifrs-standards-by-jurisdiction/#analysis

Kashif, M., Jamal, K., & Rehman, M. (2018). The Dynamics of Zakat Donation Experience Among Muslims: A Phenomenological Inquiry. *Journal of Islamic Accounting and Business Research, 9*(1), 45–58.

Khan, A. (2013). *"Contemporary Application of Law of Zakat", What is Wrong with Islamic Economics?* Cheltenham: Edward Elgar Publishing.

KPMG. (n.d.). *Zakat Tax Compliance Services*. Retrieved August 16, 2019, from KPMG: https://home.kpmg/kw/en/home/services/tax/zakat-tax-in-kuwait.html

Lukman, B., Hussain, L., & Ahmed, M. (2018). Metodologi Pengiraan Zakat di Institusi Kewangan Islam di Malaysia. *Muzakarah-12—Muzakarah Cendekiawan Syariah Nusantara*. Phuket: ISRA. Retrieved September 26, 2019, from https://ifikr.isra.my/library/viewer/10388

Nasir, N., & Hassan, S. (2005). Zakat on Business in Malaysia: Issues and Current Treatment. In B. Shanmugam, V. Perumal, & A. Hanuum Ridwa (Eds.), *Issues in Islamic Accounting* (pp. 165–178). Serdang: UPM Press.

Obaidullah, M. (2016). Revisiting Estimation Methods of Business Zakat and Related Tax Incentives. *Journal of Islamic Accounting and Business Research, 7*(4), 349–364.

Pew Research Center. (2015). *The Future of World Religions: Population Growth Projections, 2010–2050.* Pew Research Center. Retrieved August 18, 2019, from https://assets.pewresearch.org/wp-content/uploads/sites/11/2015/03/PF_15.04.02_ProjectionsFullReport.pdf

Saad, R., & Farouk, A. (2019). A Comprehensive Review of Barriers to a Functional Zakat System in Nigeria. *International Journal of Ethics and Systems, 35*(1), 24–42.

Tajuddin, T. (2017). Business Zakat Accounting and Its Assessment. *Jurnal Pengajian Islam, 10*(2), 18–30.

The World Bank. (2018, October 4). *Classifying Countries by Income.* Retrieved August 18, 2019, from The World Bank: https://datatopics.worldbank.org/world-development-indicators/stories/the-classification-of-countries-by-income.html

UNHCR. (2017). *Global Trends 2017.* UNHCR.

UNHCR. (2019, April 26). *UNHCR Unveils the Refugee Zakat Fund, a Global Islamic Finance Structure to Help Displaced Populations Worldwide.* Retrieved August 16, 2019, from United Nations High Commissioner for Refugees: https://www.unhcr.org/hk/21715-unhcr-unveils-the-refugee-zakat-fund-a-global-islamic-finance-structure-to-help-displaced-populations-worldwide.html

UNHCR. (n.d.). *Your Zakat can Shelter and Protect Refugee Widows, Orphans, and the Elderly.* Retrieved August 18, 2019, from UNHCR: https://zakat.unhcr.org//en/

Wahab, A. (2016). Zakat Obligation for Public Listed Companies. *The 18th Malaysian Finance Association Annual Conference.*

CHAPTER 19

Fintech in the MENA Region: Current State and Prospects

Ahmed Belouafi

Abstract Applying descriptive, inductive and analytical methodologies this chapter explores the current state and prospects of Fintech in the Middle East and North Africa (MENA) region—a predominant Muslim area whose financial systems are not deepening yet. The chapter is divided into three sections. Section 1 examines the premises, promises and risks of Fintech. Current state and prospects of Fintech in MENA region is the focus of Section 2. Finally, Section 3 provides a summary and concludes with a few remarks and recommendations.

Keywords Fintech • MENA • Current position • Application • Jurisdiction • Regulation

Introduction

Undoubtedly it is submitted that the world is going through an immense technological change. A change that has impacted almost all aspects of our societal and business practices; how we form relationships; buy, sell,

A. Belouafi (✉)
Islamic Economics Institute, King Abdulaziz University, Jeddah, Saudi Arabia

M. M. Billah (ed.), *Islamic FinTech*,
https://doi.org/10.1007/978-3-030-45827-0_19

discuss hot and serious issues; and conduct our daily tasks (Moore, 2016; Panetta, 2018: 3). Furthermore, according to the United Nations E-Government Survey, in 2003, 18 countries or about 10% of countries globally were without any online presence. Thirteen years later, the 2016 report found that all 193 UN Member States have delivered some form of online service, and the 2018 report found that 40 countries scored 'Very-High', with e-government development index (EGDI) values, as compared to only 10 in 2003, and 29 countries in 2016 (UN, 2016: 5; UN, 2018: xxv). On the other hand, the McKinsey Global Institute projects that the internet of things (IoTs) could reach the size of US$ 11.1 trillion, that is, the equivalent of 11% of the world economy by the year 2025, and Huawei, the Chinese tech giant, forecasts that in the same year "there will be 100 billion connected services used in every area of business and life" (McKinsey Global Institute, 2015: 4; Huawei, 2017: 28). Intel, on its part, "estimates that we will have 200 billion internet-connected things by 2030. Data will be the new sunlight as we create, replicate, and consume 44 zettabytes (or 44 trillion gigabytes) of data by 2030" (Goerlich, 2016). Based on the findings of the like of these studies and forecasts, we have been told and reminded, time and again, that we are living in a very 'transformed' era. It is the 'digital world', 'the Fintech era', 'the digitization' and 'the world of the (IoTs)'; or put it simply we are at the beginning of 'the fourth industrial revolution' which is, according to some experts (Schwab, 2016), "fundamentally different [from previous revolutions]. It is characterized by a range of new technologies that are fusing the physical, digital and biological worlds, impacting all disciplines, economies and industries, and even challenging ideas about what it means to be human".

Fintech: Premises, Promises and Risks

Premises

In contrast to the prevailing claim that the term 'Fintech' or 'Financial technology' appeared in the 1990s, Schueffel (2016: 36) found that it had been "used as early as 1972". Moreover, the writer concluded his research paper stating that "after more than 40 years that the term has been used in practice as well as literature there is no agreement as to what Fintech entails" (ibid.: 47). For this reason, the term has been defined by various experts and institutions from different angles and perspectives; using different words and phrases. The logical result of this disclosure is "all definitions have their merits [and demerits] and serve the purposes of the authors' research or business objectives" as noted by (Varga, 2017: 22). Thus, there is, yet, room for the elaboration of a comprehensive and more encompassing definition. However, it can be noticed that some of these definitions are very general and loose as they do not capture all, or least the most important, aspects of this evolving phenomenon. An example is the definition that refers to Fintech as "the use of technology to deliver financial solutions" (Arner et al., 2015: 3). This definition does not display the main elements that characterize the reality of the impact of the latest technological advancements. Thus, the definition can be applied to preceding phases in the 'industrial revolutions' as it does not indicate any idiosyncrasies about the current developments. The use of technology for financial services' provision has been with us for some time. A somewhat more elaborative definition has been provided by the Financial Stability Board (FSB). FSB defines Fintech as "technology-enabled innovation in financial services that could result in new business models, applications, processes or products with an associated material effect on the provision of financial services" (FSB, 2017: 7, 2019: 1). Another definition adds the 'competitiveness' element. Hence, the term has been defined as "an industry composed of companies that use new technology and innovation with available resources to compete in the marketplace of traditional financial institutions and intermediaries in the delivery of financial services" (Thomas & Morse, 2017: 2). A more advanced definition has added the 'cross-disciplinary' aspect to the subject. Elaborators of the definition claim that they have presented the definition to various audiences and seem to have "a better understanding on what is FinTech and its potential". Leong and Sung (2018: 75) define Fintech as "a cross-disciplinary subject that combines Finance, Technology Management and Innovation Management".

These three definitions reveal some important idiosyncrasies about Fintech premises. These are:

1. The impact is thorough and wide in its range and implications. Thus, Fintech impact is not limited to the input and/or output of its business model. It, rather, affects the foundation of the previous business model to produce a new one in its place, though this transformation does not affect 'rules of the game' and the 'core foundation' of the capitalist business model that has dominated the globe for a while, with profit maximization and self-interest as the main

driving forces. However, Fintech and other outlets of the digital world have produced a new business model that has termed 'platform capitalism business model (PCBM)' (Srnicek, 2017). A platform, by definition, 'creates value by facilitating an exchange between two or more interdependent groups usually consumers and producers'. Thus, firms involved in this business model do not make things (i.e. produce) rather "they simply connect people" (Moazed, 2016; Moazed & Johnson, 2016).

2. It is claimed that competition constitutes cornerstone in the emerging PCBM. But this element is questionable. The tech giants are, in fact, dominating the scene of the internet in the world; " Facebook is responsible for nearly twenty-five (25) percent of total Web visits, and the Google platform crash in 2013 took about forty (40) percent of Internet traffic with it" (Moazed & Johnson, 2016).
3. The cross-disciplinary feature of the development of the PCBM. This development bears the influence of several fields of investigation. While definition 3 adds this important dimension, what fields to be included in the cross-disciplinary subject is somehow problematic. Problematic in its narrowness and limitedness to technical fields in finance and technological domains.

Based on the above observations, the author of the chapter defines Fintech as:

> An ecosystem of technology-enabled firms that have been nourished by the interaction of cross-disciplinary subject among various fields, and it could result in new business model, applications, processes or products with an associated material effect on the provision of financial services.

The definition captures several important characteristics surrounding the salient features of this evolving and very dynamic industry. These are:

Fintech is an 'ecosystem' in a sense that it reflects the complex network and the interconnectedness of different parts of the system. Therefore, the subject should not be treated as fragmented and disconnected parts "swinging out" in the ocean of the prevailing system. Thus, the Fintech ecosystem tries to keep its organs intact to be able to achieve some penetration in the dominant system. To maintain its distinguishing features is not going to be easy in the long established 'monopolistic' and 'very powerful' financial and monetary system. On the other hand, the term portrays the evolving dynamism of the ecosystem as noted by some researchers; "ecosystems are subject to periodic disturbances and consequently are in a regular state of flux" (Gomez et al., 2013: 41). Indeed, that is exactly the nature of Fintech at this stage, the initial development stage.

The definition covers small and big (e.g. Apple and Facebook) tech firms as well as financial institutions who adopt pro-active policy in their dealing with these technological developments (WEF, 2017: 8). Thus, the definition encompasses maturing companies and even non-financial services companies, such as telecommunication providers and e-retailers.

Cross-disciplinary is a prime source of the progresses Fintech and other digital outlets have reached so far. Fields that fed these advances are not confined to "Finance, Technology Management and Innovation Management" as stated by Leong and Sung (2018). Other fields like politics, economic and civic powers, self-interest and profit-maximization maxims of the capitalist model played their role as well. For instance, Accenture, the global consulting company in its 2015 report, revealed that "private and institutional investors invested more than 50 billion dollars into the sector between 2010 and 2015 …and investment in financial-technology (Fintech) companies grew by 201% globally in 2014, compared to 63% growth in overall venture-capital investments" (Accenture, 2015: 3–4). At the economic and civic fronts, Emily Bell of Columbia University rightly pointed out that the power of the *TechGiants*

> resides in the databases of human activity which provide the internal engine for dynamic growth. Google can use image and sensing data, predictive analytics and mapping software to put driverless cars on the roads. Facebook is able to analyse and predict sentiment through the way people communicate with each other, Amazon knows what you might want to buy next before you know it yourself. Apple, through its smartphone technologies and payment mechanisms, knows how and when you communicate with your mother, your bank and your boss. Collectively these companies also make decisions for us, such as what news stories we see first in the morning, which services are recommended to us first, how our histories and foibles will be shown to the world. Which information will circulate freely, and which will be stopped? (Moore, 2016: i)

And, in 1994 Bill Gates made a visionary statement that states "banking is necessary, banks are not" that has become a self-reinforcing prophecy, with 6000–7000 Fintech companies across the world now trying to obtain a slice of the banking industry's profitable business (Varga, 2017: 22).

The impact is not limited to products alone but to other aspects as well: business model, applications and processes, in particular, and hence, the definition captures the main idiosyncrasies of platform capitalism as explained before.

The definition avoided the use of terms and phrases that have been portrayed and emphasized by some experts: terms like "disruption" and "transformation of existing model for the provision of financial services" as these terms carry more exaggerations to the impact of Fintech than the reality on the ground as we will see in later sections.

On the historical front, finance and technology had been developing and interacting with each other for a very long time. Historians tracing this close link reveal that this interaction goes back to the late seventeenth century through "the introduction of the telegraph (first commercial use in 1838) and the laying of the first successful transatlantic cable in 1866 (by the Atlantic Telegraph Company)" (Arner et al., 2015: 4, 2016: 1). And it is widely acknowledged that "the introduction of the Automatic Teller Machine (ATM) in 1967 by Barclays Bank marks the commencement of the modern evolution of today's FinTech" (Arner et al. 2015: 4). Paul Volker, ex-chairman of the Fed (1979–1987), considers the introduction of ATM as "The most important financial innovation that [he has] seen the past 20 years [i.e. years before the 2007–2008 financial crisis] is the ATM, that really helps people and prevents visits to the bank and it is a real convenience" (New York Post, 2019; Shepherd-Barron, 2017).

Figure 19.1 provides a brief summary of the different phases of the interaction between finance and technology. The author prefers the use of the 'interaction' rather than 'Fintech' which, according to some sources, appeared in 1972 as indicated earlier. Table 19.1, on the other hand, presents more details about the developments of the interactions between finance and technology over the past few decades.

That was a very short encounter of the interaction between finance and technology. The snapshot demonstrates the continuity and build-up process in these progresses. And this is a very important remark that we have

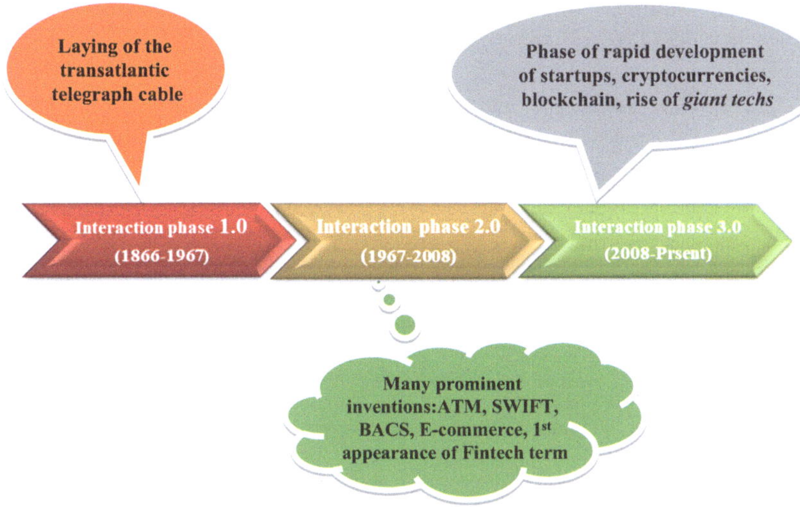

Fig. 19.1 Summary of interaction development phases between finance and technology from 1866 till present. (Source: Adapted from Arner et al. (2017: 3–7) and Leong and Sung (2018: 75))

to keep in mind in the assessment and analysis of new inventions. When they are not put in proper historical contexts, they may seem to be 'radical' and unprecedented novelties, but in reality they are just a continuity as expressed by Nick Srnicek, an expert in the historical developments of the digital inventions, "phenomena that appear to be radical novelties may, in historical light, reveal themselves to be simple continuities" (Koh, 2017).

Promises

The literature that has dealt with various aspects of the Fintech industry discussed numerous promises and risks that can arise from the evolution of this dynamic sector. The chapter discusses what it considers to be among the most important elements in each category. Figure 19.2 presents some prominent opportunities followed by a brief discussion of each item.

- Jobs. Creation of new classes of jobs is an expected outcome of these progresses. Surely, this has been the case for preceding development episodes as well. The main challenge is the overall contribution of

Table 19.1 Summary of some milestone technological developments over the past few decades (1967–2018)

Date	*Main invention (s)*
1967	The installation of the first ATM by Barclays in Enfield (North London, UK)
1968, 1970	Introduction of BACS (Payment Schemes Limited (Bacs), previously known Bankers' Automated Clearing Services) and CHIPS (2 electronic payment systems in the UK)
1971	NASDAQ (The National Association of Securities Dealers Automated Quotations exchange). The first electronic exchange that allowed investors to buy and sell stock on a computerized system
1972	First appearance of the 'Fintech' or financial technology term
1973	239 banks from 15 countries formed a cooperative utility, the Society for Worldwide Interbank Financial Telecommunication (SWIFT) to solve the problem of communicating payments across borders
1981	The invention of computing platform by Michael Bloomberg who built a computerized system to provide real-time market data, financial calculations and other financial analytics to Wall Street firms and founded media company [Bloomberg] to cater for these developments in 1981
1980–1983	The inception of online banking in the USA, the UK and other parts of advanced economies
1983	The release of the first commercial mobile phone, known as the Motorola DynaTAC 8000X, in 1983. The handset offered 30 minutes of talk time, six hours standby, and could store 30 phone numbers. The phone costs \$3995 (≈15,000 Saudi Riyals)
1993	The Financial Services Technology Consortium, a project initiated by Citicorp, an effort to overcome a reputation for resisting technological collaboration with outsiders. This project was labelled as 'Fintech'
1980s and 1990s	The development and widespread use of electronic communication networks that lead financial markets to rely more on full electronic execution through algorithmic trading to the extent that some analysts blame programme trading for the 1987 crash (i.e. 'Black Monday': 19/10/1987)
2006	Online banking had become mainstream: an overwhelming 80% of banks in the USA were offering internet banking services
2007–2008	The eruption and escalation of global financial crisis. The crisis has been regarded as a turning point for the rapid and 'revolutionary' development of Fintech; the launch of cryptocurrencies and the emergence of Blockchain technology
2010	Fiserv survey found that online and mobile banking (OMB) were growing at a faster pace than the internet
2018	The wide spread of the OMB to the extent that customers expect accounts to include free online banking, and many banks only operate on the internet

Source: Mccracken (2015), Arner et al. (2016: 9), Schueffel (2016: 36), Goodwin (2019), Sarreal (2019), and Segal (2019)

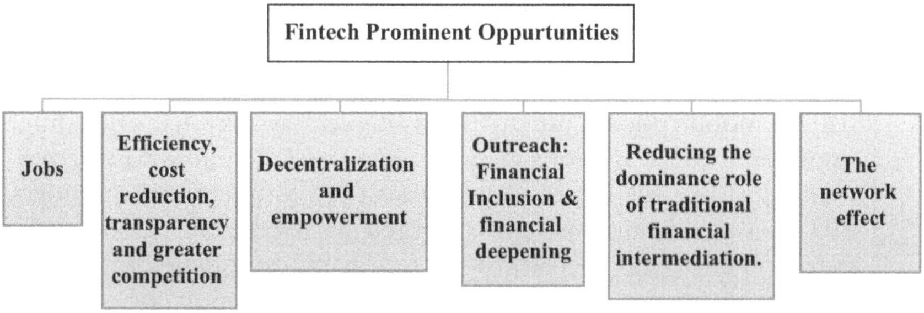

Fig. 19.2 Some prominent opportunities brought by Fintech

the 'digital sector' to the market job creation in comparison with other sectors in the economy. The results so far are not that promising, as the sector remains relatively very small. For instance, Srnicek (2017: 4) reveals.

> in the [United States (US) the technology sector] currently contributes around 6.8 per cent of the value added from private companies and employs about 2.5 per cent of the labour force. By comparison, manufacturing in the deindustrialised US employs four times as many people… This is in part because tech companies are notoriously small. Google has around 60,000 direct employees, Facebook has 12,000, while WhatsApp had 55 employees when it was sold to Facebook for $19 billion and Instagram had 13 when it was purchased for $1 billion. By comparison, in 1962 the most significant companies employed far larger numbers of workers: AT&T had 564,000 employees, Exxon had 150,000 workers, and GM had 605,000 employees. Thus, when we discuss the digital economy, we should bear in mind that it is something broader than just the tech sector defined according to standard classifications

On the other hand, Citigroup estimated that European and US banks would cut another 1.8m jobs in the next decade with the growth of Fintech (Leong & Sung, 2018: 74; Citigroup, 2016). That means in the long run the technology sector, including Fintech, will have a negative impact on the labour market.

- Efficiency, cost reduction, transparency and greater competition (Adrian & Mancini-Griffoli, 2019b). According to many researches, studies and reports (e.g. Leong & Sung, 2018), Fintech has contributed to more profitable, efficient and flexible financial services. It has also made financial services reliable, persistent and fast (i.e. immediacy benefit with increased speed and accessibility). Fintech revolution helped turn the very 'popular' device that millions of people use daily, a mobile phone, into a "point of sales" system that offers huge opportunities for millions of businesses and individuals to take payments just like the larger corporations they compete with (Landers, 2017). Crowdsourcing have emerged as invaluable resources for entrepreneurs who used to revert to a bank or an angel or venture investor to finance their new businesses. Saving on major costs and lowering transaction fees is an expected Fintech outcome. As "FinTech firms do not have the same overheads and regulatory responsibilities that traditional organizations have". Furthermore, the development of sophisticated innovations seems to be promising in this regard. For instance, Santander has estimated that "the blockchain technology could save banks £16b (≈ 20.48 $US) per year in admin costs, which can help bring the cost of traditional financial services down" (Lavie, 2018). This may be mainly due to the financial 'disintermediation' that Fintech platforms provide.

- Decentralization and empowerment constitute a major yardstick in the formation of some of the development of the Fintech revolution. At the heart of this progress is the application of artificial intelligence (AI), machine learning and big data (Panetta, 2018). Among these innovations blockchain is considered, by many quarters and analysts, as a landmark achievement in this respect. This technology had helped in solving the 'double spending' problem that hindered the development of cryptocurrencies for some time (Rosenfeld, 2014; PumaPay, 2018). Blockchain technology has also contributed to the decentralization of processes and execution of transactions and empowerment of connected parties through the distributed ledger without the intervention of a third party (e.g. a central or commercial bank). Thus, "Blockchain [has proven to be] an important FinTech innovation—it allows companies and individuals to agree and settle contracts and transactions very quickly and efficiently and removes the need for intermediaries or central counterparties" (Dillon, 2017).
- Outreach: financial inclusion (FI) and financial deepening. It is widely believed by some analysts and international institutions that FI 'opens the door for security and independence'. Not only that but financial exclusion, according to some writers, creates a cycle that a

person dwells in and he/she may pass is to his/her descendants "financial exclusion is a cycle—the more marginalised a person is, the harder it will be for them to enter the system, the more marginalised they will become. This cycle is likely to continue with their children, grandchildren and so forth" (Lavie, 2018). This assertion needs to be verified against facts not just mere prophecies. What can be said is the fact that lack of financial resources creates hardship but does not turn life into 'abyss'. For this reason, new innovations can help in the promotion of the FI cause. There are numerous studies and reports which document, in details, the potential that Fintech and the digital innovation can provide to elevate some of the obstacles that contribute to the lack of access to appropriate financial resources; see, for example, Parada and Bull (2015; DKA and FF, 2018; ICCR and WB, 2018; IMF and WB, 2019; Murthy & Fernandez-Vidal, 2019). At the level of some of the most deprived areas in Africa, Asia and Latin America, there have been some encouraging results. The case of M-PESA, mobile money, in Kenya has been highly cited in the literature as well as other initiatives elsewhere as a success story of what the digital world can offer (El-Zoghbi et al., 2019: 4–6). As a result of such evidences, the G20 document for the principles of use of technology to enhance financial inclusion asserts that "opportunities that technology offers to reduce costs, expand scale, and deepen the reach of financial services will be critical to achieving universal financial inclusion" (GPFI, 2016: i).

- Reducing the dominant role of traditional financial intermediation. Thus, the prevailing form of financial intermediation is expected, according to some analysts, to be subdued to the emergence of a new form of mediation; the 'information or data or online intermediation', "thanks to mobile money, any person with a basic phone can now make cash transfers, pay bills, and send money to family members abroad without having a bank account. This is a game-changing innovation, particularly for the world's poor as it is easy and cheap" (Chhabra & Das, 2019).
- The network effect or the idiom "when the crowd connects magic happens" (El-Gary 2015) as quoted by Cattelan (2019: 84) through the connection of the masses. The network economics has produced an ample of work demonstrating the positive effect of the network; when the number of users gets large, the 'value' of the network increases. The case of the telephone network is highly

cited in the literature as a typical example of such an effect. Some experts in this field have gone a step ahead by developing some formulae to prove the case. While, there is a general agreement that the network effect has played a potential role in the development of ecosystems like the internet and now the digital industry, there are some reservations about the extent of that effect. Furthermore, the literatures that support the positive postulate of the network effect seem to underestimate the treatment of fundamental issues; like what is meant by 'network value'? What about the social and human aspects of the members and/or users of the network? Finally, what about the 'extreme' power exalted by the 'tech giants'? There are other issues for and against the network effect, but that goes beyond the limits and scope of the chapter; see, for instance, Tongia and Wilson (2019).

Risks

As it is the case with any human developments, the 'Fintech revolution' has some merits as discussed before. At the same time, it has some perils as well; "it could invite risks to financial stability and integrity, monetary policy effectiveness, and competition standards" (Adrian & Mancini-Griffoli, 2019b). There is an ample literature (e.g. Homeland Security Enterprise, 2014; World Bank, 2016; Moore, 2016; Ortiz-Ospina, 2019; Adrian & Mancini-Griffoli, 2019a) that has explored these risks. Due to the deep penetration that the 'digitization' has on every aspect of our life, it is expected that the risks are widespread as well; they impact social, economic, political and cultural domains. It is not the intention in the limited space given to the chapter to cover comprehensively these perils. In what follows a brief discussion of some prominent risks as illustrative examples, interested readers in deep and thorough treatment should consult the appropriate literature.

1. Encroachment on privacy (data privacy and consumer protection; e.g. data misuse and manipulation by some of the tech giants in recent years). The Facebook and Cambridge Analytic Scandal (FCAS) in 2015 has been highly discussed in the media and elsewhere (Davies, 2015; Lin, 2016: 663–665). The FCAS, through 'the breach of data protection', "impacted 87 million people, and it had brought into the public discourse questions regarding appropri-

ate protection, use and access to user data" (Internet Society, 2019: 4). In 2019, *Business Insider* revealed that Facebook had "harvested the email contacts of 1.5 million users without their knowledge or consent when they opened their accounts" (Doffman, 2019). Moreover, the 'scandals' of the giants are not confined to these incidents; there is also the manipulation on income sales, through the shift of profits between countries and other techniques, for tax evasion purposes. These practices are under investigation in many jurisdictions. For instance, the OECD has recently launched a plan to prevent large multinational companies like Apple, Facebook and Amazon from avoiding taxes (Tankersley, 2019). For this and other reasons, the questions these tech giants raise are more complex and wider in range since they go far beyond the economic spectrum. Whilst there have been major questions about their economic power, and tax liability, they also raise fundamental questions about security and privacy, and their increasing impact on civic and political fronts (Moore, 2016: 3). Due to the seriousness and far-reaching implications of data privacy and consumer protection, many legislative bodies around the world are very active to develop adequate legislation that address the use of 'big data' by 'platform intermediaries' for profit maximizing and other ends. Many of these legislations are still in their development stages; the only exception, in this regard, is the EU General Data Protection Regulation (GDPR) that is in full effect. As a result, "Facebook could face a possible fine of $1.6 billion from the Irish Data Protection Authority for allegedly mishandling user data resulting in the breach of over 50 million users' personal data" (Internet Security, 2019: 8).

2. Cybersecurity and disinformation (i.e. fake news). The security council of the UN noticed that "technology firms [are] increasingly relying on algorithms and artificial intelligence to identify and remove content, concerns have been raised about how they define terrorist content, and about the perceived lack of meaningful human oversight, transparency and accountability" (CTED, 2018: 4). These algorithm techniques have shifted some of the power and role played, traditionally, by governments to the tech firms. For this reason, these firms have been blamed for their 'complacency' in checking and monitoring the contents posted by the 'far-right' and other terrorist individuals and organizations. The failure, in this respect, had contributed to very serious inflictions and fatalities in New

Zealand, Iraq, Syria and elsewhere. The use of digital currencies to pay for criminal activities has also been figured out as a major concern to regulatory and security bodies at the local and international levels (Homeland Security Enterprise, 2014; WBG, 2016: 7). On the fake news front social media providers carry major responsibility in this sensitive area. As a result, these providers have suffered a trust issue in the last few years, but the issue has been taken seriously by the outlets working in this domain (Talkwalker and HubSpot, 2019: 20). And, it seems that the taken measures are bearing some fruits. Accordingly, "Comparing H2 2018, to H1 2019, fake news mentions have dropped by 10.2 per cent. Improvements from brands and the social media platforms have helped, but there's still work to do" (ibid.). The costs of cybercrimes and fake news are huge and seem to on the rise. For instance, cybercrime in the MENA region is a factor of concern. According to a latest report that has touched upon this issue, the annual cost of the crime is about US$1.43 billion. The year 2018 saw an increase of 17% of the crime rates from previous year to reach the threshold of half a million (i.e. 500 thousand) with Saudi Arabia and UAE considered to be the highly targeted countries in the region, respectively (La Noce, 2019). And the rates are expected to increase in the coming years unless stringent and appropriate measures are put in place (ibid.).

3. Instability. Some regulatory and economic bodies have raised concern about the impact of the Fintech innovations of the stability of the financial systems. Historical records of recent decades have shown that financial innovations can have positive impact on competition, but, the same time, they can have negative impact on stability. This is partly due the regulation inadequacy to ensure stability; "regulation has periodically been superseded by innovations" as observed by (OECD, 2019) in one of its dialogues about the impact of Fintech innovations on stability. The Financial Stability Board (FSB), on its part, has conducted several studies on this issue. In one of them the board states, "technological innovation holds great promise for the provision of financial services ... [at the same time] ...This could, in turn, affect the degree of concentration and contestability in financial services, with both potential benefits and risks for financial stability" (FSB, 2019: 1).
4. Exploitation and negative impact on the well-being of societies. There have been studies that discussed the negative impact of rise of

the digitized social platforms, like Facebook on societies (Pantic, 2014: 652). They indicated to the fact that these platforms tend not to benefit the society; rather these platforms tend 'to exploit their users by treating them as workforce without benefits or as sources of data to be sold to advertisers', and the fact that "each one of us generates an immeasurable amount of data every day and many businesses (and individuals) analyse this data and generate profits from it" (Dufva, 2017; Chhabra, 2019). Moreover, other studies drew attention to the impact of the digital entities not only on the cultural and social spectrums but at the health front as well. A very recent report states that "the awareness of the impact of social media on our mental health is increasing, with platforms changing their approach, to make their communities friendlier and less toxic. Social media addiction is now a recognized affliction, changing the perception of the social media landscape. People are becoming more aware of how social media can impact their mental health, and taking individual actions to decrease their online hours" (Talkwalker and HubSpot, 2019: 14). Thus, it is apparent that the negative impact of the digital platforms on us is deeper than many analysts and majority of the users think. For this reason, there have been vocal voices calling for more intervention from government to regulate the digital sector to strike a balance between benefits and harms: "we need a more active role for governments and regulators. By updating the rules for the internet, we can preserve what is best about it—the freedom for people to express themselves and for entrepreneurs to build new things—while also protecting society from broader harms" (ibid.: 21).

5. The rise in income and wealth inequality. This is another vital issue that have received a great deal of attention. Inequality has been on the rise for some time and seems to get worse in the recent few years: "the wealth of the world's billionaires increased $900 billion in [2018], which is $2.5 billion a day, [and]26 people owned the same as [the fortunes of] 3.8 billion people" (Oxfam, 2019b). For the linkage between this afflicting phenomenon and technology, an NBER report in 2003 revealed that

> many OECD economies have experienced sharp increases in wage and income inequality over the past several decades. In the United States, for example, the college premium—the wages of college graduates relative

> to the wages of high school graduates—increased by over 25 percent between 1979 and 1995. Overall, earnings inequality also soared: in 1971, a worker at the 90th percentile of the wage distribution earned 266 percent more than a worker at the 10th percentile. By 1995 this number had risen to 366 percent. (Acemoglu, 2003)

What have been the cause and/or causes for the rise of inequality in these countries? What role have advances in technologies played in the acceleration of the phenomenon? The study reveals that some economists believe that, "although other factors including the decline in the real value of the minimum wage and globalization have played some role, the major driving force behind the changes in the U.S. wage structure is technology" (ibid.). Recently there have been more rigorous and thorough studies investigating the factors that have attributed to the rise of inequality; technological advances have been identified as one of these factors (see, e.g. Dabla-Norris et al., 2015; Oxfam, 2018, 2019a)

6. Disintermediation 'mirage'. There has been a nuisance discussion about the 'disruption' of the intermediation process in the business model of the prevailing financial system. To the extent that some of these investigations are projecting that the dawn of 'disintermediation' is 'around the corner', or at least "FinTech and platform-based competitors" are threating the profitability of some financial intermediaries (OECD, 2019). What missing and/or less discussed, in these discourses, is the fact that what the world is witnessing is a replacement of 'old and deeply established' form of intermediation with an 'intelligent' and less visible one. Lin (2016: 655) noticed that "instead of true disintermediation, where links in a financial process are eliminated, financial innovation has generally further strengthened intermediation through substitution and layering". Furthermore, "while companies like Wealth front have replaced human money managers with algorithmic programs they have simply substituted a human intermediary with a computerized one … New technology did not eliminate the need for intermediated banking and brokerage services; instead, it has simply changed the nature of those intermediaries" (ibid.: 655–656). Therefore, what the world is going through is a relative decline of well-known and practised financial intermediation and the rise of 'online and platform'

intermediation. This change of positions may lead to the monopoly and concentration of business (power) in a handful of the *BigTechs*.

In a nutshell, technology advances are not priceless. They have brought some promising benefits, but some harms have been on the rise as well. For this reason, a serious researcher must avoid general conclusions in either side: positive or negative. Thus, one is required not to fall in underestimating or overestimating the risks associated with the progresses that these technologies have brought. In addressing the question "Are Facebook and other social media platforms bad for our well-being?", Ortiz-Ospina (2019) surveyed and examined a considerable number of studies to unveil the "generalisation prototype portrayed by the media in dealing with the realities arising from the answer to this crucial question". The author ends the surveyed scientific work on this matter stating

> from my reading of the scientific literature, I do not believe that the available evidence today supports the sweeping newspaper headlines [i.e. social media has a negative impact on our well-being]. Yes, there is evidence suggesting a causal negative effect, but the size of these causal effects is heterogeneous and much, much smaller than the news headlines suggest. There are still plenty of good reasons to reflect on the impact of social media in society, and there is much we can all learn to make better use of these complex digital platforms. But this requires going beyond universal claims. (Ortiz-Ospina, 2019)

Indeed, it is very important in such a complex and nascent phenomenon to jump to general conclusions either way. Thorough and up-to-date investigations and revisions are always desirable attitudes until well-established facts are brought in crystal-clear manner. And, this may take years if not decades to reach this stage.

Fintech in the MENA Region: Current State and Prospects

Global Overview

Over the past few years Fintech and related fields of information technology witnessed a tremendous progress. According to a recent IMF-WB report, "Fintech firms have received a quarter of the financial service

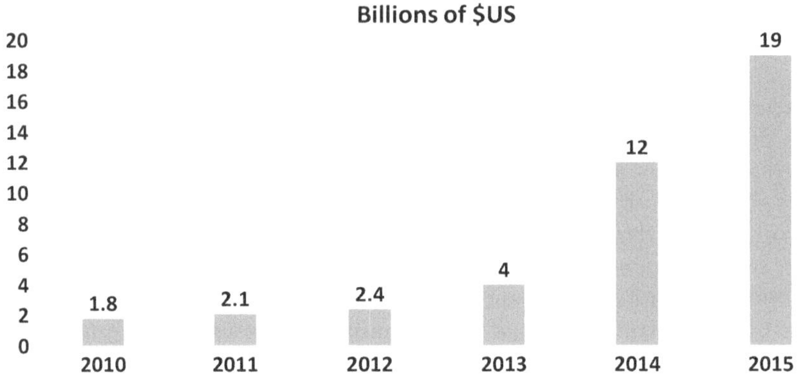

Fig. 19.3 Investment in private Fintech companies increased ten times in the past five years. (Source: Citigroup (2016: 4))

industry's venture and startup funding" (IMF-WB, 2019: 10). Investment in private Fintech companies increased by ten times within the course of six years as illustrated in Fig. 19.3.

The figures display a relatively steady growth over the first four years and close to exponential one over the last three years: 2013–2015.

E-commerce, on its part, witnessed a steady progress over the course of four years (2015–2019), and it is expected to maintain this momentum over the coming four years as depicted in Fig. 19.4.

Countries do differ in the penetration of e-commerce in their domicile. China seems to be on the leading age as the number of parties involved in e-commerce has grown drastically over the course of five (5) years (2012–2017) as portrayed in Fig. 19.5: "more than half a billion people shopped via mobile devices in 2017, with a 67.2 % penetration rate among mobile internet users" (Global E-Commerce Intelligence, 2018: 6). Thus, the number of mobile internet users, for commercial purposes, has grown slightly more than eight (5) times over five years.

And the big tech companies keep growing over time in terms of market capitalization. For the first time one of these giants has exceeded the US$1 trillion threshold as shown in Table 19.2. The other apparent characteristics of these giants is the fact that they are of US origin; 80% of the top ten largest companies are US ones.

Due to this rapid expansion of the Fintech industry and its application in October 2018, the IMF and the World Bank approved the Bali Fintech

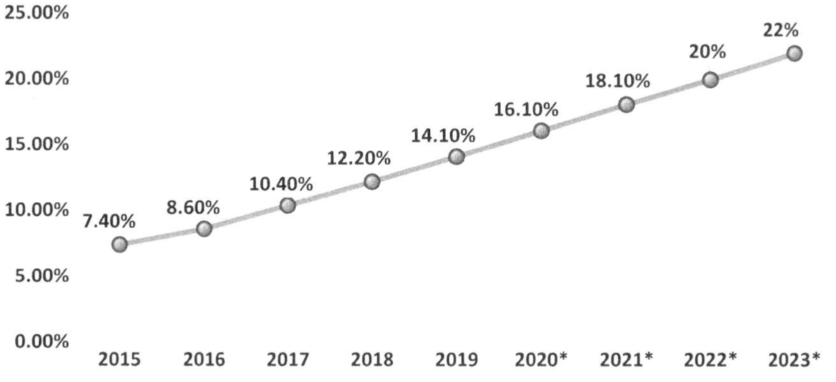

Fig. 19.4 The average growth of the share of e-commerce in relation to traditional commerce (2015–2023). (Source: Oceanx and Zid (2019: 6); (*) indicates projection)

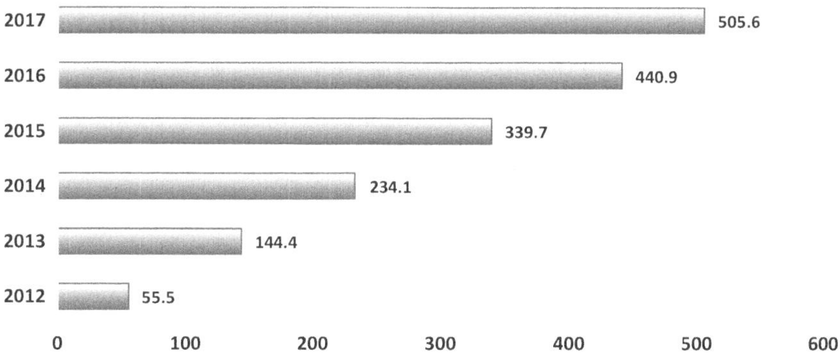

Fig. 19.5 Number of e-commerce mobile internet users in China (millions). (Source: Global E-Commerce Intelligence (2018: 6) and Jeddah Chamber (2019: 10))

Agenda (BFA) as a framework "for the consideration of high level Fintech issues by individual country members, including in their own domestic policy discussions". Moreover, IMF directors noted that "the elements of the Agenda could apply to both conventional and Islamic financial instruments and products" (IMF and WB, 2018: 3). Thus, this agenda constitutes an important part of the work that these institutions carry out. They

Table 19.2 Top ten largest companies by market capitalization (as of August 1, 2019)

Rank	*Company*	*Country*	*Sector*	*($US billion)*
1	Microsoft	USA	Technology	1058
2	Apple	USA	Technology	959
3	Amazon	USA	Consumer services	959
4	Alphabet	USA	Technology	839
5	Facebook	USA	Technology	550
6	Berkshire Hathaway	USA	Financial	496
7	Tencent	China	Technology	436
8	Alibaba	China	Consumer services	431
9	Visa	USA	Financial	389
10	JPMorgan Chase	USA	Financial	366

Source: World's Largest Companies 2019; https://www.gfmag.com/

intend to monitor and co-ordinate the progress made in this domain with member countries. For this reason, one year later these organizations published a document titled 'Fintech: The Experience So Far'. In this document it has been found that the MENA region "had a slow start in ... but the industry is ... growing rapidly" (IMF and WB, 2019: 15). The next two paragraphs discuss current state and prospects of Fintech in this region.

Current State

Fintech industry in the MENA is in its natal stages and the spread of the activities is confined to few countries. Compared with development of Fintech globally, Fintech investment in the MENA region makes up only about 1% of global Fintech venture capital investment (Mueller and Piwowar, 2019: 5). This situation may be attributed to the 'conservative' policy adopted by many governments to new ideas and inventions. And it may also be due to other factors like regulatory issues (e.g. taxation, sharia compliance and auditing) for underlying businesses that still need to be resolved in majority of jurisdictions (Sidlo, 2017: 17). Despite this slow start, the industry is evolving at an unprecedented pace. According to a very recent report compiled by MAGNiTT and Abu Dhabi Global Market (ADGM), "FinTech is the top industry across MENA by deals in 2018 and 2019" (MAGNiTT and ADGM, 2019: 2). What follows is a brief account of some of the latest developments of the Fintech industry in the region:

- MENA Fintech, which barely existed a few years ago, is now a $2 billion market. With dozens of new companies launching each year, annual growth is expected to reach $125 million by 2022, according to Beirut-based consultants MENA Research Partners (Domat, 2019).
- 2018 saw a remarkable 404 deals (13% increase from 2017) in the investment in start-ups (excl. *Souq* and *Careem*) worth 893 million USD (31% increase from 2017); and the year witnessed *Careem*'s $3.1B acquisition by Uber (MAGNiTT, 2019: 2–3).
- The number of start-ups offering financial services in the region doubled from 46 to 105 in the last three years and is expected to increase by more than 400% in 2020 from 46 in 2013 to 250 by 2020 (Wamda & Payfort, 2017: 3–4).
- Some countries are more active in this domain more than others. The IMF and WB report (2019: 15) found that "four countries (Egypt, Jordan, Lebanon, and United Arab Emirates (UAE)) account for 75 percent of FinTech start-ups", and "the UAE houses most start-ups in the Arab region 35% of all start-ups in the Arab world have headquarters (HQs) in the UAE, with which the country accounted for 28% of all deals in 2018" (MAGNiTT, 2019: 3). And according to the report, other countries are showing rapid interest in promoting the industry in their territories. This has been the case with Bahrain, Iran and Saudi Arabia.
- A survey conducted by Ernst and Young in 2015 showed that "about three quarters (73%) of adults in the MENA region would be willing to change their bank for a better digital experience and a majority declared they would increase their payment (71%), credit facilities (57%), credit card (57%), and savings (51%) usage if their online banking experience was "convenient, simple, and accessible" (Sidlo, 2017: 17). And the engagement of Saudi's in the digital world for financial services provides a typical example about the 'transformation' that is taking place in the population of some countries in the MENA region. Figure 19.6 displays out the top four categories that the Saudi adults are engaged with.

Despite the achievements and progresses made by the Fintech industry, a recent World Economic Forum/Deloitte report finds that:

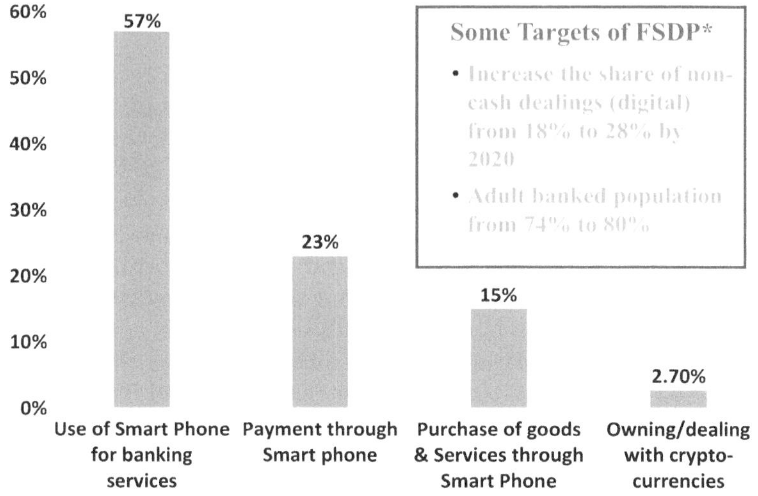

Fig. 19.6 Adult Saudis' engagement in the digital world. (Source: TREND Report (2018: 36): Saudi Digitization (Arabic); * Financial Sector Development Program (FSDP))

> Fintechs have driven a more rapid pace of technology innovation while changing expectations for what a quality customer experience can be. However, they have not meaningfully disintermediated existing providers, nor have they overturned longstanding financial services infrastructures, such as exchanges or payment networks … They have struggled to create new infrastructure and establish new financial services ecosystems … [As a result] They have been much more successful in making improvements within traditional ecosystems and infrastructure. (Deloitte, 2017: 16; WEF, 2017: 12)

Moreover, HSBC, a leading and very active bank in the MENA region, sent a comfort message to its peers in the market stating that Fintechs are not a threat to the traditional banking business model. In fact, facts on the ground indicate that the two business models are moving towards cohabitation and convergence, or collaboration, in some instances, rather than competition "for a while *FinTechs* were touted as a challenger to traditional banks but digital innovation is creating new opportunities for banks and *FinTechs* to collaborate on cutting-edge financial services solutions" (HSBC, 2019).

But they may, in the near future, create pressure on banking industry in some jurisdictions. Accenture (2016: 3) projects that "community banks [in USA] could lose up to$15 billion of revenues to FinTech companies … nearly 15 percent of the projected revenue pool for all community banks in 2020. The potential gain is also staggering, with an estimated uplift in operating income of $20 billion by 2020 for those who adopt financial technologies. This amounts to more than a 52 percent increase".

Overall, there is still a long journey for this sector to establish itself as a real 'threat and alternative' to existing business model of financial intermediation in deepening financial systems in advanced and emerging economies. Therefore, the 'hip' of high expectations that this industry is going to achieve at 'high stake levels' in less developed and some emerging economies must be treated with care.

Prospects

Fintech is expected to grow in the region with some sort of disparities between countries; UAE, Egypt, Jordan and Lebanon have been placed in the top ranking by some studies; "three in four start-ups are based in the UAE, Lebanon, Jordan or Egypt; the UAE being the most dynamic hub" (Southon, 2019). Kuwait and Bahrain are on the move. The remaining countries are still looking for ways to increase the share of the activities of

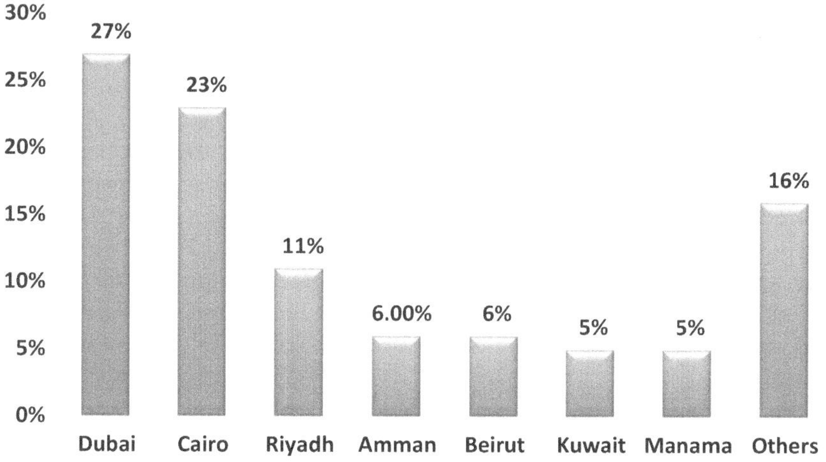

Fig. 19.7 Share of city houses of start-ups in the MENA region. (Source: https://www.zawya.com (22/10/2019))

the Fintech ecosystem in their economies. Figure 19.7 provides the latest statistics about the leading cities in the Fintech ecosystem in the MENA region.

It is apparent that Dubai is a leading city followed by Cairo and Riyadh, respectively. This is not a surprise result at all. Due to its openness and embracement for new ideas for quite some time, the UAE, via Dubai, is a leading figure in the Fintech ecosystem with "39% yearly growth in FinTech start-ups since 2012" (MAGNiTT and ADGM, 2019: 4). Based on the achievements in past few years and the numerous initiatives taking place in Dubai and Abu Dhabi, analysts predict that the UAE will continue to lead in this sector for some time in the future (MAGNiTT and MENA Fintech association). For instance, Dubai is aiming to become the first blockchain-powered city by 2020 through its ambitious "Dubai Blockchain Strategy 2020" (Zawya, 2019).

Saudi Arabia, on its part, created, in August 2019, the Saudi Data and Artificial Intelligence Authority (SDAIA). Part of this authority is the Centre for Artificial Intelligence (CAI) with a mandate to promote the application of AI in different segments of the economy. Two years before the inception of this authority, a royal decree approved the creation of the 'National Transformation Digital Unit (NDU)' as an excellence centre that will guide the digital transformation in Saudi economy as an important ingredient in the realization of the 2030 vision (https://ndu.gov.sa/about/#aboutndu).The work of the NDU covers almost all sectors of the Saudi economy including *Hajj* (pilgrimage). NDU compiled its first report about the progress made in this vital sector in the *Hajj* of 1440H (Digital Saudi, 2019a). And in August 2019 the NDU produced its biannual report about the progress made in the digital transformation programme (Digital Saudi, 2019b).There is also an important body, affiliated to the Ministry of Commerce and Investment (MCI), that has been created in 2018: the e-commerce council followed by the approval of the Council of Ministers of the Electronic Commerce Law in July 2019 (https://mci.gov.sa/; 03/07/2018;Oceanx and Zid, 2019: 14; Saudi Gazette, 2019). According to the Ministry of Telecommunications and IT, e-commerce transactions are worth 80 billion Saudi Riyals and are expected to reach 125 billion Saudi Riyals in 2025 (http://www.aleqt.com, 11/4/2019).

As far as the remaining countries, in the MENA region, are concerned, Egypt, Jordan and Lebanon are positioned in the top rank as mentioned before. Bahrain and Qatar are working pro-actively as well. It has to be noticed that almost all other countries are involved in one way or the other in introducing some 'Fintech and digital programmes' in their economies.

The ambitious initiatives show the eagerness of some countries in the MENA region to play a leading role in the Fintech and the digital world. According to a recent report published by Clifford Chance (2019: 2), a London-based LLP firm, "across the Middle East, FinTech is driven by technology-enabled innovation that improves existing financial services, but also provides routes for unbanked populations to access financial services. Government support and tech developments, together with high smartphone penetration, have contributed to the development of start-ups in the Middle East and the GCC in particular".

Who will be the 'leading figure' in the Fintech race in the MENA region? And on what basis and at which front? Results on the ground in the coming three (3) to (5) years will reveal that. However, the author of the chapter foresees that the UAE through its dynamic provinces, Dubai and Abu Dhabi, will consolidate its position due to the very early steps taken in the past few years and the pursued policies at the regulation front and elsewhere. Saudi Arabia, on the other hand, is expected to be the next leading force after UAE (Zawya, 2018) or may be Bahrain as anticipated by the Milken Institute. In its latest report about the emergence of UAE and Bahrain as 'Fintech hubs', the Institute identified three important factors that have attributed to this position (Mueller & Piwowar, 2019: 3):

1. An ecosystem conducive to new financial alternatives.
2. An ecosystem where government is at the centre of efforts to drive innovation as part of a larger remit.
3. An ecosystem particularly interested in attracting international talent as a means of stimulating innovation domestically.

On the other hand, Kuwait may emerge as a potential competitor in the Fintech race. In a report titled 'Are Kuwaiti Banks Sufficiently Prepared for the Future?', the Institute of Banking Studies in Kuwait indicated that "The mass-acceptance of mobile banking in [Kuwait] will no doubt force banks to be at the forefront of mobile banking trends in the coming years as Kuwait's young and tech-savvy population demand more mobile services from their financial institutions" (AL-Rifai, T. S. J. & Sayid, 2019: ii).

In terms of the top Fintech trends, 'Plug and Play Tech centre' predicts that the top three Fintech trends in the MENA region in the year 2019 have been security, mobile payments and online remittances, and these trends are expected to be so over the coming three to five years (La Noce, 2019). Mobile payment is expected to surge dramatically. According to GSMA, an organization representing mobile operators, "as of 2017, there were five (5) billion mobile users worldwide with 57% of users using smartphones. In the MENA region, there were 375 million mobile users in 2017, or approximately 64% of the region's population" (AL-Rifai, T. S. J. & Sayid, 2019: 11). Moreover, "The MENA region is home to 450 million people. Of that total, about half of the population is younger than 25 years old. A youthful population of such size presents an attractive and growing market of early technology adopters" (Mueller & Piwowar, 2019: 5).

Concluding Remarks and Recommendations

Though the term 'Fintech' has been with us for about five decades, and it has been used extensively in the recent past, there is still disagreement of what it entails and encompasses. The author of the chapter has made an attempt, in this regard, by defining Fintech as an 'An ecosystem of technology-enabled firms that have been nourished by the interaction of cross-disciplinary subject among various fields, and it could result in new business model, applications, processes or products with an associated material effect on the provision of financial services'. It must be emphasized that by no means this definition is the 'one better than all' or 'the end of all definitions' for such a complex and very evolving area of investigation and 'disruption'. The definition is subject to change as the apparatuses and practices of the Fintech keep changing.

Likewise, the resulting practices of the Fintech ecosystem carry out potential benefits associated with them potential risks as well. Therefore, the subject must be treated with care; 'enthusiastic and overwhelming', and/or 'passive', attitudes are non-desirable scientific stances in this respect. Weighing the benefits against the harms within a specific context of a society and/or a country is the stand that the author of this chapter believes in.

On the prospects of the Fintech in the MENA region, it is expected that the sector will grow and expand over the coming few years with countries exalting different patterns and attitudes. UAE with Dubai as the most pro-active municipality in this domain, and other 'novelties', is expected to be a leading contender in the 'Fintech race' due to the various steps and initiatives that it had taken over the past few years to establish Dubai as a

'Fintech hub' in the MENA region. What will be the consequences of this inclination? And measures will its rivals, in other MENA countries, GCC in particular, take to contest this role?

The coming years are very crucial in the development and the directions that this industry will take in this dynamic and very 'young' part of the world. For this reason, thorough and objective studies are required more than simple reports that summarize the developments in figures and charts. Exmaining the impact of such developments on the socio-cultural and economic fabric the societies are of prime importance in this regard.

Another important area of investigation is the impact of the takeover by the *tech giants* of local initiatives that seem to have been working successfully. The *Souq* and *Careem* takeovers by Amazon and Uber, respectively, are very interesting examples. Had they been good experiences for local customers and economies after the takeovers or not?

Finally, we must bear in mind, all the time, that humans are the most important asset on the planet, and the fact that each advance and/or achievement is made by them for their use and benefit, not the other way around: 'reign over' them or degrade their human specificity. As one expert nicely put amid the hot discussion about Fintech and other technological advances, we have to "constantly [remind] ourselves that all of these new technologies are first and foremost tools made by people for people" (Schwab, 2016).

References

Accenture. (2015). The Future of Fintech and Banking: Digitally Disrupted or Reimagined? Accenture.

Accenture. (2016). Fintech Playbook. Accenture and American Bankers Association. Accenture.

Acemoglu, D. (2003). *Technology and Inequality.* NBER Reporter, Winter 2003. NBER.

Adrian, T., & Mancini-Griffoli, T. (2019a). *The Rise of Digital Money.* Fintech Notes, NOTE/19/01. IMF, Washington, DC.

Adrian, T., & Mancini-Griffoli, T. (2019b, September 19). Digital Currencies: The Rise of Stablecoins. Retrieved from https://blogs.imf.org/

AL-Rifai, T., & Sayid, J. (2019). *Are Kuwaiti Banks Sufficiently Prepared for the Future?* Kuwait: Institute of Banking Studies Research.

Arner, D. W., Barberis, J. N., & Buckley, R. P. (2015). *The Evolution of Fintech: A New Post-Crisis Paradigm.* Research Paper No. 2015/047. University of Hong Kong Faculty of Law, Hong Kong, pp. 1–44.

Arner, D. W., Barberis, J. N., & Buckley, R. P. (2016). 150 Years of Fintech: An Evolutionary Analysis. *JASSA The Finsia Journal of Applied Finance*, 3, 22–29.
Arner, D. W., Barberis, J. N., & Buckley, R. P. (2017). *Fintech and Regtech in a Nutshell, and the Future in a Sandbox*. The CFA Institute Research Foundation.
Cattelan, V. (2019). Experiences in Translation: Islamic Finance and the Sharing Economy. In V. Cattelan (Ed.), *Islamic Social Finance: Entrepreneurship, Cooperation and the Sharing Economy* (pp. 71–92). London: Routledge.
Chhabra, E., & Das, B. (2019, September). Mobile Money Spreads to Asia. IMF Blog. Retrieved from https://blogs.imf.org
Chhabra, P. (2019). You, Me and (Big) Data! World Bank Blog. Retrieved from https://blogs.worldbank.org/
Citigroup. (2016). *Digital Disruption: How FinTech is Forcing Banking to a Tipping Point*. New York: Citigroup.
Clifford Chance. (2019). *Fintech in The Middle East—Developments Across MENA*. London: Clifford Chance.
Counter-Terrorism Committee Executive Directive (CTED). (2018, November). *More Support Needed for Smaller Technology Platforms to Counter Terrorist Content*. CTED Trends Alert. New York: UN Security Council (CTED).
Dabla-Norris, E., Kochhar, K., Ricka, F., Suphaphiphat, N., & Tsounta, E. (2015). *Causes and Consequences of Income Inequality: A Global Perspective*. IMF Staff Discussion Note, June 2015, SDN/15/13. IMF, Washington.
Davies, H. (2015). Ted Cruz Using Firm That Harvested Data on Millions of Unwitting Facebook Users. Retrieved from https://www.theguardian.com/
Deep Knowledge Analytics (DKA) and Future FinTech (FF). (2018). *FinTech For Social Good Industry Landscape Overview 2018*. DKA & DKA.
Deloitte. (2017). *Fintech by the Numbers Incumbents, Startups, Investors Adapt to Maturing Ecosystem*. London: Deloitte Center for Financial Services.
Digital Saudi. (2019a). *Smart Hajj: The Digital Transformation in the Hajj of 1440H*. NDU (in Arabic).
Digital Saudi. (2019b). *Indices and Achievements of The National Digital Transformation: Biannual Report 2019*. NDU (in Arabic).
Dillon, I. (2017). How Fintech is Changing the World (And How Blockchain is a Part of This). Retrieved from https://www.entrepreneur.com/
Doffman, Z. (2019, April 18). 1.5m Users Hit by New Facebook Privacy Breach as Extent of Data Misuse Exposed. Retrieved from https://www.forbes.com
Domat, C. (2019). MENA: Fintech Makes Its Mark. Retrieved from https://www.gfmag.com/magazine/
Dufva, M. (2017). Commons, Zebras and Team Economy. Retrieved from http://platformvaluenow.org/
El-Zoghbi, M., Holle, N., & Soursourian, M. (2019). *Emerging Evidence on Financial Inclusion: Moving from Black and White to Color*. Washington, DC: CGAP/WB.

Financial Stability Board. (2019). *FinTech and market structure in Financial Services :Market Developments and Potential Financial Stability Implications.* The FSB.

Financial Stability Board (FSB). (2017). *Financial Stability Implications from FinTech: Supervisory and Regulatory Issues that Merit Authorities' Attention.* The FSB.

Global E-Commerce Intelligence. (2018, May). China B2C E-Commerce Market. yStats.com, Hamburg, Germany.

Global Partnership of Financial Inclusion (GPFI). (2016). *G20 High-Level Principles for Digital Financial Inclusion.* GPFI and G20-China.

Goerlich, K. (2016). The Internet of Things and the Explosion of Life at the Periphery. Infographic. Retrieved from https://www.digitalistmag.com/

Gomez, S., Andersson, H., Park, J., Maw, S., Crook, A., & Orsmond, P. (2013). A Digital Ecosystems Model of Assessment Feedback on Student Learning. *Higher Education Studies, 3*(2), 41–51.

Goodwin, R. (2019). The History of Mobile Phones from 1973 to 2008: The Handsets That Made It All Happen. Retrieved from https://www.knowyour-mobile.com/

Homeland Security Enterprise. (2014). *Risks and Threats of Crypto-currencies.* Homeland Security Studies and Analysis Institute.

HSBC. (2019, July 15). Why Embracing FinTech is the Future for MENA Banks. Retrieved from https://www.business.hsbc.ae/

Huawei. (2017). *Digitalization: Think, Act, Accomplish.* Huawei Investment & Holding CO., LTD.

Individuals and SMEs operating in the Informal Economy. Washington: ICCR and WB.

International Committee on Credit Reporting (ICCR) and the World Bank (WB). (2018). Use of Alternative Data to Enhance Credit Reporting to Enable Access to Digital Financial Services by

International Monetary Fund (IMF) and World Bank Group (WB). (2018). *The Bali Fintech Agenda-Chapeau Paper.* Washington: IMF& WB.

International Monetary Fund (IMF) and World Bank Group (WB). (2019). *Fintech: The Experience So Far.* Washington: IMF & WB.

Internet Society. (2019, July 9). *2018 Cyber Incident & Breach Trends Report.* Internet Society'sOnline Trust Alliance.

Jeddah Chamber. (2019). *E-Commerce in Saudi Arabia: Study about the Trend of the Business Sectors (Arabic).* Jeddah: Jeddah Chamber.

Koh, S. Y. (2017, June 5). Book Review: Platform Capitalism by Nick Srnicek. Retrieved from https://blogs.lse.ac.uk/

La Noce, V. (2019). 3 Trends Reshaping Fintech in the Middle East and North Africa. Infographic. PLUGandPLAY. Retrieved from https://www.plugand-playtechcenter.com

Landers, R. (2017). How FinTech is Changing Business (and Bank Accounts). Retrieved from https://www.business.com/

Lavie, R. (2018). The Cost of Being Poor: Is Fintech the Answer? Retrieved from https://thefintechtimes.com/

Leong, K., & Sung, A. (2018). FinTech (Financial Technology): What is It and How to Use Technologies to Create Business Value in Fintech Way? *International Journal of Innovation, Management and Technology, 9*(2), 74–78.

Lin, T. C. W. (2016, January 5). Infinite Financial Intermediation. *Wake Forest Law Review, 50*(643). Temple University Legal Studies Research Paper No. 2016-06. Retrieved from SSRN: https://ssrn.com/abstract=2711379.

MAGNiTT. (2019). *The Start-up Ecosystem in the Arab World 2019*. Overview in preparation for the 10th World Economic Forum on the MENA, 6–7 April 2019. MAGNiTT, Jordan (Dead Sea).

MAGNiTT and ADGM. (2019). *MENA Fintech Venture Report* (2019th ed.). MAGNiTT& ADGM.

Mccracken, H. (2015). How the Bloomberg Terminal Made History—And Stays Ever Relevant. Retrieved from https://www.fastcompany.com/

McKinsey Global Institute. (2015). *The Internet of Things:Mapping the Value Beyond the Hype*. New York: McKinsey & Company.

Moazed, A. (2016, May 1). Platform Business Model—Definition | What is it? | Explanation. Retrieved from https://www.applicoinc.com/

Moazed, A., & Johnson, N. L. (2016). *Modern Monopolies: What It Takes to Dominate the 21st Century Economy*. New York: St. Martin's Press.

Moore, M. (2016). *Tech Giants and Civic Power. Centre for the Study of Media Communication and Power, Policy Institute*. London: King's College London.

Mueller, J., & Piwowar, M. S. (2019). *The Rise of FinTech in the Middle East: An Analysis of the Emergence of Bahrain and the United Arab Emirates*. Abu Dhabi: Milken Institute.

Murthy, G., & Fernandez-Vidal, M. (2019). *Fintechs and Financial Inclusion: Lessons Learned*. Washington: CGAP.

New York Post. (2019). The Only Thing Useful Banks have Invented in 20 Years is the ATM. Retrieved from https://nypost.com/

Oceanx and Zid. (2019). *Report about E-Commerce Retail in Saudi Arabia: Current State and the Future*. Oceanx and Zid.

OECD. (2019, June 5). Digital Disruption in Financial Markets. Retrieved from https://www.oecd.org/

Ortiz-Ospina, E. (2019, September 9). Are Facebook and Other Social Media Platforms Bad for Our Well-Being? Retrieved from https://ourworldindata.org/.

Oxfam. (2018, January). *Reward Work, Not Wealth*. Oxfam Briefing Paper. Oxfam International.

Oxfam. (2019a). *Time to end Extreme Inequality*. Oxfam International.

Oxfam. (2019b). 5 Shocking Facts about Extreme Global Inequality and How to Even It Up. Retrieved from https://www.oxfam.org/

Panetta, F. (2018). *Fintech and Banking: Today and Tomorrow*. Speech delivered at Annual Reunion of the Harvard Law School Association of Europe. Printing and Publishing Division of the Bank of Italy, Rome.

Pantic, I. (2014). Online Social Networking and Mental Health. *Cyberpsychology, Behavior, and Social Networking, 17*(10), 652–657. https://doi.org/10.1089/cyber.2014.0070

Parada, M., & Bull, G. (2015). *In the Fast Lane: Innovations in Digital Finance*. The MasterCard Foundation and International Finance Corporation (World Bank).

PumaPay. (2018). What is Double-Spending and How Can the Blockchain Prevent it from Happening? Retrieved from https://pumapay.io/

Rosenfeld, M. (2014, February 9). *Analysis of Hashrate-based Double-Spending*. Cornell University. arXiv:1402.2009v1[cs.CR]. Retrieved from https://arxiv.org/abs/1402.2009.

Sarreal, R. (2019, May 21). History of Online Banking: How Internet Banking Went Mainstream. Retrieved from https://www.gobankingrates.com/

Saudi Gazette. (2019, July 9). Approval of E-Commerce Law to spur Saudi Economic Growth. Retrieved from http://www.saudigazette.com.sa/article/571438

Schueffel, P. (2016). Taming the Beast: A Scientific Definition of Fintech. *Journal of Innovation Management, 4*(4), 32–54.

Schwab, K. (2016). The Fourth Industrial Revolution. Retrieved from https://www.weforum.org/

Segal, T. (2019, March 30). What Caused Black Monday: The Stock Market Crash of 1987? Retrieved from https://www.investopedia.com/

Shepherd-Barron, J. (2017). Meet the True Star of Financial Innovation—The Humble ATM. FT: 22/06/2017. Retrieved from https://www.ft.com/

Sidlo, K. W. (2017). *Islamic Finance 2017: State of the Art and Outlook for the Future*. The K4D Helpdesk Report.

Southon, E. (2019, February). Introduction to FinTech: A Middle East Perspective. Retrieved from https://www.dlapiper.com/

Srnicek, N. (2017). *Platform Capitalism*. Polity.

Talkwalker and HubSpot. (2019). *Social Media Trends for 2020*. Cambridge: Talkwalker and HubSpot.

Tankersley, J. (2019, October 9). Tech Giants Shift Profits to Avoid Taxes. There's a Plan to Stop Them. Retrieved from https://www.nytimes.com/

Thomas, M. L., & Morse, J. N. (2017). FinTech—Origins and Prognosis. Retrieved from quickreadbuzz.com/2017/07/26/fintech-origins-prognosis/

Tongia, R., & Wilson, E. J. (2019). The Dark Side of Metcalfe's Law: Multiple and Growing Costs of Network Exclusion. Retrieved from http://www.cstep.in/

TREND Report. (2018). *Saudi Digitization 2018 (Arabic)*. Trend.

United Nations (UN). (2016). *E-Government Survey 2016: E-Government in Support of Sustainable Development*. New York: United Nations.

United Nations (UN). (2018). *E-Government Survey 2018: Gearing E-Government to Support Transformation Towards Sustainable and Resilient Societies*. New York: United Nations.

Varga, D. (2017). Fintech, the New Era of Financial Services. *Vezetéstudomány/Budapest Management Review, XLVIII*, 22–32. ÉVF. 2017. 11. SZÁM/ISSN 0133-0179. https://doi.org/10.14267/VEZTUD.2017.11.03.

Wamda and Payfort. (2017). Fintech in MENA: Unbundling the Financial Services Industry. Wamda and Payfort.

World Bank Group (WBG). (2016). FinTech and Financial Inclusion. A Presentation. World Bank Group (WBG). Retrieved from https://slideplayer.com/slide/12218810/

World EconomicForum (WEF). (2017). *Beyond Fintech: A Pragmatic Assessment of Disruptive Potential in Financial Services*. WEF and Deloitte.

Zawya. (2018, November 20). Fintech Startups in the GCC to Attract $2bln in Private Funding. Retrieved from https://www.zawya.com/

Zawya. (2019, October 20). How Dubai is Aiming to Become the First Blockchain-Powered City by 2020. Retrieved from https://www.zawya.com

CHAPTER 20

The Risks of Islamic Fintech

Tajudeen Olalekan Yusuf

Abstract The article explores the risk factors that trail the introduction of technology into Islamic finance in Nigeria. While Islamic finance is relatively nascent in the Nigerian financial sector, it would not be out of place to underscore the impact it has made. Borrowing from its conventional counterpart, Islamic finance has largely followed the trend and development to structure and market its offerings to the Nigerian public. Typically, Islamic finance is faced by similar risk exposures as documented for its conventional counterpart which include strategic, financial, regulatory, operational, technological and political risks. The additional peculiar risk exposures are Shari'ah compliance and business partnership risks. By and large, the practical experience in Nigeria suggests herculean hurdles for Islamic finance to cross to give birth to financial Eldorado.

Keywords Islamic • Fintech • Shariah • Nigeria • Risks • Finance

---

T. O. Yusuf (✉)
Department of Actuarial Science and Insurance, University of Lagos, Lagos, Nigeria
e-mail: tyusuf@unilag.edu.ng

M. M. Billah (ed.), *Islamic FinTech*,
https://doi.org/10.1007/978-3-030-45827-0_20

Introduction

The tremendous impact that technology has had in general life has been awesome, more so in financial services. This, inadvertently, means a phenomenal challenge to financial service delivery. The problem of financial exclusion has been a recurrent decimal in the Nigerian economic landscape. The Nigeria financial services industry is beset with multifarious challenges that can only be overcome by technology. Statistics from the National Bureau of Statistics (NBS) suggest abysmal record of gross social inequality that has further fuelled insurgency in the northern part of the country.

The financial dimensions of exclusion in Nigeria suggest a dire need of technology to jump-start its economic recovery. The emerging Fintech landscape in the country galvanizes players from various industries are competing for the future of financial services. In this regard, Fintech startups have carved a niche for themselves in areas such as digital payments, microfinance, credit scoring, and remittances. Major Fintech brands in Nigeria are Paga, Interswitch, Vanso, Flutterwave, Paystack, Aella Credit and Venture Garden Nigeria (Oguh, 2017).

The Islamic finance's foray into the Nigerian financial industry coincides with the era of the development of Fintech. The experience trend of the conventional financial institutions has been replicated for Islamic financial Institutions. The risk exposure profile has been largely similar save in the areas of Shariah compliance and manpower. The intermediation process in financial market creates a series of interconnected contractual obligations and relations which alters the values of the variables in the risk equation (Akkizidis & Khandelwal, 2008).

The global financial services industry is continually transformed with the adoption of innovative technologies in the delivery of financial products and services. Innovation in finance is not a new concept, but Fintech focuses on the technological innovations that are applied to financial products and services (Rana & Akinlaso, 2018). In recent years, it has impacted the offering and consumption of products and services significantly. The advent of Fintech presents a value proposition for new opportunities and more inclusive access to financial services. Since it emergence, it continuously receives an increasing public attention and attracts growing investment interests.

Fintech promises to lower entry barriers in the financial service industry and enable nonfinancial corporations to offer financial services that were traditionally dominated by regulated financial institutions. The likes of Apple or Samsung are corporate brands synonymous to technology development, Amazon or Alibaba known as online market place, and many others whose core business is not finance have leveraged the capabilities of technology to enter the financial market place to offer payment and online lending solutions.

More so, with the aid of Fintech, incumbent financial institutions are able to adapt and develop new tech-oriented business models. While several large financial institutions switching strategies to adopt new technologies, many small and new market players are springing up to offer financial services that is powered by innovative technologies. There are now over 12,000 start-ups globally, with Fintech investments reaching $57.9 billion in the first half of 2018 (DIEDC, 2018).

The Herald of Islamic Finance

The Islamic finance segment is not left out in the global digital transformation strides. Islamic financial service providers are adapting to the new digital trend and leveraging innovative technologies to deliver financial services to their customers. Young, digitally native customers are the main stakeholders driving this change, and both large financial service providers and start-ups are responding accordingly.

More specifically, the Islamic Fintech is at the very beginning of an exciting, transformative journey for the industry that still dominated by large traditional Islamic financial institutions (IFIs). More so, the young, digitally native Muslim demographic that is on average younger than the world's non-Muslim population adds to the prospect of Islamic Fintech.

Despite the many advantages and opportunities provided by the technological innovations in finance, the Islamic Fintech like the regular Fintech solutions is exposed to many risks. The Islamic Fintech risk exposures extend beyond operational and technical risks and are interwoven in effect. It also includes technology, strategic, Shariah compliance risk, reputational risk, regulatory risk, fraud risk, data security risk and agent management or third-party risks. These risks often share similar causes and their effects are strongly related. For instance, technology risk, strategic risk, agent management risks and Shariah compliance risk can all lead to legal risk which could result in reputational risk and further financial losses.

In order for the Islamic financial services industry to be able to fully capitalize on the benefits of Islamic Fintech, it is important that the associated risks are understood and adequately addressed. The Islamic Fintech risks factors are discussed as follows.

Strategic Risk

Strategic risk refers to the actual losses that result from the pursuit of an unsuccessful business plan or the potential losses from missed opportunities (IFC-WorldBank, 2016). Strategic risks include losses that are related to business models, technology, branding, reputation, competition and economic trends.

Islamic Fintech Firms (IFFs) can be exposed to strategic risk as a result of misapprehension of market demand, misunderstanding of competition, poor product or channel design. For instance, IFFs may suffer actual losses as a result of an ineffective product, failure to respond to change in the business environment, inadequate resource allocation or poor customer judgement.

Strategic risk exposure may vary for different IFFs for some inherent heterogeneity in business models, regulatory environment, competition and market sentiment. For instance, the strategic risk exposure for a charity-based crowdfunding IFF will be distinctive to that of an equity-based crowdfunding IFF, although they are both in the crowdfunding business. So is the case for an Islamic peer-peer financing platform and an Islamic investment platform. They may exist in the same market and enjoy the same customer base, but their business models and regulatory requirements are not necessarily identical. Hence, the strategic risk exposure varies and so does the approach to their risk management.

Strategic risk if not managed appropriately could result in loss of investment for the IFF. An IFF must however identify and monitor the strategic risk indicators to their business in order to manage their strategic risk exposure. Depending on the IFF, such indicators may include drop in net revenue, decline in active customers, fall in the volume transactions per customer, drop in active agents or customers per agent, change in macroeconomic policy.

To manage strategic risk, IFFs must leverage their position in gathering and analysing customer and market data. Simultaneously, IFFs must be reviewing perspectives from customers as well as external sources such the bloggers, market reviewers and information trendsetters. See Table 20.1 for causes, effects and indicators of strategic risk in Islamic Fintech firms).

Table 20.1 Strategic risks in Islamic Fintech firms: causes, effect and indicators

Description	*Causes*	*Effect*	*Risk indicators*
The actual losses that result from the pursuit of an unsuccessful business plan or the potential losses from missed business opportunities	• Misapprehension of market demand • Misunderstanding of competition • Poor product or channel design	• Loss of investment	• Drop in Net revenue • Decline in active customers • Fall in the volume transactions per customer • Drop in active agents or customers per agent • Change in macro-economic policy

Source: Authors and IFC-WorldBank (2016)

Regulatory Risk

Regulatory risk refers to the risks associated with complying (or not complying) with the rules or guidelines that are sanctioned by the regulatory authorities in the jurisdictions where a Fintech firm operates. Examples of such regulatory provisions includes the Know Your Customer (KYC), anti-money laundering (AML), combating financing of terrorism (CFT), data privacy (PDPD or GDPR) and transaction limits (IFC-WorldBank, 2016).

Generally, regulatory risk for the IFF stems from non-compliance or violation due to change in regulatory provisions for due diligence, agent management, capital requirement, trust, interoperability, privacy and deposit insurance in some cases. For the IFFs, regulatory risk is a crucial concern, and non-compliance can have significant impact on business operations, increase regulatory oversight, invoke fines, penalties and even loss of licence.

A typical indicator for regulatory risk in IFFs is anything short of the regulatory requirement on any aspect of the business. Such indicators include the percentage of incomplete registration, percentage of rejected registration or capital inadequacy.

Table 20.2 Regulatory risks in Islamic Fintech firms: causes, effect and indicators

Description	*Causes*	*Effect*	*Risk indicators*
Risks associated with complying (or not complying) with the rules or guidelines that are sanctioned by the regulatory authorities in the jurisdictions where they operate	• Abrupt change in regulatory provisions • Poor product or channel design • Poor communication and training of personnel and agents • Weak governance	• Increased regulatory oversight • Rising cost of compliance • Penalty or fines • Loss of licence • Loss of investment	• Drop in net revenue • Decline in active customers • Fall in the volume transactions per customer • Drop in active agents or customers per agent • Change in macro-economic policy

Source: Authors, Deloitte (2018) and IFC-WorldBank (2016)

To manage regulatory risk, IFFs must ensure that their personnel, process and agents are up-to-date on regulatory provisions. The IFF may also align incentives to its personnel, agents or customers towards the fulfilment of regulatory requirements. Also products or service offers may be restricted to customers based on the level of compliance and even penalty for non-compliance where applicable Table 20.2 presents the causes, effects and indicators of regulatory risk in Islamic Fintech firms.

Operational Risk

Operational risk refers to all potential losses from inadequate or failed internal processes, employees and systems in business. Operational risk is inherent in any business. In the case of the IFF, it involves risks associated with products, business practices, damage to physical assets as well as the execution and delivery of service.

Some of the common indicators of operational risk in IFFs centre around the productivity of back office team, which is measured by delays in transaction processes such as the numbers of suspense transaction

Table 20.3 Operational risks in Islamic Fintech firms: causes, effect and indicators

Description	*Causes*	*Effect*	*Risk indicators*
Potential losses from inadequate or failed internal processes, employees and systems in business	• Poor planning • Inefficient implementation of operational procedures • Ineffective monitoring and evaluation	• Resource mismanagement • Loss of customer • Regulatory issues • Loss of funds	• Number of suspense transaction resolved • Number of days' transaction stay in suspense accounts • Decline in active customers • Time taken to resolve disputes • Drop in active agents or customers per agent

Source: Authors, Deloitte (2018) and IFC-WorldBank (2016)

resolved, number of days' transaction stay in suspense accounts or time taken to resolve disputes.

Managing operational risk requires a regular review operating manual against list of procedures being undertaken. This must be in a view to improve efficiency by adding any missing procedures, updating existing procedures as required and adding the exception use cases to all (Table 20.3).

Technology Risk

Technology risk is closely linked to operational risk. It refers to the potential loss due to technology failure that leads to the inability to implement transactions. Technology risk is inherent in IFF business as the in-core operation relies on technology infrastructure. Any technical failure leaves opportunities for fraudsters to take advantage of system inadequacies to conduct unauthorized transactions that results in loss of data and funds.

Technology risk has spill-over effect to the forms of risk, and its indicators are common across the various types of Fintech firms. For instance, a drop in the rate of successful transactions on a Fintech platform would indicate a technical failure. So are system glitches during peak service period, which indicate an insufficient capacity to cope when user requests (demand) are high at a particular time. Another common source of technology risk in IFFs is the reliance on third-party technology provider, since technology is not the core competence for most of them. They stand the risk of delays in service maintenance and failure in some cases.

Managing technology risk is crucial to any Fintech business, as it is the vehicle to deliver the firm's value proposition to users and maximize return. To manage such risk, an IFF first needs to ensure the service of competent technology talents to deliver a robust system. Secondly, the process of managing the platform must be efficient such that it calls for routine test of end-to-end transaction process. More so, Fintech platforms should have performance monitors installed to show the system traffic and raise alarm when it is approaching capacity limits. Lastly, for IFFs that rely on third-party technology, having an enforceable service-level agreement will help minimize technology service failure. Table 20.4 summarizes the causes, effect and indicators of technology risk to an IFF.

Table 20.4 Technology risks in Islamic Fintech firms: causes, effect and indicators

Description	*Causes*	*Effect*	*Risk indicators*
Potential loss due to technology failure that leads to the inability to implement transactions	• Poor technology architecture • Weak security firewall • Power failure • System faults (software and hardware) • Network connectivity failure	• Data loss • Loss of customer confidence • Reputational risk • Financial losses • Security breach • Regulatory sanctions	• Drop in transaction success rate • System glitches during peak periods • Customer reports on failed transaction • Reliance on third-party technology

Source: Authors, Deloitte (2018) and IFC-WorldBank (2016)

Financial Risk

Financial risk is an important risk factor in the Fintech firms, Islamic or otherwise. Financial risk in Fintech is defined as the potential for financial loss in all financial transitions of Fintech (Ryu, 2018). While all risks discussed in this chapter may give rise to financial losses, directly or indirectly, there are specific risks related to the financial management of an Islamic Fintech business. Financial risk for an IFF depends on the nature of Fintech activity (payments/billing, financing, investments, transfers/remittances, crowdfunding, blockchain/cryptocurrencies, institutional/B2B, insurance, etc.), area of service (innovation, regulation, financial inclusion, financial education, services or operation) and core technology (adoption/externality, mobile, blockchain, big data, biometrics, security, risk, etc.).

A brief description of five of such specific risks—namely, credit risk, liquidity risk, interest rate risk, foreign exchange risk and concentration risk—is as follows:

1. Credit risk: The risk that clients default on their financial obligation and the IFF is unable to collect on it.
2. Liquidity risk: The risk that an IFF becomes insolvent and unable to meet its cash flow obligations.
3. Interest rate spill-over risk: The risk of an interest rate hike spill over on IFF's cost of fund, while the IFF is unable to share such risk with its clients.
4. Foreign exchange risk: The risk of incurring losses from when trading currency or a mismatch of currencies in which transactions, financing or deposits are denominated.
5. Concentration risk: The risk due to excessive exposure to a particular credit counterparty or sector. For instance, if an IFF holds majority of its funds in one particular bank. Such IFF is at risk of excessive loss should the bank become insolvent.

Managing financial risk in IFFs depends on a number of factors mentioned earlier that differentiate them and the financial risk channel such as credit, liquidity, interest rate, foreign exchange or fund concentration. However, a general measure to manage financial risk in IFFs is to ensure that the financing (foreign or local) and payments are in local currency terms. Risk that cannot be avoided should be transferred or shared. Table 20.5 summarizes the causes, effect and indicators of financial risk to an IFF.

Table 20.5 Financial risks in Islamic Fintech firms: channels, effect and indicators

Description	*Channels*	*Effect*	*Risk indicators*
Potential for financial loss in all financial transitions of Fintech	• Credit risk • Liquidity risk • Interest rate risk • Foreign exchange risk • Concentration risk	• Book or real Loss • Insolvency • Loss of customer confidence • Regulatory sanctions	• Foreign exchange rate fluctuation • Interest rate fluctuation • Poor client credit rating • Fund concentration • Dropping liquidity ratio

Source: Authors, Deloitte (2018) and IFC-WorldBank (2016)

Political Risk

Political risks are external risk that often affects IFFs, significantly. It refers to the potential loss incurred from the political decisions, events or conditions in the environment where IFFs operate. Political risks have direct impacts on operational risk, strategic risk and financial risk in particular and spill over to other risks.

IFFs are exposed to political risks as a result of civil unrest, terrorism, war, corruption, unfavourable economic conditions due to fiscal or monetary policy changes by the government. These events are exogenous and beyond the control of IFFs. As such managing them requires anticipation and contingency plans in case the anticipated risk materializes. Table 20.6 summarizes the causes, effect and indicators of political risk to an IFF.

Fraud Risk

Fraud risk refers to the potential loss resulting from fraud activities. Fraud risk is a notorious risk that concern IFFs, their consumers and the market regulators. It is a multi-faceted risk that relates to several other risks. For instance, a failure in operation or flaw in technology can lead to fraud risk, which may result in financial risk. Fraud risk is also a significant driver of reputational risk.

In the global Fintech industry, large cases of fraud have been reported over the last few years that have caused financial damages worth millions

Table 20.6 Political risks in Islamic Fintech firms: causes, effect and indicators

Description	*Causes*	*Effect*	*Risk indicators*
Potential loss incurred from the political decisions, events or conditions in the environment where IFFs operate	• Political instability • Elections • War or terrorism • Economic policy	• Inaccessibility due to loss of connectivity • Inoperability of business • Loss of investment • Asset destruction • Risk spill-overs	• Election • Economic policy • Agent activity • Customer activity

Source: Authors and IFC-WorldBank (2016)

of dollars. These fraud cases have been perpetuated by Fintech service customers, agents and employees through the creation of ghost accounts to perform fraudulent transactions (Akinlaso, Adediran, Diallo, & Mahomed, 2019). As a result, funds have been stolen from Fintech providers, agents and customers.

Managing fraud risk requires regular assessment of system and processes to understand where fraud could be detected and prevented. There are three general reasons for fraud: pressure (or motivation to commit fraud), opportunity (typically because of poor systems or processes) and rationalization (that they will not be caught). An effective way to prevent fraud is to decrease the opportunity for fraud through detection technology and procedures. Table 20.7 summarizes the causes, effect and indicators of fraud risk to an IFF.

Agent Management Risk

Agent management risk refers to the potential loss to an IFF resulting from a third-party engagement in Fintech service delivery. Some IFFs employ the service of third-party agents to deliver some aspect of their services, and as a result, such IFFs enjoy benefits in terms of cost, geographical reach and scale. However, any inadequacy in the management and supervision of agents can result in potential losses for the IFF, its clients and the agent themselves. Hence, such IFF is exposed to agent management risk.

Agent management risk exposure is limited to IFFs that use the service of third-party agents. It triggers other risks such as operational,

Table 20.7 Fraud risks in Islamic Fintech firms: causes, effect and indicators

Description	*Causes*	*Effect*	*Risk indicators*
Potential loss resulting from fraud activities in Islamic Fintech business	• Misaligned business incentives • Technical lacuna • Third-party access • Lax customer on boarding procedure	• Loss of customer confidence • Loss of reputation • Regulatory scrutiny • Financial loss • Loss of investment	• Suspicious transaction report • Unverified client access ratio to total client • Unsupervised staff access

Source: Authors

technological, legal, reputational and fraud risks. For IFFs, agent management risk can be caused by a number of factors that depends on the nature of IFF's activity and service. Such factors include the distribution of agents across geographical areas and user base, agents to user ratio, agent liquidity options (in transfers and remittances service) and security, teller errors, agent-customer relationship management, training and regulatory updates, brand marketing and operating procedures.

To manage the risk from third-party agents, IFFs must first put in place a robust agent on-boarding procedure and due diligence (e.g. a regulatory licence requirement, or pre-fund capital requirement), adequate quality control process and supervision (e.g. process that detects when agents fail to meet their liquidity requirements), regular engagement with agents or the use of super agents (where liquidity is involved), agent-specific help lines. Table 20.8 summarizes the causes, effect and indicators of fraud risk to an IFF.

Reputational Risk

Reputational risk refers to the potential loss resulting from damage to the image of an IFF, its partner or stakeholder, leading to a negative perception and reduction of trust from clients and agents. An IFF can be directly exposure to reputational risk on event of frequent technology failure (that hinders customer from transacting), lack of transparency in pricing and

Table 20.8 Agent management risks in Islamic Fintech firms: causes, effect and indicators

Description	*Causes*	*Effect*	*Risk indicators*
Potential loss to an IFF resulting from a third-party engagement in Fintech service delivery	• Inadequate agent management strategy • Suboptimal agent distribution • Inefficient agent on-boarding procedure (due diligence) • Inefficient agent liquidity management • Ineffective provider-agent relation	• Loss of agents • Loss of customer confidence • Decline in sales • Regulatory scrutiny • Financial loss • Loss of investment	• Agent due diligence compliance flags • Agent-provider engagement • Agent liquidity requirement flags • Agent density • Regulatory updates

Source: Authors, IFC-WorldBank (2016) and Ryu (2018)

opaque policies, fraud, inadequate liquidity, ineffective agent management, poor customer engagement and regulatory and Shariah compliance issues.

Indirectly, IFFs are often exposed to reputational risk through other risk channels such as regulatory, financial, operational and Shariah non-compliance risks. Such exposure can affect the IFF in the form of loss of customers, reduced revenue and shareholder value, increased operating costs, legal liability, diminished brand equity.

Managing reputational risk is crucial to the success of any Fintech business and quite tricky for an IFF. This is because for a conventional Fintech firm, reputational risks emanating from regular transaction of regulatory provisions are not far-fetched and easily managed. But for an IFF, a Shariah non-compliance reputation has a severe consequence for business and its effect can be long lasting.

The foremost strategy to managing reputational risk for any IFF is rule compliance. Then setting up a public relations strategy that has contingency to manage negative press. Also a transparency culture that attracts the trust of client and partners. Table 20.9 summarizes the causes, effect and indicators of reputational risk to an IFF.

Table 20.9 Reputation risks in Islamic Fintech firms: causes, effect and indicators

Description	*Causes*	*Effect*	*Risk indicators*
Potential loss resulting from damage to the image of an IFF, its partner or stakeholder, leading to a negative perception and reduction of trust from clients and agents	*Direct* • Lack of transparency • Technology failure • Poor customer engagement *Indirect Channels* • Shariah non-compliance risks • Regulatory risk • Financial risk • Operational risk	• Public embarrassment • Loss of customer confidence • Decline in revenues • Regulatory scrutiny • Loss of investment	• Shariah compliance issues • Customer dissatisfaction • Regulatory scrutiny • Technology inadequacies

Source: Authors, IFC-WorldBank (2016), Ryu (2018) and Erdem Oz, Zahid ur Rehman Khokher, Mohammad Mahbubi Ali, and Romzie Rosman (2016)

Business Partnership Risk

Business partnership risks are the potential losses from a third-party partnership in delivering a Fintech service to end users. Partnerships are necessary in the global financial service segment for smooth and expanded service provision. Fintech firms partner with each other and with traditional financial and non-financial institutions to leverage on the existing infrastructure for operational efficiency and cost savings.

In some cases, partnerships are required by regulatory authorities to ensure stability and growth in the financial service sector. For instance, some degree of collaboration is required between banks and mobile network operators (MNOs) for mobile money and remittance operations. In such case, banks rely on MNOs for connectivity and the MNOs depend on banks to hold funds as deposit and disburse them or in trust.

For IFFs, business partnership risk exposure can include the breakdown of relationships with operational and strategic partners such as distributors, principal agents, vendors, technology providers, outlet partners and donors. The presence of a pro-active regulator can foster meaningful partnerships that support IFFs. But lack of a level playing fields in regulatory

Table 20.10 Business partnership risks in Islamic Fintech firms: causes, effect and indicators

Description	*Causes*	*Effect*	*Risk indicators*
Potential loss from a third-party partnership in delivering a Fintech service to end users	• Poor strategic planning • Loose service contracts with partners • Increasing demand ahead of capacity	• Service disruption • Loss of customer confidence • Loss of funds	• Business uptime • Partner service consistency • Technology inadequacies

Source: Authors, IFC-WorldBank (2016), Ryu (2018) and Erdem Oz, Zahid ur Rehman Khokher, Mohammad Mahbubi Ali, and Romzie Rosman (2016)

environments in which IFFs operate may lead to suboptimal partnership arrangements that result in risk exposure.

Managing business partnership risk in IFFs requires the establishment of detailed service-level partner contracts that are enforceable. The IFF should also ensure regular technical reviews with partners to ensure compliance with deliverables and planning ahead. Lastly, IFFs should incentivize partners and align incentives with deliverables to keep the service running. Table 20.10 summarizes the causes, effect and indicators of reputational risk to an IFF.

Shariah Non-compliance Risk

As defined by the IFSB, Shariah non-compliance risk (SNCR) the potential of loss that arises from the "failure of the Islamic banks to comply with the Shariah rules and principles determined by the Shariah board or the relevant body in the jurisdiction in which the Islamic Bank operates" (Erdem Oz, Zahid ur Rehman Khokher, Mohammad Mahbubi Ali, & Romzie Rosman, 2016). Drawing from this definition, Shariah non-compliance risk in IFFs is the potential loss that arises from the failure to comply to the Shariah rules as determined by the relevant authorities in the jurisdictions where the IFF operates.

Shariah is the backbone of Islamic financial institutions: it is instrumental in maintaining the confidence of stakeholders and the public at large. Shariah non-compliance risk occurs from events or transactions that are not in congruence with the tenets of the Shariah. Ensuring compliance

Table 20.11 Shariah non-compliance risks in Islamic Fintech firms: causes, effect and indicators

Description	*Causes*	*Effect*	*Risk indicators*
Potential loss that arise from the failure of an IFF to comply with the Shariah rules as determined by the relevant authorities in the jurisdictions where they operate	• Inadequate Shariah governance framework • Deviation from the tenets of Shariah	• Illegitimacy regulatory scrutiny • Loss of customer confidence • Loss of investment	• Novel business activity • Internal Shariah board competence • Communication break with Shariah board members • Diminishing autonomy of internal Shariah board

Source: Authors and Erdem Oz, Zahid ur Rehman Khokher, Mohammad Mahbubi Ali, and Romzie Rosman (2016)

with the Shariah is a necessary condition for the legitimacy of an IFF. As such, Shariah non-compliance risk is a principal risk and a distinctive risk factor for an IFF. It is also a significant implication for reputational risk.

Managing Shariah non-compliance risk requires a regular track of status of transactions and processes for Shariah non-compliant events. It is important to regularly engage internal Shariah compliance functions to ensure timely sharing of information and proper coordination to handle any emerging Shariah compliance matters. It also requires procedures to ensure purification of non-permissible income through income de-recognition. Table 20.11 summarizes the causes, effect and indicators of reputational risk to an IFF.

Cyber Security Risk

Cyber security risk refers to the potential loss due to security compromise in the transaction operations of IFFs. Security risks are unpredictable and not unique to IFFs. It presents a major challenge because of the potential systemic risks and interaction with other risks. Increased connectivity and new entrants that may not well equipped with security infrastructure can increase the entry points for cyber criminals and the potential for successful attacks.

Security breaches can lead to direct financial losses for IFFs, data privacy breaches or through denial of services that triggers reputational and

Table 20.12 Cyber security risks in Islamic Fintech firms: causes, effect and indicators

Description	*Causes*	*Effect*	*Risk indicators*
Potential loss due to security compromise in the transaction operations of IFFs	• Weak security framework • Outdated security systems • Third-party security system	• Financial loss • Data privacy • Regulatory scrutiny • Loss of customer confidence	• Outdated security infrastructure • Reliance on third-party security

Source: Authors and Lukonga (2018)

regulatory risks (Akinlaso et. al, 2019). Table 20.12 summarizes the causes, effect and indicators of reputational risk to an IFF.

Conclusion

The foregoing discussion presents the peculiar background to the integration of technology to the Nigerian financial industry which commenced about five years ago. Though starting later than Kenya and South Africa, the most populous black nation on Earth has attracted steady investment and destination for Venture Capital investors. The dire abysmal scorecard in financial exclusion statistics has further accelerated Fintech integration into the conventional financial setting. This has been further boosted by the foray of Islamic financial institutions into the Nigerian financial sector. The attendant risk exposures faced by Islamic Financial Institutions (IFIs) include strategic, financial, regulatory, operational and regulatory. Others are Shariah-compliance and Business Partnership risks. These risks, though while typical under conventional setting, have their impact on IFIs in a peculiar sense due to their nature of product design and packaging. The management of these risks is also peculiar; requiring special approach and methodology.

References

Akinlaso, I. M., et al. (2019). Blockdentity: A Future Beyond Digital Identity. In U. A. Oseni & S. N. Ali (Eds.), *Fintech in Islamic Finance: Theory and Practice* (1st ed., p. 76). London: Routledge.

Akkizidis, I., & Khandelwal, S. K. (2008). *Financial Risk Management for Islamic Banking and Finance*. New York: Palgrave Macmillan.

Deloitte. (2018). *Fintechs and Regulatory Compliance: The Risk Management Imperative*. Deloitte.

DIEDC. (2018). *Islamic Fintech Report 2018 Current Landscape*. Dubai.

Erdem Oz, et al. (2016). Shariah Non-Compliance Risk in the Banking Sector: Impact on Capital Adequacy. *IFSB Working Paper Series, 5*(March).

IFC-WorldBank. (2016). *Digital Financial Services and Risk Management*. IFC World Bank. Retrieved from www.ifc.org/financialinclusionafrica%0AC

Lukonga, I. (2018). Fintech, Inclusive Growth and Cyber Risks: A Focus on the MENAP and CCA Regions.

Oguh, C. (2017). Africa's Fintech landscape. Retrieved from http://www.financialnigeria.com/africa-s-Fintech-landscape-blog-214.html

Rana, O., & Akinlaso, I. M. M. (2018). How Blockchain Can Impact the Muslim World: Food. *IFN Fintech*. Retrieved from https://www.ifnFintech.com/how-blockchain-can-impact-the-muslim-world-food.html

Ryu, H. (2018). Understanding Benefit and Risk Framework of Fintech Adoption: Comparison of Early Adopters and Late Adopters, pp. 3864–3873.

CHAPTER 21

TakafulTech for Business Excellence and Customer Satisfaction

Kazi Mohammad Mortuza Ali

Abstract Insurance vis-à-vis takaful represents a tool of prime importance in modern economies. It enables the insureds to reduce and better manage their risk exposures. The basic feature of an insurance contract is that the insured buys a future promise of payment contingent upon the occurrence of specified events. This means the insured pays his consideration from the very beginning of the contract. But before the insurer is called to "perform its part", the security profile of the insurer may have changed with time. Therefore, the long-term reliability of an insurance/takaful company must be beyond doubt. This has led the regulatory authority to enact regulations aimed at securing the long-term reliability of insurers. The concern for consumer protection has expanded the scope of insurance supervisory body, and therefore, greater consideration may be given to insurance consumer protection measures. Supervisory body need to frame rules/regulations, guidelines to ensure customer protection measures. Strong commitment, integrity and honesty are essential qualities for all positions within the insurance industry. Further, to keep up with the times, on-going training and retraining of key personnel is a necessity. The

K. M. M. Ali (✉)
Bangladesh Institute for Professional Development, Dhaka, Bangladesh

M. M. Billah (ed.), *Islamic FinTech*,
https://doi.org/10.1007/978-3-030-45827-0_21

government regulatory body need to ensure that the insurers and *Takaful Operators (TO)* adhere to the basic rules and ethics of business.

Keywords Risk • Fintech • Takaful • TakafulTech • Customer • Satisfaction

Introduction

Takaful is a community-based business, whereby the policyholders or the participants contribute to a common fund and those who suffer losses are paid from that fund. This makes takaful a method of cooperation amongst the policyholders. TOs are the custodians of policyholder's money, and they are supposed to protect the best interest of the policyholders. They need to treat the customers fairly and friendly and at the same time must provide the services timely. Takaful is essentially a business of trust between the operators and the participants. This trust cannot be developed, if operators rely mostly on commission-centric approach for business development. The only way they can build trust and confidence is through customer centricity. This has to be built into the culture of every employee of takaful operators. This has to be reflected in the day to day servicing of the policies, in meeting participants' grievances, in the settlement of claims, in pricing the product, in the observance of business ethics and in the behavior and attitude of takaful agent, employees, managers and everybody.

Customer service is an attitude, a culture and a collective way of providing best service and addressing customer grievances speedily. Sales agents need to explain the features and benefits of the product and its conditions, warranties, restrictions to the prospective and existing policyholders. Honesty and integrity are important hallmarks of takaful sales person. Salesmen need to be taught continuously on how to deal with policyholders by keeping constantly in touch with them, to know their feeling. Participants should be kept satisfied for all the time. Even if they are unsatisfied, they become the greatest source of learning, for the organization.

Living up to the expectations of participants and timely delivery of services to them are the hallmarks of good governance. This is necessary to ensure accountability and transparency in functioning of organizations dealing with services to people. Takaful is essentially a service industry where expectations of participants are ever increasing toward quality. Besides continuous awareness program to safeguard the interest of policyholders, it is necessary to codify time limit in every phase of dealing with customers. Appropriate use of information and communication technology can ensure timely delivery of services to the participants while helping towards orderly growth of business.

Ensuring timely delivery is a core competence of an operator of takaful business. This creates sustainable competitive advantage for a company. It is a deep proficiency and requires coordination of several departments and sections. It allows to differentiate takaful operators from others and set strategies that unify the entire organization. In order to ensure timely delivery of services, all the departmental and sectional heads need to understand how customer's value is created through unique capabilities of the company. Then it is necessary to develop unique capabilities and qualities that are difficult for competitors to copy. Takaful operators need to create a strategic roadmap that set goals and yardsticks for competence building. Core competency should be developed in the areas of product development, distribution, underwriting, claims management, risk management and so on (1).

Need for Digitization

Information technology has revolutionized the way takaful business is being conducted. In the Western world, information technology has proved to be essential not only for growing the insurance business but also for sustaining it. Insurance companies who have redefined their strategy in response to the growing relevance of technology have managed to stay afloat smoothly in the business. Information technology has not only made the insurance world more connected but also made business development more accessible. The most powerful asset of the digital age is data and data is really a new asset (2).

With a single click on *Google*, we have lots of information accessible to us. This increased access to information has been radically changing our lives since the last decade. The momentum of IT innovation is dramatically shifting towards digital transformation.

(1) *The role of Takaful is to safeguard the hazards of life and the property as well. It also protects a person's risk and liability arising in day to day life.*

(2) *Don Tapscott, "Why Blockchain is a big opportunity for property?" Fintech, September 2018.* (Issue 20)

The millennial generation is becoming the driving force for change. Millennials, born from 1980 to 2000, grew up with *Amazon, Google* and social media accessible via mobile devices and computers in their hands. They have an entirely new framework. Smartphones have created an expectation that data should be available anytime and anywhere.

Application development for mobile devices is growing at a blistering pace. E-commerce and e-insurance are rapidly gaining ground. Insurers are keen to use technology to gain more information of their customers and potentially offer them low-cost insurance solutions. In the information era, takaful sector is expected to witness best international practices, product innovation and penetration which will lead to future growth with the aim of providing prompt service to the policyholders in the most cost-efficient manner.

Takaful operators are now trying to establish virtual offices that can provide takaful solutions to clients at their doorsteps. Companies have launched digital insurance wallets to empower customers to make digital transactions. Some operators are looking at digital claim settlements in the future. Digitization has made it easier for operators to indulge in direct selling of policies to customers. Thus digitization should be used to increase customer satisfaction.

Digital technologies provide new opportunities for additional premiums, enhanced customer experience and selection of risks in a better fashion. Loss prevention efforts also get a boost. Takaful operators, therefore, must explore different ways to access and process data from devices and sensors and streamline real-time data from social media and external sources. Communication strategies in the information era have to be innovative to secure competitive advantage. Awareness of value of takaful solutions must be made more explicit to the public at large. Information sharing through efficient communication strategies coupled with the development of client-based product is crucial for competitiveness of takaful sector (3).

Takaful industry all over the world is embracing new technology. They are using technology not just to replace manual work by technology-based work but also to understand the customers better and serve them better. A large number of takaful operators are no longer pushing products. They are developing products with the help of customer's feedbacks and experiences. Distribution channels are getting developed, keeping in mind the customer choices. Even sales process is getting automated by operators. Therefore, TOs need to adopt to the new rules of the game if they want to sustain growth in future.

Today's customers are going to be profoundly net-savvy. Not just the young generation, even the older generations have developed a habit of visiting websites of service providers to acquire more information about products and services. Takaful sector is not an exception. Almost all takaful companies have launched similar products in the mat. This has not helped the prospective participants to choose the right product as per need and satisfaction.

(3) *Communication is a golden key to success in the insurance and takaful industry. The competitive pressure and the battle for market share has compelled takaful operators to improve communication and technological capabilities to a greater extent.*

It would be a natural curiosity of the people to study the product features of the operators and the price of the products, before making the actual purchase. The websites of the insurance companies are extremely useful and user-friendly to give this information very quickly. Web aggregators compare the prices of insurers and takaful operators, and these help the customers to buy appropriate products.

Social media enables the customer to compare the service qualities of the insurers and operators. The focus of the takaful operators, therefore, has to shift towards "customers" from "products". This shift is possible only through information technology. The market is huge; customer base is also pretty large for all the insurers. Information technology can help to understand diverse market segments, their needs and preferences and also their grievances against the insurers, if any. Therefore, customers have to be engaged on a continuous basis. The job of engaging the customers cannot be totally delegated to the intermediaries. New age customers want interactions directly with the operators. Since customers are many in numbers, it is not humanly possible to engage them through employees and agents only.

The takaful operators all over the world are making little use of the advanced digital technology. They are using technology more as a disruption tool. They have understood that information technology has the potential to change the way insurance/takaful business has so far been carried out. They are using more of *Fintech* and *InsurTech*, which are nothing but technological solutions of complex problems. This is because many complex problems cannot be solved by using the present level of information technology. Digitalization is now playing significant role in developing the economy of a country (4).

Role of Information and Communication Technology (ICT)

We cannot ignore the role **"Information and Communication Technology"** plays in the continued success of business and providing excellent service to customers. While today's focus on customer management is being driven by real business needs and market demands, in most cases it is actually being enabled by information and communication technology. The most successful takaful companies of today are those who make full use of IT's potentials in customer management and other areas.

Information and communication technology has now become an integral part of business processes. Therefore, takaful operators need to change their perceptions and understand how IT fits into the takaful business and in particular implements customer-focused data. This will have a major effect on the establishment and continued success of customer management strategies. We need to realize how taking a holistic view, that is, integrating *ICT* within the business more effectively can bring major commercial rewards. We need to understand how ICT can drive up the quality of customer services and enhance contribution of digital economy to GDP.

(4) *Malaysia has set 20% target of digital economy contribution to its gross domestic product.*

Historically, senior executives and the ICT department tended to work in isolation. Senior managers of many organizations even today view ICT as a necessary evil and an element of increasing overhead expense. Senior executives of takaful operators are used to some extent to focus on business issues such as cost control, market share, business growth and profits. We need to realize now that *IT* can drive the business forward and improve our overall profitability. In order to get full benefits of an effective ICT system, TOs need to undertake the following tasks:

(a) Data warehouse to provide centralized repositories of data structured in ways that make sense for business development.
(b) Analyze all available data/particularly customer-related data to enhance customer satisfaction and customer management strategies.
(c) Call center operations be brought together with communication and IT in frontline dealings with customer covering everything, that is, dealing with complaints, providing customer support services and so on.
(d) Use data for marketing activities and analyzing customer behavior.
(e) Implementation process of ICT solutions should be expedited.

In fact, ICT and the business are now so closely linked that its successful deployment is dependent on a sound understanding of the business processes. A customer management strategy can provide the impetus necessary to explore the current relationship between ICT and key business drivers. The gap between the two needs to be bridged if we choose to take a holistic view of ICT and our business.

The ultimate goal ought to be to develop a homogenous infrastructure that unites both ICT and business process of Takaful operators. While reshaping our ICT infrastructure, it is important to focus on the needs of the business first, and explore to achieve in areas of customer management. We need to define and formulate an appropriate business strategy and then adapt our ICT infrastructure around this. We should not think big and start small. ICT systems should support customer management works in a planned and incremental way. We need to monitor at each stage and develop a customer-focused ICT infrastructure in a well-managed and cost-effective way (5).

ICT can perform a variety of roles associated with customer service in a "tactical" way. In implementing ICT, it is vital to consider the core administration systems. To acquire or build a system that is more appropriate for takaful, TOs have to consider a number of options:

(a) Is it to be developed 100% in-house?
(b) Are they going to buy a package application?
(c) Can they use a third-party administration service?

(5) *"Technology for the sake of technology does not matter, if it does not impact the customer" Fintech, May 2019.* (Issue 28)

To answer these questions, TOs should be clear about both requirements and the extent to which the options under consideration meet those requirements. They need to assess, where we are and where we need to go? For an accurate assessment, TOs need to ask themselves the following facts and realities:

(a) Can the existing system handle all the features of the products without manual intervention?
(b) Does the present system provide their people with all the information and facilities they need to deal efficiently with their customers?
(c) Can the present system be relied upon to provide online service?
(d) Are they open to customers for 24 hours and 7 days a week?
(e) Can the system process the expected volume of policies within a time frame?
(f) How much effort is required to integrate new products they develop in the future into the system?
(g) How much time and effort will it take to implement the IT solutions and system?
(h) How much help, in terms of process design and management information, can the system give in managing the operation?
(i) What is the cost of implementing and running this service or package?
(j) Whether sales people are equipped with laptops or smartphones, and to what extent they use it during field visit?
(k) Whether a modem to a laptop computer gives almost instant access from any location?

Information and communication technology underpins a variety of tasks and, as such, is a great enabler of customer service. It can change the ways they do business and provide services to the customers. In order to derive maximum benefits from IT department, TOs must carefully consider issues such as system functionality; volume of transactions; data to be collected, stored and analyzed; future product development; time for practical implementations; business relationship with customers and sales people; and, of course, cost involvement. The key issue is the management culture and attitude.

If takaful operators want to be a leader in business and customer service, they should have a clear view on data required to meet customers' needs and to manage the process. Takaful operator's objective should be to maximize value for the customers at reasonable cost. The technologies available for customer management are moving rapidly. However, the old methods are not dying. In fact, technologies often supplement and enhance existing technologies. It is necessary to recognize that the aim of customer management is to meet the needs of present and future customers. Therefore, call centers should be upgraded with new technology as well as with new staff having experience in customer management.

Application of Fintech and InsurTech

Fintech usually refers to technology start-ups that are already disrupting sectors like mobile payments, money transfers and asset management. Takaful industry has been slow in discovering the power of *Fintech*, but some developed countries like the UK, Germany, France and the USA have started investing in *Fintech* quite generously. The technology which is used by the insurance industry of those markets is also known as InsurTech. In the days of rapidly changing customer behavior and financial regulations, Fintech has much to offer to the insurance and takaful industries of emerging economies. Fintech is also making it possible for people all over to access financial services to mass people far away from the service provider (6).

There is no industry-accepted definition of InsurTech. InsurTech refers to deploy specific tech-led innovation in activities within the insurance value chain and leverage different forms of funding. InsurTech is a subset of Fintech. New high-tech start-ups (InsurTech) are increasingly targeting insurance, especially personal lines distribution. In response, operators have two options of setting up in-house innovation section or partnering with large tech firms and investing in InsurTech start-ups. While some failures are inevitable, InsurTech can enable takaful operators to upgrade digital capabilities.

Some of the technologies used by InsurTech start-ups are not especially new. But the carbonation of technical progress—which facilitate *Big Data* and smart analytics—and the widespread use of digital, internet-enabled devices are allowing start-ups to influence the way in which it is designed, priced and sold, as well as how they engage with customers (7).

Takaful operators can use technology to provide digitally enabled services that involve more frequent interaction with customer contact. The provision of these value added service facilitates collection of data that can be used to improve underwriting and pricing decisions. The network effects associated with new technology have grown significantly over recent years, driven by better infrastructure, smartphones, sensors and so on. Recent surveys suggest that insurers are most worried about big tech companies disrupting the insurance industry. In principle, these firms have the financial strength, technological expertise and customer-centric focus to offer a serious competitive challenge to small insurers and takaful operators.

New technology is bringing about change in the takaful industry, most notably by enabling enhanced data capture and analytics capabilities. *Big Data*, *Artificial Intelligence (AI)/Cognitive Computing*, Telematics and the *Internet of Things (IoT)* are having impact all along on the insurance value chain. Digitalization is helping in the design and pricing of new and existing insurance products. The growing proliferation of new data about insureds, collected via sensors and smart devices, permits more granular underwriting of individual risk.

(6) *Andy Kearns "Five ways Fintech is helping the unbanked and under banked" Fintech, May 2018.* (Issue 16)
(7) *Technology is to improve financial activities. It is a new category of digital motion that the takaful operators will have to adopt.*

Distribution channels should respond to changes in consumer preferences. Price comparison websites, which have been used in neighboring countries for quite some time, are providing consumers with more information on products and costs. They often sell a product directly through online service with no agent or broker involvement (8).

InsurTech is all about knowing each customer more intimately and then offering those personalized insurance products and services. InsurTech enables the insurers in developing direct contact with customers, often with the help of Artificial Intelligence (AI), *Fintech*, vis-à-vis InsurTech manifesting itself in cutting-edge technologies like *Internet of Things (IoT)*, business analytics and telematics. It is enabling insurers to engage with customers on a regular basis and improve customer experience manifold. There is little dearth of tech talent in our country. Despite this, some tech start-ups are already catering to the needs of financial sector. They have not come to be of much use to the insurance industry because the insurers here have already established different kinds of business models through agents and so-called employer of agents.

Use of advance digital technology will not reduce the importance of agents, brokers and Bancassurance partners. It will help them in selling the right products and giving the right kind of services. But sales people will have to learn new skills to stay relevant in the industry. They need to be extremely knowledgeable in the field. It is true that technology alone cannot bring great business or improve persistency ratio. However, the employees will have to be customer sensitive and so also be able to give top quality advice to their customers.

High level of information technology should act as enablers of the company. Operators will have to develop the mindset to use analytic and Artificial Intelligence (AI) more and more in procuring business, delivering of desirable services and retention of customers. Tomorrow's leaders of insurance will be those who are willing today to change the present model of product development, distribution, customer engagement and skill development. In this respect experience of Malaysia, Singapore and even India will help to formulate prudent strategy and future action plan (9).

Blockchain and Artificial Intelligence

Blockchain technology first used in Bitcoin is a new type of distributed consensus system that enables transactions to be quickly validated and securely maintained through cryptography, computational power and network users, removing the need for a trusted centralized authority. The blockchain provides an immutable record and audit trail of transactions and agreements that are replicated on computers around the world, thereby eliminating a single point of failure. Thus blockchain facilitates building a trust and will bring insurance to mass people. A 2015 study by the World Economic Forum found that 58% of surveyed executives and experts from the information and communication technology sector believe that 10% of global GDP will be stored on blockchain technology by the mid-2020.

(8) *K. M. Mortuza Ali- "How to Proceed with E-insurance" Fintech- March 2019.* (Issue 26)
(9) *K. M. Mortuza Ali- "E-Insurance and its role in Business Expansion" Fintech- February 2019.* (Issue 25)

Insurance industry observers believe that the innovative distributed ledger could introduce a variety of improvements and efficiencies to the takaful landscape, including establishing a level of accountability and transparency that hitherto was impossible mitigating risk and fraud, streamlining back-office operations, introducing new products, lowering costs, and providing easier and improved data access to parties.

We are well aware that the technology revolution is a threat as well as an opportunity for the traditional insurance/Takaful industry. Emerging digitization and innovation are starting points to transforming to takaful industry as the new era of transformation needs to focus to measure, control, and price risk, engage with customers, optimize company's efficiency and has to swiftly penetrate to the insurable population to spread insurance and takaful.

We should leverage the upcoming technology and convert negatives like "**life insurance is sold not bought**" into a positive like "**Life Insurance has to be bought and bought again**". Yes, this is possible because the entire insurable population is likely to be tech savvy population in future and only with advent of modern technology we can win hearts of customers. We shall have to attract this technology savvy population to have an amazing and world class electronic insurance (E-insurance) experience. *Artificial Intelligence, Blockchain, Machine Learning* and *Big Data* are becoming most beneficial to Fintech solutions (10).

Advances in technology are bringing about change in the traditional value chain and reconfiguring the competitive landscape. After a slow start, business organizations are responding to the implications of the digital transformation. Some are re-positioning their business models, by investing in tech-led start-ups, especially those focused on distribution. Unfortunately, we have not been pioneers in technology adoption. However, there are signs that the insurance sector is gearing up now. Successful insurers will be those that leverage new technology to acquire new customers, improve underwriting and increase efficiency. Such innovation is crucial in responding to current and future competitive threats and achieve business excellence (11).

It is necessary to realize that we do not have enough time to adjust to the changing risk environment shifts in customer attitudes and accelerating advances in technology. When we utilize new technology more fully and intelligently, (the latest information and communication technology), it presents an opportunity to reinforce its relevance to its clients. We, therefore, should continue to embrace both incremental and sometimes more radical innovations. This is because advances in technology are impacting all points along the value chain of life insurers and takaful operators and re-shaping the competitive landscape.

New generation consumers are likely to be more self-directed in their insurance decisions and want to interact through various channels when buying insurance.

(10) *Mohammad Asif, "Fintech Dynamism: From disruption to restoration" Fintech, December 2018.* (Issue 23)
(11) *Imran Farhad, "Fintech Inclusion and coverage of Fintech" Fintech, February 2019.* (Issue 25)

On the other hand, several surveys indicate that consumers often continue to value the personal interaction and expert advice of agents and brokers, especially when it comes to complex insurance of life and health risks. In many countries like Bangladesh, traditional intermediaries still represent the dominant channel through which insurance policies are sold. In these areas, technology is being applied to improve the efficiency and effectiveness of agents and brokers (12).

Policy servicing and claims management is also becoming more efficient, as machine learning and pattern recognition are used to analyze handwritten and unstructured documents to expedite and detect false claims. Insurers are also experimenting with blockchain technology (digital distributed ledgers) which is cryptographically secure to improve the efficiency of processes within and among existing departments, such as in claims management and retakaful contracts. Here, blockchains offer benefits of speedier connectivity between counterparties and potential for reduced fraud and loss expenses. All of which will help to lower overall costs.

While blockchain might not be the end-all-be-all to problems faced by takaful operators, it does provide foundational technology that promotes trust, transparency and stability. Blockchain is in the early stages of adoption, but there are already a handful of ways that insurers are leveraging the technology to mitigate the challenges.

(a) Blockchain can potentially eliminate suspicious and duplicate transactions by logging each transaction. Through its decentralized digital repository, it can verify the authenticity of customers, policies and transactions by providing historical records. This makes it more difficult for hackers to corrupt and steal files.
(b) Blockchain can properly manage, share and monetize large amounts of data. The benefit is that the technology can store static records

and/or data without central coordination and the data can be viewed by all parties. Streamlined data can also make risk assessment timelier and more accurate.

(c) Blockchain can handle the increase in third-party transactions and claims made through personal digital devices. Blockchain helps reduce administrative costs through automated verification of claims/payments data from third parties.

It is nice to see insurance companies and takaful operators are starting to embrace the benefits of blockchain. Organizations such as Swiss Re, Allianz, Munich Re and Zurich have launched the Blockchain Insurance Industry Initiative, which aims to explore the potential of distributed ledger technologies to better serve clients through faster, more convenient and secure services.

A report of Earnest Young (EY) "Blockchain in insurance: applications and a path to adoption" observes that "the insurance industry must make investments now to be in a position to take advantage of efficiencies and opportunities blockchain technology can deliver long term benefits". The insurance industry will still have obstacles to overcome, but blockchain's ability to provide complete accountability, transparency and superior security will help insurers to save time and money, as well as improve customer satisfaction. As higher levels of trust are established between the insurer and the insured, stronger relationships will be built as well.

(12) *Faisal Mahmud, "Why Insurance Sector in Bangladesh should opt for intelligent software?" Fintech, July 2017.* (Issue 6)

Hurdles to Be Faced

Technology has become inseparable from human livelihood and has occupied an undisputable and unstoppable space in replacing human intelligence. In the competitive environment, one who uses efficient technology to optimum level can take up the driving seat. Change is accelerating and upcoming new technology is challenging and overriding existing technology and making it redundant. This so-called new technology is wiped away with a better one just as a passing cloud. This is an ongoing phenomenon, and what we perceived as *big* and as an innovation yesterday has become *small* and obsolete today due to the advent of better technology of tomorrow.

The general hurdles before the takaful operators in leveraging new technology are:

(a) High operational cost.
(b) Legacy issues with regard to old and complex data.
(c) Lack of data security system.
(d) Operation of multiple systems and complicated spreadsheets.
(e) Possibility of cybercrime/cyber fraud and third-party attack.
(f) Changing phase of technological transformation is fast and we are not clear where to start and where to stop.
(g) While transforming technology, we need to ensure existing service is not hampered. There is no stop of service changes and parallel service to existing customers is a challenge.
(h) Low penetration and slow phase of business growth keeps them thinking before scaling up investment in technology.
(i) Lack of continuous learning and training among employees and stakeholders.
(j) Lack of talents and lack of continuity.

Under the circumstances, takaful operators need to shift focus on investing in technology very rationally. Consolidation of efforts and collaboration among peers and stakeholders is required to meet this objective. Flexibility and personalization in customer experience interface between operator and customers will continue with more seamless engagement encompassing desktops, smartphones, tablets and wearables. This will imply a simpler user facility. TOs will have to shift towards actively managing risk as well as carrying it through *Big Data* and the increasing prevalence of connected sensors.

Through internet of things (IOT), customers and takaful operators will be able to constantly share insights with each other simultaneously. Technology has to reach a stage when a member is added by birth, in a family; a quote for new insurance should reach the family and at the same time when death is registered, immediately claim amount should reach the claimant's bank account. This is a dream today but ought to be real in the near future. The single most fundamental impact of Fintech in insurance has been the shift to customer by using modern technology. Among the emerging technological tools, two prominent technologies that will be a challenge to takaful operators are blockchain technology and Artificial Intelligence.

Opportunities of New Technology in Takaful Sector

It is generally apprehended that the insurance/takaful industry is vulnerable to large-scale disruption caused by technology trends. It is, therefore, necessary to examine how transformational and disruptive the tech-led innovation will be for takaful sector in general and in particular. It is felt that recent changes in technology are likely to prove persistent and that they can be an enabler rather than a major competitive threat to insurance companies and takaful at least in the near term. The world is flat now. There is no geographical business. If there is any new technology anywhere in the world, it will eventually come to any country within few weeks (13).

Ultimately there are reasons to be hopeful that InsurTech/Fintech will prove to be a positive development for the insurance sector. Our investments in InsurTech will help to stimulate innovation, identify priorities and complement digital insurance strategies. Bringing in experience and ideas, other companies/industries can also be a valuable tool to aid the cultural transformation of both employees and agents/brokers. Indian and Iranian experience in e-insurance can be of much help to go ahead.

The regulatory authority can play an important role in shaping the adoption of new technology and integration of InsurTech into the landscape. In monetizing the potential of technology, insurance/takaful sector could face regulatory challenges on data protection and privacy, providing incorrect advice and records retention. It is important that one should continue to innovate, embrace new ideas and remain flexible in order to respond as technology advance and customer risk preferences and profiles shift. Successful companies are likely to benefit from a balanced innovation portfolio. Therefore, the takaful sector needs to go forward with moderate application of InsurTech which is now a buzzword in the insurance world.

Insurance sector, vis-à-vis takaful sector, is still at a nascent stage and has only begun its attempt at grasping technology. We have recently realized the benefits of marrying technology with takaful. There is a whole lot of innovation happening in different industries that are yet to be introduced in takaful. Some major technological innovations will decide, the degree of success or failure of takaful operators in future. These are the internet, blockchain, big data and advanced analytics.

(13) *Shaquib Ahmed, "How far is the Bridge?" Fintech, October 2018.* (Issue 21)

In our current day, we are able to gather more and more data without understanding how to make use of it. Big Data refers to huge data sets that are so large and complex that traditional data processing tools are inadequate to make sense of them. Though most organizations in the insurance and takaful sector do not have the capabilities (yet) to make use of big data, they are sitting on top of a casket of gold that they do not yet have a key to open. Big Data is the treasure of knowledge that we can bank upon to arrive at suitable products, risk models and customer segments, among numerous other attributes.

To predict the direction of the business and make sense of it, analyzing data is of utmost importance. It can transform how insurers do business. Actuarial science has been at the forefront of predicting risk in the insurance industry, and though they continue to be drivers of profit for the insurer, advanced analytics in insurance delve far beyond the boundaries of traditional risk prediction and actuarial science. If we invest in advanced analytics today, we will be revolutionizing and leading in the insurance industry future.

Consumers generally obtain information about insurance policies through advertisements, sales people, family, friends, neighbors and acquaintances. They tend to perceive very little difference among brands of takaful solutions available in the market. However, many buyers have access to a more trusted experiential source of information. Here, buyers share their brand experience, which is then accessible to a larger audience.

In the traditional market, customers are routed to agents on the basis of their perceived business value. Today, online social networks provide a larger platform to socialize and exchange information and opinions. This renders the traditional method of market segmentation almost meaningless. Social analytics integrate, analyze and enable enterprises to act on intelligence that is gathered from online conversations occurring across professional and consumer-generated media sites.

This helps and enables individuals and enterprises to attribute online conversations to specific parts of their business. Enterprises can extract important insights, sentiments, hidden patterns, trends and unknown correlations from customer-centric conversations and proactively act upon them to drive business outcomes. Consumers are increasingly using social channels. In this regard modern technology is playing a key role in servicing customers in the insurance business. Consumers expect service when and where they want it and through the channels they prefer. Sharing informative content on social media will help to better educate consumers in policy retention also.

Policy guidelines for social media need to be formulated. The social strategy must be closely aligned with the overall business objectives. If we have the right strategy, then with the right choice of partners, we can redesign our communication system and build stronger relationships with our customers to sustain in the long run.

Social Analytics and *Big Data* thus can deliver a concoction of benefits in the long run by generating insights to business intelligence. This paves the way for expansion of the takaful business. Social media considerations should play a significant role in overall business strategy. Takaful operators need to be a key part of the decisions that guide tactical directions and operations. Firstly, goals ought to be set and guidelines for social media should be established. Marketing and sales people need to be motivated to develop a plan as to how social media can work for takaful operators. The strategic plan should be guided by a comprehensive set of capabilities to analyze and predict social media activity. *Research and Development* department should be entrusted with this important role to play efficiently.

Fintech is a new category of digital platform that the takaful operators will have to adopt. Takaful needs strict regulation. Apart from internal audit and external audit, it needs Sharia audit. As the Fintech industry grows worldwide, it is felt that we need regulations for financial sector including takaful sector for internal control, audit disclosers and compliences.

The best solution for ensuring efficient regulations is to enable tech-based automated management and record-keeping. This has led to the need for appropriate technology for regulators, which will facilitate regulatory compliances. The term *RegTech* has been getting a lot of attention recently. Appropriate development of *RegTech* can ease *Fintech Operations* and save a lot of money.

RegTech is the answer for regulators in interpreting and complying with voluminous regulations, and also help the takaful operators save times and money. Now *RegTech* has the promise of making that process more efficient and cost-effective. RegTech solutions will enable the takaful operators to have smooth compliance while reporting regulators, sharia auditors and the sharia supervision council/board. Reports will be more transparent and proactive to improve governance and achieve business excellence. RegTech solutions will also help to protect financial health of takaful companies and prevent disruptions of the market agility and integrity (14).

RegTech solutions will work best in identifying risk areas and its tools for management. These include legislation and gap analysis, health checks, management information, transaction reporting, regulatory sharia reporting activity monitoring and training. Takaful companies will have better customer satisfaction and be more confident in the process of continuous growth. This will also help to educate desk employee, sales force and the participants as well.

(14) *Abdullah Al Mamun, "RegTech the Big New Frontier" Fintech-September 2019.* (Issue 32)

References

Douglas, R. (2018, December). *Reinvesting the Institution of Insurance in a Networked World*. AOA Seminar, Hongkong.

From Policyholders to Valued Customers. (1998). Swiss Re Life and Health.

Fulfilling the Promise of Microinsurance. (2013–2015). ICMIF Development Strategy Paper 2013–2015.

Insurance in the Emerging Markets: Overview and Prospects of Islamic Insurance. (2008). *Sigma, 5*.

Insurance in the Information Era. (2017). *The Journal of Insurance Institute of India, V*(1), July–September.

Life Insurance: Focusing on the Consumer. (2013). *Sigma, 6*.

Mobile Insurance Distribution Spreading Globally. (2015). *Swiss Re*, May.

Rahman, M., & Sarker, S. (2019). Digital Financial Ecosystem to Create Unprecedented Financial Inclusion. *Fintech*, April (Issue 27).

Ramli, M. (2016). *Crowd Takaful the New Fintech Initiative*. World Takaful Report-2016, Finance Forward.

The Takaful Industry: Adapting the Fundamental Change. (2017). The International Takaful Summit-2017.

PART IV

Islamic FinTech: Its Challenges and the Professional Way Forward

CHAPTER 22

The Challenges of Cryptocurrencies and the Shariah Paradigm

Hurriyah El Islamy

Abstract Overreliance on centralized system, that is, the ecosystem built on trust and thus there ought to be a trusted party for the mechanism to work, was seen as the crux that prevented the existence of an effective and true electronic payment system, that is, one that's truly non-reversible. Bitcoin was introduced as an answer to that (Nakamoto, Bitcoin: A Peer-to-Peer Electronic Cash System. *bitcoin.org*, 2008). It gave rise not only to a whole new system of electronic payment akin to the more original mode of trading, it also gave birth to the new world of cryptography. What's interesting is that despite its wider global acceptance, such initial introduction of cryptocurrency raised many issues more than the issues its introduction sought to resolve. The questions raised and issues arise not only from the commercial but also regulatory point of view. As Islamic finance is growing and due to the borderless and nationless nature of cryptocurrencies, it becomes necessary that we also examine it from Shariah view point. Hence, in this chapter, after the general discussion of cryptocurrency and its characteristics, we take for case study the two celebrated cryptocurrencies before we will see how Shariah perceives

H. El Islamy (✉)
Badan Pengelola Keuangan Haji, Jakarta, Indonesia

M. M. Billah (ed.), *Islamic FinTech*,
https://doi.org/10.1007/978-3-030-45827-0_22

cryptocurrencies and how cryptocurrencies are being regulated. Thereafter, we highlight issues and challenges, and we put forward our recommendations and the way forward for the issues and challenges surrounding the cryptocurrencies.

Keywords Cryptocurrency • Blockchain • Challenges • Regulations • Shariah

Introduction to Cryptocurrency

Literally, cryptocurrency is a term made of two words, that is, crypto and currency. The word crypto is a short form of cryptography that connotes the IT system used as medium for transacting in the virtual world and known for its ability to generate asset and to ensure security of such asset trading. Literally, however, it is the Latinized form of Greek *kryptos* that means hidden or concealed as in a thing that kept secret. As for currency, it refers to certain units generally acceptable as mode of exchange, the value of which is usually preset by the regulator in a given jurisdiction which can be pegged or otherwise to the like of it from other jurisdiction or a basket of select currencies and so on.

As for cryptocurrency, the term will usually give inference to the advance medium of exchange, notably done over the Internet or the virtual world, which supposed to have the characters of currency albeit its existence on the virtual world exclusively. Such understanding has widened the perception of what's included as cryptocurrency. Hence, the inclusion of Libra that despite the use of cryptography technology is not by itself an asset and thus is lacking the characteristic of a 'commodity' which was deemed to be one of the essential characteristics of cryptocurrencies. We will examine that deeper at the later part of this chapter. For the purpose of the discussion in this chapter, let's agree on the simple understanding of cryptocurrency (Rosic, 2018) being "an internet-based medium of exchange which uses cryptographical functions to conduct financial transactions."[1]

[1] We adopted this more general definition to facilitate the points of discussion in the chapter and also to move away from product inspired definition such as "digital asset that is

Cryptocurrency: The Characteristics

Careful analysis of cryptocurrencies reveals the three essentials that qualify an object as cryptocurrency. They are as follows:

(a) It is an asset.
(b) It is medium of exchange
(c) It uses cryptography technology such as blockchain technology.

It is interesting to note that such characteristics of cryptocurrencies bring its notion closer to the concept of 'currency' in Shariah as opposed to the conventional and prevailing market practice with respect to currency. Dirham and dinar being the currency used during the period of the Prophethood and khilaafaat were made of gold and silver, respectively. They were minted to represent the value of the respective precious metal. They were both assets/commodities as well as media of exchange. Most cryptocurrencies, Bitcoin included, squarely fall within the Islamic notion of currency being commodities as well as the media of exchange. And as with the case of most cryptocurrencies including, most notably, Bitcoin, the assets have intrinsic value and have limitation of availability. By intrinsic value means each of the Dinar and Dirham and the Bitcoin are valued based on its value as commodity, not based on certain value or figure dictated by centralized authority which does not represent the true value of such medium of exchange as an asset. By limitation of availability means the supply of each gold and silver as well as Bitcoin has limitation and is not endless.

One celebrated feature of Bitcoin is the decentralized nature of the payment system, the very reason it was invented and introduced in the first place. This feature, however, has been somehow downplayed. It is arguable that to allow this as the determining or crucial part that differentiates cryptocurrencies from others would exclude any claim of any asset backed, as opposed to asset generating, system of electronic payment for being part a cryptocurrency. That will, for example, disqualify Libra and all other electronic payment systems which have an operation backed by non(virtual) asset or fiat money, a system that government of a country or regulator

constructed to function as a medium of exchange, premised on the technology of cryptography, to secure the transactional flow, as well as to control the creation of additional units of the currency" (Chohan, 2017).

most likely adopt if they will introduce 'cryptocurrency' of their own. In brevity, it is highly difficult, if not impossible, not to include any role of a 'trusted' party as a component of electronic payment system that is backed by fiat money. That's the natural consequence of deployment of non-asset and/or non-commodity as the backbone of the system as the absence of intrinsic value necessitates the presence of a 'party' to enable extrinsic value to be conferred.

The similarities and the differences between Bitcoin and Libra are further discussed in the later part of this chapter. Choosing Bitcoin as a case study for this chapter is a no-brainer. As for Libra, its contrast to Bitcoin is one of the reasons for its selection as case study as that helps to highlight several points of discussions this chapter seek to demonstrate. Furthermore, Libra has the potential to be a game changer in the whole sphere and may even shake the traditional banking and payment system outside the virtual world, hence, too dominant an impact to be ignored.[2]

Cryptocurrency: Case Study

Bitcoin and Libra

Generally, people regard Bitcoin as digital money, coin that has cash value but available only in virtual world. It was described as the world's best performing currency as the value of one Bitcoin has increased tremendously since it was released in 2009 to its all-time high of $19,783.06 on 17 December 2017 (Morris, 2017). The price started to plunge in February 2018. On 15 November 2018 Bitcoin's market capitalization fell below the$100 billion mark and its price stood at $5564.70 (Huang, 2018). On 12 October 2019 the value stood at 8318.65 at 02.00 GMT (Coindesk, 2019). As a coin has such high value, it is not uncommon for people to transact in fraction of the coin, usually referred to as millibitcoin (mBTC), microbitcoin (μBTC, sometimes referred to as a *bit*) and satoshi.

On the other hand, until recently Libra was seen as a more promising digital currency. To be backed on Facebook gigantic social network, "the effort, should it succeed, threatens to upend the traditional, lucrative plumbing of e-commerce and would likely be the most mainstream application yet of cryptocurrency" (Andriotis, Hoffman, Rudegeair, &

[2] At least that was the case until its development and progress were halt by the US government indefinitely and Facebook's major partners exited from the project.

Horwitz, 2019). Officially announced on 18 June 2019, the ambitious plan to create an alternative financial system that relies on a cryptocurrency called Libra was expected "to be the most far-reaching attempt by a mainstream company to jump into the world of cryptocurrencies" (Isaac & Popper, 2019). Facebook also introduced Calibra. It's a digital wallet planned for Libra. Through Calibra, Facebook planned to provide financial services that would enable people to access and participate in the Libra network. It was announced that Facebook planned to launch Calibra in 2020, that it would get the support from Mastercard, Visa, Paypal, eBay, Uber, Lift, Spotify and some others, and it would be available in Messenger, Whatsapp and as a standalone application (ALvares, 2019). It was not, however, an easy sailing for Facebook. Since the announcement, it has "ruffled feathers and sparked fears among governments all over the globe" (Telford, 2019) until finally the effort came to a complete halt when the House of Financial Services Committee and other congressional leaders sent a letter to Facebook Founder and Chief Executive asking Facebook, its Chief Operating Officer and the Chief Executive Officer of Calibra to agree to a moratorium on any movement forward on Libra and Calibra reasoning that since "Facebook is already in the hands of over quarter of the world's population, it is imperative that Facebook and its partners immediately cease implementation plans until regulators and Congress have an opportunity to examine these issues [exposure to massive scale of the risks and the lack of clear regulatory protections which could pose systemic risks that endanger U.S. and global financial stability] and take action."[3]

Be that as it may, it is not the political and regulatory issues surrounding Libra that are of interest for the discussion in this chapter. It is selected for the case study as it has similarities and salient contrast to Bitcoin that made the two the best illustrations as to how the regulations and Shariah should afford different approach and treatment to the two.

The Similarities Between Bitcoin and Libra

Both Bitcoin and Libra are referred as cryptocurrency even though that may not necessarily be accurate. Such reference is because both currencies are built on cryptography technology, namely, the blockchain. Both

[3] The full text of the letter available on the website of the US House Committee on Financial Services.

Bitcoin and Libra are (and/or intended to be) medium of exchange. Another similarity between the two is that Bitcoin and Libra blockchain are pseudonymous and allow users to hold one or more addresses that are not linked to their real-world identity (Nakamoto, 2008). And that's about it; the two currencies do not share anything else in common.

The Differences Between Bitcoin and Libra

When we discussed the three characteristics of cryptocurrencies, Bitcoin has all these three essentials. Libra, on the contrary, despite being built on cryptography technology, on blockchain, is more akin to e-cash or digital cash.[4] Here are how Libra differs from Bitcoin and other commodity/asset kinds of cryptocurrencies:

First, it is not per se an asset. Section 2 of Libra Whitepaper states that the reserve is the asset and it requires to be backed by a reserve to give it an "intrinsic" value. That's the very same character fiat money has. Without any reserve, Libra unit has zero value, and hence, it is unlikely that it could be utilized for trading purposes. Bitcoin, on the other hand, is asset. Obviously one cannot turn Bitcoin into building materials or jewellery, but otherwise it is being accepted for trade and as a means of exchange in the manner commodity is albeit it is limited in the virtual realm. As with other commodities, its price increases when the demand does and vice versa.

Second, unlike commodity, Libra units are endless. The unit could be issued when certain parameters are met or based on the discretion of the operator. There will be no issue of scarcity nor will there be any potential of diminishing or limitation of supply. Commodity, on the other hand, is usually grown or mined. Bitcoins, like most metals, are mined. It's a mistake to think that Bitcoin's supply is endless. The protocol for Bitcoin halves the reward for adding the block every 210,000 blocks. That means, once the limit of 21 million Bitcoins reached, there will be no more Bitcoin to mine and record keeping will only be rewarded by transaction fees.

Third, Libra, like fiat money, does not have intrinsic value. Like fiat money which paper or coin represents the value stated on the cash, not the value of the paper or coin itself, the value of Libra unit is based on fiat money used as the underlying. Bitcoin, however, has intrinsic value. Each

[4] For discussion on e-cash from legal and Shariah view point, see El Islamy, 2002.

part of the coin is valued for the fraction it represents just like people do gold and silver.

Fourth, even though Facebook claims that its blockchain technology is decentralized, the fact that Libra unit does not have intrinsic value makes it mandatory that certain mechanism has to be put in place to set the value of the unit something akin to that for fiat money. Bitcoin, on the contrary, decentralized in its true sense. Not only that it was set to be such, it is also because as with any other commodity of similar nature used or could be utilized as medium of exchange, it does not need an authority or a trusted party to conferred its value: it already has one, intrinsically.

Those differences should attract different regulatory treatments and so would the Shariah perception of them. Let us first see how Shariah views them before we see how the regulators from around the globe respond to cryptocurrencies.

Cryptocurrency: Shariah Views

Shariah has given clear guideline of what is lawful and unlawful based on the teachings of the Qur'ān and the Sunnah. It is not at human's pleasure to hold something halal as haram and vice versa (Al Quran 7: 32–33). Being the way of life sanctioned by Allah the One and Only God, Shariah governs all aspects of humans' life including the spiritual and the day-to-day life. However, it differentiates the fundamental approach to the two: with respect to spiritual aspects of life, the believers are not obliged to undertake any obligations unless ordained by Shariah, whereas the fundamental principle that governs other aspects of life is permissible and the believers have the freedom to transact unless there is express prohibition in the Shariah that puts some limitations and/or prohibitions in any particular matter.

There are very limited items which are prohibited by Shariah due to its substance and the prohibition could be extended by way of analogy. Cryptocurrencies are not prohibited items by substance or by way of analogy; thus, they are permissible (*halal*). Can a ruling on a substance which originally is permissible (*halal*) become prohibited (*haram*)? Yes, and that could be due to several factors such as due to the transgression of rules in the manner and/or dilution with prohibited substance that made it impossible to separate the two. With respect to cryptocurrencies, while it is *halal* by substance, can the haram ruling applies due to other reasons or external factor? The answer is yes but that would make prohibited transaction void without affecting the permissibility nature of cryptocurrencies, for example, if there is element of *riba*, *gharar* or *maysir* in a transaction where a cryptocurrency is used as part of transaction; hence even though the cryptocurrency is halal, the transaction is haram. The permissibility ruling of cryptocurrencies does not change albeit the ruling of the overall transaction.

The basic principle of Islamic contract law is that everything is presumed to be lawful, unless it is definitely prohibited. Hence, as with other new innovations, Bitcoin and Libra are to be presumed halal and remain so unless and until it is proven that they or any components that constitute them are prohibited by or contravenes Shariah injunctions. That especially so because the usage of Bitcoin or Libra in transactions is a matter of transactional nature (*muamalah*) and there is no revelation in a form of Qur'anic verses or hadith or other sources of Shariah that impose an injunction prohibiting it as such.

Now that we have determined the original ruling of cryptocurrencies, we need to ascertain the parameters that will apply in any given transactions using the cryptography. Shariah sets different set of treatments when one is dealing in commercial transaction in a form of trading of commodities and when the gist of the transaction is to trade or transact in currencies or both.

Let's take the following four scenarios as the illustrations for the foregoing discussion:

(a) A trades his sheep for goat from B.
(b) A trades his gold for goat from B.
(c) A trades his class 1 gold for class 2 gold from B.
(d) A trades his gold for silver from B.

To ensure the clarity of understanding the illustrations, it is important to note that goats and sheep are regarded as commodities while golds and silvers, despite being commodities, are also used and recognized as media of exchange.

When a person trades a commodity for another commodity, such as the scenario given in the first illustration above, the most important aspect for such transaction to be valid is the consent of the parties (Al Quran 4: 29). Each of the parties has the freedom and the right to deal in such transaction in any manner both parties agreed, and it is valid even if there is delay in delivering one or both of the commodities to each other and it remains valid even if there is disparity of pricing in the two. This illustration applies if, and only if, Bitcoin and other asset-regarded kinds of cryptocurrencies are treated as commodities,[5] and despite its use in trade and/or for trading purposes, they do not represent currency and/or media of exchange.

The same concept and ruling are applicable when the exchange or trade involves the trading of commodity for cash or currency as given in the second illustration above. In such arrangement, each of the party has the right to determine how, when and the price of the transaction. Any delay in delivering one or both of the object of trade and fixing the price above or below the cash/currency value is allowed and will not avoid the transaction. In other words, when A trades his gold for goat from B, the transaction is valid and binds both parties even if the trade is not done on spot, or the price paid by instalments, or A is paying more than the market value of similar goat that may be sourced from the market and vice versa. This applies to Bitcoin and/or Libra when they are used as the payment mode for purchases of non-currency such as things or services. In such instance, the value of each item being exchanged, the time and mode of delivery are as per the parties agreed terms. The original ruling here is halal even if the transactions involves price disparity and/or delayed delivery as long as those are accepted and agreed by the parties.

The third illustration, however, involves exchange of two commodities treated as cash/media of exchange. When it comes to such transaction and any similar transactions where the subjects to be exchanged are, despite having the essence of being commodity, regarded as media of exchange, Shariah imposed the following restrictions: the trade has to be "yadanbi-yadin, sawaanbisawain", that is, has to be done on spot basis and for the same quantity. Both restrictions, that the trading has to be on spot basis and for the same objects are applicable when the parties will exchange the same kind of medium of exchange. Hence, in the third illustration, for such trade to be effective and binding, the two restrictions have to be fulfilled and that despite the absence of parity in pricing of the golds due to the difference in quality. It is not allowed to delay delivery of any of the

[5] It is interesting to note that it has been argued that in the USA, cryptocurrencies are commodities within the provisions of SAFT and thus subject to regulation by the CFTC (Concannon et all, 2019). The China government went extreme into stating that Bitcoin cannot be regarded as currency because it is not issued by monetary authority and does not have legal status of being compulsory used and accepted as currency. The US Commodities Futures Trading Commission has also adopted the approach describing Bitcoin as a commodity (Comply Advantage, 2019).

objects of trade, and it is also prohibited to trade the same kind of medium of exchange with a lower quantity; it has to be exactly for the same quantity irrespective of quality. Hence, it is prohibited to trade in the following:

(a) spot exchange of 1 ounce of A class gold with 1.2 ounce of B class gold even if those represent price parity;
(b) spot exchange of US$50 old notes with US$49 new notes;
(c) exchange of 1 ounce of gold for 1 ounce of gold with delay in delivery of one of the items;
(d) future exchange of 1 ounce of gold for 1 ounce of gold;
(e) exchange of US$50 for US$50 with delay in delivery of one of the items; and
(f) future exchange of US$50 for US$50.

As for the fourth illustration, the trade is valid when done on spot basis. This is as instructed in the following hadith of the Prophet PBUH:

> *Gold with gold, silver with silver, burr with burr, sya'ir with sya'ir, tamr with tamr, salt with salt must trade on equal weight and on spot. If trade is between two different kinds then you can trade as you wish provided it has to be spot.* (Narrated by Bukhari and Muslim No. 1587)

If we were to make an analogy between cryptocurrencies with conventional media of exchange, Bitcoin could be regarded as both commodity and medium of exchange, while Libra only fits for the latter. Consequently, the rulings applicable to gold and silver are applicable to Bitcoin and the likes of Bitcoin from among cryptocurrencies duly regarded as assets. Being afforded the same treatment as gold and silver means Bitcoins should be subjected to the same *ribawi* injunctions that require, among others, exchange of the same kind has to be for the same quantity (regardless of quality) and on spot basis. As for exchange with other kinds of *ribawi* commodities, quantity may differ, but it has to be done on spot basis. As for Libra, if it would be introduced in the manner its Whitepaper presents, then it will be equal to fiat money that takes the exclusive form in the virtual world, and thus, the Shariah ruling applicable to fiat money shall apply to Libra accordingly.

The question that remains is whether Bitcoin was intended to be the medium of exchange or would be regarded solely as commodity. If the latter is confirmed, then it will gain the huge potential of Shariah-compliant trade where the restrictions which are applicable with respect to *ribawi* items are not necessarily applicable. At a glance, that may not seem plausible considering Bitcoin was intended as "electronic payment system based on cryptographic proof instead of trust." If that's the case, irrespective of owner's intent, the restrictions applicable on *ribawi* items are applicable because, by way of analogy, the restrictions apply even when gold or silver are bought as jewellery with the intent to be kept as investment as opposed to its usage as the media of exchange. However, careful reading of Nakamoto's Bitcoin Whitepaper does not infer that Bitcoin is to be regarded as currency the way we understood fiat money (Nakamoto, 2008). It's a medium to affect electronic payment without the need for a trusted party. A payment system requires an object to be exchanged to affect payment. Such object could be fiat money or commodity. Hence, it is plausible that despite the main objective of Bitcoin is to serve as decentralized payment system creation, it could also have been intended to be virtual commodity (Nakamoto, 2008). Such point could be further analysed as an interesting topic for future study. As for the purpose of this chapter, it suffices to deduce that due to its very nature, Bitcoin is to be given the same treatment as gold and silver and Libra is as fiat money. It should be subjected to the same *ribawi* injunctions that require, among others, exchange of the same kind has to be for the same quantity (regardless of quality) and on spot basis. As for exchange with other kinds of *ribawi* commodity, quantity may differ but it has to be done on spot basis. Otherwise, Bitcoin is to be given the same treatment like other halal commodities, an option that is not available for Libra. It is permissible for people to transact and/or trade with it or by using it. The standard Shariah injunctions on sale and/or contracts apply. In any case, we should not use Bitcoin, Libra or any other cryptocurrencies in transactions involving fraud (*gharar*) or for speculative purposes (*maysir*) just like we should not use fiat money or gold to commit fraud or unethical transaction nor should we use it to gamble.[6]

[6]It is interesting to note that Libra Whitepaper reveals that "[t]he assets in the Libra Reserve will be held by a geographically distributed network of custodians with investment-grade credit rating to provide both security and decentralization of the assets. ... Interest on the reserve assets will be used to cover the costs of the system, ensure low transaction fees and support further growth and adoption. The rules for allocating interest on the reserve will be set in advance and will be overseen by the Libra Association. Users of Libra do not receive a return from the reserve." That could raise the issue of participation by investors whose mandate is Shariah-compliant and/or select to observe the use of its fund in a manner that

Cryptocurrency: Regulatory Approach

Cryptocurrencies are generally regarded as new kids on the block. Many talk about it, some uses it and even speculates with it, a few avoid it, and we have a large size of population in the world that do not even know what it is and it is not surprising that in developing countries or rural areas people may not even have heard of it. Despite that, many regulators from both developed and developing countries are quickly expressing their stance with respect to cryptocurrencies.

In the USA, as the government and the regulators usually leave online commercial-related activities to be regulated by the concerned industry, one may think that would also be the case with cryptocurrencies. Wrong! On the contrary, regulators jump into regulating this aspect of the previously unregulated virtual world. Some claimed the right to regulate on the argument that it is currency and therefore to be treated the way fiat money do. Some claimed the right to regulate because it is securities. Others extended their authority based on either the movement of asset or security, or with respect to prevention of money laundering. The disparate approaches taken by different agencies within the USA have led to confusion on the part of blockchain companies about the jurisdiction and regulatory regimes to which their products and services will be subject (Weinstein, Cohn, & Chelsea Parker, 2019). Some existing regulation were invoked to regulate cryptocurrency; yet, some state government chose to issue regulation to afford exemptions and the like in order to facilitate development and promotion of cryptocurrencies and/or encourage players to choose such state as the base for the new business and/or startups due to the more friendly regulatory regime. Consequently, as noted in Comply Advantage (Comply Advantage, 2019),

> [i]t's hard to find a consistent legal approach to cryptocurrencies in the United States. Laws governing exchanges vary by state, and federal authorities actually differ in their definition of the term 'cryptocurrency'. … the IRS … regards cryptocurrencies as property and has issued tax guidance accordingly. the Securities and Exchange Commission (SEC) has indicated that it considers cryptocurrencies to be securities.

does not contradict Shariah. Such deployment of reserve may also attract the view that will prohibit the system as an entirety on the basis of the obligation to prevent the accomplishment of what's prohibited by Shariah (*SaddDzara'i*).

The good news is that the Justice Department is coordinating with SEC and CFTC over future cryptocurrency regulations to ensure effective consumer protection and more streamlined regulatory oversight and there are other initiatives undertaken by the Federal Authorities to better regulate cryptocurrencies.

The UK regulator, on the other hand, had not extended its authority upon cryptocurrencies. The transfer, purchase and sale of cryptocurrencies fall outside the regulatory remit of FCA. Consequently, any such investor won't have access to the Financial Ombudsman Service or the Financial Services Compensation Scheme if something goes wrong (FCA, 2019). Slowly, but surely, the UK government looked into the aspects of cryptocurrencies. In August 2014, the UK government announced a major programme of works looking into the benefits and risks associated with digital currencies and the underlying technology, with a particular focus on the question of regulation. In November 2014, the government published a call for information to gather views and evidence on those questions. On 31 July 2019, the FCA issues its finalized policy statement on cryptocurrencies.

China, however, has an interesting approach. Acknowledging the importance to lead in the area of new technology, in June 2018, China Banking and Insurance Regulatory Commission issued a working paper, which stated that "the sovereign cryptocurrency shall be deemed as a legitimate digital currency issued by the PBOC", which "has value as a fiat currency and can be used as a medium of exchange... while the non-sovereign cryptocurrency shall not be regarded as 'currency'; it's merely a digital symbol programmed and issued by market participants with agreed protocols. It is essentially similar to a kind of commodity that can be circulated" (Gong & Yu, 2019). China does not recognize Bitcoin as a fiat currency. It is instead being treated as a kind of virtual commodity. The People's Bank of China, the primary regulatory body policing cryptocurrencies in China, has issued the Joint Notice on the risks Associated with Bitcoin in 2013 that defined the nature of Bitcoin:

Bitcoin has four major features including. (1) no centralized issuer, (2) limited issuance volume, (3) no geographical boundaries, and (40 anonymity. Despite being call 'currency', Bitcoin is not a currency in nature because it is not issued by monetary authorities and does not possess the legal status of being compulsorily used and accepted. Judging from its nature, Bitcoin should be regarded as a specific virtual commodity; it does not have the same legal status as a fiat currency, and it cannot and should not be circulated in market as fiat currency. (PBOC Circular, 2013)

It is interesting to note how the government of China went into a great length trying to elaborate and differentiate between sovereign cryptocurrency and the non-sovereign cryptocurrency, that Bitcoin cannot be treated as currency because it is not sovereign, that Bitcoin does not have the characteristic applicable to currency and so on and so forth while it is clear that the true reason for curbing Bitcoin and any other non-sovereign cryptocurrencies is about asserting authority and retaining the power to issue fiat money digitally and otherwise.

In Indonesia, Bank Indonesia, the Indonesia's Central Bank, on 13 January 2018 released a statement that warns all parties not to sell, buy or trade virtual currency. The press release states (BI, 2018):

> Bank Indonesia affirms that virtual currencies, including bitcoin, are not recognized as legitimate instrument of payment, therefore not allowed to be used for payment in Indonesia. This is in line with Act No. 7/2011 on The Currency which states that currency shall be money of which issued by the Republic of Indonesia and every transaction that has the purpose of payment, or other obligations which need to be fulfilled with money, or other financial transactions conducted within the territory of the Republic of Indonesia, has to be fulfilled with Rupiah.

BI cited Bank Indonesia Regulation No. 18/40/PBI/2016 on Implementation of Payment Transaction Processing and Bank Indonesia Regulation No. 19/12/PBI/2017 on Implementation of Financial Technology as the basis to forbid all payment system operators and financial technology operators in Indonesia to process transactions using virtual currency. The reasons given were because BI viewed that "[o] Ownership of virtual currency is highly risky and loaded with speculations, considering there is no authority responsible, no official administrator, no underlying assets to base the virtual currency price, and that the trade value is highly volatile" (BI, 2018).

Cryptocurrency: Issues and Challenges

Now that we have seen how Shariah perceives cryptocurrencies and how the regulators react to the market and the industry, it becomes apparent that Shariah being the rules that was established more than 1400 ago remains relevant and could address the legality aspect of the cryptocurrencies, and yet the newly introduced man-made law has mixed reaction and poses uncertainty to a large extent. The latter poses one of the biggest issues faced by most regulators across the globe. While many felt and correctly so thought that this area should be regulated, the real question is to what extent? Too heavy regulation will deter development of advance technology and could also cause high expense which was initially one of the reasons for the cryptocurrencies to be developed and the players wish to avoid. Proper assessment should be undertaken too before any decision enforced or policy introduced so as not to kill a player who might have invested heavily for the offerings. The risk is not imaginary, but it's real, and Facebook is an example where it looks like its cryptocurrency initiative might have collapsed before it could see the light of day.

Yet, the steep reaction was for reasons. "Global privacy regulators, central bankers and finance ministers have voiced concerns" (Schulze & Choudhury, 2019), and no doubt sudden growth of this niche industry will also increase potential abuse and/or fraud by the so-called players. Other issues related to cryptocurrencies vary from the lack of Shariah pronouncement of "halal" status that may deter its usage by some potential investors, to the issue of traceability that unlike cash, the use of internet makes it possible to track the transaction and hence potentially raises the issue of privacy and/or data privacy to public acceptance and awareness.

If we were to divide the major issues and challenges surrounding cryptocurrencies and the industry, they are of three prongs: (1) issues and challenges faced by the regulators, (2) issues and challenges faced by the players and (3) issues and challenges faced by the public.

The issues and challenges posed and/or faced by the regulators mainly because cryptocurrencies are yet to be fully understood by most regulators. Understanding the system itself is one thing, trying to regulate its unique aspects considering that it is borderless, nationless, the issue of traceability, are quite another. Often among the regulators themselves, it becomes unclear who should regulate and what would be the best approach to adopt when a situation falls within the authority of multiple regulators. Which of the regulators' claims should prevail when a transaction involves parties from different continents and the wallets and/or other parts of the facilities are elsewhere, in other countries miles away from the parties. If there is an alleged breach of law, how to determine and where an offender should be tried and so on and so forth. The list can go on and yet the answers are not necessarily as easy or straightforward. It perhaps calls for the sovereigns to sit together, have experts highlighting to them the risks and aspects that need to be governed and have the rules embedded transparently and clearly in a form that have wider coverage, in a form of treaty, for example.

As for the players, it is not uncommon that players in a given jurisdiction face the potential of being exposed and be subjected to overlapped and multiple regulations in a country where they are and elsewhere. That's usually coupled with the uncertainty in terms of the applicable rules: whether the traditional ones are applicable to cryptocurrencies and/or on anything that relates to it too. Those uncertainties consequently put them in the unclear position in terms of customers' rights and protection. They may also be subjected to multiple regulators and/or law from another jurisdiction which they are not aware of. A transaction may have tax obligation or trigger certain other obligations and/or even attract potential law enforcement action in a country where the players may not have set their foot in. Those are among the issues and challenges cryptocurrencies players have to face in addition to technical issues and challenges they may face in relation to the use of the system. Those could not be solved by each country, and/or authority continues to pass regulations in areas each of them claims to fall within its authority to regulate, nor can heavy regulation address the issue. At the stage where authorities and/or law enforcement agencies have yet to fully understand the extent they should regulate, perhaps the best way to do is to ensure all players are made aware of the terms and conditions that they must mutually agree among themselves, including those terms which reconcile differences that otherwise present in a transaction. Furthermore, the authorities and law enforcement agencies should agree on the terms that allow for handling of a case and/or enforcement to be done in the best manner seen in a case to case basis. That as opposed to simply asserting authority and forcing enforceability each time each of them sees fit so as to potentially pose the risks of multiple sanctions on a single action being unfairly imposed.

The effort, however, should not stop there. Enacting regulation that aims to provide clarity and certainty to players and/or setting rules to allow adult players to make well-informed decisions is as important as setting mechanism to ensure availability of protection and its conferment. Terms for deterrence must be made clear and known too to discourage foul players from abusing and/or misusing the system and/or breaching the agreed-upon procedure and/or to cause repercussion to other players.

Last but not least, efforts should be made to educate the public about cryptocurrencies, the advantages they have to offer and the risks they pose and to create awareness too. Both are still lacking but needed because ignorance could be misused and systemic crime could be prevented.

Recommendation and Way Forward

The basic principle is that a thing which is not forbidden is deemed lawful. That's based on the maxim "lawfulness is a recognised principle in all things." In other words, everything is presumed to be lawful, unless it is specifically prohibited by law.[7] Despite the lawful ruling of cryptocurrencies from Shariah view point, the issues and challenges we mentioned earlier will continue until and unless the regulators, the players and the public are prepared to better understand cryptocurrencies, the system and the objectives they aim to serve. The regulators need to play its role too. It must strive to introduce regulations which are transparent, fit for the purpose and create robust environment which result in the balance between the need for proper regulations and for the growth of the industry. Creating public awareness is important, but there is also a need to create standards that confer protection on their rights while ensuring interoperability and protect end users too. It is important to strike the right balance and maintain the focus on the regulatory objectives. The latter should always constitute the basis of any regulation. Although it is inevitable for one to wonder how can we regulate a technology designed to be decentralized through a centralized institution?

As the technology develops in one hand, the law makers including through judiciary continues to shape the take of technology. In the USA, in *Securities and Exchange Commission v. W. J. Howey Co.*, 328 U.S. 293 (1946), for example, the Howey test has been applied to cryptocurrencies. Consequently, intrinsic value in the USA becomes less relevant, whereas in Shariah it could make a whole lot difference in deciding proper treatment. Speculation (its presence or absence) is less important too, whereas in Shariah it is prohibited.

[7] This dictum is based on the Qur'ānic verse 2:29 and further 31:20. This is expressly stated in the hadith read as follows: "Wherever Allah has declared lawful in His book is lawful, and wherever He has declared unlawful is unlawful, and wherever He has remained silent are forgiven. Then accept those bounties of Allah because Allah does not forget anything. Then the Prophet (PBUH) recited the verse (of Surah Maryam): Your Lord never forgets anything."

The way forward could be projected from the current state. Libra, unlike Bitcoin, is not an asset. It won't and can't be regarded as commodity. It is proposed to be used as a medium of exchange over blockchain technology; however, it does not have intrinsic value, and the value is based on fiat money used as the underlying, hence making Libra closer, in terms of nature, to e-cash or digital cash than cryptocurrency for the lack of the character of being an asset. It is akin to e-cash one would have talked about 20 years ago except it will be based on basket of currency and run by a group of self-declared "regulator" as opposed to a central bank and it will run on the technology so advance and unheard of two decades ago. Despite the highly enthusiastic start, the way forward is bleak and the road ahead is rough for Facebook to launch Libra, and if at all that will happen, the most likely scenario of Libra will be a continuous tug of war game with the regulators from across the globe. Facebook should have known that "currency" is the sovereigns' holy grail and any attempt to create new system that would subordinate the existing one will always be met with resistance.

Unlike Libra, Bitcoin was a new kid on the block with a humble start. Except for his pseudonym, we don't even know the very individual who created it. It sparked excitement, obviously, as most new things do when they have just received the limelight. Nakamoto had made brilliant move by putting much emphasis on these, among others, that unlike fiat money, Bitcoin has intrinsic value, that it is a commodity and it is decentralized—away from every aspect the sovereigns and/or financial regulators would traditionally claim as their exclusive authority.

Today, more than a decade after Nakamoto implemented and released the Bitcoin software as open-source code, Bitcoin continues to "excite" the virtual realm and stays at the top of the rank of cryptocurrencies despite the "rollercoaster" ride it's experienced most notably in 2018 (Chance, 2018). This and the years to come stand as evidence on a salient feature of Bitcoin which Nakamoto intended the most out of its introduction, albeit it's mostly belittled by many when they discussed on cryptocurrencies, that is, the decentralized aspect of the system; that payment system, most notably one offered in virtual world, could be offered without the presence of a trusted person. It also proves that when there are more honest players manning the system, it can stand alone and it can serve the market and the industry needs for such payment system with all features there were thought could only be done top down, through the order of the sovereign down to its subjects or by being regulated by the authority or agency that has been conferred with the authority over currency.

Nomayo (2019) illustrates the adoption of Bitcoin across the globe through that image and others and his paper. Nakamoto did not emphasize on the distribution in his paper. Perhaps he did not expect the impact Bitcoin would have at the time of writing; or perhaps it was intentionally omitted because such discussion will highlight the impact Bitcoin could have should the manner of its distribution had been carefully planned, strategized and implemented rather than being left to the market as it is.

Be that as it may, Nakamoto and his Bitcoin should have inspired many more techno geniuses to come up with independent systems to populate the virtual world. It's doable; it could surpass the border limitation we have in real world and the restrictions we know in traditional market. If it is a completely new technology that one proposed to introduce, he or she could consider some element of convergence between the virtual and real world to be the bridge until people are comfortable with the new technology. When anything bad happens in the real world such as war, natural disasters and any other force majeure that can cause physical and complete destruction, one would feel a bit relief to know that some or perhaps significant amount of his wealth stays safe in the virtual world and is accessible from any part of the globe for as long as he or she has the access to the internet (and his/her password).

Now that all has been said, there is only one thing which I would like to put as a challenge to the techno geniuses—at the moment, what remains in virtual world remains there. One's wealth stays exclusively in the virtual world untouched when he dies and no one else knows his password. Even the court sanction given as a proof of eligibility to inheritance won't provide the heirs with access to his wealth in the virtual realm. He would have shared his password had he known his time has come but how many of us would know such time. Even worse, he could still be alive, but he simply forgot his password. It is a very simple issue but it is most annoying too. So let me end this chapter by noting that the emergence between the virtual and reality hasn't yet materialized so as to have the former equally reflected in the latter and with that I welcome anyone who can prove that the emergence can be done.

References

Alvares, E. (2019). Facebook's Calibra Cryptocurrency Wallet Launches in 2020. *Engadget*. Retrieved July 8, 2020, from https://www.engadget.com/2019/06/18/facebook-calibra-libra-cryptocurrency-digital-wallet/

Andriotis, A., Hoffman, L., Rudegeair, P., & Horwitz, J. (2019). Facebook Building Cryptocurrency-Based Payments System. *The Wall Street Journal*. Retrieved July 8, 2020, from https://www.wsj.com/articles/facebook-building-cryptocurrency-based-payments-system-11556837547

Andriotis, A., & Rudegeair, P. (2019). Mastercard, Visa, eBay Drop Out of Facebook's Libra Payments Network. *The Wall Street Journal*. Retrieved July 8, 2020, from https://www.wsj.com/articles/mastercard-drops-out-of-facebook-s-libra-payments-network-11570824139?mod=cx_picks&cx_navSource=cx_picks&cx_tag=contextual&cx_artPos=5#cxrecs_s

Baraniuk, C. (2019). Libra: Could Facebook's New Currency Be Stopped in its Tracks? *BBC News*. Retrieved July 8, 2020, from https://www.bbc.com/news/business-49090753

BBC. (2017). Bitcoin's Rollercoaster Ride after Hitting $17,000. *BBC*. Retrieved July 8, 2020, from https://www.bbc.com/news/business-42275564

BI. (2018, January 13). Bank Indonesia Warns All Parties Not to Sell, Buy, or Trade Virtual Currency. Retrieved October 19, 2019, from https://www.bi.go.id/en/ruang-media/siaranpers/Pages/sp_200418.aspx?__hstc=172477884.47f4fea8ab884286c11d72f5acbded2a.1515888000091.1515888000092.1515888000093.1&__hssc=172477884.1.1515888000094&__hsfp=528229161

Chance, D. (2018). Bitcoin's Rollercoaster Ride Finally Comes Off the Tracks. *Independent.ie*. Retrieved July 8, 2020, from https://www.independent.ie/business/technology/news/bitcoins-rollercoaster-ride-finally-comes-off-the-tracks-37537429.html

Chohan, U. W. (2017). Cryptocurrencies: A Brief Thematic Review. *Economics of Networks Journal, Social Science Research Network*. Retrieved July 8, 2020, from https://papers.ssrn.com/sol3/papers.cfm?abstract_id=3024330

Coindesk. 2019. Bitcoin. https://www.coindesk.com/price/bitcoin. Accessed on 12 October 2019.

Comply Advantage. (2019). Viewed on 14 October 2019. Retrieved July 8, 2020, from https://complyadvantage.com/knowledgebase/crypto-regulations/cryptocurrency-regulations-united-states/

Concannon, D., Valdez, Y. D., & Wink, S. P. (2019). The Yellow Brick Road for Consumer Tokens: The Path to SEC and CFTF Compliance. In *Blockchain & Cryptocurrency Regulation 2019* (Global Legal Insights). London: Global Legal Group Ltd.

El Islamy, H. (2002). *E-Business: An Islamic Perspective*. Kuala Lumpur: A.S. Nordeen.

El Islamy, H. (2019). Executive Board Member of Hajj Fund Management Agency of Indonesia and Shariah Board Member and Strategic Adviser of Islamic Fintech Alliance. This Chapter is Written in Loving Memory of Adlin bin Hisyamuddin, the IT Genius Who Worked on Several Cryptocurrencies Projects, Whose Brilliant Ideas Immortalised in Those Coins.

FCA. (2019a). Cryptoassets. *Financial Conduct Authority*. Retrieved July 8, 2020, from https://www.fca.org.uk/consumers/cryptoassets

FCA. (2019b). Policy Statement PS19/22: Guidance on Crypto Assets. Retrieved July 8, 2020, from https://www.fca.org.uk/publication/policy/ps19-22.pdf

Gong, L., & Yu, L. (2019). China. In *Blockchain & Cryptocurrency Regulation 2019* (Global Legal Insights). London: Global Lead Group Ltd.

Holmes, A. (2019). Facebook's Cryptocurrency Push Takes a Big Hit as PayPal Cuts Ties with Libra. *Business Insider*. Retrieved July 8, 2020, from https://www.businessinsider.sg/paypal-drops-out-of-facebook-libra-cryptocurrency-project-report-2019-10/?_ga=2.13905463.1683141069.1571078649-843707746.1570858444&r=US&IR=T

Huang, E. (2018). Bitcoin Market Cap Falls below $100 Billion First Time Since October 2017. *CNBC*. Retrieved July 8, 2020, from https://www.cnbc.com/2018/11/15/bitcoin-market-cap-falls-below-100-billion-for-first-time-since-2017.html

Isaac, M., & Popper, N. (2019). Facebook Plans Global Financial System based on Cryptocurrency. *The New York Times*. Retrieved July 8, 2020, from https://www.nytimes.com/2019/06/18/technology/facebook-cryptocurrency-libra.html?action=click&module=Top%20Stories&pgtype=Homepage

Libra Whitepaper. (2019). Libra White Water. Retrieved July 8, 2020, from https://libra.org/en-US/white-paper/#the-libra-blockchain

Morris, D. Z. (2017). Bitcoin Hits a New Record High, But Stops Short of $20,000. *Fortune*. Retrieved July 8, 2020, from https://fortune.com/2017/12/17/bitcoin-record-high-short-of-20000/

Nakamoto, S. (2008). Bitcoin: A Peer-to-Peer Electronic Cash System. *bitcoin.org*. Retrieved July 8, 2020, from https://bitcoin.org/bitcoin.pdf

Nomayo, O. A. (2019). Visualizing Bitcoin Adoption across the Globe. *bitcoinist.com*. Retrieved July 8, 2020, from https://bitcoinist.com/bitcoin-adoption-visual-map/

Partz, H. (2019). UK Financial Regulator FCA won't Regulate Bitcoin and Ether. *Coin Telegraph*. Retrieved July 8, 2020, from https://cointelegraph.com/news/uk-financial-regulator-fca-wont-regulate-bitcoin-and-ether

PBOC. 2013. The Circular of the People's Bank of China, Ministry of Industry and Information Technology, China Banking Regulatory Commission, China Securities Regulatory Commission, and China Insurance Regulatory Commission on the Prevention of Risks from Bitcoin. Last modified 6 December 2013. http://www.miit.gov.cn/n1146295/n1652858/n1652930/n3757016/c3762245/content.html. Accessed on 19 October 2019.

Rosic, A. (2018). What is Cryptocurrency. *blockgeeks.com*. Retrieved July 8, 2020, from https://blockgeeks.com/guides/what-is-cryptocurrency/

Schroeder, P., & Johnson, K. (2019). Facebook Vows Libra Currency will Wait for Approval as U.S. Airs Worries. *Reuters*. Retrieved July 8, 2020, from https://www.reuters.com/article/us-usa-facebook-libra/facebook-vows-libra-currency-will-wait-for-approval-as-us-airs-worries-idUSKCN1UA1PF

Schulze, E. (2019). Swiss Group that's Supposed to Oversee Privacy for Libra says it Hasn't Heard from Facebook at All. *CNBC*. Retrieved July 8, 2020, from https://www.cnbc.com/2019/07/16/fdpic-says-facebook-has-not-contacted-about-libra-data-protections.html

Schulze, E., & Choudhury, S. R. (2019). Facebook's Dream of a Global Cryptocurrency Raises Political Stakes—For the Regulators Themselves. *CNBC*. Retrieved July 8, 2020, from https://www.cnbc.com/2019/08/26/facebooks-libra-cryptocurrency-raises-political-stakes-for-regulators.html

Telford, T. (2019). Why Governments around the World are Afraid of Libra, Facebook's Cryptocurrency. *The Washington Post*. Retrieved July 8, 2020, from https://www.washingtonpost.com/business/2019/07/12/why-governments-around-world-are-afraid-libra-facebooks-cryptocurrency/

The Law Library of Congress. (2018). *Regulation of Cryptocurrency around the World*. USA: Global Legal Research Center. Retrieved July 8, 2020, from https://www.loc.gov/law/help/cryptocurrency/world-survey.php#indonesia

Treasury H. M. (2015). Digital Currencies: Response to the Call for Information. Viewed on 14 October 2019. Retrieved July 8, 2020, from https://assets.publishing.service.gov.uk/government/uploads/system/uploads/attachment_data/file/414040/digital_currencies_response_to_call_for_information_final_changes.pdf

Waters, M., Maloney, C., Clay, L., Green, A., & Lynch, S. F. (2019). Committee Democrats Call on Facebook to Halt Cryptocurrency Plans. *The U.S. House Committee on Financial Services*. Retrieved July 8, 2020, from https://financialservices.house.gov/news/documentsingle.aspx?DocumentID=404009

Webb, K. (2019). Facebook's Cryptocurrency Project Suffers Massive Blow as Mastercard, Visa, eBay, and others Withdraw from Libra. *Business Insider*. Retrieved July 8, 2020, from https://www.businessinsider.sg/mastercard-ebay-stripe-leave-facebook-libra-cryptocurrency-project-payapl-2019-10/?r=US&IR=T

Weinstein, J. M., Cohn, A., & Chelsea Parker, C. (2019). Promoting Innovation through Education: The Blockchain Industry, Law Enforcement, and Regulators Work towards a Common Goal. In *Blockchain & Cryptocurrency Regulation 2019* (Global Legal Insights). London: Global Lead Group Ltd.

CHAPTER 23

Digital Technology and Its Impact on Islamic Social Finance Literacy

Irfan Syauqi Beik and Laily Dwi Arsyianti

Abstract Indonesia is one of five middle-income countries that remains trapped in the area where the richest 10 percent of their population continue to conquer a much greater share of the national income than 40 percent of the poorest. Fighting poverty and injustice are the main objectives of Islamic finance, and thus the society may live with good welfare and reach maqasid sharia. Within the Islamic finance sector, digital technology has emerged in the middle of this nascent industry. Financial sector has utilized the commencement of digital services to enhance its coverage, especially when government is promoting financial inclusion. This paper also elaborates Islamic social finance industrial solution to improve digitalized application as well as justifiable recommendations that followed it. Daily lifestyle of middle class population has switched the payment system, from manually transferring money through conventional banking services

I. S. Beik (✉)
IPB University (Bogor Agricultural University), Bogor, Indonesia

BAZNAS, Jakarta, Indonesia
e-mail: irfan_beik@apps.ipb.ac.id

L. D. Arsyianti
IPB University (Bogor Agricultural University), Bogor, Indonesia

M. M. Billah (ed.), *Islamic FinTech*,
https://doi.org/10.1007/978-3-030-45827-0_23

into employing e-banking facilitation for social funds-related transaction. A simple transaction leads to tremendous growing of the shifting social class penetration. This phenomenon has put BAZNAS to target 30 percent of *zakat* and charity transactions are done via digital platform in 2020. As a result, in 2020, the *zakat* literacy index survey showed that the surveyed Indonesia's population has a moderate level of literacy, with a score of 66.78. Basic knowledge of *zakat* contributed the highest score among the dimensions. It seems that *zakat* institutions still have a homework to bring Islamic social finance literacy into society, particularly via digital frameworks.

Keywords Digital • Finance • FinTech • Islamic • Social finance • Literacy

Introduction

Indonesia is one of five middle-income countries that remains trapped in the area where the richest 10 percent of their population continue to conquer a much greater share of the national income than 40 percent of the poorest (Oxfam, 2014). Globally, it is also reported that the elites are progressively becoming richer, leaving a pernicious effect toward the poorest. This widening inequality gap is potentially creating impoverishment and famine. The wealthiest people are obtaining their fortunes at the expense of the rest of society, which left the deterrent effect of the rest of society living a better life. Fighting poverty and injustice are the main objectives of Islamic finance, and thus the society may live with good welfare and reach maqasid sharia. Both economic and social motives are merely in the favor of the welfare of society. While the financial sector has attracted many professionals, regulators, and academicians, the real sector has also been practicing toward the favor of micro-, small-, and medium-sized markets, but social sector has not much been attracted by many of them. The Islamic financial sector reached 8.24 percent in 2017 (Otoritas Jasa Keuangan [OJK], Snapshot of Indonesia Islamic Banking, 2017), while the household, wholesale and retail, construction, and process manufacturing sectors reached 40.67 percent, 11.49 percent, 7.77 percent, and 7.51 percent, respectively, placing them among the top four economic sectors in Indonesia. The Islamic social sector is still at 1.57 percent of its potential that should reach 3.4 percent of the gross national product (GDP) (BAZNAS, 2018). From the fact that Islamic social finance is still far behind other sectors, dissemination of the products is highly recommended. Within the Islamic finance sector, particularly digital technology has emerged in the middle of this nascent industry. The financial sector has utilized the commencement of digital services to enhance its coverage, especially when the government promotes financial inclusion. Turkey's ETHIX, UK-based Path Solutions, Malaysia's Investment Account Platform (IAP), Dubai's Commodity Murabahah Trading Platform (CMTP) and Nasdaq Dubai Murabahah Platform are some of Islamic finance platforms adopted by many financial institutions in today's 4.0 era. Meanwhile, the real sector has employed many digital technology applications that support their activities by conveniently providing simple actions to do various transactions. In Indonesia there are Gojek and Bukalapak, which are part of local provenience of the real sector employing digital savvy. Furthermore, the social sector should also join the other sectors engaging with the techs. The global population is moving toward middle-class groups who are relatively familiar with the growth of digital technology. The middle class may use digital technology in the creation of life chances (Blagoev, 2015).

In term of digital technology utilization, Islamic social finance within the financial industry is still in its blossoming stage. Although Indonesia has been crowned as the most generous country by the World Giving Index 2018, its prime contribution was voluntary activities, compared with the other 143 countries. Meanwhile, for donating money Indonesia is only placed second, and for helping strangers is in 97th place. Thus, Islamic social finance still needs to spread its wings, especially to attract donors to give money to trustworthy and accountable institutions. Being a volunteer does not necessarily mean being free of compensation, because volunteers were given all facilities provided in the field. Volunteers may get money for expenses, limited to food, drink, even travel and any equipment they need to buy (www.gov.uk).[1] According to this hypothetical assumption, the first priority aspect to using the techs is to improve the Islamic social finance literacy of society. Literacy is the first stage of education, including in terms of financial education (Hogarth, 2006).

This study aims to identify possible industrial solutions for employing digital technology as a tool to improve the literacy rate of Islamic social

[1] https://www.gov.uk/volunteering/pay-and-expenses

finance, particularly in developing countries such as Indonesia. This paper also elaborates an Islamic social finance industrial solution to improve digitalized application as well as justifiable recommendations that followed it. Lastly, this paper provides today's reality of its application in this industry.

Islamic Social Finance

In general, Islamic social finance offers almsgiving (represented by *zakat*), endowment funds (represented by *Waqf*), charity (represented by *sadaqa*), and interest-free loans (*qardhasan*) (Rehman, 2019). All products are aimed to bridge the gap between the *have* and the *have-not* groups, thus circulating wealth not only among certain groups in society but also disbursing money more widely.

Almsgiving, which is an obligation for Muslims, has strong a objective and points directly at the *Muzakki* (the have group). The recipient groups (*mustahiq*) are specifically focused on. They are *faqir* (the poor), *miskin* (the needy), *amylin* (*zakat* administered), *riqab* (slave), *gharimin* (highly in debt and bankruptcy), *mualaf* (converter/reverted to Islam), *ibn sabil* (traveller), and *fi sabilillah* (wayfarer). The groups are eligible to receive funds from *Muzakki* directly or indirectly through *amilin* (*zakat* administered) to fulfil their needs. Particular attention is paid to the needs that attain to *maqasid sharia*, such as protection of *diin* (religion), *aql* (intellectual), *nafs* (life), *nasl* (offspring), *maal* (wealth).

The *Muzakki* must disburse their surplus through both productive and consumptive schemes. Productive schemes have particularly encouraged the *mustahiq* to uplift their class becoming *Muzakki*. The programs mainly consist of social entrepreneurship, micro and small businesses, with development community activities such as education for human development, skill improvement through various soft-skill trainings, and supervision for product development. Meanwhile, the consumptive scheme purposely targets those who are not productive anymore, senior citizens, or those who are incapable of producing any products or provide any services. The management of *zakat* is usually conducted by *amil*, which is specifically appointed to effectively and efficiently distribute *zakat* from *Muzakki* to *Mustahik* around the globe.

In 2018 there were 604 *amil zakat* organizations in total, spread throughout Indonesia (BAPPENAS, 2019). One of them is the government/state-owned organization, the National Board of *Zakat* (*Badan Amil Zakat Nasional*-BAZNAS). BAZNAS organizations consist of the central BAZNAS at national level, thirty-four provincial BAZNAS, and 514 municipal- and district-level BAZNAS. There are also privately-owned *zakat* administered, i.e., private *Zakat* institutions (*Lembaga Amil Zakat*-LAZ).

Another form of social fund are endowment funds, which is represented by *Waqf*, but has not been much explored by Indonesia. There are 358,710 *Waqf* land units, which are 1,538,198,586 sq. meters in total. Most of the lands are idle, while are supposed to be cultivated or utilized for productive activities. However, Muslims in Indonesia have realized and recognized that *Waqf* revival has the potential to create a just and sustainable society (Ihsan & Adnan, 2017) because its perpetuity value becomes the uniqueness of *Waqf* (Candra & Ab Rahman, 2010).

The *Waqf* fund is collected by *nazir* who also manage the operation of its utilization. Its management must be conducted with prudence, be sustainable yet profitable, and achieve growth in order to keep the value of the *Waqf* fund from declining in any way. The Indonesia Board of *Waqf* (*Badan Waqf Indonesia*-BWI) acts as a regulator as well as organizer of the *Waqf* fund. Currently there are 192 *Waqf* organizations that have been licensed by BWI (BAPPENAS, 2019). Fifteen of them are Islamic Finance Institution-Cash *Waqf* Institutions (*Lembaga Keuangan Syariah Pengelola Waqf Uang* LKS-PWU). Also, 66 percent of them are sole *nazir*, 16 percent are *nazir* organizations, and another 18 percent are incorporated *nazir*.

Charity is another form of Islamic social finance that can be disbursed for any kind of product or services that can be consumed by anyone, including non-Muslim recipients. Unlike *zakat*, charity as well as *Waqf* is not limited to those who wealthy. People with lower incomes are eligible to give charity as well. Charity can also take a non-monetary form, such as voluntary work, giving a smile, and helping senior citizens. Charity also does not need a specific officer to operate the funds. However, particular organizations can organize the funds, including *amil* and philanthropy organizations.

Meanwhile, the monetary form of charity in Indonesia includes money given into a charity box which has been put in masjid or *mushola*,[2] the money given through the box circulated during *Jumat* prayer, and money

[2] Prayer rooms, smaller than masjid, which usually also have been used to conduct every prayer, except *Jumat* prayer.

collected during *arisan*[3] or *majlis ta'lim*[4] (Arsyianti, Kassim, & Adeyemi, 2018). Actually, *zakat* is an obligatory monetary charity for eligible Muslims and *Waqf* is a voluntary charity which has perpetual value. Therefore, charity is the umbrella form for *zakat* and *Waqf*.

Lastly, *qardhasan* is also a part of Islamic social finance. It means giving loans for free. The term "for free" indicates that the borrowed money has no repayment requirement to be added with extra interest. "And if the debtor is in a hard time (has no money), then grant him time till it is easy for him to repay. but if you remit it by way of charity, that is better for you if you did but know." (Al-Baqara (2): 80). Imam Muslim also narrated that Rasulullah (blessings and peace be upon him), once said that whoever allows more time for a debtor who is in difficulty or who waives the debt, Allah will shade him with His shade.

The Global Report on Islamic Finance 2017 has identified each financial sector in the Islamic financial industry to what extent their contribution is a catalyst for shared property. Islamic social finance has been encouraged to enhance community empowerment for sustainable Islamic social funding instruments. The aforementioned instruments (*zakat*, *Waqf*, *sadaqa*, and *qardhasan*) play a vital role in eradicating poverty and providing social protection in a dignified manner for wider social and inclusive impacts. The instruments, apart from public–private partnerships and market-based solutions, foster harmonious relationships between economic sectors and environmental interests (Islamic Development Bank Group [IDBG], 2017).

All forms of Islamic social finance have been developed widely in Indonesia within the last decade, in parallel with the monetary and real sectors which have dominated the Indonesia economy for centuries. Although the regulations have been developed and revised, infrastructure in supporting Islamic social finance has not much improved, in which an effective and efficient manners that pursuit mutual gains between developing the regulations and building the Islamic social finance infrastructure should not be an issue for the government. The development of Islamic social finance also needs to be supported with the updated, familiar, and

[3] A micro-financing scheme for the Indonesian community, provided by a small group of people, usually with common interests, who gather together at a specified time. The main objective is to strengthen *silaturahmi* (brotherhood) among them (within a community).

[4] A Muslim community who gather at an agreed time to share or hear Islamic knowledge or preaching. The speaker can be one of them, or an invited preacher outside the community, usually available in one specific neighborhood.

widely recognized tools that strengthen harmonious relationships among the economic sectors, namely digital technology.

Digital Technology

Gottfried Wilhem Leibniz, a German mathematician, proposed a computing system using binary code (combination of 1 and 0) that inspired the American Standard Code for Information Interchange to digitized objects, known as digital technology, in the mid-twentieth century (Encyclopedia.com, 2019).[5] These days telecommunications relies massively on digital methods for transferring messages. The most extensively acknowledged technologies that enable this transmission is through fiber optics. Fiber optics utilize light instead of electricity to deliver optical signals. For a comprehensive infrastructure and digitalized system, digital technology can only be developed by support from the Indonesia government.

Indonesia will undergo a revision on the e-commerce road map under Presidential Regulation No. 74/2017 and the management of electronic transactions and systems under Government Regulation No. 82/2012, particularly to accommodate micro-, small-, and medium-sized enterprises (MSMEs). Indonesia is expected to become a giant "Komodo dragon" in digital transactions within the next twenty years, and that the amount will reach 172 billion US dollars as estimated by the Hinrich Foundation and the Centre for Strategic and International Studies (CSIS).[6]

Over the last five years in Indonesia, from 2012 to 2017, consumer behavior for spending has been shifting from product category into service category. Consumer good services and traveling have become the second and the third position after food, beverages, and tobacco on their spending in 2017, according to Euromonitor International.

Digital financial services have become more affordable and convenient, especially for low-income people, as they offer inclusiveness and broader accessibility (Haider, 2018). For example, the dissemination of e-tailing in Indonesia had become similar to China in 2010 (Das et al., 2018) with the

[5] Encyclopedia.com. (2019). Digital Technology. https://www.encyclopedia.com/history/dictionaries-thesauruses-pictures-and-press-releases/digital-technology. Retrieved on July 12, 2019, 15:38 GMT+7.

[6] R. Aisyah (2019). Indonesia Aims to be a Regional Digital Technology Hub in 2020, *Jakarta Post*. Retrieved from https://www.thejakartapost.com/news/2019/02/20/indonesia-aims-to-be-regional-digital-technology-hub-in-2020.html on February 20, 2019, 05:59 pm.

indicators of retail spending, Internet penetration, and urbanization. Digital-savvy, mobile first market, young consumers help explain the growth of this industry, especially for MSMEs. Therefore, it is expected that poverty will reduce more speedily through the improvement of economic outcomes and livelihoods, than in non-digital technology utilized industries.

The development of digital technology has offered more timely, secure, faster, and convenient transactions as it goes along with developing the individual's experience in financial transactions. Thus, people's literacy on finance as well as their competencies, confidence, and experience toward it are improved, and create better economic opportunities ([OECD] International Network on Financial Education, 2018).

According to Venkataramani et al. (2017), Indonesia should focus on its foundational infrastructure at the beginning, followed by the improvement of awareness which later becomes the trust of Indonesian society toward digitization. Next, the homework is to prepare a viable and qualified capital of a readily hirable workforce.[7] Hiring good talent is still an obstacle to developing this industry, especially by knowing that 9 million Indonesian people are looking for jobs abroad—the "brain drain." Subsequent steps that should have attracted Indonesia's attention are developing an innovation ecosystem before looking for supporting local potentials of the monetary, real, and social sectors (Table 23.1).

Table 23.1 Involved economic sectors

Economic sectors	Sectors with economic motives	Financial sector: Banks, financing institutions, insurance, capital markets, etc. Real sector: Manufacturing, agriculture, tourism, transportation, communication, trading, construction, etc.
	Sectors with social motives	• ZIS and other social religious fund managed by BAZNAS • *Awqaf* managed by BWI • Hajj fund managed by BPKH

Source: Sudibyo (2018)

[7] T. Astandu (2019). Same Old Issues Slow Indonesia's Digital Economy, *Jakarta Post*. Retrieved from https://www.thejakartapost.com/academia/2019/03/18/same-old-issues-slow-indonesias-digital-economy.html on March 18, 2019, 09:05 am.

To the extent of the potential application of digital technology in the financial industry, which can be juxtaposed with the development of Islamic social finance, Blagoev (2015) studied the growth and emergence of the middle class/bourgeoisie, their life chances and digitized world. The global dispersed social relations have attracted the middle class to applied innovative practices in fusing global opportunities. To the degrees of flexibility, autonomy, and innovative orientation toward the environment, the digitized world will be widely accepted by this group, especially when it narrows or eliminates the stratification of classes in the society.

In term of age, this is expected to relate to tech savvy; at the context of giving charity, Leliveld and Risselada (2017) found that Donators were younger than Keepers. Donators denote to those who always donate regularly whenever they earned money, while Keepers are those who always keep money whenever they earned money, in the sense of distributing their money. Another study done by Arsyianti and Kassim (2016) found that age has not been proven to be significantly differentiate between those who gave charity regularly and those who do not, with the frontier age being 45 years old. The Indonesian population on average was at the age of 28.3 years old in 2019.[8] Therefore, applying digital technology is not a difficult matter to Indonesian people in the Islamic social finance industry.

Haider (2018) added regulations as the first priority to build a supporting system for digital technology application, not limited to financial services. Regulations can overcome the barriers of low (financial) literacy and numerical skills.

Financial Literacy

Financial literacy indicates the rate of an individual's knowledge of finance. Financial knowledge can be improved through financial education, either at the higher level or from the middle level of education. Although some research, such as done by Mandell and Klein (2009), shows that financial education has made no different effect between those who have taken a financial course and those who have not. Financial literacy can also improve an individual's expectation on their future financial condition (Martin, 2007). Yet financial education was still continually searched even for those

[8] Worldometers (2019). Indonesia Population. Retrieved from https://www.worldometers.info/world-population/indonesia-population/ on July 16, 2019, 7:46 am.

who have taken financial course. Nevertheless, the financial literacy survey is put on Indonesia's financial inclusion program (Ministry of Finance, 2013) in order to embrace wider groups applying formal financial transactions, through online or offline operators.

The Islamic financial literacy rate, in general, is still low for Indonesia, i.e. 8.11 percent, as of 2017. Meanwhile, the financial literacy rate, according to the National Survey on Financial Literacy 2013, is only 21.84 percent. It means that every one hundred Indonesian people, only around 21–22 of them are financially literate. However, for a specific Islamic Social Finance literacy there is as yet no provided data.

Financial literacy for Islamic Social Finance should intentionally be developed through intensified programs. Financial literacy can drive individuals' preference toward their financial portfolio (Setyawati & Suroso, 2016). Apparently, skills and behavior collegially link to literacy, beside knowledge (Hung et al., 2009; Lusardi, 2008; Mitchell, Lusardi, & Curto, 2010). Albeerdy and Gharleghi (2015) have studied the correlation between financial socialization agents and financial literacy which, however, shows a weak relationship between the two. Therefore, literacy in this paper includes skills and behavior as its key points to deepen the meaning of knowledge that a society has.

Digital Technology Best Practices for Islamic Social Finance Literacy

The *Mustahik* and *Muzakki* database systems are applied in the case of BAZNAS. The *Mustahik* database system integrates several available data, such as from the Ministry of Social Affairs (104 million people at the bottom 40 percent), develops special applications for the data centre, and for BAZNAS data centre of *Mustahik* and its impact factor. Meanwhile, the *Muzakki* database system is supported by Dukcapil data (e-KTP, or electronic identification card number), special applications for the data centre, and potential targets of *Muzakki* and their dissemination (Beik, 2019).

Collecting and distributing social funds in BAZNAS is now easier and more affordable. The digital technology platforms are initialized both internally and externally. BAZNAS has also utilized social media. Social media as a catalyst of financial literacy has been demonstrated in Uzbekistan where media are socializing factors for young students (Isomidinova, Singh, & Singh, 2017). Skills and behavior as part of literacy can be improved through widening social networks in United States (US) (Hung et al., 2009).

Fig. 23.1 Zakat digital channel. (*Source*: Beik, 2019)

Figure 23.1 depicts Indonesia's *amil* institution's digital channel platform that is adopted to collect and distribute *zakat* funds as well as charity. The platform accommodates social media, and external and internal sources of application to deliberate the knowledge and behavior of *Muzakki* and *Mustahik*.

Partners and tools that are used in *zakat* digital channel platforms include Facebook, LINE, Google, Play Store, and App Store donation platforms. These giant social media players were selected due to the wide range of users, the effective target of (at the least) middle-class users, and efficient utilization of cashless, paperless, and immediate transactions. As of June 2019, Facebook as a media to socialize via electronic systems has grabbed 42.99 percent of social media share in Indonesia.[9] Meanwhile, 88 percent of Indonesian people are widely utilizing YouTube,[10] which is the highest frequency of social media penetration, followed by WhatsApp and Facebook; 150 million people spend eight hours and thirty-six minutes per day to communicate online.[11] The statistics showed that using social

[9] GlobalStats (2019). Social Media Stats Indonesia. Retrieved from http://gs.statcounter.com/social-media-stats/all/indonesia on July 18, 2019, 02:36 pm.

[10] Statista (2019). Penetration of leading social networks in Indonesia as of 3rd quarter 2018. Retrieved from https://www.statista.com/statistics/284437/indonesia-social-network-penetration/ on July 18, 2019, 02:43 pm.

[11] E. Wong (2019). How Indonesians Embrace the Digital World, *Jakarta Post*. Retrieved from https://www.thejakartapost.com/academia/2019/03/18/how-indonesians-embrace-the-digital-world.html on March 18, 2019, 04:03 pm.

media to boost the literacy of Islamic social finance, at this time and particularly by BAZNAS, is precisely right on target.

External sources of applications that are employed by BAZNAS include e-commerce, banking facilitation, apps, and start-up FinTech corporations. There were an estimated 1.8 billion people worldwide purchasing goods via e-commerce in 2018.[12] For example, Bukalapak, one of the biggest online marketplaces, has facilitated their customers—buyers and sellers—to pay *zakat* via BAZNAS using their platform. Online banking, mobile banking, apps, and their automated teller machines (ATMs) have been also providing online users with a friendly platform to accommodate their customers paying *zakat* via BAZNAS. For example, at the end of every transaction, a pop-up message will appear, and their customers are asked whether they are willing to pay *zakat*.

Other than those external source, BAZNAS engages with internal sources of digital application. The B-landing page, *Muzakki* corner, *zakat* calculator, games, and apps are some of the internal sources of application that are employed by BAZNAS. *Muzakki* can directly transfer their *zakat* funds through BAZNAS accounts at appointed banks via the BAZNAS website. BAZNAS has targeted to simplify *zakat* and the charity payment system. Since it has been launched, the *zakat* collection via digital platforms has increased from 2 percent in 2017, 6 percent in 2018, 15 percent estimated in 2019, to become 30 percent in 2020.[13] Meanwhile, Dompet Dhuafa, one of the private *amil* organizations, published the fact that the use of digital platforms for *zakat* and charity transaction has been increasing 200 percent per month with an estimated volume up to around 8000 transactions.[14]

[12] J. Clement (2019). E-commerce worldwide: Statistics & Facts in Statista. Retrieved from https://www.statista.com/topics/871/online-shopping/ on March 12, 2019.

[13] Puskas BAZNAS (2019). BAZNAS target 30 percent of *zakat* is collected via digital. Retrieved from https://www.puskasbaznas.com/news/928-baznas-target-30-percent-of-*zakat*-is-collected-via-digital on February 25, 2019.

[14] U. N. Fadillah and A. Sasongko (2019). TrenDonasi Online di DompetDhuafaAlamiPeningkatan in Republika On Line. Retrieved from https://www.republika.co.id/berita/dunia-islam/wakaf/prndvu313/tren-donasi-online-di-dompet-dhuafa-alami-peningkatan on May 17, 2019, 09:41 pm.

Impact on *Zakat* Collection and Distribution as a Projection of Islamic Social Finance Literacy

As a digital platform progressively employed by both *Muzakki* and *Mustahik*, BAZNAS has stimulated their collection from 2012 until 2020 which might reflect the growth of Islamic social finance literacy. The *zakat* literacy index survey (BAZNAS, 2020) showed that the surveyed Indonesia's population has a moderate level of literacy, with a score of 66.78. Basic knowledge of *zakat* contributed the highest score among the dimensions. Meanwhile the advanced knowledge got the lowest score. The highest score was about the basic concept of *zakat*, followed by the concept of *asnaf*. In the meantime, the lowest score was literacy about *zakat* regulation. Therefore, it is obvious that Indonesian society is not yet familiar with *zakat* regulations where there are stated that formal *zakat* institutions have been appointed by Indonesia regulations. The aforementioned literature reviews have clearly elaborated that literacy is not only about knowledge, but also includes skills and behavior. According to their income, *Muzakki* is divided into five social classes: elite, affluent, high middle, mid middle, and low middle. Meanwhile, *Mustahik* is divided into only two classes which basically are the targeted group for distributed funds, i.e. the poor and the needy.

Since the middle class has been growing rapidly in Indonesia,[15] there might be quite a big shifting of class penetration from low-middle-class in 2012 to becoming mid-middle-class in 2020. Currently, the middle class of 60 million is expected to reach 85 million in 2020. Mid-middle-class people are shifting to high-middle-class.

Digital platform technology has become all of society's preference for every transaction. Whether for purchasing goods, financial transactions, or highlighting the importance of lifestyles and experiences, the Indonesian people are predicted to grow enormously, especially the middle class who should be more aware of Islamic social funds (Table 23.2).

[15] Kementerian KeuanganRepublik Indonesia (2019). These are the impacts and opportunities of Indonesia as a middle-income country. Retrieved from: https://www.kemenkeu.go.id/en/publications/news/these-are-the-impacts-and-opportunities-of-indonesia-as-a-middle-income-country on January 22, 2019, 05:01 pm.

Table 23.2 Social class penetration as Islamic social transactions grown immensely through digital platforms

Social class		*2012*		*Projection 2020*		*Shift*		
		Million people	*%*	*Million people*	*%*	*Million people*	*%*	
Muzakki	Elite	2.5	3.67	6.9	8.74	4.4	5.07	23.85
	Affluent	6.6		16.5		9.9		
	High middle	23.2	44.00	49.3	62.78	26.1	18.78	
	Mid middle	41.6		68.2		26.6		
	Lower middle	44.4		50.5		6.1		
Mustahik	The needy	65.4	52.33	47.9	28.48	-17.6	-23.85	-23.85
	The poor	64.5		28.3		-36.2		

Source: Sudibyo (2018)

Conclusion

Digital technology has been widely used in developing countries such as Indonesia, Uzbekistan, and Malaysia. This utilization is not limited to e-commerce for selling and buying products, but also for financial services, including Islamic social finance services. The daily lifestyle of the middle-class population has switched the payment system from manually transferring money through conventional banking services, into employing e-banking facilitation for social funds-related transactions.

A simple transaction leads to tremendous growth of the shifting social class penetration. This phenomenon has made BAZNAS target 30 percent of *zakat* and charity transactions which were done via digital platforms in 2020, where the middle class is familiar with the digitized world. Behavior and skills, then, cannot be separated from literacy. Thus, Islamic social finance literacy can also be estimated by people's targeted behavior or mastery of skills. Islamic social finance literacy survey leads us to give more effort to introduce formal *zakat* institutions to the society. According to the survey, most of them were still paying *zakat* informally via masjid. This left *zakat* institutions to instill the concept of Islamic social finance into the society, specifically via digital frameworks.

References

[BAPPENAS], Kementerian Perencanaan Pembangunan Nasional. (2019). *Masterplan Ekonomi Syariah Indonesia 2019–2024*. Retrieved from https://ubico.id/wp-content/uploads/2019/05/Masterplan-Ekonomi-Syariah-Indonesia-2019-2024_Terbaru.pdf

[IDBG], Islamic Development Bank Group. (2017). *Global Report on Islamic Finance: A Catalyst for Shared Prosperity?*. Retrieved from http://www.tkbb.org.tr/Documents/Yonetmelikler/Global-Report-on-Islamic-Finance-Islamic-Finance-A-Catalyst-for-Shared-Prosperity-Dr-AhmedMohamedAli.pdf

[OECD] International Network on Financial Education. (2018). *Digitalisation and Financial Literacy*. Retrieved from http://www.oecd.org/finance/G20-OECD-INFE-Policy-Guidance-Digitalisation-Financial-Literacy-2018.pdf

Albeerdy, M. I., & Gharleghi, B. (2015). Determinants of the Financial Literacy Among College Students in Malaysia Muhammad. *International Journal of Business Administration, 6*(3), 15–24. https://doi.org/10.5430/ijba.v6n3p1

Arsyianti, L. D., & Kassim, S. (2016). Regular Charity Giving Behaviour Among Low-Income Households in Indonesia. *Intellectual Discourse, 1*(24), 133–156. Retrieved from http://journals.iium.edu.my/intdiscourse/index.php/islam/article/view/653/556

Arsyianti, L. D., Kassim, S., & Adeyemi, A. A. (2018). Enhancing Financial Education: Debt-Taking and Charity-Giving Context in Indonesia. *Li Falah: Jurnal Studi Ekonomi dan Bisnis Islam, 3*(2), 32–49.

BAZNAS [Centre of Strategic Studies, National Board of Zakat]. (2020). Report of Survey on Zakat Literacy Index.

Beik, I. S. (2019). *Pengembangan Sistem Pengelolaan Zakat Nasional*. Enrekang: BAZNAS.

Blagoev, D. (2015). Middle Classes Undergoing Transformation in a Digitizing World. *International Journal of Communication, 9*, 2784–2800. Retrieved from https://ijoc.org/index.php/ijoc/article/viewFile/3074/1454

Candra, H., & Ab Rahman, A. (2010). Waqf Investment: A Case Study of Dompet Dhuafa Republika, Indonesia. *Jurnal Syariah, 18*(1), 163–190.

Das, K., et al. (2018). *The Digital Archipelago: How Online Commerce Is Driving Indonesia's Economic Development*. Retrieved from https://www.mckinsey.com/~/media/McKinsey/Featured Insights/Asia Pacific/The digital archipelago How online commerce is driving Indonesias economic development/The-digital-archipelago-Executive-summary.ashx

Departemen Keuangan. (2013). *Financial Inclusion: Strategi Nasional Keuangan Inklusif (SNKI)*. Jakarta: Ministry of Finance Republic of Indonesia. Retrieved from http://www.fiskal.depkeu.go.id/2010/adoku/2013%5Cpublikasi%5Cpkrb%5CFinancial Inclusion (SNKI).pdf

Haider, H. (2018). *Innovative Financial Technologies to Support Livelihoods and Economic Outcomes*. Retrieved from https://assets.publishing.service.gov.uk/media/5b6c552ee5274a297e35fa39/Digital_financial_services.pdf

Hogarth, J. M. (2006). *Financial Education & Economic Development*. Retrieved from http://search.oecd.org/daf/fin/financial-education/37723380.pdf

Hung, A. A., et al. (2009). *Defining and Measuring Financial Literacy*. WR-708. Retrieved from https://www.rand.org/content/dam/rand/pubs/working_papers/2009/RAND_WR708.pdf

Ihsan, H., & Adnan, M. A. (2017). A Study of Accountability Practice in Dompet Dhuafa Waqf of Indonesia. *Islamic Economics, 30*(2), 13–32.

Isomidinova, G., Singh, J., & Singh, K. (2017). Determinants of Financial Literacy: A Quantitative Study Among Young Students in Tashkent, Uzbekistan. *Electronic Journal of Business and Management, 2*(1), 61–75. Retrieved from http://www.apu.edu.my/ejournals/ejbm/journal/2017/Paper6_Determinants_Of_Financial_Literacy_A_Quantitative_Study_Among_Young_Students_In_Tashkent.pdf

Leliveld, M. C., & Risselada, H. (2017). Dynamics in Charity Donation Decisions: Insights from a Large Longitudinal Data Set. *Science Advances, 3*(9). https://doi.org/10.1126/sciadv.1700077

Lusardi, A. (2008). *Household Saving Behavior: The Role of Financial Literacy, Information and Financial Education Programs*. Working Paper. Retrieved from http://www.nber.org/papers/w13824

Mandell, L., & Klein, L. S. (2009). The Impact of Financial Literacy Education on Subsequent Financial Behavior. *Journal of Financial Counseling and Planning, 20*(206), 15–24. Retrieved from http://www.eric.ed.gov/ERICWebPortal/contentdelivery/servlet/ERICServlet?accno=EJ859556

Martin, M. (2007, June 15). *A Literature Review on the Effectiveness of Financial Education*. Federal Reserve Bank of Richmond Working Paper No 07-03. https://doi.org/10.2139/ssrn.2186650

Mitchell, O., Lusardi, A., & Curto, V. (2010). Financial Literacy Among the Young: Evidence and Implications for Consumer Policy. *Pension Research Council WP*, 1–35. https://doi.org/10.2139/ssrn.1476982

Otoritas Jasa Keuangan [OJK]. (2017). *Snapshot of Indonesia Islamic Banking*. Retrieved from https://www.ojk.go.id/en/berita-dan-kegiatan/publikasi/Documents/Pages/Snapshot-of-Indonesia-Islamic-Banking-Development-2017/Indonesia Islamic Banking Snapshot 2017 (V3).pdf

Oxfam. (2014). *Working for the Few: Political Capture and Economic Inequality*. Retrieved from https://www-cdn.oxfam.org/s3fs-public/file_attachments/bp-working-for-few-political-capture-economic-inequality-200114-en_3.pdf

Rehman, A. A. (2019). *Islamic Finance for Social Good: Sustainable Development in Islamic Social Finance, UNDP*. Retrieved from https://www.undp.org/

content/undp/en/home/blog/2019/IFN_ANNUAL_GUIDE_2019_Islamic_Social_Finance.html

Setyawati, I., & Suroso, S. (2016). Sharia Financial Literacy and Effect on Social Economic Factors (Survey on Lecturer in Indonesia). *International Journal of Scientific & Technology Research, 5*(2), 92–102. Retrieved from http://www.ijstr.org/final-print/feb2016/Sharia-Financial-Literacy-And-Effect-On-Social-Economic-Factors-survey-On-Lecturer-In-Indonesia.pdf

Sudibyo, B. (2018). *The Role of BAZNAS in the Development of Halal Industry*. Bogor: BAZNAS.

Venkataramani et al. (2017). Unleashing Indonesia's Digital Potential. ATKearney. Retrieved from https://www.kearney.com/documents/20152/1875957/Unleashing+Indonesia%C3%A2%E2%82%AC%E2%84%A2s+Digital+Potential-+The+Case+for+a+Clear+Road+Map.pdf/0df1c282-4195-1f3c-d763-9fab11dea697?t=1548349134459

CHAPTER 24

The Direction of Future Research on i-FinTech

Kazi Md Tarique and Mezbah Uddin Ahmed

Abstract The effect of the fourth industrial revolution, coupled with three core technological drivers, namely, automation, disintermediation and decentralization, has bought about an unprecedented change in the global financial industry. The global Fintech investment has reached $57.9 billion in the first half of 2018 (Islamic Fintech report-2018). Top-ranked financial institutions have accepted the need for change and they are now investing in data analytics, artificial intelligence (AI) and Big Data. Moreover, 77% of them have targeted to introduce blockchain in the system by 2020.

Keywords Fintech • Shariah • Islamic • Literature • Review • Research • Direction

K. Md. Tarique
University of Liberal Arts Bangladesh (ULAB), Dhaka, Bangladesh

M. U. Ahmed (✉)
International Shari'ah Research Academy for Islamic Finance (ISRA), Kuala Lumpur, Malaysia
e-mail: mezbah@isra.my

M. M. Billah (ed.), *Islamic FinTech*,
https://doi.org/10.1007/978-3-030-45827-0_24

Introduction

The Islamic financial industry aspires to grow its asset base to $3.9 trillion by 2023 according to Thomson Reuters. The adoption of Fintech in this industry is still in its nascent stage. This is largely due to its domestic and OIC-based nature. However, the promising youths associated with this industry are driving the growth of Islamic Fintech. According to the i-Fintech Report—2018, about 90 Islamic Fintech start-ups globally are delivering financial solutions to customers. Among them, 65 are providing peer-to-peer technology solutions to facilitate consumer and business solutions and another 14 are using blockchain technology for deposits and transfers. Demographically, Indonesia, US, UAR and UK host the largest number of Islamic Fintech start-ups. Governments of some Islamic countries are supporting Islamic Fintech such as DIFC's $100 million Fintech fund and Bahrain's regulatory sandbox. There are also some private sector initiatives such as the Islamic Fintech Alliance in Singapore and the Turkey-based Al Barakah Bank's Accelerator arm to support Islamic Fintech.

Methodology

Like the Islamic Fintech industry, academic research on Islamic Fintech is also in its nascent stage. To conduct this study, the authors used some keywords and synonyms for the literature search in Google scholar. The keywords used are "Islamic Fintech", "Fintech and Islamic Banking", "Fintech and Blockchain", "Fintech and Crowdfunding", etc. In the first phase, 50 articles were selected based on title and keywords. The articles that were not in English were rejected. In the second phase, a careful review of the abstract of the selected 50 papers was conducted to ensure the relevance of this study and also to avoid duplication. Finally, the authors selected 30 articles deemed to be suitable and relevant for this book chapter. The time frame of the literature search started in May 2019 and ended in August 2019.

Analysis of the Selected Articles

To present the findings of this study, at first, the authors looked at the patterns and themes of the selected 30 papers. A systematic analysis of literature helped to group the articles into seven themes. The themes are the following:

I. i-Fintech and Islamic Banking (T1)
II. i-Fintech and Bitcoin (T2)
III. i-Fintech and Blockchain (T3)
IV. i-Fintech and Crowdfunding(T4)
V. i-Fintech Financial Inclusion and Zakat (T5)
VI. i-Fintech and SME (T6)
VII. i-Fintech in miscellaneous issues (T7)

In order to show few details of the selected articles, Table 24.1 is presented with authors, year and title under seven themes. To support Table 24.1, two figures were presented. Figure 24.1 contains the number under each theme. Figure 24.2 shows a 3D pie chart that shows T-1–T7 in percentage. Figure 24.3 depicts the number of paper according to year of publishing.

i-Fintech and Islamic Banking

A systematic literature review revealed only two papers that linked Fintech with Islamic banking. The effect of financial technology on the banking system of Indonesia has been analyzed by Darussalam et al. (2019). The study interviewed Islamic banking customers to find out the strength, weakness, opportunity and threats (SWOT) for Islamic banks after the adoption of Fintech. The study found that the introduction of Fintech will surely improve the services of Islamic banks in Indonesia even though the infrastructure is poor. Fintech will also open up different business opportunities despite fears of cybercrime. In another paper, Todorof (2018) critically examined whether current Fintech activities adhere to Shariah principles or not. The study found that the use of Fintech will help Islamic banks to provide better service and thus increase market share. The study also revealed that Shariah-compliant crowdfunding, remittance and Mobile wallet help financial inclusion for the poor Muslim population around the globe. Overall, the digitalization of Islamic banks will save cost and time for both banks and their customers.

i-Fintech and Bitcoin

The popularity of cryptocurrencies especially bitcoin has surged in the recent past. Individual investors are quite excited but central banks around the globe are showing their cautious reaction. The pertinent question now

Table 24.1 Distribution of selected articles under different themes

Author/year	*Title*
i-Fintech and Islamic Banking	
Darussalam, Tutuko, Dahlan, Hudaifah, and Tajang (2019)	Islamic Financial Technology Towards the Advancement of Islamic Banking in Indonesia
Todorof (2018)	Shariah-Compliant Fintech in the Banking Industry
i-Fintech and Bitcoin	
Bergstra (2015)	Bitcoin And Islamic Finance
Bakar and Rosbi (2018)	Robust Framework Diagnostics of Blockchain for Bitcoin Transaction System: A Technical Analysis from Islamic Financial Technology (I-Fintech) Perspective
Evans (2015)	Bitcoin in Islamic Banking and Finance
Meera (2018)	Cryptocurrencies from Islamic Perspectives: The Case of Bitcoin
i-Fintech and Blockchain	
Elasrag (2019)	Blockchain for Islamic Finance: Obstacles & Challenges
Lacasse, Lambert, and Khan (2017)	Blockchain Technology—Arsenal for a Shariah-Compliant Financial Ecosystem?
Hussen and Ibrahim (2018)	New Business Model for Malaysian Ar Rahnu Using Blockchain as Sustainable Business
Nor, Rahman, Rahman, and Abdullah (2017)	Blockchain Sadaqa Mechanism for Disaster Aid Crowd Funding
Alzubaidi and Abdullah (2017)	Developing a Digital Currency from an Islamic Perspective: Case of Blockchain Technology
Habib and Ahmad (2019)	Using Blockchain and Smart Contracts for Waqf Institutions
i-Fintech and Crowdfunding	
Biancone, Secinaro, and Kamal (2019)	Crowdfunding and Fintech: Business Model Sharia Compliant
Abdullah and Oseni (2017)	Towards a Shariah Compliant Equity-Based Crowdfunding for the Halal Industry in Malaysia
Alma'amun, Shafiai, Shahimi, and Adnan (2018)	Waqf-Based Crowdfunding: A Case Study of Waqfworld. Org
Saiti, Musito, and Yücel (2019)	Islamic Crowdfunding: Fundamentals, Developments and Challenges
i-Fintech Financial Inclusion and Zakat	
Yahaya and Ahmad (2018)	Financial Inclusion Through Efficient Zakat Distribution for Poverty Alleviation in Malaysia: Using Fintech & Mobile Banking

(*continued*)

Table 24.1 (continued)

Author/year	*Title*
Firmansyah and Ramdani (2018)	The Role of Islamic Financial Technology (Fintech) Start-Up in Improving Financial Inclusion in Indonesia Case: Angsur
Wulan, Khairunnisa, and Bahri (2018)	Internal Audit Role in Digital Zakat Finance (Case Study at a Zakat Institution in Indonesia)
Yahaya and Ahmad (2019)	Factors Affecting the Acceptance of Financial Technology Among Asnaf for the Distribution of Zakat in Selangor – A Study Using Utaut
Friantoro and Zaki (2018)	Do We Need Financial Technology for Collecting Zakat
i-Fintech and SME	
Fatturroyhan (2018)	Go-Mudaraba: The Solution of Poverty and Unemployment in the Digital Era
Rumondang (2018)	The Utilization of Fintech (P2P Landing) as SME's Capital Solution in Indonesia: Perspective in Islamic Economics (Qirad)
i-Fintech in Miscellaneous Issues	
Lajis (2019)	Fintech and Risk-Sharing: A Catalyst for Islamic Finance
Manaf and Amiruddin (2019)	Fintech and the Challenge of Digital Disruption in Takaful Operation
Miskam and Eksan (2018)	Big Data and Fintech in Islamic Finance: Prospects and Challenges
Jamil and Seman (2019)	The Impact of Fintech on the Sustainability of Islamic Accounting and Finance Education in Malaysia
Miskam, Shahwahid, and Sholehuddin (2018)	Catching the Fintech Wave in Islamic Finance: Regulatory Approach for Malaysia
Firmansyah and Anwar (2018)	Islamic Financial Technology (Fintech): Its Challenges and Prospect
Rusydiana (2018)	Developing Islamic Financial Technology in Indonesia

Fig. 24.1 Analysis of the articles by title (number)

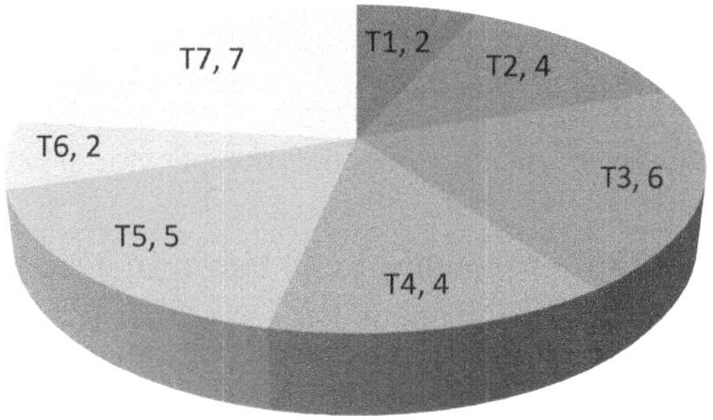

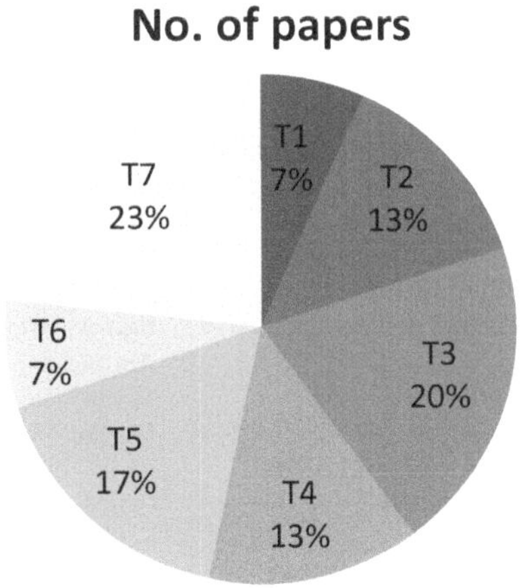

Fig. 24.2 Analysis of the articles by title (in percentage)

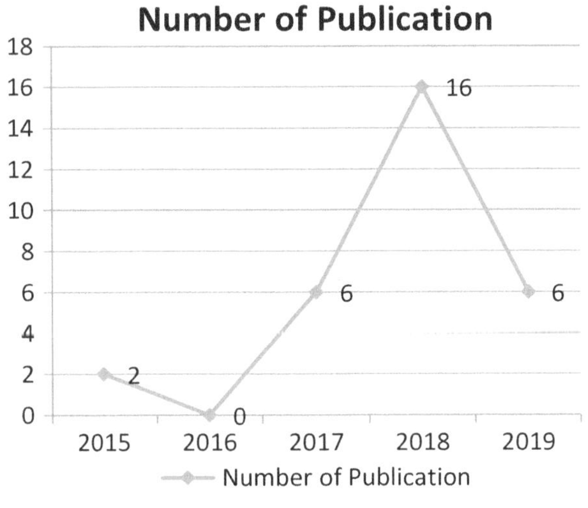

Fig. 24.3 Number of publication per year

is the Shariah compliance of bitcoin and its applicability in Islamic finance. According to Meera (2018), cryptocurrencies that are not backed by real assets are not Shariah-compliant. Bitcoin is neither real money nor fiat money. There is a possibility of misuse of bitcoin due to lack of intrinsic value and zero supervision. Furthermore, it may violate Maqsid al-Shariah by contributing to socioeconomic injustice due to presence of mysir and gharar (Bakar & Rosbi, 2018; Meera, 2018). Bergstra (2015) also echoes the same by commenting that bitcoin will fail the requirement of Islamic financial contract. However, Evans (2015) asserts that bitcoin that is based on a blockchain management system can conform with maslahah (social benefit) through risk-sharing as opposed to risk-transferring and also can avoid riba.

i-Fintech and Blockchain

The popularity of blockchain technology is gaining momentum among Islamic financial institutions (IFIs). Authorities in Dubai are planning to implement blockchain in the public and private sector by 2020. Blockchain, as a tamper-proof ledger, not only cuts intermediaries but also reduces cost and increases reach and speed. Lacasse et al. (2017) inquired whether IFIs can use blockchain to enhance transparency in Islamic finance contracts. The study found that the use of blockchain can improve transparency in financial contracts for Islamic banks and also ensure better corporate governance. Alzubaidi and Abdullah (2017) examined the possibility of introducing an Islamic digital currency through the use of blockchain. They concluded that it is possible to introduce an Islamic digital currency but it requires further Shariah scrutiny.

Nor et al. (2017) looked at the use of blockchain in disaster management. The study proposed that a crowdfunding platform can be created to collect saqadah to help distressed people in need at the time of natural calamity. Blockchain technology will be used to raise fund. Hussen and Ibrahim (2018) suggested the use of blockchain to facilitate Ar-Rahnu (pawn broking) operations. It will help provide continuous and consistent cash flow to Ar-Rahnu provider. Habib and Ahmad (2019) looked at the use of blockchain in Waqf institution. With lack of transparency and proper management, most of the Waqf institutions are suffering an image problem. The blockchain technology can be used to increase the innovation and efficiency in Waqf institutions. Lastly, Elasrag (2019) examines the challenges and obstacles in adopting blockchain for Islamic finance. He found four major challenges: scalability (technical, trusting a network (Behavioral), innovation (Business) and modern regulation (Legal).

i-Fintech and Crowdfunding

Worldwide crowdfunding has become an important source of financing for projects that otherwise would never receive the fund. Fintech is playing an important role in the success of crowdfunding. Biancone et al. (2019) try to understand the concept of Shariah-compliant crowdfunding. They assert that combining the principles of Islamic finance with crowdfunding and Fintech can enhance the ecosystem of the entrepreneurial ecosystem in the Islamic world. Abdullah and Oseni (2017) examine· the Shariah compliance of crowdfunding for the Halal industry in Malaysia. Their study found that not all equity-based crowdfunding projects are Shariah-compliant. There is a need for a unique Shariah-compliant equity crowdfunding for a sustainable halal industry. Alma'amun et al. (2018) stressed for the need for web-based crowdfunding for waqf institutions. Lastly, Saiti et al. (2019) proposed two different P2P models, namely, Mudharabah-and Murabahah-based crowdfunding projects. However, there are some challenges related to regulatory issues, fraud cases and Shariah issues in P2P crowdfunding projects.

i-Fintech-Financial Inclusion and Zakat

The literature search revealed a few papers that discussed financial inclusion through i-Fintech. Firmansyah and Ramdani (2018) proposed an innovative Fintech start-up called "Angsur". The aim of this Fintech-based start-up is to provide micro-lending to undergraduate students of Indonesia with financial difficulty. The micro-lending contract will be based on Murabahah principle. The project will donate 2.5% of sales margin to slum dwellers as Sadakah. Yahaya and Ahmad (2018) shed light on the use of Fintech for effective distribution of Zakat to achieve financial inclusion. They argued that effective distribution of Zakat is always under question due to lack of proper distribution management system. The use of Fintech such as mobile banking can help send Zakat money to appropriate receiver efficiently and effectively and thus ensure financial inclusion for those who do not have access to formal banking.

Wulan et al. (2018) investigated the impact of the digital Zakat Finance System of the Zakat Institute of Indonesia. The study found that there is huge potential for Zakat collection through digital means in Indonesia. Using the digital platform will not only help accumulate a huge amount of Zakat fund but also ensure effective and efficient distribution of Zakat fund among the poor and the needy. However, the study suggested that an audit mechanism is also necessary to prevent any sort of corruption. Yahaya and Ahmad (2019) in another study try to explore the factors that influence the acceptance rate of mobile banking as a means of Zakat distribution among Zakat receivers. The study used UTAUT (Unified theory of acceptance and usage of technology) model to understand acceptable behavior. The data was collected from the state of Selangor, Malaysia. The study found that performance expectancy, social influence, facilitating conditions and Zakat receivers' intention have a positive influence on the use of mobile banking by Zakat receivers. Lastly, Friantoro and Zaki (2018) questioned the need for financial technology in collecting data. The author conducted a SWAT analysis of financial technology as a means for collecting Zakat in Indonesia. The study found the strengths and opportunities are far greater than threats and weaknesses.

i-Fintech and Small and Medium Enterprise (SME)

Financing small and medium enterprise has become an area of concern and popular research topic for long. Fatturroyhan (2018) proposed a Fintech-based solution to the problem of SME financing using Madarabah principle. The author designed an online Fintech platform based on crowdfunding principle named "Go Mudarabah". The purpose of this platform is to connect the wealth owners (Rab al-Maal) with a poor but creative business manager (Mudarib). The author concluded that if developed, the platform can solve the financing problem of the underprivileged SME owners. Rumondang (2018) proposed a similar Fintech-based platform to facilitate SME financing, but based on lending (Qirad). The author argued that Shariah- based lending through Fintech platform can provide financing for SME owners in a shorter time and more simple terms.

i-Fintech in Miscellaneous Issues

Literature search has revealed a few papers on Islamic Fintech that cannot be grouped into earlier categories. So, the papers are grouped into "others" category. Miskam and Eksan (2018) discussed the application of Big Data for decision making in Islamic financial institutions with the help of Fintech. Big Data not only help to understand the behavior of customers but also helps to prevent fraud and other financial crimes. As mentioned earlier, understanding customer habits can help institutions to provide personalized services to the customers. Big Data algorithm can help in audit, reporting and compliance issues, which will ultimately reduce overhead cost (Miskam & Eksan, 2018).

Lajis (2019) discussed the use of Fintech in risk-sharing-based Islamic financing model. As opposed to risking transferring conventional financing model the author proposed a Fintech-based platform/marketplace. This platform will act as a delivery channel for risk-sharing-based financial intermediation, trade finance, social finance and discretionary mutual takaful. The Fintech-based platform will provide reliability and trust, reduce operating cost and enhance financial inclusion (Lajis, 2019). Manaf and Amiruddin (2019) discussed the effect of Fintech on Takaful industry of Malaysia. Takaful companies normally used to sell products through agent marketing. Now, they need to shift to a digital platform to survive. Even though the older generation still prefers dealing with agents while buying insurance, but tapping into the growing younger-generation digital transformation is essential (Manaf & Amiruddin, 2019).

The advent of Fintech, cryptocurrency, crowdfunding, etc., has changed the landscape of the financial service industry including Islamic Finance. Miskam et al. (2018) investigated the impact of Fintech technology on a legal and regulatory system on Islamic Finance Industry of Malaysia. The findings of this research showed that Fintech in Islamic Finance has bought both opportunities and risk to financial stability. The policymakers now need to benefit from the opportunity but at the same time they need to remain vigilant to guard the industry against emerging risk (Miskam et al., 2018).

Firmansyah and Anwar (2018) surveyed Islamic Fintech firms located in Indonesia and Singapore to analyze the opportunities and challenges faced by them. The study found that Islamic finance supported by the development of technology along with the availability of the smartphone has an immense opportunity. The main challenge in Islamic Fintech industry is found to be regulation by governing authorities (Firmansyah & Anwar, 2018). In a similar study, Rusydiana (2018) claims that Islamic Fintech has huge potential in Indonesia. The challenges are lack of policy instrument guarding the Fintech work process and lack of human resources for Fintech. Last but not least, Jamil and Seman (2019) also identified the issue of talent shortage in managing Fintech system in Islamic financial institutions. They investigated the Malaysian governments' response to this talent shortage in Islamic financial institutions. The study recommended that government of Malaysia should intervene in the education system through policy reform that enables graduates working in Islamic financial institutions to cope with the disruptive change brought by the Fintech wave (Jamil & Seman, 2019).

Future Research Direction

Research interest in i-Fintech is a recent phenomenon among academics. It is only in the last 3–4 years that conferences are being arranged on i-Fintech and papers are being published. So far, our review reveals that most of the selected papers are qualitative in nature. So, there is ample scope for quantitative/empirical research in this field. The published papers also lack econometric rigor in methodology. Thus, further research on i-Fintech should be carried out using sophisticated econometric tools. Other areas for research could be customer satisfaction in i-Fintech users, data security, accessibility and infrastructure development for i-Fintech.

References

Abdullah, S., & Oseni, U. A. (2017). Towards a Shari'ah Compliant Equity-Based Crowdfunding for the Halal Industry in Malaysia. *International Journal of Business and Society, 18*(S1), 223–240.

Alma'amun, S., Shafiai, M. H. M., Shahimi, S., & Adnan, M. S. A. (2018). Waqf-Based Crowdfunding: A Case Study of Waqfworld.Org. *International Journal of Islamic Economics and Finance Research, 1*(1), 12–19.

Alzubaidi, I. B., & Abdullah, A. (2017). Developing a Digital Currency from an Islamic Perspective: Case of Blockchain Technology. *International Business Research, 10*(11), 79–87.

Bakar, N. A., & Rosbi, S. (2018). Robust Framework Diagnostics of Blockchain for Bitcoin Transaction System: A Technical Analysis from Islamic Financial Technology (i-FinTech) Perspective. *International Journal of Business and Management, 2*(3), 22–29.

Bergstra, J. A. (2015). *Bitcoin and Islamic Finance.*

Biancone, P. P., Secinaro, S., & Kamal, M. (2019). Crowdfunding and Fintech: Business Model Sharia Compliant. *European Journal of Islamic Finance*, (12).

Darussalam, A. Z., Tutuko, B., Dahlan, A., Hudaifah, A., & Tajang, A. D. (2019). Islamic Financial Technology Towards the Advancement of Islamic Banking in Indonesia. *Nisbah: Jurnal Perbankan Syariah, 4*(2), 171–181.

Elasrag, H. (2019). *Blockchains for Islamic Finance: Obstacles & Challenges.*

Evans, C. (2015). Bitcoin in Islamic Banking and Finance. *Journal of Islamic Banking and Finance, 3*(1), 1–11.

Fatturroyhan, F. (2018). *Go-Mudaraba: The Solution of Poverty and Unemployment in the Digital Era.*

Firmansyah, E. A., & Anwar, M. (2019, January). Islamic Financial Technology (FinTech): Its Challenges and Prospect. In *Achieving and Sustaining SDGs 2018 Conference: Harnessing the Power of Frontier Technology to Achieve the Sustainable Development Goals (ASSDG 2018).* Atlantis Press.

Firmansyah, H., & Ramdani, A. (2018). *The Role of Islamic Financial Technology (FinTech) Start-up in Improving Financial Inclusion in Indonesia Case: Angsur.* 3rd International Conference of Integrated Intellectual Community (ICONIC).

Friantoro, D., & Zaki, K. (2018). Do We Need Financial Technology for Collecting Zakat? In *International Conference of Zakat.*

Habib, F., & Ahmad, A. U. F. (2019). Using Blockchain and Smart Contracts for Waqf Institutions. In *Financial Technology and Disruptive Innovation in ASEAN* (pp. 225–244). IGI Global.

Hussen, M. Z. B., & Ibrahim, J. B. (2018, July). New Business Model for Malaysian ArRahnu Using Blockchain as Sustainable Business. In *2018 International Conference on Information and Communication Technology for the Muslim World (ICT4M)* (pp. 110–113). IEEE.

Jamil, N. N., & Seman, J. A. (2019). The Impact of FinTech on the Sustainability of Islamic Accounting and Finance Education In Malaysia. *Journal of Islamic, Social, Economics and Development (JISED), 4*(17), 74–88.

Lacasse, R. M., Lambert, B., & Khan, N. (2017). Blockchain Technology-Arsenal for a Shariah-Compliant Financial Ecosystem. *Journal of Business and Economics.*

Lajis, S. M. (2019). Fintech and Risk-Sharing: A Catalyst for Islamic Finance. In *Islamic Finance, Risk-Sharing and Macroeconomic Stability* (pp. 237–254). Cham: Palgrave Macmillan.

Manaf, A. W. A., & Amiruddin, N. (2019). Fintech and the Challenge of Digital Disruption in Takaful Operation. *Asia Proceedings of Social Sciences, 4*(1), 1–3.

Meera, A. K. M. (2018). Cryptocurrencies from Islamic Perspectives: The Case of Bitcoin. *Bulletin of Monetary Economics and Banking, 20*(4), 1–18.

Miskam, S., & Eksan, S. H. R. (2018). *Big Data and FinTech in Islamic Finance: Prospects and Challenges.*

Miskam, S., Shahwahid, F. M., & Sholehuddin, N. (2018). *Catching the Fintech Wave in Islamic Finance: Regulatory Approach for Malaysia.*

Nor, R. M., Rahman, M. H., Rahman, T., & Abdullah, A. (2017). Blockchain Sadaqa Mechanism for Disaster Aid Crowd Funding. In *Proceedings of the 6th International Conference on Computing and Informatics* (pp. 400–405).

Rumondang, A. (2018, April). The Utilization of Fintech (P2P Landing) as SME's Capital Solution in Indonesia: Perspective in Islamic Economics (Qirad). In *International Conference of Moslem Society* (Vol. 2, pp. 12–22).

Rusydiana, A. S. (2018). Developing Islamic Financial Technology in Indonesia. *Hasanuddin Economics and Business Review, 2*(2), 143–152.

Saiti, B., Musito, M. H., & Yücel, E. (2019). Islamic Crowdfunding: Fundamentals, Developments and Challenges. *Islamic Quarterly, 62*(3), 469.

Todorof, M. (2018, August). Shariah-Compliant FinTech in the Banking Industry. In *ERA Forum* (Vol. 19, No. 1, pp. 1–17). Springer Berlin Heidelberg.

Wulan, M., Khairunnisa, H., & Bahri, E. S. (2018). Internal Audit Role in Digital Zakat Finance: Case Study at a Zakat Institution in Indonesia. In *International Conference of Zakat*.

Yahaya, M. H., & Ahmad, K. (2018). *Financial Inclusion Through Efficient Zakat Distribution for Poverty Alleviation in Malaysia: Using FinTech & Mobile Banking*.

Yahaya, M. H., & Ahmad, K. (2019). Factors Affecting the Acceptance of Financial Technology Among Asnaf for the Distribution of Zakat in Selangor – A Study Using UTAUT. *Journal of Islamic Finance, 8*, 35–46.

Index[1]

[1] Note: Page numbers followed by 'n' refer to notes.

M. M. Billah (ed.), *Islamic FinTech*,
https://doi.org/10.1007/978-3-030-45827-0

The manufacturer's authorised representative in the EU is Springer Nature Customer Service Centre GmbH, Europaplatz 3, 69115 Heidelberg, Germany. If you have any concerns regarding our products, please contact ProductSafety@springernature.com

Printed and bound by CPI Group (UK) Ltd, Croydon, CR0 4YY
30/09/2026
02225456-0015